AppleScript
THE MISSING MANUAL

*The book that
should have been
in the box*

OTHER MACINTOSH RESOURCES FROM O'REILLY

Related titles

AppleScript: The Definitive Guide

Mac OS X: The Missing Manual, Panther Edition

Running Mac OS X Panther

Learning Unix for Max OS X Panther

Mac OS X Panther in a Nutshell

Modding Mac OS X

Mac OS X Panther Pocket Guide

Mac OS X Power Hound

Macintosh Books Resource Center

mac.oreilly.com is a complete catalog of O'Reilly's books on the Apple Macintosh and related technologies, including sample chapters and code examples.

oreillynet.com is the essential portal for developers interested in open and emerging technologies, including new platforms, programming languages, and operating systems.

Conferences

O'Reilly brings diverse innovators together to nurture the ideas that spark revolutionary industries. We specialize in documenting the latest tools and systems, translating the innovator's knowledge into useful skills for those in the trenches. Visit *conferences.oreilly.com* for our upcoming events.

Safari Bookshelf (*safari.oreilly.com*) is the premier online reference library for programmers and IT professionals. Conduct searches across more than 1,000 books. Subscribers can zero in on answers to time-critical questions in a matter of seconds. Read the books on your Bookshelf from cover to cover or simply flip to the page you need. Try it today with a free trial.

AppleScript
THE MISSING MANUAL

Adam Goldstein

POGUE PRESS™

O'REILLY®

Beijing · Cambridge · Farnham · Köln · Paris · Sebastopol · Taipei · Tokyo

AppleScript: The Missing Manual
by Adam Goldstein

Copyright © 2005 O'Reilly Media, Inc. All rights reserved.
Printed in the United States of America.

Published by O'Reilly Media, Inc., 1005 Gravenstein Highway North, Sebastopol, CA 95472.

O'Reilly books may be purchased for educational, business, or sales promotional use. Online editions are also available for most titles (*safari.oreilly.com*). For more information, contact our corporate/institutional sales department: (800) 998-9938 or *corporate@oreilly.com*.

Editors:	Chuck Toporek
	Sarah Milstein
Production Editor:	Genevieve d'Entremont
Cover Designer:	Ellie Volckhausen
Interior Designer:	Phil Simpson

Printing History:

February 2005:	First Edition.

 This book uses RepKover™, a durable and flexible lay-flat binding.

ISBN: 0-596-00850-3

[M]

Table of Contents

Foreword ix

The Missing Credits xi

Introduction.. xv

Part One: AppleScript Overview

Chapter 1: Setting Up AppleScript 3
The Script Menu 4
Working with the Scripts You Have 17

Chapter 2: Using Script Editor 21
The Script Editor Look 22
Script Formats 30
Setting Script Editor's Preferences 35

Chapter 3: Building a Script from Scratch 39
Getting Started 39
Commanding Other Programs 43

Part Two: Everyday Scripting Tasks

Chapter 4: Manipulating Text 53
String Notation 54
Getting Text Back from Dialog Boxes 54

Linking Strings Together 56
Multiline Strings 58
Scripting TextEdit 59
Adding Word Count 64
Commanding Microsoft Word 66
Running Scripts from Text 72

Chapter 5: Controlling Files 75
File Path Boot Camp 76
Displaying Folders 78
Moving Files Around 88
Backing Up Files 91
Deleting Files 94
Picking a File from a Dialog Box 97
Saving Files 100

Chapter 6: Creating Lists 105
Common List Commands 106
Displaying Lists 107
The Ever-Useful every Keyword 109
List Processing 112
Joining Lists Together 115
Inputting Lists 119
Getting Lists from Other Programs 120

Chapter 7: Organizing and Editing Graphics 125
Scripting iPhoto 126
Controlling Photoshop 131
Image Events 137

Chapter 8: Playing Sound and Video 147
Scripting iTunes 147
Speaking and Listening 155
Scripting QuickTime 164

Chapter 9: Internet and Network Scripting 171
Internet Connect 171
Safari 175
Address Book 183
Mail 186
iChat Control 191
URL Access Scripting 195
Recalling Passwords 197

Chapter 10: Organizing Information in Databases 203
Record Notation 203
Making a Simple AppleScript Database 204
Getting File Information 206
Scripting FileMaker Pro 209

Part Three: Power-User Features

Chapter 11: Linking Scripts to Folders with Folder Actions 221
Enabling Folder Actions 221
Built-in Actions 222
Running Your Own Actions 229

Chapter 12: Scripting Programs That Don't Have Dictionaries 237
Enabling GUI Scripting 239
GUI Scripting Basics 239
Controlling Menus 240
Clicking Buttons 241
Deciphering Interface Hierarchies 245
Fake Typing 248

Chapter 13: Mixing AppleScript and Unix 251
Terminal 252
Unix Without Terminal 256
Running Superuser Commands 258
Running AppleScripts from Unix 259
Scheduling AppleScript Commands 261

Chapter 14: Testing and Debugging Scripts 265
First Line of Defense: The Compiler 265
Noting Important Events 266
Preventing Errors 271
Isolating and Handling Errors 273
The Xcode Debugger 275

Chapter 15: AppleScript Studio 281
What Is AppleScript Studio? 281
Making a Program 283

Part Four: Appendixes

Appendix A: AppleScript Support in Common Programs 299
Databases 299
Email Programs 300

Graphics Editors 300
Page Layout Programs 301
Plain Text Editors 301
Word Processors 302
Web Browsers 302

Appendix B: Moving from HyperCard to AppleScript........................303

Data Types 304
Dialog Boxes 304
Existence 305
Numbers 305
Pausing 306
Ranges 306
Repeat Statements 306
Subroutines 307
Variables 307

Appendix C: Where to Go from Here 309

Web Sites 309
Discussion Lists 310
Books 311

Index 313

Foreword

I created the Missing Manual series in 1999, and then I went on to write or edit the first 25 books. But strange as it may sound, I've rarely been as excited as I am about this book, which I didn't write *or* edit.

That's because I'm the discoverer of its author.

Or, rather, he discovered me. At a book signing in New York City. Adam had come all the way from his home in New Jersey just to meet me. Of course, I was flattered, even if he was only 14 years old.

I found it kind of charming when he described himself a programmer. I thought to myself: *Isn't that cute? He probably did a little HyperCard stack.*

That will be the *last* time I ever underestimate someone based on his age.

It turns out that Adam Goldstein is not just a gifted Mac programmer; he's an absolutely amazing writer. Little by little, over the months, we corresponded. He'd send me a book proposal here, a Mac OS X tip for my book there. More than once, I emailed him to ask: "Do you *swear* to me that you didn't have any parental input on this?"

Because his writing was everything I strive for in my own stuff, and too rarely find in other authors' material: authoritative, clear, light-hearted, encouraging, beautifully structured.

And funny. Not funny as in forced, but funny as in sardonic, as in wry. After reading Adam's definition of inheritance in Chapter 5, for example, you'll never look at a Subaru the same way again.

Anyway, Adam grew on me like ivy. I eventually asked him to give my own *Mac OS X: The Missing Manual* manuscript a tech read. His comments added so much to the book that I wound up hiring him to write some advanced discussions for the book (on FileVault and journaling, for example).

And once again, his writing was so clear, so enthusiastic, and so funny that offering him a Missing Manual title of his own was a no-brainer.

You're holding the result. If this isn't the clearest, most patient, most skillfully taught AppleScript book ever published, I'll eat my mouse.

If you've never written a line of software code, this book will blow your mind open to the possibilities. If you have an iPod, don't miss the tip in Chapter 8, which shows you how AppleScript can turn any text, from your dissertation to a downloaded *New York Times* article, into a spoken recording, for your jogging pleasure.

And if you work in Photoshop, the timesaving automation tips in Chapter 7 alone will pay for this book—about 685 times over.

I'd like to extend my warmest congratulations to Adam for attaining such amazing writing and teaching skills at such a young age, and to you for having the wisdom to choose this book.

So what's next for this brilliant young writer? Getting his driver's license. Adam Goldstein, the writer who will one day eat my lunch, has just turned 17.

David Pogue is the weekly tech columnist for the New York Times, an Emmy award–winning corresponding for CBS News, and the creator of the Missing Manual series.

The Missing Credits

About the Author

 Adam Goldstein is the teenage founder of GoldfishSoft (*www. goldfishsoft.com*), a software company specializing in games and utilities for Mac OS X. He has worked on several books for O'Reilly, including *Mac OS X: The Missing Manual* (as technical editor) and *Mac OS X Power Hound* (as co-editor). In his spare time, Adam attends high school in New Jersey, where he is a captain of the Quizbowl team and is engaged in various other nerdy endeavors.

He welcomes feedback about this book by email: *mail@goldfishsoft.com*. (If you need technical help, however, please refer to the sources in Appendix C.)

About the Creative Team

Chuck Toporek (editor) is the author of *Inside .Mac*, the *Mac OS X Panther Pocket Guide* (and all its previous incarnations for earlier versions of Mac OS X), and is a coauthor of *Mac OS X Panther in a Nutshell*. He's a senior editor with O'Reilly Media, Inc., responsible for all of the non–Missing Manual Mac OS X–related books published by O'Reilly. Chuck resides in Portland, Oregon, where he spends his free time sipping coffee and enjoying the grandeur of the Pacific Northwest. Email: *chuck@oreilly.com*. Web: *http://homepage.mac.com/chuckdude*.

Rose Cassano (cover illustration) has worked as an independent designer and illustrator for 20 years. Assignments have ranged from the nonprofit sector to corporate clientele. She lives in beautiful Southern Oregon, grateful for the miracles of modern technology that make working there a reality. Email: *cassano@uci.net*. Web: *www.rosecassano.com*.

Ellie Volckhausen (cover designer) has been at O'Reilly for several years, and has discovered that the sooty phalangist from Van Diemen's Land is the same animal as the Common Brushtail Possum from Tasmania.

Paul Berkowitz (technical reviewer) has tech-edited other O'Reilly AppleScript books, including *AppleScript: The Definitive Guide* by Matt Neuburg, and has also done some technical proofreading of AppleScript-related documentation for Apple and Microsoft. He is the author of the AppleScript chapter in *Office 2004 for the Mac: The Missing Manual*. He is well known as the author of over 100 Apple-Scripts for Entourage—including major script programs for exporting and importing just about everything—and programs for syncing Entourage to Apple's

Address Book and iCal. In his "other life," he is a classical pianist and Professor of Piano at the University of California in Santa Barbara, where he now lives happily ever after.

John Gruber (technical reviewer) is a freelance writer, Web developer, designer, and Mac nerd. He combines those interests on his Web site, Daring Fireball (*http://daringfireball.net*), which is widely regarded as "not bad." John lives in Philadelphia with his lovely wife, Amy, and their young son Jonas.

Lydian Meredith (technical reviewer) has been working and playing with Macs since 1988, in academia, business, and publishing. Currently she runs her own publishing bureau in London and lurks in several Mac User lists, including some for AppleScript.

August Trometer (technical reviewer) is the creator and developer of the podcasting client iPodderX, as well as the creator and administrator of the .Mac portal Web site, *dotmac.info*. A former restaurant owner, he now works as a software and Web developer. He lives in Indianapolis, Indiana. Email: *BlueGus@mac.com*. Web: *http://dotmac.info*.

Linley Dolby (copyeditor) spent several years in the production department at O'Reilly before moving to Martha's Vineyard to pursue a freelance career. She now helps whip technical books into shape for several companies, including O'Reilly and Pogue Press. Email: *linley@gremlinley.com*.

Genevieve d'Entremont (production editor) has been at O'Reilly for two years now, but she still doesn't understand why people are so fascinated by technological minutiae. In her spare time, she reads novels and dreams of spending the rest of her days on a tropical beach, sipping Mai Tais and reading more novels.

Acknowledgments

The Missing Manual series is a joint venture between Pogue Press (the dream team introduced on these pages) and O'Reilly Media, Inc. (a dream publishing partner).

The first person to whom thanks is due is Marcia Palmer, my Kindergarten math teacher, who introduced me to Logo before I even knew how to read. Logo was my earliest experience with computer programming, and I've never lost interest.

More recently, I owe a great deal to Chuck Toporek, whose editorial comments on this book were far and away the most thorough I've ever received. Chuck was flexible when scheduling became tight, incredibly helpful in getting the book into production, and in innumerable other ways the best editor anyone could possibly imagine.

I also owe tons of thanks to Sarah Milstein, Missing Manual Superwoman, for her own ultra-helpful comments. Without Sarah's input, this book would have been yet another techy AppleScript guide, rather than a beginner-friendly Missing Manual. (And of particular note, I'd like to thank Sarah for being open to me writing an AppleScript book in the first place.)

The four technical editors also were top-notch. Paul Berkowitz's insightfulness and personal AppleScript expertise were particularly helpful, as were John Gruber's wonderfully constructive suggestions. Lydian Meredith brought the helpful perspective of a first-time scripter, and August Trometer's careful testing caught several important glitches that would have slipped through otherwise. Altogether, these technical editors made the book far better.

My parents, Risa and Eliot, have been amazingly helpful in their own right. They signed my book contract since I'm too young to do it myself, and had few qualms about letting me write a book while school was in session. They offered me endless supplies of food, shelter, and—most importantly—love, without which it would have been hard to write anything at all.

My sister, Hannah, offered all of the above (with the exception of food and shelter). So did all four of my grandparents: Ben, Ruth, Roseanne, and Jim.

Last of all, I am eternally indebted to David Pogue, God of Technical Writing, for his willingness to let a high schooler work with him. Letting me tech-edit, edit, and finally write a book in the Missing Manual series was unbelievably magnanimous of him. And had it not been for the inspiration of David's *own* books, I never would have been interested in technical writing in the first place.

The Missing Manual Series

Missing Manuals are witty, superbly written guides to computer products that don't come with printed manuals (which is just about all of them). Each book features a handcrafted index; cross-references to specific page numbers (not just "see Chapter 14"); and RepKover, a detached-spine binding that lets the book lie perfectly flat without weights or cinder blocks.

Recent and upcoming titles include:

- *Mac OS X: The Missing Manual* (Tiger Edition) by David Pogue
- *FileMaker Pro 7: The Missing Manual* by Geoff Coffey
- *iPhoto 4: The Missing Manual* by David Pogue and Derrick Story
- *iMovie 4 & iDVD: The Missing Manual* by David Pogue
- *iPod & iTunes: The Missing Manual*, 3rd Edition, by J.D. Biersdorfer
- *GarageBand: The Missing Manual* by David Pogue
- *iLife '04: The Missing Manual*, by David Pogue, et al.
- *Google: The Missing Manual* by Sarah Milstein and Rael Dornfest
- *Switching to the Mac: The Missing Manual* by David Pogue
- *Mac OS X Power Hound, Panther Edition* by Rob Griffiths
- *Dreamweaver MX 2004: The Missing Manual* by David Sawyer McFarland

- *Office 2004 for Macintosh: The Missing Manual* by Mark H. Walker and Franklin Tessler

- *AppleWorks 6: The Missing Manual* by Jim Elferdink and David Reynolds

- *Windows XP Home Edition: The Missing Manual,* Second Edition by David Pogue

- *Windows XP Pro: The Missing Manual* by David Pogue, Craig Zacker, and Linda Zacker

- *Windows XP Power Hound* by Preston Gralla

- *Excel: The Missing Manual* by Matthew MacDonald

- *Photoshop Elements 3: The Missing Manual* by Barbara Brundage

- *QuickBooks 2005: The Missing Manual* by Bonnie Biafore

Introduction

AppleScript is a powerful computer language that's been around since the days of Mac OS 7. Despite its maturity, however, AppleScript is often looked down upon by snooty Mac programmers for being too simple, too easy to learn, and too much like English.

Of course, those are precisely the traits you *want* in a computer language. If you're an everyday Mac user—not some fancy-schmancy computer science Ph.D.—AppleScript is by far the easiest language to use for automating your Mac.

AppleScript has been around long enough to become a stable, powerful, and—most importantly—nearly bug-free language. It grew out of the old HyperCard project (Appendix B), whose goal was to make programming accessible to regular computer users. HyperCard was a big success, but Apple stopped making new versions after a few years.

Meanwhile, Apple took much of what it learned from HyperCard and applied it to its new techno-baby: AppleScript. Since its creation, AppleScript has been the heir to HyperCard's dream of a simple, powerful language that non-programmers can use. Despite nine major revisions and countless minor ones, Apple-Script's approach today is much the same as it was 10 years ago—and that's a good thing.

Uses for AppleScript

Of course, what really matters is what you can *do* with AppleScript. The answer? Just about anything you can do yourself.

AppleScript is a language with which you create individual *scripts*—little software robots that send commands to different programs on your computer. In fact, scripts do much of what you can do with a keyboard and mouse.

"But why should I learn an entirely new language just to do the things I do myself?" you ask. Luckily, AppleScript has several advantages over a human computer user:

- **AppleScript eliminates repetitive jobs.** One of AppleScript's greatest strengths is its ability to automatically perform similar jobs over and over again. With AppleScript, you can automatically rename all the files in a folder (page 113), save all your open TextEdit documents at once (page 103), or rate every song in your iTunes library (page 148), for example. Best of all, AppleScript will never get repetitive stress disorder—or complain that you're making it work too hard.

- **AppleScript automates complicated workflows.** Another great ability of AppleScript is managing jobs that take place in multiple programs. For instance, AppleScript can take a picture from the Finder, bring the image into Photoshop, correct color tones, and shrink the file down to a suitable size for a Web site, all without breaking a sweat (page 133).

- **AppleScript can do stuff in the background.** Sometimes you might want to have a program that works without you asking, and AppleScript can do that too. If you have a screensaver running, for example, AppleScript can automatically set your iChat status to Away without you having to touch your keyboard or mouse (page 191).

- **AppleScript works even when you're not.** If you're on vacation, AppleScript can take over some of the jobs you'd normally do yourself. For instance, you can create a simple AppleScript that automatically puts excess junk from your Desktop into a different folder (page 88).

- **AppleScript's much faster than you are.** Unless you're some sort of computational Superman, AppleScript is always faster than you; while it might take you 10 minutes to rename all the files in your Documents folder, for example, AppleScript can do it in less than 10 seconds.

UP TO SPEED

The Meaning of "AppleScript"

The term *AppleScript* causes some confusion, mainly because it can be used as virtually any part of speech. Originally, it referred to a language, just like *English*, *Swahili*, or *Java*. Later, *AppleScript* became a more general noun, referring to any program written in the language. Nowadays, you'll hear people refer to an *AppleScriptable* program (one that can be controlled by AppleScript), or the task of *Apple-*

Scripting (using AppleScript to accomplish a job). In some circles, you'll even hear it used an expression of nerdy surprise ("Why, I'll be AppleScripted!").

Keep in mind, too, that the word *script* has similar connotations. When it comes to AppleScript, a *script* is a document written in the language, and *scripting* is the act of writing such a script.

Advantages and Disadvantages

AppleScript is by no means the *only* scripting language for OS X. Nonetheless, AppleScript has several advantages that make the best option for many jobs:

- **It's more like English than any other Mac language.** AppleScript's greatest advantage is that it uses grammar that closely resembles the commands you'd give to your seven-year-old son. (A typical command, for example, would be "say cheese", which would have your computer speak the word "cheese" out loud.)

  If you've never learned a computer language before, you'll be grateful that AppleScript doesn't bother with semicolons, curly brackets, and all the other annoyances of more advanced computer languages. Even better, AppleScript is *not* case-sensitive—a feature you can appreciate only if you've ever had to search through reams of code just to find a mis-capitalized command name.

- **It works with the same programs that you do.** Virtually every big-name Mac program supports AppleScript commands: Microsoft Word, Adobe Photoshop, FileMaker Pro, and so on. Lots of free programs support AppleScript, too: TextEdit, Address Book, Mac OS X Mail, iPhoto, and many more.

Note: For a list of common programs that work with AppleScript, see Appendix A.

- **It works with other computer languages, too.** AppleScript isn't just a little software island; it's got bridges to virtually every other programming language on Mac OS X. If you're a serious Unix hacker, for example, you can mix AppleScript commands right into your Unix programs (page 259). And this cross-pollination works the other way around, too: you can mix Unix commands into your AppleScript programs just as easily (page 254).

- **Lots of people use it.** There are several popular gathering places for AppleScripters online, where you'll find useful pre-made scripts for free. If you're having a problem, chances are that someone else has had the same problem and posted a fix somewhere on the Web. And if you simply can't work a problem out, AppleScript's large community means that someone else can almost always help you fix it. (Appendix C has a list of these resources.)

Despite all its advantages, however, AppleScript isn't perfect. Several trade-offs had to be made to make it more like English, for example, and the language sometimes reveals all too well that it was designed with 10-year-old computers in mind. Here are some of AppleScript's biggest weaknesses:

- **Commands are sometimes inconsistent between programs.** Because AppleScript has changed so many times over the years, some commands work differently in different programs. This isn't a complete showstopper, though; it just means you may have to dig deeper into a program's dictionary (page 44) to find the right command.

• **Some programs don't support AppleScript at all.** Certain programs, unfortunately, don't take advantage of all that AppleScript has to offer. Programs that show up in this category are usually old, free, and/or made by a company that doesn't make Mac support a top priority.

Still, all hope is not lost. If a program you use regularly doesn't work with AppleScript out of the box, you may find that someone on the Internet has written a plug-in that adds AppleScript support. And as a last resort, you can use Apple's own GUI Scripting feature (page 238) to bend non-scriptable programs to your will.

• **It's slower than most other languages.** In exchange for all the power AppleScript grants you, the language has an unusually high overhead for running commands. In the real world, it probably won't make much of a difference—AppleScript is still dozens of times faster than you are. But if speed is of utmost importance to you (say, you work in a mathematical or scientific field), you might want to look elsewhere for a language that better suits your needs.

• **It only works with Macs.** Furthermore, if you write scripts that take advantage of new AppleScript features, your scripts will only work in Mac OS X. Of course, if you're only going to write scripts for your computer, this isn't a big deal. But if you need to exchange scripts with Windows or Linux users, you'll need to find a cross-platform language.

In total, AppleScript is wonderful if you're an everyday Mac user who wants to automate things, but it's useless if you need your scripts to run on Windows.

About This Book

Like most software these days, AppleScript doesn't come with a printed manual. To find your way around, you're expected to use Apple's Help Viewer program (in your Applications folder). But as you'll quickly discover, the help pages are tersely written, offer very little technical depth, lack useful examples, and provide no tutorials whatsoever.

The AppleScript Language Guide (*http://developer.apple.com/documentation/ AppleScript/Conceptual/AppleScriptLangGuide/AppleScriptLanguageGuide.pdf*) is hardly any better. It hasn't been updated since the days of OS 8.5, and it reads more like an encyclopedia than a help file. Of course, it's wonderful to have a complete guide to the language for *reference*, but it doesn't help much when you're learning the language.

The worst part of both documents, however, is that they're *virtual* help files: you can't mark your place, underline important passages, or read them in the bathroom (unless, of course, you take your laptop in there with you). And there's no more than a passing mention of powerful new features like multimedia support (page 147), GUI Scripting (page 238), or AppleScript Studio (page 281). The purpose of this book, therefore, is to serve as the AppleScript manual that should have accompanied your computer.

What You'll Need

This book covers the AppleScript features found in Mac OS 10.3 ("Panther"). If you have an earlier operating system, visit *www.apple.com/macosx/upgrade/* for information on how to upgrade.

Furthermore, you may want a copy of these other programs that are used with some of the scripts in this book:

- **Adobe Photoshop CS ($650).** Photoshop is the staple of any graphic pro's software library, and its AppleScript support is nearly unbeatable. If you don't feel like spending your retirement savings on software, just use the free 30-day trial version from *www.adobe.com/products/tryadobe/main.jsp#product=39*.

- **FileMaker Pro 7 ($300).** FileMaker is a powerful database program that can organize virtually *any* kind of information. You can download a 30-day trial version from *https://www.filemaker.com/downloads/trial_download.html*, and that'll work just as well.

POWER USERS' CLINIC

Other Languages

If AppleScript just doesn't cut it for a certain task, you have plenty of other options. OS X comes with one of the most complete sets of languages around, and you can add even more languages by installing the Xcode Tools (page 275). Here's a look at alternatives to AppleScript:

- **Perl** is famous for its power, flexibility, and totally alien-looking grammar. Many Web sites use Perl scripts for processing credit card payments, for example—and it works on virtually every operating system available. If you need to throw together programs that you can run anywhere, this might be your language. Check out *Programming Perl*, Third Edition (O'Reilly) for details.

- **Python** is known for its simplicity and clever design. Some people use it for whipping up quick prototypes of future programs, while others use it for making scripts that run Web sites. You can find out more in a book like *Learning Python*, Second Edition (O'Reilly).

- **Shell scripting** is a method of linking together various Unix commands (page 252). Among Unix hackers, it's a popular method for automating computer tasks, much as AppleScript is for Mac fans. You can find numerous examples in a book like *Wicked Cool Shell Scripts* (NoStarch Press).

- Languages like **PHP, JavaScript,** and **ActionScript** are used on numerous Web pages to control the look of these Web sites. Each language has specific uses (PHP is often used for managing online databases, for example) and disadvantages (ActionScript works only if the Flash plug-in is installed, for example). None of these languages, unfortunately, can easily work with AppleScript. You can find online tutorials for all three at *www.theopensourcery.com/ostutor.htm*.

- **C, C++,** and **Objective-C** are the languages that are used to create the vast majority of commercial software programs. Microsoft Word, Adobe Photoshop, TextEdit, Safari, and virtually ever other program you use daily were written using at least one of these three languages. These C-based languages are known for being fast, powerful, and hard to learn—and you need the Xcode Tools to use them. Visit *http://cprog.oreilly.com/* for more.

- **Java** is intended to let you write a program on one operating system and have it run on all others. It's used a lot online (for programs like games and chat rooms), and it requires that you install the Xcode Tools to program in it. You can find out more in a book like *Learning Java*, Second Edition (O'Reilly).

- **Microsoft Word 2004 ($230).** Word is the time-tested, cross-platform standard for word processing documents. It's available as part of the Microsoft Office 2004 suite ($400), which also includes PowerPoint (for presentations), Excel (for spreadsheets), and Entourage (for emailing and creating calendars). You can download a free 30-day trial of the whole package from *www.microsoft.com/ mac/default.aspx?pid=office2004td.*

Tip: Many of the scripts in this book will work with an earlier version of these programs, but the scripts may behave somewhat differently. It's a good idea, therefore, to download the free trial copies of the newest versions, so you can follow along easily with the scripts in this book.

About the Outline

This book is divided into four parts, each containing several chapters:

- **Part 1, AppleScript Overview** covers the basics of using AppleScript to control your Mac. You'll learn how to crack open the scripts that Apple gives you for free—and how to change what they do. These three chapters also explain the purpose of the built-in Script Editor program, and show you how to make the most of your time there.

- **Part 2, Everyday Scripting Tasks** explains how to use AppleScript for automating typical jobs: renaming files, organizing your iPhoto library, playing music, and so on. These are also the chapters where you'll learn about AppleScript's different ways of storing information, such as lists, numbers, and database records.

- **Part 3, Power-User Features** takes you beyond the basics into truly time-saving territory. You'll learn how to make the Finder run scripts whenever you open a folder, and how to work around the scripting limitations in programs like System Preferences. These chapters also show you how to mix AppleScript with other powerful tools, to squeeze the most power possible from your scripts.

- **Part 4, Appendixes** offers three useful references. Appendix A lists the Mac OS X programs that play best with AppleScript, so you can figure out which programs to avoid and which ones to use. Appendix B shows you how to move HyperCard stacks into Mac OS X, using AppleScript to ease the transfer. Finally, Appendix C sends you off into the great universe of advanced AppleScript books and Web sites.

Along the way, you'll get a lot more out of this book if you have the free Missing CD, where you'll find all the scripts from this book prewritten for you. Using that, you won't have to retype all the long scripts by hand, and you'll save yourself both time and typos. Page 24 has instructions for downloading the Missing CD.

About → These → Arrows

Throughout this book, and throughout the Missing Manual series, you'll find sentences like this one: "Open the System folder → Libraries → Fonts folder." That's shorthand for a much longer instruction that directs you to open three nested folders in sequence, like this: "On your hard drive, you'll find a folder called System. Open it. Inside the System window is a folder called Libraries. Open that. Inside *that* folder is yet another one called Fonts. Double-click to open it, too."

Similarly, this kind of arrow shorthand helps to simplify the business of choosing commands in menus, such as → Dock → Position on Left. That instruction is just another way of saying, "Click the Apple menu to open it, navigate to the Dock submenu, and then choose Position on Left."

About MissingManuals.com

At *www.missingmanuals.com*, you'll find news, articles, and updates to the books in this series. But if you click the name of this book and then click the Errata link, you'll find a unique resource: a list of corrections and updates that have been made in successive printings of this book. You can mark important corrections right in your own copy of the book, if you like.

In fact, the same page offers an invitation for you to submit such corrections and updates yourself. In an effort to keep the book as up-to-date and accurate as possible, each time we print more copies of the book, we'll make any confirmed corrections you've suggested. Thanks in advance for reporting any glitches you find!

In the meantime, we'd love to hear your suggestions for new books in the Missing Manual line. There's a place for that on the Web site, too, as well as a place to sign up for free email notification of new titles in the series.

 When you see a Safari® enabled icon on the cover of your favorite technology book, that means it's available online through the O'Reilly Network Safari Bookshelf.

Safari offers a solution that's better than e-Books: it's a virtual library that lets you easily search thousands of top tech books, cut and paste code samples, download chapters, and find quick answers when you need the most accurate, current information. Try it free at *http://safari.oreilly.com*.

The Very Basics

To use this book, and indeed to use a Macintosh computer, you need to know a few basics. This book assumes that you're familiar with these terms and concepts (if you're not, pick up a book like *Mac OS X: The Missing Manual*):

- **Clicking.** This book gives you three kinds of instructions that require you to use the mouse that's attached to your Mac. To *click* means to point the arrow cursor at something on the screen and then—without moving the cursor at all—to press and release the clicker button on the mouse (or laptop trackpad). To *double-click*, of course, means to click twice in rapid succession, again without moving the cursor at all. And to *drag* means to move the cursor while keeping the button held down.

When you're told to ⌘-*click* something, you click while pressing the ⌘ key (which is next to the Space bar). Such related procedures as *Shift-clicking*, *Option-clicking*, and *Control-clicking* work the same way—just click while pressing the corresponding key at the bottom of your keyboard.

- **Menus.** The *menus* are the words in the lightly striped bar at the top of your screen. You can either click one of these words to open a pull-down menu of commands (and then click on a command) or click and hold the button as you drag down the menu to the desired command (and release the button to activate the command). Either method works just as well.

Note: Apple has officially changed what it calls the little menu that pops up when you Control-click something on the screen. It's still a contextual menu, in that the menu choices depend on the context of what you click—but now it's called a *shortcut menu*. That term not only matches what it's called in Windows, but it's more descriptive. Shortcut menu is the term you'll find in this book.

- **Keyboard shortcuts.** Every time you take your hand off the keyboard to move the mouse, you lose time and potentially disrupt your creative flow. That's why many Mac pros use keystroke combinations instead of menu commands whenever possible. ⌘-P opens the Print dialog box, for example, and ⌘-M minimizes the current window to the Dock.

When you see a shortcut like ⌘-Q (which quits the current program), it's telling you to hold down the ⌘ key and, while it's down, type the letter Q, and then release both keys.

If you've mastered this much information, you have all the technical background you need to enjoy *AppleScript: The Missing Manual*.

Part One:
AppleScript Overview

Chapter 1: Setting Up AppleScript

Chapter 2: Using Script Editor

Chapter 3: Building a Script from Scratch

1

Setting Up AppleScript

Although AppleScript is fast and free, perhaps the *best* part about it is that it gets installed right along with Mac OS X. You don't need to download any files, install any CDs, or configure any nasty system files to get AppleScript to work. In fact, you've got an AppleScript folder tucked inside your Applications folder, right this very moment (Figure 1-1).

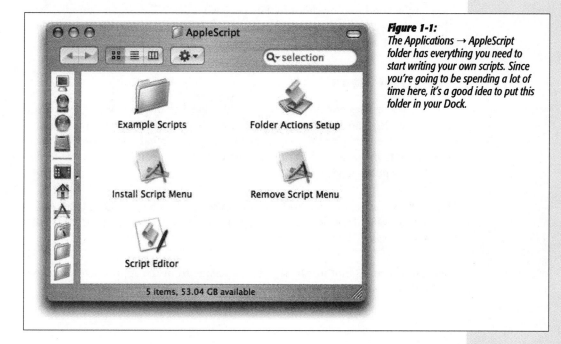

Figure 1-1:
The Applications → AppleScript folder has everything you need to start writing your own scripts. Since you're going to be spending a lot of time here, it's a good idea to put this folder in your Dock.

Whenever you install Mac OS X—or buy a new Mac—you'll find these five icons in your AppleScript folder:

- **Example Scripts** is simply an *alias* (shortcut) to your Library → Scripts folder. This folder contains more than 100 example scripts for you to run, examine, and edit (page 5).

- **Folder Actions Setup** turns on the powerful *folder actions* feature of OS X. Once it's on, you can make the Finder run your very own scripts whenever you open a folder, add an icon to a folder, remove an icon from a folder, and so on. (A full explanation of Folder Actions appears on page 221.)

- **Install Script Menu** adds a new icon to the right side of your menu bar. With this menu in place, you can easily run your favorite AppleScripts from any program you want (read on for details).

- **Remove Script Menu** *hides* the menu that appears when you double-click Install Script Menu.

- **Script Editor** is AppleScript Central. From there you can open, edit, and run your scripts, and save them in any number of special formats. Script Editor coverage starts on page 21.

Now that you know what you've got, it's best to spend some time getting acquainted with all the AppleScript stuff that's already on your Mac. Pop open a new Finder window—by choosing File → New Finder Window, for example—and then click the Applications folder icon in the Sidebar. Once in the Applications folder, open the AppleScript folder, and you're ready to explore.

The Script Menu

To get your first taste of AppleScript, double-click Install Script Menu. When you do so, a curled-parchment icon appears right in your menu bar. (This icon is a recurring theme in Mac OS X that means, roughly, "What you're looking at has something to do with AppleScript.") Simply click the menu bar icon once to display the Script Menu (Figure 1-2).

Tip: All the scripts that appear in the Script Menu come from the Library → Scripts folder. And, as described on page 15, that means you can add your *own* scripts to the Script Menu in addition to tweaking the existing ones.

You can run any script just by selecting its name from the appropriate submenu. The following sections provide a breakdown of what the scripts do.

Address Book Scripts

Here, you'll find a single **Import Addresses** script, designed to move your contacts into Mac OS X's Address Book from other applications, such as Entourage, Outlook Express, Palm Desktop, Eudora, Claris Emailer, and Netscape. If you've got a lot of friends, this script saves you from having to re-enter all their names, phone numbers, and email addresses by hand.

Note: The scripts in the Helper Scripts submenu (just above **Import Addresses**) are off-limits to mere mortals. If you try to run any of the **Helper Scripts**, Mac OS X simply tells you to use the **Import Addresses** script instead.

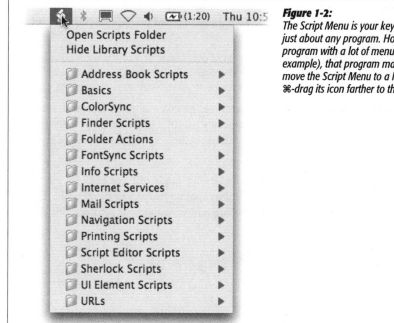

Figure 1-2:
The Script Menu is your key to running AppleScripts from just about any program. However, if you're using a program with a lot of menus (Word or Photoshop, for example), that program may clip off the Script Menu. To move the Script Menu to a less clip-prone position, simply ⌘-drag its icon farther to the right.

Basics

In this submenu, you'll find three small, handy scripts:

- **AppleScript Help** launches Help Viewer and displays a fairly random list of every AppleScript help file on your Mac.

Tip: To see a more orderly list of such files in Help Viewer—organized by Apple for quick reference—choose Library → AppleScript Help and then click Browse AppleScript Help.

- **AppleScript Website** opens the AppleScript home page (*www.apple.com/applescript/*) in your default Web browser.

- **Open Script Editor** launches the Script Editor program from your Applications → AppleScript folder. See page 21 for more on this powerful program.

ColorSync

This submenu contains almost 20 different scripts for working with ColorSync (a technology for matching colors between pictures, computer screens, printers, and so on). When you select a script from this submenu, it presents a short dialog box explaining what it does. Here are some of the highlights:

- **Build profile info web page** presents an Open dialog box for picking a folder of pictures. Once you've done so, the script generates a Web page containing each image, along with a description of which *profile* (color settings) it uses.

Tip: Even if you don't use ColorSync, this script can be quite handy; it's a great way to quickly generate a Web page from the pictures in a folder.

- **Mimic PC monitor** adjusts your screen so the color settings are similar to those of a Windows PC. (This script is especially useful if you're a Web designer, since it shows you how your Web pages will likely look to Windows users all over the world.)

- **Remove profile from image** takes any special color settings out of a picture, so you're left with the raw, unfiltered colors that were there to begin with. If you're trying to gauge the accuracy of your digital camera's color settings, this script is a helpful tool.

Tip: To learn more about ColorSync, visit *www.apple.com/colorsync/*.

Finder Scripts

This submenu contains a bunch of timesaving scripts for working with files in the Finder:

- **AboutFinder Scripts** simply presents a dialog box explaining how the scripts work.

- **Add to File/Folder Names** lets you tack the same prefix or suffix onto every item in the active Finder window (Figure 1-3).

Note: If there aren't any Finder windows open, this script (and all the other **Finder** scripts) works with the files or folders on your desktop instead. That means, for example, that the **Add to File Names** script appends your chosen extension to every file on the desktop if there aren't any Finder windows open.

- **Change Case of Item Names** lets you make every file and folder in the current Finder window either all uppercase or all lowercase. If you pine for the days of DOS—where every file name was in capital letters—this script is for you.

- **Finder Windows – Hide All** minimizes all your Finder windows, one at a time, to the Dock.

Tip: A faster way to minimize all your Finder windows is to simply Option-click the yellow minimize button in any *single* Finder window. That way, the windows all minimize simultaneously, rather than one at a time.

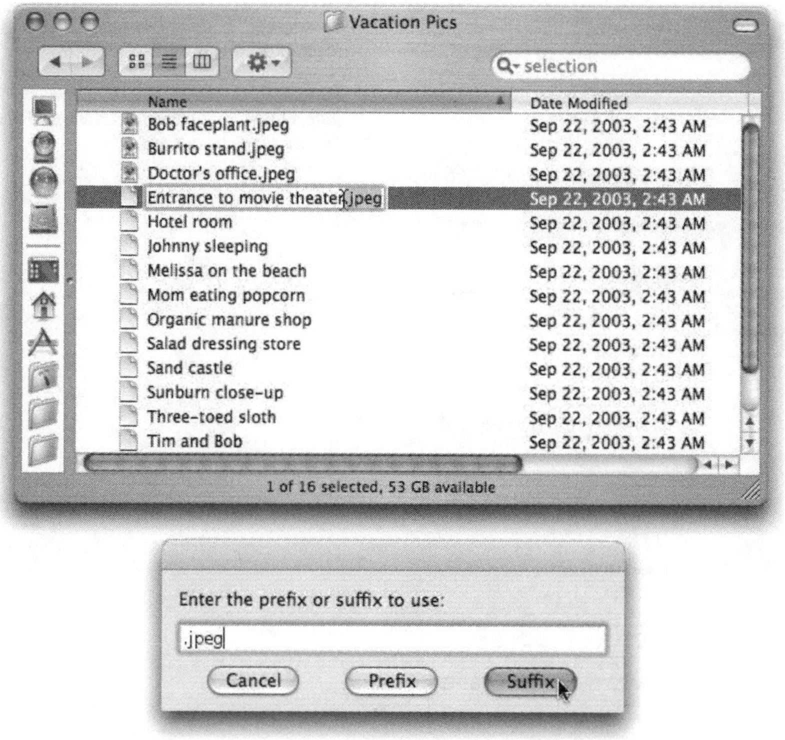

Figure 1-3:
If you have a lot of files that you're bringing over from Mac OS 9 or your digital camera, there's a good chance that they're missing file extensions (abbreviations like .jpeg and .txt that let them open in Mac OS X). The hard way to add these extensions is to rename each file by hand (top).

The easy way: in the Script Menu, choose Finder Scripts → Add to File Names, enter the file extension you want to append, and click Suffix (bottom).

- **Finder Windows – Show All** brings back all your Finder windows from the Dock.

- **Replace Text in Item Names** does a find-and-replace on every file name, folder name, or both in your active Finder window (Figure 1-4).

- **Switch to Finder** brings the Finder to the front and hides every other program.

Tip: You can accomplish the same task by Option-⌘-clicking the Finder icon in the Dock.

• **Trim File/Folder Names** cuts off any prefix or suffix you specify (by clicking Trim Start or Trim End, respectively). It's basically the reverse of the Add to File/Folder Names command described earlier.

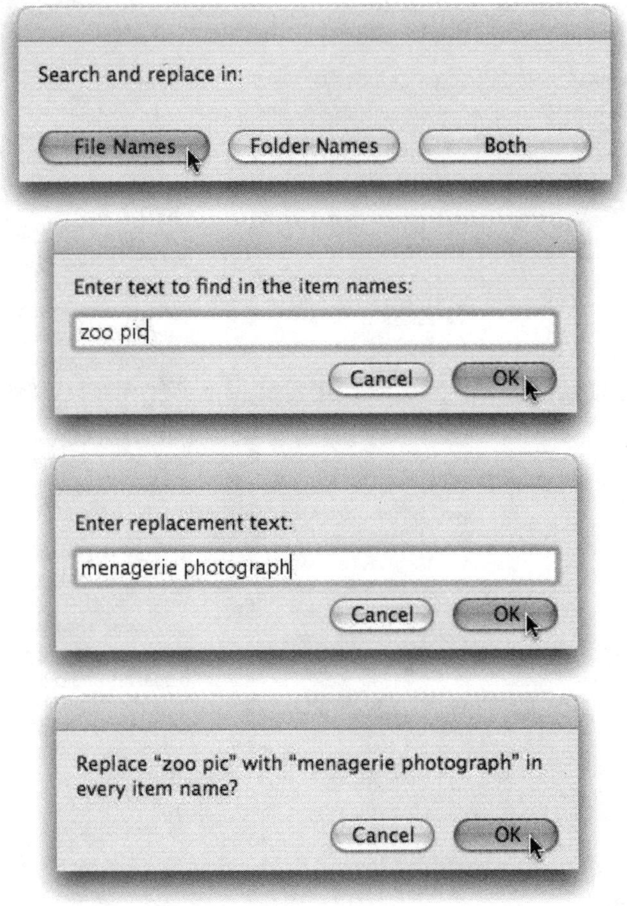

Search and replace in:

File Names   Folder Names   Both

Enter text to find in the item names:

zoo pic

Cancel   OK

Enter replacement text:

menagerie photograph

Cancel   OK

Replace "zoo pic" with "menagerie photograph" in every item name?

Cancel   OK

Figure 1-4:
Batch-renaming items is a four-step process. Top: Choose whether you want to apply the operation to files, folders, or both.

Second from top: Enter the text you want to replace (it's not case-sensitive).

Second from bottom: Enter the text you want to substitute.

Bottom: Confirm your choice and watch in amazement as AppleScript renames all the files that match your text.

Folder Actions

These scripts turn on and off *folder actions*—scripts that run automatically in the Finder—either for the entire system or just for a specific folder. (Folder action coverage begins on page 221.)

FontSync Scripts

If you spend your life doing visual layout or printing, you may have come across *FontSync profiles* (little summaries of all the fonts on someone's computer). You can easily generate such profiles (using **Create FontSync Profile**) or compare your own profile to someone else's (using **Match FontSync Profile**) to see if you have the same fonts. Beyond that, though, there's not much you can do with the Apple-Scripts found in this submenu.

Info Scripts

The two scripts in this submenu are pretty much duplicates of existing Mac OS X features:

- **Current Date & Time** displays a dialog box with—you guessed it—the current date and time. The only real benefit to this command is that it has a Clipboard button; when you click that, the date and time information is copied to the Clipboard, so you can paste (⌘-V) that information into a document window, such as one from TextEdit, Mail, or Microsoft Word.

- **Font Sampler** displays every font you have on your computer in its own type-face (Figure 1-5). Of course, you can always preview your fonts with Font Book (found in your Applications folder), but that's not nearly as fun as being able to see how all your fonts look at once.

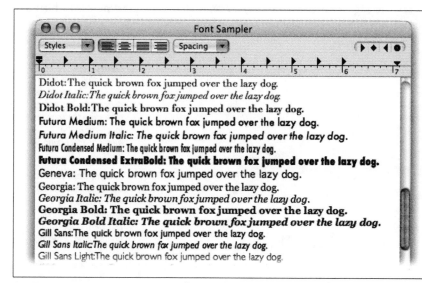

Figure 1-5:
Each sentence here is supposed to contain every letter of the alphabet, so you can see exactly how each letter appears in each typeface. Of course, whoever programmed this feature forgot that the sentence "The quick brown fox jumped over the lazy dog" is missing the letter "s" (it should say "jumps" instead of "jumped").

Internet Scripts

With the exception of the first script in this folder, these scripts go out and troll the Internet to fetch information for you:

- **About Internet Services Scripts** presents a dialog box with a link to additional Web services. (See page 200 for more about using AppleScript with Web services.)

- **Current Temperature by Zipcode** gives you the temperature outside your house in both Fahrenheit and Celsius, assuming you live in the United States.

- **Stock Quote** fetches a 20-minute delayed stock quote for the ticker symbol of your choice.

Tip: If you don't know a company's ticker symbol, visit *http://finance.yahoo.com/* to look it up. But if you want to quickly see how *Apple's* stock is performing, just click the OK button when the dialog box appears. (The script automatically inserts AAPL, Apple's ticker symbol, into the dialog box.)

Mail Scripts

This submenu contains a collection of scripts that work with Mac OS X's built-in Mail program (page 186).

Note: If you use a different email program, you're out of luck; these scripts work *only* with Mail.

- **Count Messages in All Mailboxes** is a convenient way to tell how much spam you've been getting. Of course, that's not what this script is *meant* for—it's just supposed to tell you how much email you have in each mailbox. If you're like most people, though, your spam count will far outweigh anything else you have in your mailboxes, rendering this count almost useless.

- **Crazy Message Text** is a great way to send electronic greeting cards, birthday wishes, or ransom notes (Figure 1-6).

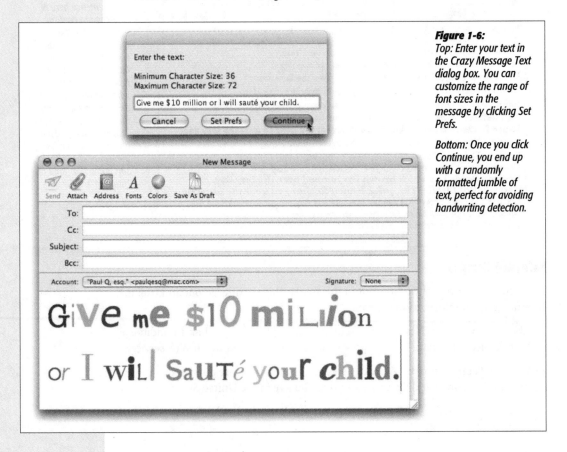

Figure 1-6:
Top: Enter your text in the Crazy Message Text dialog box. You can customize the range of font sizes in the message by clicking Set Prefs.

Bottom: Once you click Continue, you end up with a randomly formatted jumble of text, perfect for avoiding handwriting detection.

- **Create LDAP Server** is worthless unless you're on a corporate network. If you are, though, you may have access to an *LDAP server* (basically, a virtual employee directory). Your network administrator can help you fill out the dialog boxes.

  Once you've set up an LDAP server in Mail, you'll be able to type the first few letters of an employee's email address and have the rest of the address filled in for you automatically. (Of course, it might not be worth all that trouble to configure an LDAP server if you've already got all your contacts in Address Book.)

- **Create New Mail Account** prompts you for everything you need to set up a new email account. There's not much benefit to this multi–dialog box script, however, when you can set up a new account all at once in Mail → Preferences → Accounts.

- **Create New Message** takes you, dialog box by dialog box, through everything you need to make a new email message. The only benefit of using this script (instead of creating a new message in Mail itself) is that you don't have to bring Mail to the front first.

- **Display All Accounts and Preferences** puts together a new email message containing every imaginable statistic about your email settings. This script even attaches a copy of Mail's preference files for your perusing pleasure.

- **Get Size of IMAP Mailbox** is perfect for figuring out how full your .Mac mailbox is—if you've signed up for Apple's .Mac service (page 92), that is. Simply select an email account, let Mail synchronize its database with your mail server, and wait a few minutes. When Mail is done calculating, you'll see a new email message telling you how much space your email is taking up on the server.

- **Import Addresses** is identical to the Address Book version described on page 5. In other words, this script lets you import your contacts from a third-party program—like Microsoft Entourage—into Mac OS X's Address Book. (Once you do so, all your old contacts will be available in Mail as well.)

Note: The **Helper** scripts aren't much help here either. Just like in the **Address Book** scripts, you can't run these **Helper** scripts yourself.

- **Manage SMTP Servers** lists all the outgoing email servers that Mail is set up to use but that *you're* not using to send mail. If you deleted an email account but forgot to delete all the server settings that went with it, for example, this script can help you track down the orphaned settings.

- **Rule Actions** lets you run AppleScripts whenever email that matches certain criteria arrives. Check out **Help with Rule Actions** for more information on using this powerful feature, or see page 190 for an example of rule actions in action.

All the AppleScripts found in the **Scripts Menu** submenu only work from *within* Mail: just select an email message and choose the script you want to run. For more detailed explanations, check out the sidebar "Secrets of the Script Menu" on page 19.

Navigation Scripts

This subfolder contains scripts that let you jump to a particular folder in the Finder, right from the menu bar of any program.

Tip: If the folder you want to open doesn't have its own dedicated script, just choose from the extended folder listing in Open Special Folder.

Printing Scripts

Each of these scripts helps you send something to your printer:

- **About "Convert"/"Print Window" Scripts** provides some tips for using these scripts with multiple files at once.

- **Convert to PDF/PostScript** takes any graphics or plain text files you've selected in the Finder and converts them to either PDF or PostScript format. This is a great tool if your Mac is connected to a shared printer on your network, for example, but you don't want to shell out hundreds of dollars for a dedicated PostScript converter (a necessity for using many network printers). Instead, just use this PostScript-converting script and send the resulting file directly to your printer using Printer Setup Utility (in your Applications → Utilities folder).

I see the regular Script Menu in the upper-right corner of my screen, but I also see one in the regular menu bar of some of my programs. What's the deal?

You've just come across one of AppleScript's quirks. The *global* Script Menu—the one you see in the menu bar from all your programs, and the one that this chapter talks about—is a fairly new development in the world of Apple-Script. As far as old programs like AppleWorks and BBEdit are concerned, the global Script Menu might as well not ex-

ist. These programs have their *own* script menus and don't add their private scripts to the global Script Menu.

Luckily, some programs are kind enough to put their scripts in program-specific script menus and *also* in the global Script Menu (Mac OS X–native programs like Mail and Address Book, for example, fall into this category). These programs give you the benefits of both approaches: you get a script menu that you can use when you're working within the program—often with keyboard shortcuts for useful scripts—but you also get the global Script Menu with the same exact scripts, so you can run them from *another* program.

Of course, there's a third category—the one that just about every other program fits into. These programs (TextEdit, Microsoft Word, Photoshop, and iChat, just to name a few) lack script menus of their own. In these cases, any program-specific scripts you create must be placed into the *global* Script Menu, because the program has nowhere to store them in its own menu bar.

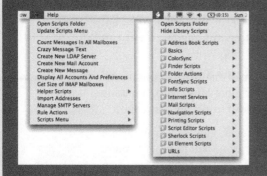

- **Print Window** is a handy replacement for the old Print Window command from Mac OS 9's Finder. This script lets you generate a printout of all the items inside any folder you choose (with no icons, alas), to post on your refrigerator perhaps.

Tip: The **Print Window with Subfolders** script is the same, except that it prints a list of all the folders' *subfolders* as well.

Script Editor Scripts

This submenu is filled with dozens of helpful scripts for getting the most out of Script Editor. For a quick summary of what the scripts do, choose "About these scripts." Or, for a more detailed explanation of using these scripts while writing your own code, turn to page 28.

Sherlock Scripts

OK, "scripts" is a bit of a misnomer—there's only one script here. Nonetheless, it's a useful one: **Search Internet** lets you enter any text and have Sherlock check the results from five search engines simultaneously. The results come back in an easy-to-browse list, ranked by how relevant each site is to your search terms.

UI Element Scripts

The scripts in this menu are all demonstrations of AppleScript's *GUI Scripting* capability, for controlling programs' interfaces. These scripts probably won't make much sense to you, however, until you've read Chapter 12, which explains how GUI Scripting works.

Note: You can't run any of these scripts right from the Script Menu; you have to run them from Script Editor (page 24) instead.

URLs

This final set of scripts provides quick links to some Web sites. All of these scripts use your default Web browser—which for most Mac OS X users is Safari, unless you specify a different browser (such as Camino, Firefox, or even Internet Explorer) in Safari → Preferences → General.

- **Apple Stock Quote (Yahoo)** displays detailed financial information for Apple Computer.

Tip: If you want a stock quote for any *other* company, choose Internet Scripts → Stock Quote (page 9). Unfortunately, using that other script doesn't provide any of the detailed news, graphs, and statistics that Apple's *own* stock quote script does.

- **Apple Store** brings you straight to Apple's online retail shop, *http://store. apple.com/.*

- **AppleScript Related Sites** contains scripts for jumping to three of the most popular AppleScript sites on the Web. (See page 309 for more AppleScript-related Web sites.)

- **CNN** takes you right to the popular online news site.

- **Download Weather Map** fetches an up-to-the-minute weather map of the continental United States and saves it as *weathermap.jpg* on your desktop. The script then goes one step further and opens the file in your favorite image viewer (by default, the Preview program). Figure 1-7 has the details.

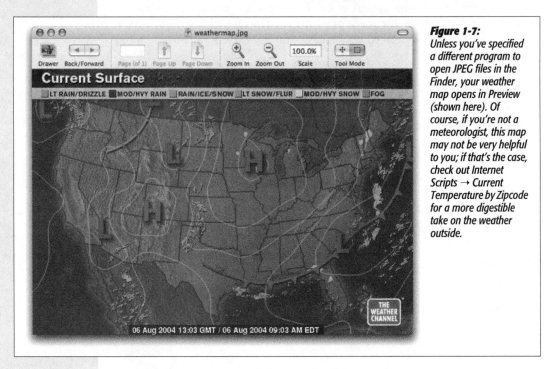

Figure 1-7:
Unless you've specified a different program to open JPEG files in the Finder, your weather map opens in Preview (shown here). Of course, if you're not a meteorologist, this map may not be very helpful to you; if that's the case, check out Internet Scripts → Current Temperature by Zipcode for a more digestible take on the weather outside.

- **Macintouch** brings you to the popular in-the-know Mac news site.

- **MacWeek** is a poor title for this script, as it actually takes you to MacCentral, a news site run by *Macworld* magazine.

Customizing the Script Menu

At this point, you probably think the Script Menu is a pretty handy tool for running the scripts on your Mac. However, the Script Menu is much more than just a tool for launching the scripts that come with Mac OS X. Hidden behind its humble icon in the menu bar is enough power to keep any Mac person engrossed for hours.

For example, you can:

- **Add new scripts to the Script Menu.** Or, if you're a clutter nut, you can *remove* some of the useless scripts that come with the menu.

- **Rearrange the submenus.** Since the Script Menu just mirrors a folder that lives on your system (found in Macintosh HD → Library → Scripts), you can move scripts around and customize the Script Menu to suit your needs.

- **Tweak the scripts themselves.** Fix Apple's spelling oversights (page 9), for instance, or insert AppleScript commands of your own into the built-in scripts.

Adding new scripts

After you use the Script Menu for a while, you'll probably get bored with the selection of scripts that Apple ships along with Mac OS X. Luckily, you can take any script you want—for example, an AppleScript you write yourself, or one you download from a Web site listed on page 309—and add it to your Script Menu.

Say you want a script that'll speak the time and temperature out loud. You can search online for an AppleScript that does just that, and once you download the script, you can add it to your Script Menu as follows:

1. **Download the script you want from the Internet.**

   In this case, the script you want is available from *http://files.macscripter.net/ scriptbuilders/Utilities/SayYourTimeAndTemperature.sit.*

Note: If the downloaded file doesn't expand itself automatically, simply double-click its icon in the Finder.

---

2. **Open the Macintosh HD → Library → Scripts folder.**

   This is the Library folder that's located at the root of your Mac's hard drive (not to be confused with your *personal* Library folder, described on page 16).

3. **Drag the script you just downloaded and drop it into any of the folders in the Finder window.**

   Because this new script uses the Internet to access its information, an appropriate folder would be Internet Services.

Tip: You can put the script in whichever folder you want, and you can even *name* it whatever you want. For this script (originally named **SayYourTimeAndTemperature**), a more concise name might be **Time and Temp**, for example. (To rename a file, select it, press Return, type the new name, and press Return again.)

---

4. **Open the Script Menu and run your new script (Figure 1-8).**

   The script opens Address Book in the background to find your home address and then "speaks" out loud the temperature and time for your area (using the default system voice you've chosen for your Mac via System Preferences → Speech → Default Voice).

Rearranging submenus

It's nice that Apple took the time to organize the scripts in the Script Menu into different submenus, but sometimes it seems like their choices were just plain random. Why, for example, aren't the **Finder** scripts and **Navigation** scripts combined in the same folder when both sets of scripts work with the Finder?

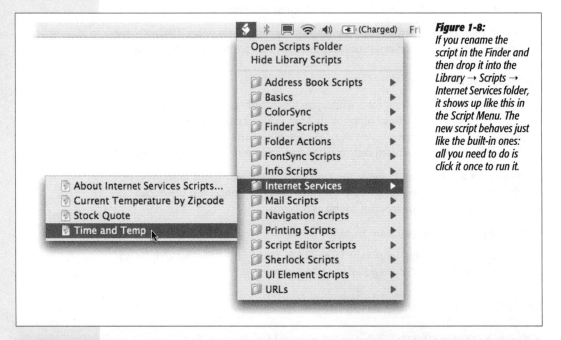

Figure 1-8:
If you rename the script in the Finder and then drop it into the Library → Scripts → Internet Services folder, it shows up like this in the Script Menu. The new script behaves just like the built-in ones: all you need to do is click it once to run it.

The Mystery of Open Scripts Folder

Why is it that whenever I choose Open Scripts Folder from the Script Menu, the Finder shows me an empty window? I know that I have scripts—they all show up in the Script Menu—but I can't seem to get to them using the Open Scripts Folder command.

This strange behavior is all Mac OS X's fault, mainly because there is more than one Scripts folder. All the built-in scripts (the ones you've been looking at in the Script Menu) are stored in Library → Scripts, in the root level of your hard drive. On the other hand, when you choose Open Scripts Folder, the Finder goes to the Library → Scripts folder found within your *Home* folder.

Luckily, if you place or save scripts into your Home → Library → Scripts folder, they'll *also* appear in the Script Menu (below the ones from the Library → Scripts folder). This gives you an opportunity to fix the behavior of the Open Scripts Folder command: just move all the existing scripts (from Library → Scripts) into your Home → Library → Scripts folder. From now on, you'll see every script in the Script Menu, but when you choose Open Scripts Folder, you'll *also* see the correct scripts in the Finder.

This workaround has one unfortunate side effect: if you move the scripts into your Home folder, none of the other people who use your computer will be able to access the scripts from *their* accounts.

Luckily, you can override the Script Menu and put scripts into whatever folders you'd like. To move some scripts from one Script Menu category to another, simply open the Library → Scripts folder, and drag the scripts into a different subfolder (Figure 1-9).

Tip: Your scripts don't *have* to be inside a subfolder at all; if you'd like, you can just leave them floating in the Library → Scripts folder. That way, they'll appear directly in the Script Menu—you won't have to navigate through submenus to get to them .

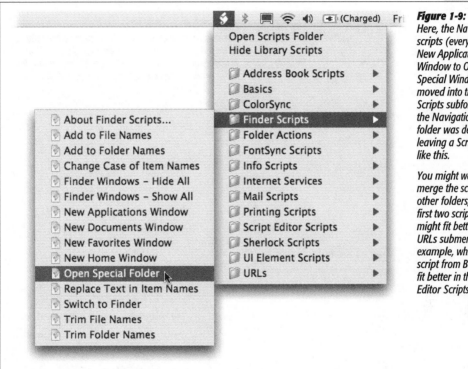

Figure 1-9:
Here, the Navigation scripts (everything from New Applications Window to Open Special Window) were moved into the Finder Scripts subfolder. Then, the Navigation Scripts folder was deleted, leaving a Script Menu like this.

You might want to merge the scripts from other folders, too. The first two scripts in Basics might fit better in the URLs submenu, for example, while the last script from Basics might fit better in the Script Editor Scripts submenu.

Working with the Scripts You Have

As you'll quickly realize from using the Script Menu, your Mac is teeming with dozens of free, built-in scripts. You can run, rename, and organize these scripts, as described on the preceding pages.

But if you're just starting to learn AppleScript, these scripts can be lifesavers. Not only can you examine how the scripts work, but you can also make *changes* and see how they affect the scripts' behavior. Best of all, if you get stuck when writing a new AppleScript, you can copy some of the code from the Script Menu's scripts and paste that code right into your *own* script.

Opening a Script

The first step in working with a script, of course, is opening it up. Fortunately, this is an easy process: just double-click the script in the Finder. The script opens in Script Editor, the all-purpose AppleScript program described in Chapter 2.

When you're just learning AppleScript, you might as well start by looking at a simple script. Double-click Library → Scripts → Navigation Scripts → New Application Window.scpt, and Script Editor opens the script file in a new window (Figure 1-10).

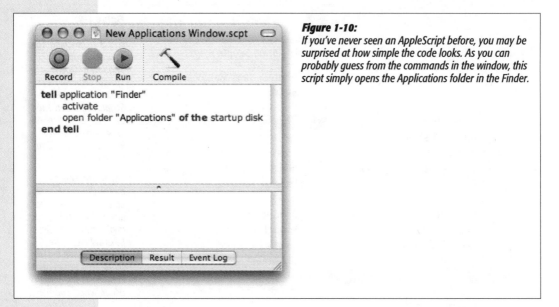

Figure 1-10:
If you've never seen an AppleScript before, you may be surprised at how simple the code looks. As you can probably guess from the commands in the window, this script simply opens the Applications folder in the Finder.

At this point, you can click the Run button to see what the script actually does (in this case, the script opens a new Finder window and takes you to the Applications folder).

Analyzing How It Works

The next step in working with a script, of course, is understanding how the script actually works. Some commands are self-evident, while others require you to examine a program's *dictionary*—its master command list (page 44)—to understand exactly what's going on. Luckily, the commands in the New Applications Window script are all pretty simple:

- **tell application "Finder"** instructs Mac OS X that the commands that follow should be run by the Finder.

- **activate** brings the Finder to the front, much as you would by clicking its Dock icon. Unlike clicking the Dock icon, however, the *activate* command doesn't automatically open a new Finder window; for that stunt, you'll need the next command.

- **open folder "Applications" of the startup disk** tells the Finder to open a new window, displaying the Applications folder of your main hard drive. (If you already have the Applications folder open, this command simply brings that window forward.)

- **end tell** directs the Finder to go about its regular business, ignoring further AppleScript commands.

POWER USERS' CLINIC

Secrets of the Script Menu

The Script Menu, simple as it may seem, has a number of completely hidden tricks up its sleeve. All these shortcuts can save you time, annoyance, and confusion:

- **Click any submenu to jump right to that folder in the Finder.** For instance, if you wanted to open up the Mail Scripts folder, you could just click on the Mail Scripts submenu of the Script Menu.

- **Shift-click any script to jump right to it in the Finder.** This is a great trick when you want to quickly

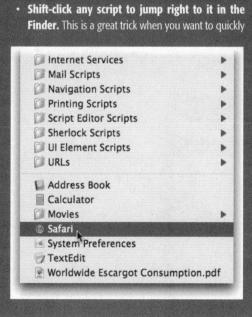

rename a script: Shift-click its name to switch to the file, start editing its name by pressing Return, and then press Return again when you're done editing. Presto—the new name now shows up in the Script Menu.

- **Option-click any script to open it in Script Editor.** Once there, you can examine the script to see how it works, or edit it to change how it works. Either way, page 21 has more details on Script Editor.

- **Add files *besides scripts* to your Scripts menu.** Yes, you read that right. Your Scripts menu is perfectly content to *display* programs, files, folders, and aliases, and they'll all show up in your Script Menu (shown here). To make your items appear on the *bottom* of the Script Menu, put them in your Home → Library → Scripts folder (rather than just Library → Scripts).

Using this trick, you can turn your Script Menu into a fast, free application and file launcher. There's just one caveat: don't try to add big folders to the Script Menu. If you do, the menu may spend *minutes* burrowing into your folders, trying to figure out how to display all their items. Instead, add the individual files and programs you'll need and leave the rest of the folder somewhere else.

Changing What It Does

Now that you understand how the script works, you can change it to better suit your needs. To make the script open the Users folder, for example, you'd follow this procedure:

1. **Replace *Applications* with *Users*.**

   File names have to be surrounded in double quotes, so make sure you don't delete the quotation marks.

2. **Click the Run button to test your script.**

   You should see the Finder come forward and display the Users folder.

3. **Choose File → Save As (Shift-⌘-S).**

   Name the file New Users Window.scpt, make sure the File Format is set to Script, and save it in the Library → Scripts → Navigation Scripts folder.

4. **Open your Script Menu, and run your new script from the Navigation Scripts submenu.**

   If you did everything correctly, your new menu item opens the Users folder in the Finder (Figure 1-11).

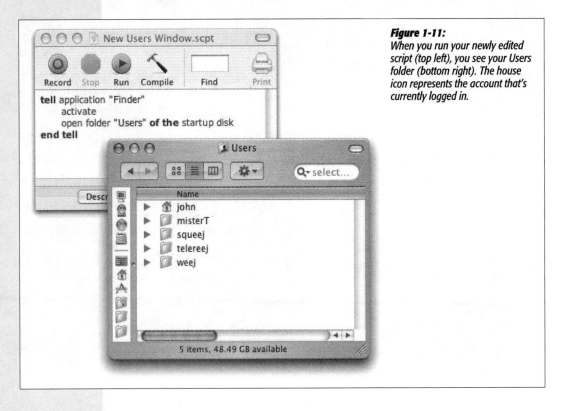

Figure 1-11:
When you run your newly edited script (top left), you see your Users folder (bottom right). The house icon represents the account that's currently logged in.

Using Script Editor

If you're going to write and edit AppleScripts, you're going to need some sort of program to help you out. For that, Apple has graciously supplied you with the aptly named Script Editor program. Script Editor is AppleScript's bread and butter—the program you'll use for just about everything as you learn the language. It's a text editor, script runner, documentation viewer, and antifreeze solution, all rolled into one. And although there are other AppleScript editors available (listed on page 38), you'll be best off sticking with Script Editor for now—if only because it's free and included with your computer.

You can start Script Editor in several ways:

- **Double-click its icon in the Applications → AppleScript folder.**

  Since you're going to be using Script Editor a lot, you might even like to store its icon in the Dock or the Finder's Sidebar, where you'll have easy access at a moment's notice.

- **Open a script anywhere on your computer.**

  You can drag a script from your Library → Scripts folder to Script Editor's icon, for example.

- **In the Script Menu, choose Basics → Open Script Editor.**

  This is the best method if you're tight on screen space, because you don't have to open any new windows.

The Script Editor Look

As you can see from Figure 2-1, Script Editor's window is fairly basic, especially when compared to something like Photoshop or Microsoft Word. Along the top of the window, you'll see a toolbar with four simple buttons (Record, Stop, Run, and Compile), with an area beneath for you to type in your script.

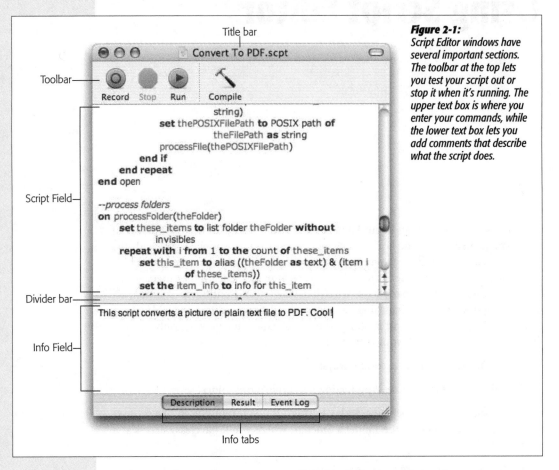

Figure 2-1:
Script Editor windows have several important sections. The toolbar at the top lets you test your script out or stop it when it's running. The upper text box is where you enter your commands, while the lower text box lets you add comments that describe what the script does.

Unfortunately, Apple gave many of Script Editor's tools nerdy, programmer-y names (Event Log, anyone?). This section of the book, therefore, is meant to clear up what all the buttons and doodads in Script Editor's interface do.

The Toolbar

The four buttons you see at the top of your window make up the toolbar. They're all modeled after the buttons on an old audiocassette recorder (alright, all of them except Compile, which actually comes from Xcode, one of Apple's programmer tools [page 275]).

Tip: You can run the same toolbar actions by using the commands or keyboard shortcuts in Script Editor's Script menu.

Record

Strange as it may sound, you don't need to write AppleScript commands yourself to get a working script. If you simply click the Record button, Script Editor tries its best to write out the appropriate AppleScript commands *for* you, based on what you're doing with your Mac. That's a much easier arrangement than, for example, hand-typing a series of complicated commands yourself.

Note: Unfortunately, using this recording trick is rarely the best way to create AppleScripts. That's because recording is based on what's currently happening on screen, so you can't make "general scenario" scripts that perform *different* tasks depending on what's happening at the moment.

Say you have a daily routine: you open a Finder window, navigate to the Applications folder, and turn on Column View. This is a perfect task to automate with AppleScript. All you'd need to do is click the Record button in Script Editor, go about your routine, and then click the Stop button in Script Editor when you're done. You'd end up with a script that looks something like this, without even having to write a single line of code yourself:

```
tell application "Finder"
    activate
    make new Finder window to startup disk
    set target of Finder window 1 to folder "Applications" of startup disk
    set current view of Finder window 1 to column view
end tell
```

Note: You can download this script, and all the other examples in this book, from the Missing Manual Web site. See the AppleScript Examples CD sidebar on the next page for instructions.

Since this is a full-fledged script, you can run it again and again without having to perform all the tasks manually. You could then save this script in your Script Menu (page 15), and you'd be able to easily run the script from any program.

Note: Unfortunately, most programs (TextEdit, Photoshop, iTunes, and so on) don't support AppleScript recording. If you spend a lot of time in programs that *do,* however (BBEdit, QuickTime, and the Finder, for example), you'll be glad that you can create scripts without writing the code yourself.

Stop

As its name implies, this toolbar button halts whatever's in progress inside Script Editor's brain. If you've finished recording a series of Finder actions, for example, this is the button to click to let AppleScript know you're done. Or, if you've got a script that just won't seem to finish, this button lets you cut it off midstream.

Run

When you click this button, Script Editor first makes sure your commands are all valid. If they are, Script Editor then runs every command in your script, one at a time, until it reaches the end.

Tip: If something goes wrong while your script is running (say, you realize it's deleting your entire Home folder), simply click the Stop button. Next time you click Run, the script starts from the very beginning again—*not* from the point where it stopped last time.

Compile

In programming lingo, *compiling* a file just means turning it into something you can run. For example, when you compile a script, Script Editor goes line by line through the code to make sure every AppleScript command is spelled and used correctly.

Note: If AppleScript finds an error while compiling your script, Script Editor will likely display a cryptic error message. See page 266 for an explanation of what these messages mean.

UP TO SPEED

AppleScript Examples CD

A few examples make any learning process easier-and this book is no exception. Throughout these pages, you'll find references to AppleScript files on something called the AppleScript Examples CD.

You can download these files right now. First, visit *www.missingmanuals.com*. At the top of the page, click the Missing CD button.

You arrive at a page listing the downloadable files for the entire Missing Manual Series. Under the AppleScript heading, click to download the "AppleScript examples CD" disk image. It contains all the sample scripts you'll work with in this book.

When the download is complete, you'll find on your desktop a file called AppleScript Examples.dmg. That's the disk image file, shown here at lower left.

When you double-click it, you'll find a second icon on your Desktop, resembling a hard drive icon, shown here at lower

right. (If Safari is your Web browser, just relax and wait as the icon opens automatically.) This is the actual "CD" icon. If you open it up, you'll find all the files for this book. You can copy them to a folder on your hard drive, if you like.

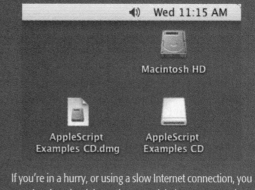

If you're in a hurry, or using a slow Internet connection, you can also download the various tutorial pieces one at a time. You'll find them listed under the appropriate chapter headings on the Web site.

Even though clicking the Run button automatically compiles a script for you, it's still a good idea to click the Compile button yourself first to catch all the errors. That way, when you finally do click the Run button, you can be sure that your script *will* run—so you can walk away from your Mac and make a cup of coffee, for example.

Tip: If you're a speed freak, using the mouse to click the Compile button is a big waste of time. Instead, just press ⌘-K; it accomplishes the same thing, but you don't have to move your hand off the keyboard.

True power users, on the other hand, use the *secret* keystroke: Enter. Rather than inserting a new line (as it does in, say, TextEdit), pressing Enter in Script Editor simply compiles the script for you. As you write your own scripts, get into the habit of hitting Enter before you click Run to save time.

(Something to remember if you come from Windows: the Enter key on a Mac is *not* the same as Return.)

Customizing the toolbar

What's on the toolbar now is great—if you're happy to accept what Apple gives you right out of the box. However, if you're the sort of person who paints your car seven different colors, you'll be happy to know that Script Editor lets you customize its toolbar to the hilt.

For starters, you can move around the icons that are already there by ⌘-dragging them. If you'd like to completely get rid of a toolbar icon, ⌘-drag it *off* the toolbar—the icon disappears in an animated poof of smoke.

Just as easily, you can add new icons. Simply choose View → Customize Toolbar (or Option-⌘-click the pill button in the upper-right corner of a Script Editor window), and drag any icons you want right into the toolbar. When you're finished, click Done to make the customization sheet disappear.

Tip: If you're interested in *searching* your scripts, drag the Find box from this customization sheet into Script Editor's toolbar. From then on, simply enter your search criteria into the Find box and press Return to search the script. (If you keep pressing Return, you'll continue jumping to the next occurrence of whatever it was you searched for.) This trick saves you a few seconds over mousing up to Edit → Find.

GEM IN THE ROUGH

The Divider Bar

The humble divider bar lies in between your Script Field and Info Field, as shown in Figure 2-2. Of course, you probably know that you can drag the divider bar up or down to change the sizes of the two fields that border it. However, there are two tricks that make the divider bar an even more useful tool:

- **Double-click it to send it all the way to the bottom of the window.** That way, you'll see just your Script Field—perfect if you have a small screen and need to enter a lot of commands.

- **Option-double-click it to send it all the way to the top of the window.** That's a handy arrangement if you need to enter a lot of comments in the Info Field, for example.

No matter which trick you use, you can bring the divider bar back to the middle of the window by double-clicking it again.

If you're tight on screen space, you're probably annoyed at how *big* the toolbar is, not which icons are on it. Luckily, Script Editor gives you a choice of six toolbar sizes, from the slimmest bar of text (perfect for small-screened iBooks) up to the large icon-and-text display you see now (perfect for, say, that new 30-inch screen you just bought). Figure 2-2 has the details.

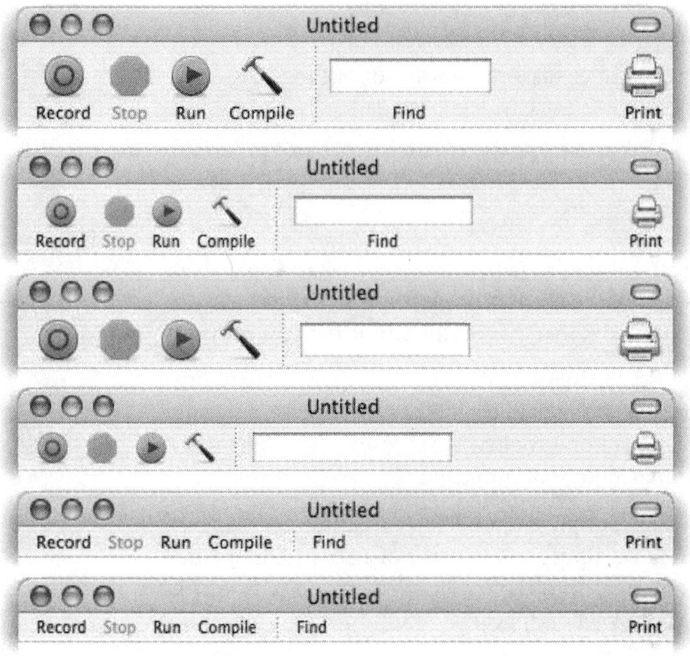

Figure 2-2:
The many looks of Script Editor's toolbar. ⌘-click the pill-shaped button to switch between: big icons and text, small icons and text, big icons, small icons, big text, and small text. Note that if you're using a text-only setting, the Find button brings up the Find dialog box.

If you're *really* squeezed for screen real estate, you can completely hide the toolbar: simply choose View → Hide Toolbar, or click the pill-shaped button in the upper-right corner of the window. (You can bring the toolbar back by choosing View → Show Toolbar or by clicking that pill-shaped button again.)

The Script Field

The Script Field, located right beneath the toolbar, is where your AppleScript commands go. You enter them, one command per line, and click Compile when you're done. That's when the fun begins.

For starters, the Script Field uses *colored* text. When you type commands in at first, they're purple. As soon as you click Compile or Run, though, the text turns blue, black, and gray—assuming your script compiled correctly (page 24). Here's what the colors mean:

- **Blue text** is what Script Editor uses to indicate AppleScript commands. Keep an eye out especially for blue *bold* text, which indicates special AppleScript keywords like *of, to,* and *set.*

Tip: If you're just getting started with AppleScript, examine existing scripts' blue text for examples of commands you can use in your *own* scripts.

- **Black text** is what Script Editor uses for specific AppleScript values—numbers, for example, or the text between quotation marks.

- **Gray text** is reserved for AppleScript *comments*—pieces of English narration that let you describe what's going on in a certain section of your script (page 42).

This colorizing feature is a great way to tell whether a script has any typos, for example. Since a script won't compile *at all* if it has any typos, a colorized Script Field indicates that your script has passed the compiler's inspection (Figure 2-3).

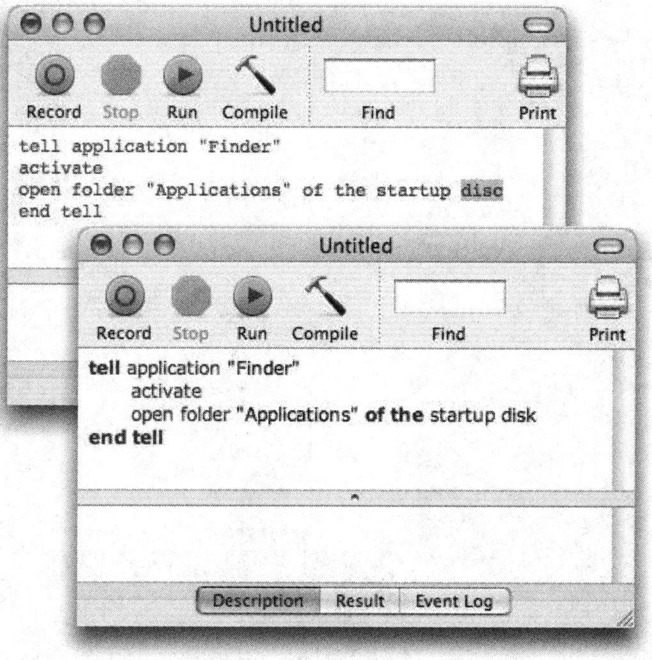

Figure 2-3:
The even-width Courier font (top) indicates that a script hasn't been compiled successfully. In this case, the word "disk" was misspelled, so the compiler selects it.

Once the typo is fixed and the script is compiled again (bottom), the script changes color and uses the Verdana font. (You can customize the font, size, and color settings as described on page 36.)

The Script Field also supports the full range of text operations that TextEdit does. You can drag text around within the Script Field, for instance, or drag a particularly long URL out of your Web browser and into the Script Field. You can easily find pieces of text in your script using the Edit → Find menu, too. And you can even spell check your script by choosing Edit → Spelling → Check Spelling.

Tip: If you'd like Script Editor to check your spelling as you enter commands, choose Edit → Spelling → "Check Spelling as You Type."

Mega Shortcut Menu

The Script Field has one of the most complete shortcut menus available in any program, ever. Simply Control-click inside the Script Field. (Alternatively, summon the commands from the Script Editor Scripts submenu of the Script Field.)

Each command in the menu's lower portion automatically writes out a section of code for you:

- **About These Scripts** presents a simple dialog box explaining, very roughly, how the scripts work. The information it shows mostly applies to running these scripts from the Script Menu (page 4), however.

- **Comment Tags** (page 42) surround the selected text in parentheses and asterisks, indicating to Apple-Script that the text should be ignored.

- **Action Clauses** let your script ignore errors pro-duced by other programs or wait a period of time before proceeding.

- **Conditionals** let your script run commands when certain criteria are met (page 47). For example, if you wanted to display a dialog box *only* when Text-Edit is open, you would use a conditional statement to enclose your commands.

- **Dialogs** inserts commands used for presenting dialog boxes. You can have up to three buttons in a dialog box, with or without a place to enter text (page 60).

- **Error Handlers** let your script deal with problems that arise while it's running (page 274). If there's a possibility that the Finder might quit in the middle of your script, for instance, you'd use an error handler to make sure your script doesn't quit too.

- **Folder Actions Handlers** are preassembled chunks of text for writing *folder actions*—scripts that are trig-gered automatically by the Finder (page 221).

- **Image Manipulation** lets you create scripts that auto-matically resize, zoom, and rotate images. Page 137 shows you how to get started writing graphics scripts.

- If you want your script to go through each item in a folder, **Iterate Items** and **Repeat Routines** can help. A batch-renaming script would use an iterating or repeat command so the script could rename every file as it went through a folder (page 113).

- **String Comparison** checks whether two pieces of text are equal, optionally ignoring capitalization, etc.

- **Tell Blocks** let you address commands at a certain program, rather than at Mac OS X itself.

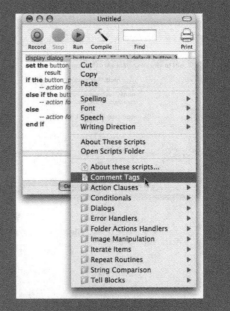

When you're first learning AppleScript, Script Editor's shortcut menu is invaluable. You can use the menu to drop in pieces of AppleScript code that you're unfamiliar with, as a way of learning new commands. As you become more experienced with AppleScript, you might use the shortcut menu to enter complicated commands you already know, just to save time.

Even better, you can add your *own* items to the shortcut menu by dragging them to your Library → Scripts → Script Editor Scripts folder—or edit the scripts that are already there.

The Info Field

The Info Field lies at the bottom of your window, and it's one of the least-used pieces of Script Editor's interface. That's because it's a passive display—you rarely click it, and it mostly displays tangential information on the status of your script. Right beneath the Info Field, there are three tabbed buttons (Description, Result, and Event Log), which let you switch between the Info Field's three modes. To change modes, simply click one of those tabs, or press ⌘-1, ⌘-2, and ⌘-3, respectively.

Description

The Description tab lets you enter a short comment about what your script does. If you're planning to distribute your script over the Internet, for example, you might enter copyright information here, too.

The reason most people don't use the Description tab, though, is that they can enter comments right *inside* a script (page 42). If you wrote a particularly complicated math operation, for example, you'd probably rather mention how it works right *next* to each command, rather than refer to the code from the Description tab.

Tip: The Description tab does have one advantage over the Script Field, though: you can drag files into it. When it comes time to save your script, just choose Script Bundle as the format (page 34), and you can distribute your script with all the attached files intact. (To open one of the attached files later, just drag it out of the Info Field and into the Finder.)

You might find this trick useful if you ever want to attach your photo to a script—or, even weirder, you could attach an audio file you've recorded, so other people can *hear* your comments rather than read them.

Result

When a script has finished running, it might be left with a piece of information— the value from a math operation, for instance, or the button someone clicked in a dialog box. The Result field is where Script Editor dumps that leftover information, waiting for you to read at your leisure.

If you're writing your own scripts, though, you probably want that leftover information brought *to* you, so you don't have to switch into Script Editor and look at the Result field to find it. Figure 2-4 shows the difference.

Event Log

If you're testing out a complicated script, the Event Log keeps track of important things that happen while the script is running. For example, if your script batch-renames files in the Finder (page 113), the Event Log keeps track of every file that was renamed.

Note: In order to make the Event Log display such events, you must switch to it *before* your script starts running.

On its own, the Event Log would be a great tool for checking how your scripts run. However, Script Editor includes a far more advanced tool—the Event Log *History*—that lets you see the Event Logs of *previous* scripts and what time they ran (page 269). Because of that—and because the Event Log History is quite easy to browse through—most self-respecting AppleScript programmers use the Event Log History instead of the puny, underpowered Event Log at the bottom of a script window.

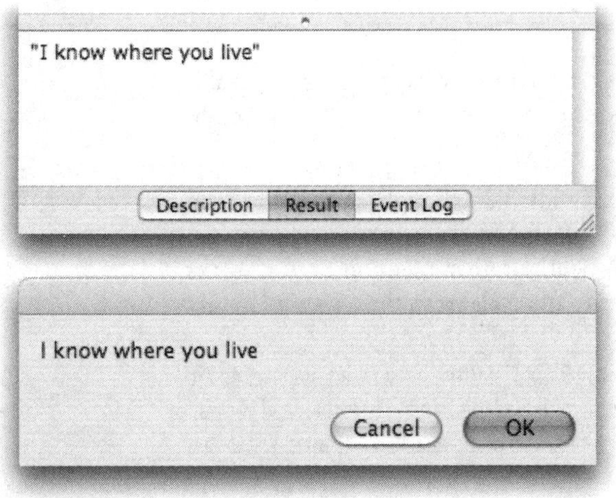

Figure 2-4:
Two approaches to displaying the result of a script. Top: Leave the information loose at the end of your script, and it'll be shown in the Results field. If you use this approach, you won't know when your script is done, and you'll have to switch into Script Editor to see the result.

Bottom: Use the display dialog command (page 40) to display the result, and you'll know exactly when your script is done.

Script Formats

When you double-click one of the scripts in, say, your Library → Scripts → Finder Scripts folder,Script Editor opens a new window containing the AppleScript code for that script. On the other hand, if you double-click one of the scripts in your Library → Scripts → ColorSync folder, the script *itself* runs rather than opening up in Script Editor.

That might seem like a minor difference, but it highlights an important fact of AppleScript life: scripts come in different formats. If you hope to make it through the jungle of AppleScript files available on the Web (page 309)—and, perhaps, to post your own scripts there—you first have to understand the different formats AppleScript supports.

You can open any AppleScript-supported file by dragging it onto Script Editor's icon in the Finder or Dock. To *save* a script in a different format, you use the File Format pop-up menu in the Save dialog box (Figure 2-5).

There are three main formats:

- **Script files,** which get a *.scpt* file extension.

- **Applications,** which get a *.app* file extension (just like regular Mac OS X programs).

- **Text documents,** which get the lengthy *.applescript* file extension.

Note: Two other minor formats—called *bundles*—are also available. Page 34 explains how and when to use these.

The following sections give you a better idea of when you should save a script as a particular script type.

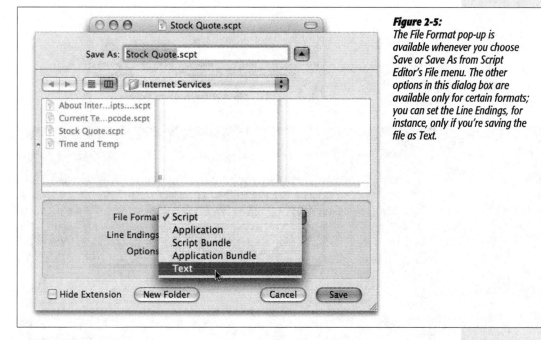

Figure 2-5:
The File Format pop-up is available whenever you choose Save or Save As from Script Editor's File menu. The other options in this dialog box are available only for certain formats; you can set the Line Endings, for instance, only if you're saving the file as Text.

Script Files

So far, the scripts you've been using for most of this book—the ones located in your Library → Scripts → Basics folder, for example—are stored as .scpt files (Figure 2-6). When you double-click a .scpt file, the script automatically opens in Script Editor.

If you plan to use your scripts in the Script Menu (page 15), use this format. To save a file in .scpt format, simply choose Script from the File Format pop-up menu (Figure 2-5).

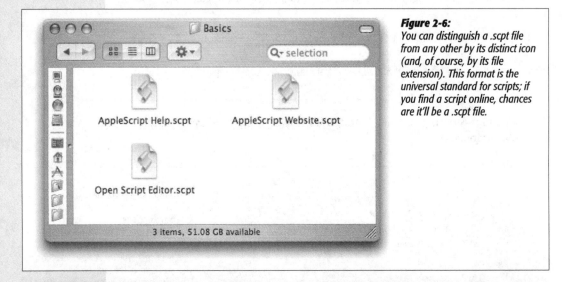

Figure 2-6:
You can distinguish a .scpt file from any other by its distinct icon (and, of course, by its file extension). This format is the universal standard for scripts; if you find a script online, chances are it'll be a .scpt file.

The Navigation Bar

If you open long, involved scripts with Script Editor (say, the Stock Quote script included with Mac OS X), you might get annoyed at the time-consuming process of scrolling up and down just to find a certain section of code. Luckily, Script Editor includes an easier way to get where you need to go: the Navigation Bar.

To display the Navigation Bar, simply choose View → Show Navigation Bar. You'll see a thin new strip just below the toolbar, containing two pop-up menus.

The left menu lets you choose which scripting language to use for the script. Unless you've installed third-party languages (page 44), the only choice you'll have in this menu is AppleScript.

The menu on the right, though, is where the action is. Here, you can choose from the different *properties* (page 48) and *subroutines* (page 85) in your script, which are the building blocks of advanced AppleScript code. Just select a particular handler from the menu, for example, to jump right to that line of code in the script.

It turns out the Navigation Bar in Script Editor is actually a close approximation of the Navigation Bar in Xcode (page 275). If you ever tire of the overwhelming power, simply choose View → Hide Navigation Bar.

Applications

An application, is a double-clickable program that gets saved with a .app file extension. (Of course, when you view an AppleScript application in the Finder, you'll likely notice that its extension is hidden, just like all the other applications in your Applications folder.)

With Script Editor, you can create your *own* applications using AppleScript code. For example, you could take the **Current Temperature by Zipcode** script (page 9), save it as an application, and then run it just by double-clicking its Finder icon (Figure 2-7).

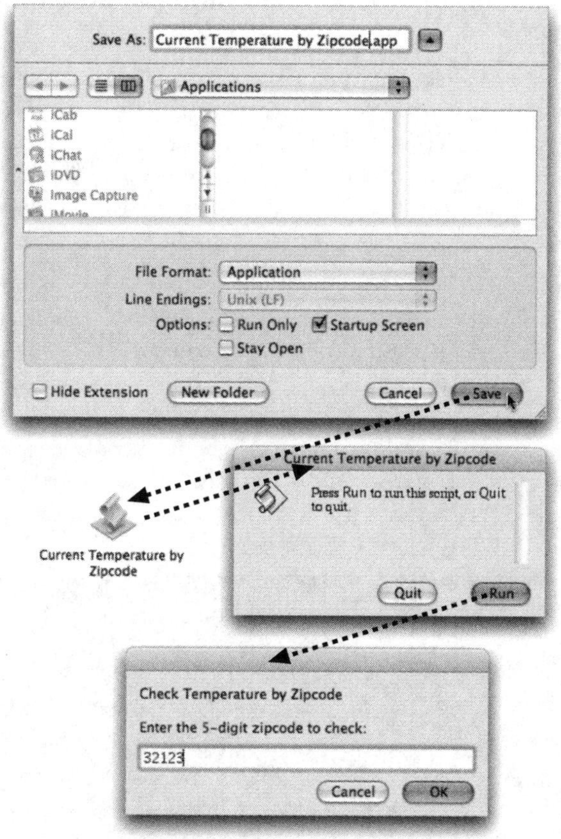

Figure 2-7:
Top: Choose Application from the File Format pop-up menu, and select any options you'd like from the bottom. Turning on Run Only will keep other people from reading your code, while turning on Stay Open will keep your program running even after it's done with its commands.

Middle left: When you click Save, you get a double-clickable icon.

Middle right: If you turned on the Startup Screen option, the application will present a dialog box before it runs its commands.

Bottom: When you click Run, your application finally runs its code.

AppleScript applications have all the other benefits of normal programs, too: you can put them in your Dock; they'll show up in the Apple menu's Recent Items; and you can launch them when you log in by dragging them into your System Preferences → Accounts → Startup Items pane.

Note: You can even make AppleScript applications that support drag-and-dropped files. These mini-applications are known as *droplets,* and page 141 shows how to write them.

Plain Text Documents

If you choose Text from the File Format pop-up menu, you'll get a file that ends in .applescript. This extension signifies that the script is nothing more than a plain old text file. Even though you can double-click the file's icon to open it in Script Editor, you can also drag the file into TextEdit, BBEdit, Microsoft Word, or any other text-processing program.

"But why would I save a script as a text file when I can just save it as an application?" you ask. The biggest benefit is that it creates a teeny, tiny file, as shown in Table 2-1. If you want to send a big script as an email attachment, a plain text file is much quicker to download than an application. And once your friend *has* downloaded the .applescript file, she can open it in Script Editor and re-save it as either a script file or an AppleScript application.

There's one more benefit to using a plain text file: Windows and Mac OS 9 users can open it, too. Just choose Windows Line Endings in the Save dialog box, and send the script to all your Mac- and PC-using friends. (Of course, Windows people can't *run* the AppleScript file, but at least they can see the beauty of your code.)

Note: When you save a file as plain text, it loses all the syntax coloring that Script Editor applied (page 27). If formatting is important to you, choose File → Print → Save As PDF instead. You'll get a convenient PDF file—rather than a text file—with all the color and formatting intact.

POWER USERS' CLINIC

Bundling Files

As mentioned earlier, there are two other formats that AppleScript supports: Script Bundles and Application Bundles. The point of using a *bundle* is that all the auxiliary files that your commands use (movies, images, sounds, and so on) can be hidden from view, stored *inside* the script or application. Then, if you choose to distribute your script over the Internet, you can be sure that all the auxiliary files get distributed as well.

Once you save a file as a bundle, you can crack it open in the Finder by Control-clicking its icon and choosing Show

Package Contents from the shortcut menu. Then navigate to the Contents → Resources folder, and drop any files there. Now, when you launch the script, it'll have direct access to those files (using the *path to me* command, described on page 166).

The best part of this arrangement is that you can move your bundle around—on your hard drive or over the Internet—and keep all the files intact. You can even rename the bundle itself (but not the files inside), and the script or application will still work properly.

Table 2-1. Script format comparison

Script type	What happens when you double-click it?	Can Windows open it?	Typical file size
.scpt file or script bundle	Launches Script Editor	No	12 KB
Application or application bundle	Runs itself	No	60 KB
Plain text file	Launches Script Editor	Yes	4 KB

Setting Script Editor's Preferences

Now that you've been using Script Editor for a little while, the boring text coloring is probably starting to get to you. Or maybe you're just sick of reading your scripts in a 12-point font. No matter what your complaint, chances are Script Editor can make things better for you.

Start out by opening Script Editor → Preferences (⌘-,). You'll see five buttons in the toolbar, each for a different aspect of Script Editor's behavior. Click the category you want to customize (Figure 2-8), and continue reading.

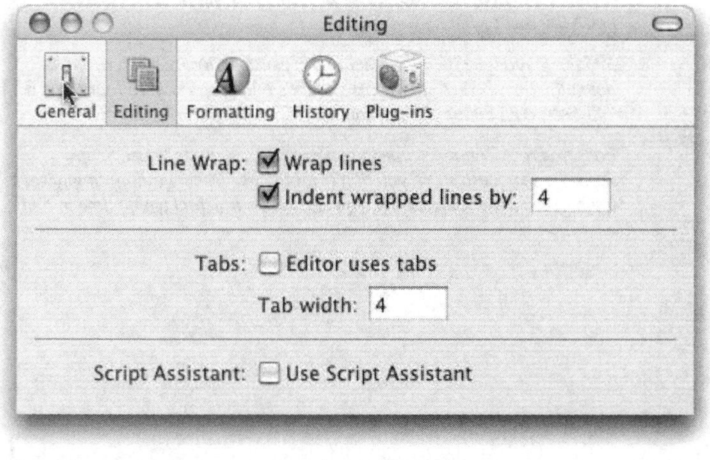

Figure 2-8:
Script Editor's Preferences window. Click a toolbar button to jump right to that particular pane.

General

Fresh out of the box, your Mac comes with only one language you can use in Script Editor: AppleScript. That's why Script Editor automatically understands your AppleScript commands when you create a new script and click Run.

However, some people install other programming languages—like JavaScript—for use in Script Editor (page 44), and that's where the Default Language pop-up menu comes in. With this menu, you can select what language you want to use for *all* new scripts. (If you ever want to override this setting for a single script, just use the Navigation Bar [page 32].)

Editing

The three sections of the Editing pane allow you to customize how text appears in Script Editor's windows. The Line Wrap preferences, for example, let you set whether text that's too long for one line continues onto the next one (Wrap Lines on) or scrolls off the side of the window (Wrap Lines off). If you've turned Wrap Lines on, you can even set how many space-widths the overflowing lines are indented.

The Tabs section, on the other hand, let you choose whether your script should be indented at *all*. If you turn off "Editor uses tabs," all your commands will end up flush against the left side of the Script Field. (Or, at least that's the idea; as of Mac OS X v10.3, this setting worked so inconsistently that it was pretty much useless.)

Finally, turning on the Script Assistant enables Script Editor's secret autocomplete feature. With the Script Assistant, you don't have to remember the full names for AppleScript commands; you just type the first few letters, and the Assistant does the rest (Figure 2-9).

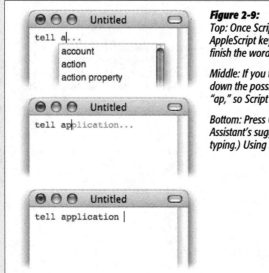

Figure 2-9:
Top: Once Script Assistant is turned on, you can just type the first letter of an AppleScript keyword. Script Editor presents you with its best guesses to finish the word.

Middle: If you type the next letter of the word, Script Assistant narrows down the possibilities. In this case, there's only one keyword that starts with "ap," so Script Editor fills it in lightly.

Bottom: Press Option-Escape to confirm that you want to use Script Assistant's suggestion. (If you don't want to use its suggestion, simply keep typing.) Using Script Assistant, you can cut your actual typing time in half.

Formatting

If you're bored with Script Editor's coloring scheme, this is the preference pane for you. Simply select the kind of text you want to customize—Language keywords, for example—and then double-click the little color swatch to open the Color palette and change its color. (If you'd like, you can also double-click an item's Font entry to change its font.) Figure 2-10 shows one possibility.

As you go through the types of text, modifying them to your liking, the Category column updates itself with the fonts' new look. Click Apply to make your changes take effect, or click Revert to go back to the previous settings.

Note: The fonts you set in Script Editor are also the ones used for AppleScript commands in Xcode (page 275).

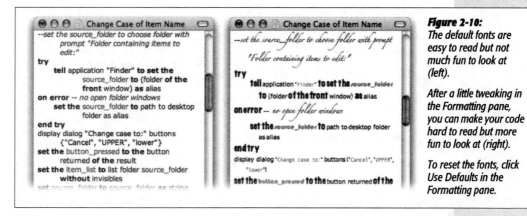

Figure 2-10:
The default fonts are easy to read but not much fun to look at (left).

After a little tweaking in the Formatting pane, you can make your code hard to read but more fun to look at (right).

To reset the fonts, click Use Defaults in the Formatting pane.

History

When you choose Window → Result History (Option-⌘-R), you see a list of the results from the past few scripts you've run. You can set how many results are listed there by changing the "Maximum entries" setting in the History pane of Script Editor's preferences.

Tip: If you run a lot of scripts, you can even set the History to display "Unlimited entries," meaning that the Result History window will show every single script's results since you last launched Script Editor.

On the other hand, if you don't care what your scripts' results are, you can just turn off the Enable Result History checkbox altogether.

You can set the same preferences for the Event Log History, too (page 269).

Plug-ins

Script Editor is useful on its own, but there are plug-ins to add even *more* features (such as those available from the Web sites listed on page 309). For example, the HetimaOsaxOpener plug-in adds a new item to the File menu for opening any scripting additions you have installed on your Mac (page 50). Here's how you'd install this plug-in:

1. **Quit Script Editor.**

   You should always quit a program (⌘-Q) before installing new plug-ins for it.

2. **Download the plug-in you want.**

   HetimaOsaxOpener, for instance, is available from *http://hetima.com/soft/ hetimaosaxopener.html*.

3. **Drag the plug-in into the Library → Application Support → Apple → Script Editor folder.**

    If the folder doesn't exist already, create it yourself.

Note: If don't want other users of your computer to have access to the plug-in, drag it to your *Home →
Library → Application Support → Apple → Script Editor* folder.

---

4. **Relaunch Script Editor.**

    If you installed the plug-in correctly, you should see a confirmation dialog box. Click Enable.

5. **Choose Script Editor → Preferences → Plug-ins.**

    The new plug-in appears in the list here. (You'll also see the new Open OSAX item in the File menu.)

If you ever want to disable a plug-in, just turn off its checkbox in the Plug-in preferences, and relaunch Script Editor.

POWER USERS' CLINIC

Other AppleScript Editors

Script Editor is great for writing AppleScript commands, and every script in this book works just fine with it. Like most features in Mac OS X, however, there are alternatives to Script Editor that pack more power:

- **Smile** (free), from Satimage Software, is a nice alternative to Script Editor that packs a few extra features. Smile includes a more powerful Find feature than Script Editor, for example, and lets you quickly locate the definition of any AppleScript keyword—a great timesaver. You can even step through scripts line by line, to test how each command works. To download Smile, visit *http://www.satimage.fr/ software/en/downloads_software.html.*

- **Script Debugger** ($190), from Late Night Software, is an amazingly powerful, full-featured script editor. You'll find just about everything you could dream of:

incredible customizability, tons of convenient keyboard shortcuts, and the ability to run individual lines at your leisure. If you spend a lot of time with AppleScript, Script Debugger (*www.latenightsw.com/sd3.0/ index.html*) can make your work much easier.

- **Xcode** (free) is Apple's souped-up programming tool, the main attraction of the Xcode Tools. It has line numbering, great search capabilities, and the ability to pause commands, among other powerful features. See page 275 for instructions on installing and using the Xcode Tools.

In addition to these programs, you can write scripts in just about any text editor you want. As long as you save the files as plain text (page 34) and use the *osascript* command in the Terminal to run them (page 259), you can use programs like TextEdit and BBEdit—or even Unix editors like *pico* and *vi* (page 254)—to write AppleScripts.

Building a Script from Scratch

So far, you've been on a quick tour of all the AppleScript stuff that comes with Mac OS X. You've learned how to add the Script Menu to your menu bar, how to use Script Editor, and even how to tweak one of the Script Menu's scripts. Now, you'll finally break free from the limits of your built-in scripts and start creating your *own* AppleScripts from scratch.

When most people refer to "scripting," this is what they're talking about: writing a new script all by themselves. With Script Editor as your trusty tool, you can link commands in the order *you* prefer, making it possible to create totally customized scripts to deal with the tasks you perform every day.

Before you can write the next blockbuster AppleScript, though, you first need to learn the basics. That's what this chapter's for: teaching you how to create your first simple script from the ground up.

Note: The example scripts from this chapter can be found on the AppleScript Examples CD (see page 24 for instructions).

Getting Started

Just as you can't surf the Web without a Web browser, you can't create Apple-Scripts without a script-editing program. The aptly named Script Editor (in your Applications → AppleScript folder) is the simplest program for the job, but feel free to try any of the other editors listed on page 38.

Before you start diving into the following sections, the first thing you'll need to do is *launch* Script Editor (page 21). With this blank scripting slate before you, it's possible to accomplish such neat tasks as:

- Displaying a dialog box using a single line of code (see below)

- Performing basic arithmetic (see the next page)

- Getting the contents of your Clipboard (the place where Mac OS X stores information when you choose Edit → Cut or Edit → Copy [see the next page])

But that's only the beginning. So strap on that beanie with the propeller on top, and get ready to write your first lines of AppleScript.

Displaying a Simple Dialog Box

As you saw on page 6, dialog boxes are the most common way for AppleScript to interact with you. That's because, on their own, scripts can't display complex interface elements like pop-up menus, checkboxes, or toolbars. As you're starting out in AppleScript, therefore, you'll use the *display dialog* command even more than you breathe.

Here's how:

1. **With Script Editor open, type the following command in the Script Field:**

   ```
   display dialog "Hello! I'm your first AppleScript."
   ```

   As you type in the command, you'll notice it appears as a bunch of purple text. That's Script Editor's way of telling you that it hasn't checked your command for AppleScript compliance yet.

2. **Click the Compile button.**

   That tells Script Editor, "Make sure I didn't make any typos in my AppleScript commands" (page 24).

3. **Click Run.**

   Under the hood, AppleScript sees your *display dialog* command and realizes that it has to put together a dialog box with your provided text. After a fraction of a second, you see the fruits of AppleScript's labor (Figure 3-1).

Note: If you *don't* see that dialog box, see page 266 for an explanation of what may have gone wrong.

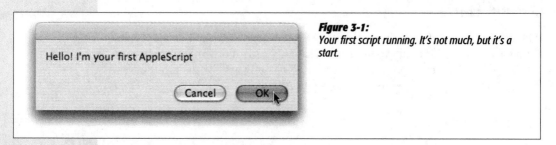

Hello! I'm your first AppleScript

Cancel   OK

Figure 3-1:
Your first script running. It's not much, but it's a start.

No matter which button you click (Cancel or OK), AppleScript dismisses your dialog box. If you start to suffer from dialog box withdrawal, though, simply click Run again to redisplay the dialog box.

Displaying Numbers

In general, the *display dialog* command just presents whatever follows it. In the previous example, you typed a *string* (a series of characters surrounded by double-quotes), so *display dialog* showed that.

On the other hand, you can just as easily use a *number* with the *display dialog* command, since AppleScript automatically converts (or *coerces*) the number to its textual representation. For example, if you opened a new script window (File → New) and ran this command:

```
display dialog 4.52
```

you'd see a dialog box with 4.52 in it.

The fun doesn't stop there, though. If you'd like, you can put math expressions after the *display dialog* command, like this:

```
display dialog (1 + 3 - 9)
```

When you run that command, AppleScript figures out the value of the expression (in this case, 1+3–9), and displays the result in a dialog box: –5.

Note: AppleScript supports the full range of operations you'd perform on a pocket calculator: addition (symbolized by a + sign), subtraction (indicated by a – sign), multiplication (shown with an *), and division (shown with a /).

Just like your middle school math teacher taught you, AppleScript follows the proper order of mathematical operations: parentheses first, then multiplication and division, and finally addition and subtraction. That means that *4+2*3* would come out to 10, whereas *(4+2)*3* would come out to 18.

To avoid confusion, experienced scripters use parentheses even when they're not strictly necessary. That single change can save you hours of time trying to track down math errors.

More than One Command

So far, you've been writing scripts with a single command in them—known by geeks as "one-liners." If you were restricted to one command per script, though, you'd have quite a time trying to write that workflow-integration script you've been dreaming about.

Luckily, AppleScript lets you put as many commands as you want in your script. When you click Run, AppleScript runs the first command, waits for it to finish, runs the second command, waits for it to finish, and so on. Here's a simple example:

```
display dialog "This script shows the text on your clipboard. Click OK to
proceed."
display dialog (the clipboard) -- This command runs after you click OK
display dialog "Thank you for running Clipboard Viewer."
```

Note: Before running this script, you should copy some text to your clipboard, or else the script will fail and report an error. Since you already have Script Editor open, you might as well double-click a word or two in the script and use Edit → Copy (⌘-C) to copy that text to your Clipboard. When you run the script, the words you copied will show up in the second dialog box.

This script shows three dialog boxes, one at a time.

- **The first dialog box** explains what the script does. If you're creating a new script, it's often a good idea to have an explanatory dialog box at the beginning.

- **The second dialog box** displays the contents of the Clipboard. Any text you've copied (using, for example, the Edit → Copy command) is shown onscreen.

Tip: In AppleScript, all you need to do to get the contents of the Clipboard is write *the clipboard*.

The text after the two hyphens is a *comment*—something that AppleScript ignores. See the "Making Comments" sidebar (page 42) for more about this feature.

- Finally, **the third dialog box** displays a goodbye note. This, of course, is completely optional in your own scripts.

Note: If, at any point, you click the Cancel button in a dialog box, the script stops running. In fact, that's just about the *only* way to make a script stop running while a dialog box is open; if you attempt to click the Stop toolbar button, Script Editor just beeps.

UP TO SPEED

Making Comments

When you're reading through a script, many of the commands are probably pretty self-evident. Unfortunately, there can also be some that seem totally foreign. In those cases, you can use a *comment*—a section of text in plain English—to remind yourself how the commands work.

AppleScript supports two kinds of comments: single-line and multi-line. No matter which kind of comments you use, AppleScript ignores what's inside—they're there solely for your benefit.

You'd write a single-line comment like this:

```
display dialog "Watermelon" --a dialog box
```

AppleScript understands that everything from the double-hyphen to the end of the line is a comment. To AppleScript, therefore, the previous command is identical to this one:

```
display dialog "Watermelon"
```

You'll often see a single-line comment used to clarify how a particular command works.

On the other hand, a multi-line comment is useful for explaining how a big *chunk* of your script works. It could look something like this:

```
(* Please note that this script may
irrevocably erase your ENTIRE hard drive.
Use with caution, or on someone else's
computer. *)
```

Everything between the parentheses and asterisks is understood to be a comment—no matter how many lines it spans. You'll often see multi-line comments in the scripts that come with your Mac, since they contain Apple's copyright information.

Commanding Other Programs

Unless you plan to display dialog boxes in Script Editor all day, you're probably feeling pretty constrained by AppleScript right now. Yeah, you can display cool *stuff* in your dialog boxes, but that won't be enough to automate your Mac.

Luckily, you can use AppleScript to do other things—and one of the most powerful is the ability to control other applications. This feature alone unlocks a world of possibilities:

- **Automate your favorite word processor,** so you can save all unsaved documents with a single click (page 103).

- **Apply color-correction settings automatically** using Adobe Photoshop (page 133).

- **Convert song files in iTunes automatically** while you recline in your lounge chair (page 152).

Before you can write any of those complicated scripts, however, you must learn the basics of program control. This section, therefore, introduces the basics of how to send commands to specific programs, rather than just to Mac OS X itself.

Using tell Statements

When you want to target a program with your commands, you have to let Apple-Script know which program to talk to. For such purposes, the *tell* statement is your best friend.

Say you want the Finder to open your Home folder, so you can copy some files onto your desktop. To do this, enter these commands in Script Editor, then click Run:

```
tell application "Finder"
    activate
    open home
end tell
```

Everything after the *tell* command is directed at the program you specify—in this case, the Finder. The *activate* command brings the program forward, while the *open home* command tells the Finder to open a new Finder window and for your Home folder. Finally, once AppleScript reaches the *end tell* command, it lets the Finder off the hook and stops sending it commands.

Note: If you want to send a *single* command to a program, you can put the entire *tell* statement on one line, like this:

```
tell application "Finder" to activate
```

That way, you don't have to spell out the entire thing on multiple lines, like this:

```
tell application "Finder"
    activate
end tell
```

Opening a Dictionary

If you hope to do real work with the Finder, being able to open windows or display dialog boxes is really just small potatoes. For more complex tasks, you have to read the Finder's *dictionary*—a list of all the commands it can accept. Every program that AppleScript can command has a dictionary, too, so it's helpful to take some time to explore.

To access a program's dictionary, follow these steps:

1. **Open Script Editor, and choose File → Open Dictionary (Shift-⌘-O).**

   A dialog box appears, with a list of every program on your Mac that Apple-Script can control.

2. **Scroll down to the program whose dictionary you want to open.**

   Alternatively, type the first few letters of the program's name. For example, just type "Fin" to jump down to the Finder.

Note: If you want to open the dictionary of a program, but you don't see its name in the Open Dictionary dialog box, click Browse. You'll get a standard Open dialog box, which you can use to navigate to the appropriate program on your hard drive.

POWER USERS' CLINIC

Apple Events

When you tell the Finder to *activate,* Mac OS X sends a tiny virtual packet—known as an *Apple Event*—from Script Editor to the Finder. Such packets are the foundation of AppleScript; every single command you write gets translated into an Apple Event before it's sent off to the appropriate program.

Not only does Mac OS X send Apple Events between programs, but Apple Events are often sent within the *same* program. For example, Script Editor's Recording feature (page 23) works by picking up Apple Events that occur as you interact with individual programs on your Mac.

If you'd like to see the actual guts of an Apple Event—not a pretty sight—a program like AE Monitor (*http://software.oxalyn.com/aemonitor/*) can help. With AE Monitor installed, you can track all the Apple Events flying around your system—to see where they're coming from and where they're heading to, for example. If you have a spare afternoon, set up AE Monitor and just use your Mac

as usual; you'll be amazed at the number of Apple Events your Mac is sending.

Of course, this is all possible because Apple Events are a standard for communicating between Mac programs. That means they work in Mac OS 9 *and* Mac OS X—and that's why you can send AppleScript commands back and forth between programs running in the Classic environment (a Mac OS 9 emulator) and in Mac OS X. Most of all, this standards-compliance means that AppleScript isn't the *only* language you can use for controlling programs. Other languages, such as Late Night Software's version of JavaScript (*http://latenightsw.com/freeware/JavaScriptOSA/index.html*) can control other programs using Apple Events, too.

Now, that's not to say you should start using other languages to control Mac programs—AppleScript is still the easiest and most supported Mac scripting language around. However, if you happen to have JavaScript code that you've written for a Web site, the ability to also automate *programs* with JavaScript is a big plus.

3. **Click Choose.**

The program's dictionary opens, as shown in Figure 3-2.

Tip: If you're a speed freak, there are two other ways to open a program's dictionary. The first is to drag the program's icon onto Script Editor's Dock icon. No dialog boxes, no navigating—just a quick way to bring up the program's dictionary.

The second trick is even sneakier than the first. If the program whose dictionary you want to open is *already* in the Dock, just ⌘-drag that program's icon onto Script Editor's icon. (For instance, if you wanted to open the Finder's dictionary, you could just ⌘-drag its Dock icon onto Script Editor's). Time saved: 2.7 seconds.

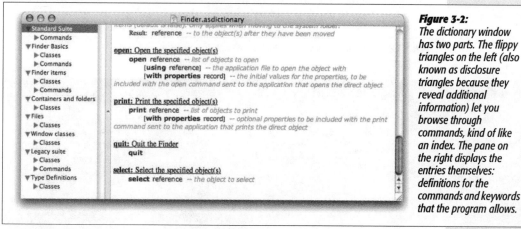

Figure 3-2:
The dictionary window has two parts. The flippy triangles on the left (also known as disclosure triangles because they reveal additional information) let you browse through commands, kind of like an index. The pane on the right displays the entries themselves: definitions for the commands and keywords that the program allows.

Looking for the Commands You Want

Now, suppose you want to make a script that checks whether you have a Home → Current Work folder and then displays a dialog box that tells you its findings. To make such a script, you must first figure out the appropriate AppleScript commands.

For this job, the Finder's dictionary is your best reference. That's because the dictionary *determines* which commands you can use, so you're likely to find the best command for your job there.

When you're looking through a dictionary, it's always a good idea to check the dictionary's *Standard Suite* first. In the world of AppleScript, the Standard Suite is a set of commands common to most scriptable programs. The commands listed there are AppleScript mainstays (*open, close,* and *delete,* for example)—the sorts of commands that give AppleScript its reputation for being like English. To open the Standard Suite, just click the flippy triangle next to its name. Then, to browse the list of possible commands, click the triangle next to *commands.*

Tip: If the mouse is too slow for you, you can navigate a dictionary using just the keyboard. Use the arrow keys to scroll over a particular suite, and reveal the suite's contents with the right arrow key. If you want to pop open the suite's *commands* at the same time, press Option-right arrow while the suite's heading is selected.

When you're done sifting through the commands with the up and down arrow keys, select the heading of the suite again and press the left arrow key. In an instant, the contents of the suite disappear.

Checking whether the folder is already there

As your eyes wander down the left column in the Finder's dictionary, you'll come across the *exists* command. Click it once, and you'll see a brief description of how it works: "Result: boolean -- true if it exists, false if not." This is precisely the command you'd use to check if a folder is already there.

Note: A *Boolean* value is simply one that can be only true or false.

GEM IN THE ROUGH

Script Editor's Library

As you write more scripts, you'll spend a lot of time reading dictionaries. Unfortunately, the method Apple suggests for examining them (choosing File → Open Dictionary, then scrolling pages and pages to find the right program) can be time-consuming, especially if you have a lot of programs.

Luckily, Script Editor includes a shortcut for examining dictionaries: the Library window, which you can open by choosing Window → Library (Shift-⌘-L).

The Library window contains a list of common scriptable Mac OS X programs. You can open a program's dictionary by selecting its name and clicking the bookshelf icon, or just by double-clicking the program's name.

If you often find yourself reading a particular program's dictionary, you can add the program to the Library window by clicking the + button in the toolbar, and then navigating to the program in the Open dialog box. Conversely, you can remove a program from the Library window by selecting its name and pressing the – button in the toolbar.

Finally, the script icon in the toolbar (the one farthest to the right) is a convenient way to create a new script for an application in the Library list. For example, if you select iCal and then click the Script icon, a new script window pops open

with the following code, ready for you to enter additional commands:

```
tell application "iCal"

end tell
```

Enter the following script to test out the *exists* command:

```
tell application "Finder"
    if the folder "Current Work" of home exists then
        display dialog "The Current Work folder is already there."
    end if
end tell
```

This might not look quite like English, but it's pretty close. Here's how the commands work:

- **tell application "Finder".** This is the equivalent of saying "heads up" to the Finder. It sends all the commands that follow to the Finder instead of to Mac OS X itself.

- **if the folder "Current Work" of home exists then.** This command searches in your Home folder for a folder named Current Work. If this folder exists, the script runs every command inside the *if* statement (everything from *if* to *end if*).

Note: In AppleScript, you need to put the names of specific items (folders, programs, and so on) in quotation marks after the items they refer to—like *folder "Current Work", application "Finder",* and so on.

However, some special items are represented by AppleScript keywords, like *home* and *current application.* These terms are placeholders for a specific folder or application, so they don't use quotation marks. (To represent their special status, keywords like these also get colored blue in the Script Field [page 27].)

- **display dialog "The Current Work folder is already there."** This command is placed inside the *if* statement, which means it's run only if the Current Work folder already exists.

- **end if.** This marks the end of the *if* statement. Because of that, any commands that follow are run regardless of whether the Current Work folder already exists.

- **end tell.** This marks the end of the *tell* statement. Any commands that follow are sent to Mac OS X itself, rather than to the Finder.

Now run the script. If the script finds a Current Work folder in your Home folder, it displays a dialog box; otherwise, the script ends silently and you see nothing at all.

Displaying the other dialog box

At this point, your script works fine. However, it only does half the job; if there *isn't* a Current Work folder, the script just ends without letting you know. To fix this problem, you need to insert a few commands in your script (new lines are shown in bold):

```
tell application "Finder"
    if the folder "Current Work" of home exists then
        display dialog "The Current Work folder already exists."
```

```
        else
            display dialog "The Current Work folder can't to be found."
        end if
    end tell
```

If you have a Current Work folder, the first dialog box ("The Current Work folder already exists.") is displayed. However, if you *don't* have a Current Work folder, the first dialog box is not displayed, and the *else* statement—which shows the second dialog box—takes over instead.

Note: That's how all *if-else* statements work: if the *if* portion is true, the commands that follow *if* are run. On the other hand, if the *if* portion is false, the script runs the commands that follow *else* instead.

It's the same sort of logic you'd use when deciding what to wear outside: "If it's raining, I will wear a raincoat. Else, I will wear a T-shirt."

Understanding Dictionaries

Dictionaries are some of the most useful references in AppleScript, since they list the meanings and usage of everyday AppleScript keywords. Unfortunately, dictionaries can be hard to decipher, and their strange jargon confounds many beginners. If you find yourself tossed in the sea of programmer-speak, this sidebar can help you regain your land legs.

First of all, a dictionary is broken down into multiple sections, called *suites*. The most common—the Standard Suite—lists AppleScript commands that you'll use over and over again in multiple programs. Don't worry too much about suites, though: they're just there for organizing large numbers of commands, and they don't have any bearing on how commands work.

Within many suites, you'll find two sections—classes and commands—when you click the flippy triangle next to a suite's name. A *class* is the AppleScript equivalent of a noun—like *disk* and *folder*. A *command,* on the other hand, is like an AppleScript verb—*delete* or *restart,* for example.

As with English, you make complete AppleScript statements by connecting verbs and nouns. In the script on page 47, for example, you check whether a folder exists by using the AppleScript class (or noun) *folder,* and using the command

(or verb) *exists.* Once you realize that you're just building sentences, the whole concept of "programming" should lose some of its stigma.

Finally, certain commands have *results.* You can think of a result like the answer to a question; if you ask AppleScript whether a file exists, for instance, the result will be either *true* or *false.* Obviously, different commands will have different results—some will be files, some will be numbers, and some will be lists, for example. The great part about dictionaries, though, is that they're nice enough to tell you what *kind* of result you can expect from a particular command: just look next to the word "Result" at the bottom of a command's entry.

Don't get too cocky, though. Many commands in dictionaries have *options*—the AppleScript equivalent of prepositional phrases. Options add extra features to a particular command, letting you make the command more targeted (at a particular disk or folder, for instance). You can tell something's an option because it's surrounded in brackets in its dictionary entry—like *to location* for the *duplicate* command (page 92). Keep in mind, though, that an option is just that: optional. You never have to use an option with a particular command if you don't want to.

Displaying a Window in the Finder

So far, your script lets you know whether it finds a Current Work folder or not. That's useful, but it would be even better if the script could open a Finder window showing you the contents of the Current Work folder if it exists.

To do that, you have to go back and sift through the Finder's dictionary—and again, the Standard Suite is the best place to start, since the commands there are both simple and powerful. As you browse the command list, you'll come across the *open* command—and its definition, "open: Open the specified object(s)," reveals that it will do just what you want (Figure 3-3).

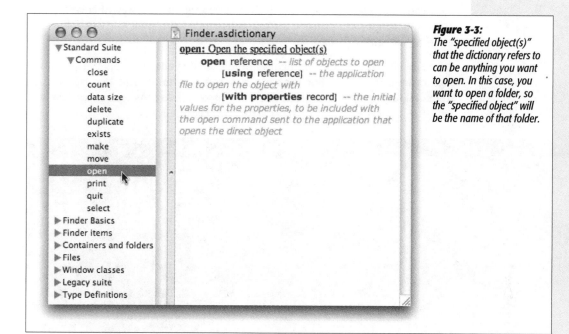

Figure 3-3:
The "specified object(s)" that the dictionary refers to can be anything you want to open. In this case, you want to open a folder, so the "specified object" will be the name of that folder.

Now you can build an updated script:

```
tell application "Finder"
    if the folder "Current Work" of home exists then
        activate
        open folder "Current Work" of home
    else
        display dialog "The Current Work folder 'can't be found."
    end if
end tell
```

Here's how the two new lines work:

- The **activate** command (page 19) brings the Finder forward.

Tip: To open a program without bringing it forward, use the *launch* command instead of *activate*.

- **open folder "Current Work" of home** does the same thing that double-clicking the Current Work folder would do: it opens a Finder window to display the Current Work folder's contents.

Now that you know how to display dialog boxes, read programs' dictionaries, and use *if* statements to run code selectively, you're well on your way to creating truly timesaving scripts. On page 89, for example, you'll learn how to *create* folders, in addition to opening them.

Before going on, though, you might want to exercise your new AppleScript knowledge to keep it flexible. For example, you could write a script that opens your Home folder, or write a script to display a series of jokes. As with most things in AppleScript, the only limit is your tolerance for geekiness.

POWER USERS' CLINIC

Scripting Additions

So far, you've looked up two commands in a dictionary: *exists* and *open*. You might be wondering, though, which dictionary has the entries for commands like *display dialog*.

As it turns out, general AppleScript commands (like *display dialog*) are stored in files called *scripting additions*. You can examine scripting additions' dictionaries the same way you'd examine the Finder's dictionary: by choosing File → Open Dictionary.

The *display dialog* command is stored in the Standard Additions dictionary included with your Mac—a scripting addition that contains commands for user interaction, network jobs, and other miscellaneous tasks. If you use Script Editor's Library window (page 46), you can just double-click the item called StandardAdditions.osax to open the Standard Additions dictionary.

Not all scripting additions come with your Mac, though. If you ever find AppleScript lacking in a certain feature—say, the ability to use logarithms—there's a good chance someone *else* has created a scripting addition to plug the hole. Check out *www.osaxen.com* for a comprehensive list of third-party scripting additions—including ones that do every-

thing from spell checking to complex math operations. Once you've downloaded a scripting addition, just drag it into the Library → ScriptingAdditions folder (creating the folder if necessary) to make the new commands available to all your scripts.

(And a side note: among AppleScript geeks, another term for "scripting addition" is *osax*, which stands for Open Scripting Architecture Extension. For the ultimate in obscurity, memorize the plural form: *osaxen*.)

Unfortunately, if you use commands from third-party scripting additions, your scripts might not work properly on other Macs. The workaround: use script *bundles*—self-contained files that let you distribute scripting additions along with your scripts (page 34). Of course, if you *purchased* a third-party scripting addition, make sure it's legal to distribute before you go bundling it with all your scripts.

If after a while you find it hard to keep track of all the scripting additions on your Mac, install the HetimaOsaxOpener plug-in (page 37) to keep them organized in Script Editor's File menu. That's a much easier way of opening scripting additions than, for example, the Open Dictionary dialog box.

Part Two:
Everyday Scripting Tasks

Chapter 4, *Manipulating Text*

Chapter 5, *Controlling Files*

Chapter 6, *Creating Lists*

Chapter 7, *Organizing and Editing Graphics*

Chapter 8, *Playing Sound and Video*

Chapter 9, *Internet and Network Scripting*

Chapter 10, *Organizing Information in Databases*

Manipulating Text

Since the ancient days of DOS, text has always played an important role in computing. Even today, 20 years after the first Mac came out, every computer Apple ships comes with a keyboard. What's more, Mac OS X's Unix core is strictly based on text: preference files are in plain text, and the commands you issue in Terminal (page 252) are all, well, text.

The importance of text isn't lost on AppleScript, though. From its dialog box capabilities to the Text Suite—a standard set of AppleScript keywords that deals with the details of words, characters, and paragraphs (page 65)—AppleScript handles text the way Mac OS X does: simply and powerfully. For example, you can harness AppleScript's text mojo to do things like:

- Add a word count feature to TextEdit (page 64)

- Shrink all the fonts in a document simultaneously (page 69)

- Type and run AppleScript commands in just about *any* program—not just Script Editor—using an application's Services menu

AppleScript's text features *are* quite powerful, but they're not always easy to learn—especially if you're reading Apple's geeky help files (page 5). Thankfully, you don't have to; just continue reading this chapter instead.

Note: The example scripts from this chapter can be found on the AppleScript Examples CD (see page 24 for instructions).

String Notation

In AppleScript, pieces of text are stored in a format called *strings*. A string can contain as many letters, numbers, spaces, and punctuation marks as you'd like. In AppleScript, strings are typically placed between double quotes, like so:

```
"Yam farmer"
"5504.45"
"What the *#@&?!"
```

However, you won't get much use out of strings unless you can *store* them for later use—rather than having to constantly recreate them. To store a string, you use the *set* command, like this:

```
set welcomeMessage to "Take your shoes off before entering the building."
```

In the previous example, *welcomeMessage* is a *variable*: a name given to a stored value (page 56). Variables come in handy when you have a long string you want to recall later. Rather than having to type in *all* that text each and every time you want to use it, you just substitute the variable name anywhere you want the string to appear, like this:

```
set welcomeMessage to "Take your shoes off before entering the building."
display dialog welcomeMessage
```

In the previous example, AppleScript notices the *welcomeMessage* variable that follows the *display dialog* command, and substitutes in the value that you *set* on the previous line. That's why running the previous script would display a dialog box that says "Take your shoes off before entering the building."

Note: When using variables, it's important to remember that you must *set* a variable before you can access it later on in your script. If you switched the two lines in the previous script, for example, AppleScript would display an error, because you would be referring to a variable (with *display dialog*) before you told AppleScript what the variable should contain (with *set*).

AppleScript's set-before-you-access requirement leads many programmers to set all the variables that a script will use at the very *beginning* of the script. Under this arrangement, if you refer to a variable *later* in your script, you can be sure that it's already been defined at the script's start, thereby avoiding "variable not defined" errors.

Getting Text Back from Dialog Boxes

So far, all you've done with dialog boxes is display information. That won't help you much if you want to get feedback to use in your scripts, though. Luckily, the *display dialog* command supports an extra option—*default answer*—which lets you type text into your dialog boxes as well. Try running this script:

```
display dialog "Enter your name:" default answer "Sylvester"
```

A dialog box appears on screen, with a text-entry field inside (Figure 4-1).

Still, even though you can enter text in your dialog boxes with the *default answer* option, you can't *capture* the text you entered and reuse it elsewhere in the script.

Or so you might think.

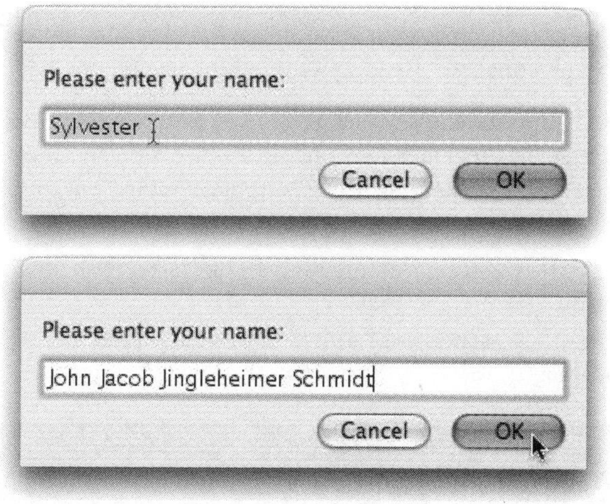

Figure 4-1:
The default answer option is all you need to add a text field to a dialog box. Whatever you put in your script after default answer will be what appears in this dialog box at first (top), although you're free to delete the text and enter anything you'd like instead (bottom).

Luckily, using the power of variables, you *can* store the response to your dialog boxes for later use. Try running this script:

```
set userResponse to the text returned of (display dialog "Enter your name:" ¬
    default answer "Sylvester")
display dialog userResponse
```

Note: The ¬ symbol, shown in the previous example, simply means "this command continues on the next line." This line-continuation symbol has no bearing on how AppleScript interprets your script, so you could theoretically retype the previous script as follows, and it would work exactly the same way:

```
set ¬
userResponse ¬
to the text returned ¬
of (display dialog ¬
"Enter your name:" ¬
default answer "Sylvester")
display dialog userResponse
```

In this book, scripts employ the line-continuation symbol because certain commands are simply too long to fit within the pages' margins. When entering these commands yourself, you can either type the ¬ symbol as written (by pressing Option-Return) or omit the ¬ symbol altogether and instead just type broken-up commands on a single line.

In this script, AppleScript sets the *userResponse* variable to the text you enter in the dialog box. Then on the next line, that text is echoed back to you in a new dialog box.

Linking Strings Together

In the previous script, the second command simply spits back whatever text is in the dialog box's text field when you press OK. It would be much cooler, however, if the script could give you a personalized greeting—something like Figure 4-2.

To achieve this feat of textual impressiveness, you have to use a feature known as *concatenation*—linking multiple strings together into one. In AppleScript, the way you concatenate strings is with an ampersand (&), which tells AppleScript to "put together the strings on my left and right." Here's what the improved script would look like:

```
set userResponse to the text returned of (display dialog "Enter your name:" ¬
    default answer "Sylvester")
set theGreeting to "Hey, " & userResponse & "!"
display dialog theGreeting
```

UP TO SPEED

Variable Usage

So far, you've used variables to store values for later lines in your scripts. Variables have restrictions and quirks all their own, however, and it's important to understand them so you can effectively write your own scripts.

For one, variable names can't be the same as preexisting AppleScript keywords. That means you can't write:

```
set text to "WiFi"
```

because *text* is an AppleScript keyword.

On the other hand, you're free to write:

```
set theText to "WiFi"
```

because the word *theText* has no significance in Apple-Script. In fact, no two-words-squashed-together-as-one have any meaning in AppleScript, and that's why you'll often see variable names like *myNumber, lastItem,* and *theAnswer.*

You can include letters, numbers, and underscores (_) in your variable names, as long as the first character of the name isn't a number. Keep in mind, though, that variable names can't be more than 251 characters long—anything longer, and you'll see the dialog box shown here.

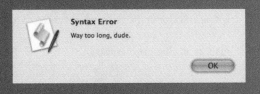

Once you've *set* a variable, you just insert its name in your script to access the corresponding value. That's why you can write *display dialog userResponse,* for example, if you've set the *userResponse* variable earlier in your script.

Finally, you can set the same variable more than once in a script. If you wanted to, you could write something like this:

```
set myNumber to 4
set myNumber to (myNumber + 8)
set myNumber to (myNumber / 2)
```

In that example, the value of *myNumber* after the first line would be 4, after the second line it would be 12 (4+8), and after the third line it would be 6 ([4+8]/2).

Note: Whenever you concatenate more than two strings (as in this example), you have to use ampersands between *each* item.

When the script runs, it combines the three strings—"Hey, " whatever is entered as *userResponse,* and the exclamation mark—together. The result is that all three items appear together as one big string (*theGreeting*) in your final dialog box, as shown at the bottom of Figure 4-2.

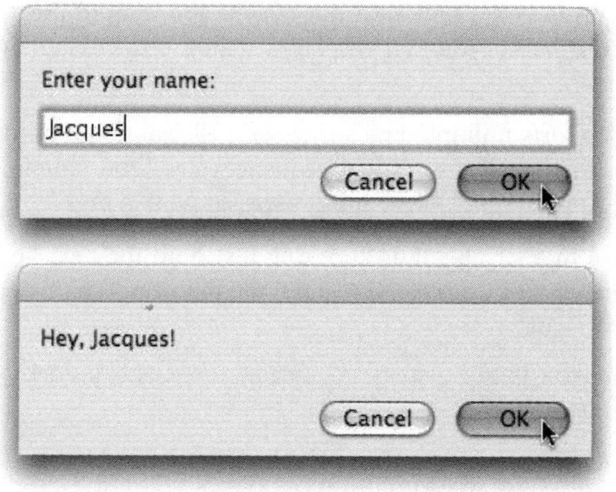

Figure 4-2:
Top: As in the previous scripts, you enter your name in the first dialog box.

Bottom: However, when the second dialog box appears, you get a personalized welcome message, courtesy of AppleScript's text-handling capabilities.

There are other uses for concatenation, too:

• **Pulling the results of multiple commands into a single string.** For example, if you wrote a script to administer computerized history tests, you could make your script concatenate all your responses together to create a summary of your answers.

• **Inserting punctuation into strings.** You could use concatenation to surround a famous quote with quotation marks, for example.

• **Mixing numbers into strings.** Just as you can concatenate two strings together, you can concatenate a string to a *number.* You might find that useful if you're writing a script to manage kitchen utensils, since you can combine the word "fork" with the number of clean forks left, for example.

As you become more and more familiar with AppleScript, you're sure to find many other ways to put concatenation to work for you. Just remember: if you're concatenating more than two items together, you must use a separate ampersand between every two items.

Multiline Strings

If you've spent any time working in a word processing program like TextEdit or Microsoft Word, you already know that text often spans multiple lines. Unlike typewriters from days of old, you don't have to hit the Return key when you reach the end of a line. Instead, the text just wraps around to the next line, and you continue typing until you reach the end of a paragraph.

There are, however, certain times when you might like to break text up onto multiple lines—such as typing your mailing address at the top of a letter—and for that, the trusty Return key is right there by your side. But what if you want to use such multiline strings in *AppleScript*, so you can display a dialog box containing a friend's address, for example?

Thankfully, AppleScript supports multiple-line strings as well, but you'll need to enlist some help from *escape sequences*. Escape sequences are little chunks of slashes and letters that tell AppleScript, "Please insert a special symbol here."

To insert a newline symbol in a string—thus knocking text onto the next line— you use the \n escape sequence. For example, if you ran the following script, you'd see the dialog box shown in Figure 4-3:

```
set multiLiner to "To whom it may concern,\nI want my money back.\nThanks."
display dialog multiLiner
```

Note: If you find the \n sequence too geeky, you can instead just type Return in the middle of a string. For example, you could rewrite the above script as follows:

```
set multiLiner to "To whom it may concern,
I want my money back.
Thanks"
display dialog multiLiner
```

and it would work exactly the same way. Still, you'll often see older scripts use the \n sequence, so remember that it works the same way.

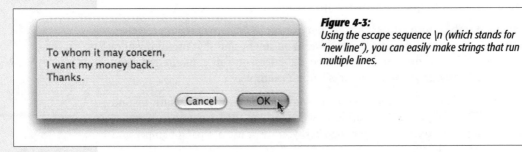

Figure 4-3:
Using the escape sequence \n (which stands for "new line"), you can easily make strings that run multiple lines.

There are other escape sequences you can use in your strings, too (Table 4-1 has a list of the most common). Such escape sequences allow you to make AppleScript

---

strings that match what you could create in a TextEdit or Microsoft Word document. That way, you can display dialog boxes with all sorts of punctuation inside—not just letters and numbers.

Table 4-1. *AppleScript escape sequences*

Sequence	What it represents	Example string
\n	A newline character.	"1: Shine shoes\n2: Eat lunch"
\r	A "carriage return"–the way that certain older Mac programs indicate that text should continue onto the next line. Some programs use \n to break a line, some require \r, and some will accept either (you have to test the program to see which one it accepts).	"1: Shine shoes\r2: Eat lunch"
\t	An indentation character (the same as pressing Tab); this character will show up as a single space in a dialog box but will show up as a *true* tab in a program like TextEdit or Microsoft Word.	"Cost\t\Number sold\ tProfit"
\"	A double quote within a string.	"She said, \"Hello\" to me."
\\	A *single* backslash character.	"The haiku said: AppleScript is good. \\ Concatenation is a \\ quite long word indeed."

Note: You should type each string example from Table 4-1 on a single line.

Scripting TextEdit

TextEdit is a free word processor installed on your Mac, and it is—in many ways—the ideal Mac OS X program. TextEdit supports drag-and-dropped text and files, allows complex typographical control, and can check your spelling automatically as you type. Best of all, you can control TextEdit with AppleScript, opening up a whole new world of possibilities beyond just typing:

- Create a new TextEdit document with a single click, rather than having to mouse up to File → New (page 61).

- Insert the current date into a new TextEdit document automatically (page 62).

- Add a word count feature to TextEdit, so you can brag to your friends about the length of your business memos (page 64).

To understand TextEdit's scripting abilities, you first have to open its dictionary to see the list of commands it can accept (page 44). In Script Editor, choose File → Open Dictionary (Shift-⌘-O), scroll down to TextEdit, and click Open. As you can see from the left pane of Figure 4-4, TextEdit has a rather lengthy—and quite detailed—dictionary. Take the time to peruse all the scripting suites now, so you can get a feel for what AppleScript and TextEdit can do together.

Extreme Dialog Boxes

As you already know, dialog boxes play a critical role in how you interact with your scripts. Thus far, however, you've only used one extra option in your dialog boxes: *default answer* (page 54). Although that's useful for getting user responses, there are far more options you can tack onto the end of your *display dialog* commands to make them truly powerful user feedback tools:

- The **buttons** option lets you specify which (and how many) buttons you want to appear at the bottom of the dialog box. You can specify a list (page 105) of between one and three buttons of your choice. (If you don't specify *any* buttons, you'll end up with the usual Cancel and OK buttons.) The following example displays a dialog box with Nope and Yep for buttons:

  ```
  display dialog "Got Milk?" buttons ¬
      {"Nope", "Yep"}
  ```

- The **default button** option sets the button that pulses blue in your dialog box. The default button is also the button that you can press Return or Enter to select. (If you don't specify a default button, OK is used.) For example, if you wanted to designate the Yep button as the default, you could write this:

  ```
  display dialog "Got Milk?" buttons ¬
      {"Nope", "Yep"} default button 2
  ```

- The **with icon** option lets you specify a small image—either *stop* (a stop sign), *note* (a cartoony face with a bubble coming out of its mouth), or *caution* (a yield sign)—to appear inside your dialog box. For a quick dose of graphical fun, try this:

  ```
  display dialog "Got Milk?" buttons ¬
      {"Nope", "Yep"} ¬
      default button 2 with icon note
  ```

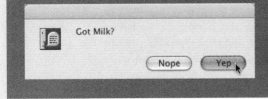

- The **giving up after** *X* option lets you hide the dialog box if there's no response after *X* number of seconds. To keep your dialog box onscreen for a maximum of 3 seconds, you would type this:

  ```
  display dialog "Got Milk?" buttons
  {"Nope", "Yep"} ¬
      default button 2 with icon note ¬
      giving up after 3
  ```

(Keep in mind that you can add as many or as few of these options as you'd like. You could specify an icon, for example, but decide not to use any custom buttons.)

There's more to dialog boxes than just displaying information, though. If you insert the phrase *text returned of* or *button returned of* before the *display dialog* command, you can have your script figure out what text you typed—or what button you clicked—when the dialog box was onscreen. To store the clicked button in a variable called *dialogResponse,* you could type this:

```
set dialogResponse to the button ¬
returned of (display dialog "Got Milk?" ¬
buttons {"Nope", "Yep"})
```

Note that you have to surround the entire *display dialog* command in parentheses, or else AppleScript will throw a fit.

Finally, if you want a dialog box to appear on top of every running program, you should direct your command at the SystemUIServer program, like this:

```
tell application "SystemUIServer"
    activate
    display dialog ¬
        "Your computer will crash ¬
        in 4 seconds."
end tell
```

Regardless of what program is running or how many programs you have open, this dialog box will appear in front of all of them. (Of course, your computer won't crash if you run that AppleScript—it's just a silly text message.)

Create a New TextEdit Document

Since you need a document to do anything useful in TextEdit, you might as well learn how to create a *new* document to hold that text. The trouble is, there's no *create* command in TextEdit's dictionary for making a new document.

This sort of dilemma, unfortunately, is fairly common in AppleScript. To find a command that does what you want, you have to look for synonyms of "create" instead: *generate, produce,* and—aha!—*make.* Once you find a synonym that's listed in the dictionary, just click it to read its definition in the right pane (Figure 4-4).

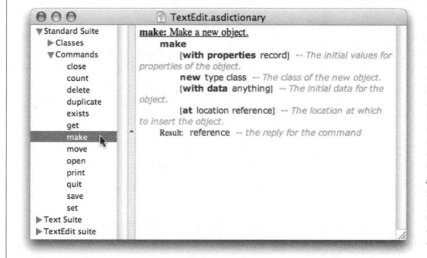

Figure 4-4:
When you select a specific command (make, in this case) Script Editor shows the command in blue in the right pane. All the indented pieces below the command are additions you can append to the command. Optional additions (with properties, with data, and at) are in brackets, while required additions (new) aren't surrounded with brackets.

When you read the entry for *make*, you'll find that it has only one required addition: *new.* In other words, any command you write has to say *make new <something>*. Now the problem is, what should you put in place of *something*?

As it turns out, TextEdit's dictionary can help you find this bit of information, too. If you scroll through the Classes lists on the left, you'll come across a few nouns (page 48): *character, paragraph,* and *word,* for example. Finally, at the very bottom of the TextEdit Suite, you'll come across the term you want—*document*—which lets you create a new file. Now you have all the information you need to write your script:

```
tell application "TextEdit"
    activate
    make new document at the front
end tell
```

Note: The *at the front* portion of this script tells TextEdit where to place the new document window (in this case, TextEdit brings the new document window in front of any other TextEdit windows you have open). If you didn't have that little snippet, TextEdit would get confused by the plain *make new document* command and would show you an error dialog box, because it wouldn't know where to place the new window.

Adding Text to a New Document

Of course, there's nothing the previous script does that you can't do yourself by choosing File → New. What *can* set your script apart, however, is automatically adding text to your new document—which is particularly helpful when you're typing a letter and want to insert the date at the beginning, for example.

The key to modifying your script like this, again, is the *document* entry in Text-Edit's dictionary. If you look under the Properties heading in the right-side pane, you'll find the keyword *text,* which is described—quite creatively—as "the text of the document." This is precisely the property you should use to insert a string into your new TextEdit document:

Note: If you look carefully in TextEdit's dictionary, there are actually *two* entries for *document.* The first entry, in the Standard Suite (page 45), simply represents a generic Mac OS X document. The second entry, in the TextEdit suite, represents TextEdit's personal kind of document. You can safely use properties from *either* entry when sending AppleScript commands to TextEdit documents.

```
tell application "TextEdit"
    activate
    make new document at the front
    set dateString to "Created: " & current date
    set the text of the front document to dateString
end tell
```

Here you added two new lines of code to the AppleScript (both are marked in bold):

- **In the first new command, you create the *dateString* variable.** This variable concatenates "Created: " and the *current date* command, resulting in a string something like "Created Wednesday, January 12, 2004 2:29:15 PM."

- **The second line tells TextEdit to insert the text from the *dateString* variable into the front document.** This is where the *text* property comes into play. By telling your newly created document to set its *text* property to a particular string (in this case, the current date), you effectively *insert* that string into the document.

When you run this script, therefore, TextEdit obediently opens, creates a new document, and then adds a line for the current date.

Adding Formatting

Now you're getting somewhere. There are only two minor issues left with your script:

- It doesn't insert a new *line* after the date.

- It doesn't format the date in a different font and size than the rest of the document.

Once you clear these issues up, the script will be quite useful for making new documents—like business letters—with the date already inserted.

Inserting a new line after the date

To place a new line after the date, you have to modify the *dateString* variable in your script. Therefore, change the following line:

```
set dateString to "Created: " & (current date)
```

to:

```
set dateString to "Created: " & (current date) & return
```

Tip: If you'd like, you can access specific properties of the *current date* command from your script. For example, if you want to insert only the current *time*–not the entire date–you could rewrite the previous command like this:

```
set dateString to "Created: " & time string of (current date) & return
```

Simply typing *& return* is enough to append a new line to your text, and thereby to insert a new line in TextEdit.

Note: Using *return* accomplishes the same thing as the more foreign-looking \r escape sequence (page 59)–that is, it inserts a new line.

Changing the font and size

Finally, to change the font and size of your text, you have to make AppleScript set the appropriately named *font* and *size* properties of your TextEdit document. The following, therefore, is what your final script should look like:

```
tell application "TextEdit"
    activate
    make new document at the front
    set dateString to "Created: " & (current date) & return
    set the text of the front document to dateString
    set the font of the first paragraph of the front document to "Zapfino"
    set the size of the first paragraph of the front document to 14
    --You can change the font and size to anything you want
end tell
```

When you run the script, you'll end up with a document that looks like Figure 4-5.

At this point, you have a fully functional script. What now?

If you're content to run your script from Script Editor for the rest of your life, go take a hot bath—there's nothing left for you to do. On the other hand, if you want to run your script from *elsewhere* on your Mac, try one of the following tricks:

- **Save your script for use in the Script Menu.** In Script Editor, choose File → Save, type whatever name you want for the script (like "DateDoc"), and then navigate to the Library → Scripts folder. Save your script in one of the subfolders here, and you'll be able to run the script anytime from the menu bar, using the system-wide Script Menu described on page 4.

Note: Before you click Save, make sure the File Format is set to Script (page 31).

- **Save your script as a double-clickable program.** In Script Editor, choose File → Save As. For the File Format, choose Application, and save the script somewhere on your hard drive. When you double-click this new application in the Finder, Mac OS X runs your code (page 33).

- **Put your script in the Dock.** This option requires you to complete the previous trick first. Once you've done so, navigate to your new application in the Finder, and simply drag it into the right side of the Dock. Whenever you want to run your code from now on, just click the Dock icon.

Of course, you can perform these three tricks with *any* script you have—not just this TextEdit script.

Figure 4-5:
Your own convenient business-letter starter. If you'd like, you can modify the script so it automatically adds "to whom it may concern," or some similarly business-sounding phrase to your document.

Adding Word Count

If there's one feature that TextEdit lacks over its competitors, it's the ability to count the number of words in a document. With all the powerful searching, typographical, and speech tools TextEdit has, it almost makes you wonder whether an Apple programmer was just sick the day he was supposed to program that feature.

Thankfully, AppleScript comes to your aid—again. You can write a short script that not only counts the number of words in your document but also counts the paragraphs and even the number of *characters* in your document—great for tricking people into thinking you've written a lot for your term paper.

The key to all this text-based power is the *Text Suite,* a section of many programs' dictionaries that deals exclusively with the nitty-gritty of text (like counting individual characters). You'll find the Text Suite in the dictionaries of professional programs like Microsoft Word (page 66)—but more immediately, you'll also find the Text Suite in *TextEdit's* dictionary. By employing the Text Suite as described in the following pages, you can write a script to count the number of words in any TextEdit document

Employing the Text Suite

If you open TextEdit's dictionary (page 59) and browse the lefthand pane, you'll find that the Text Suite already includes entries for *word, character,* and *paragraph.* These are the fundamental nouns (or *classes*) of AppleScript's text handling. By using those keywords as follows, you can create a script to add a basic word count feature to TextEdit:

```
tell application "TextEdit"
    activate
    --Count the characters:
    set allCharacters to every character of the front document
    set numberOfCharacters to (count allCharacters)
    set characterText to "Characters: " & numberOfCharacters
    --Count the words:
    set allWords to every word of the front document
    set numberOfWords to (count allWords)
    set wordText to "Words: " & numberOfWords
    --Count the paragraphs:
    set allParagraphs to every paragraph of the front document
    set numberOfParagraphs to (count allParagraphs)
    set paragraphText to "Paragraphs: " & numberOfParagraphs
    --Assemble the text for the dialog box:
    set dialogText to characterText & return & wordText & return ¬
        & paragraphText
    display dialog dialogText
end tell
```

Here's how the script breaks down:

- The commands following **Count the characters** get a list of all the characters in the frontmost TextEdit document, count the number of items *in* that list (see the sidebar "The count Command" on page 67), and then put together a string something like "Characters: 932" based on how many characters there are in the document.

- The commands after **Count the words** do the same thing, just for words instead of characters.

- The commands after **Count the paragraphs** do the same thing too, but for paragraphs instead of words.

Note: In AppleScript terms, a *paragraph* is any block of text that has a return or newline character after it (page 59). That means that even an *empty* line is considered a paragraph in AppleScript.

- The commands after **Assemble the text for the dialog box** concatenate all the previous strings you created, putting each string on its own line.

- Finally, the script displays the dialog box that lets you know the script has completed its word-counting mission (Figure 4-6, bottom).

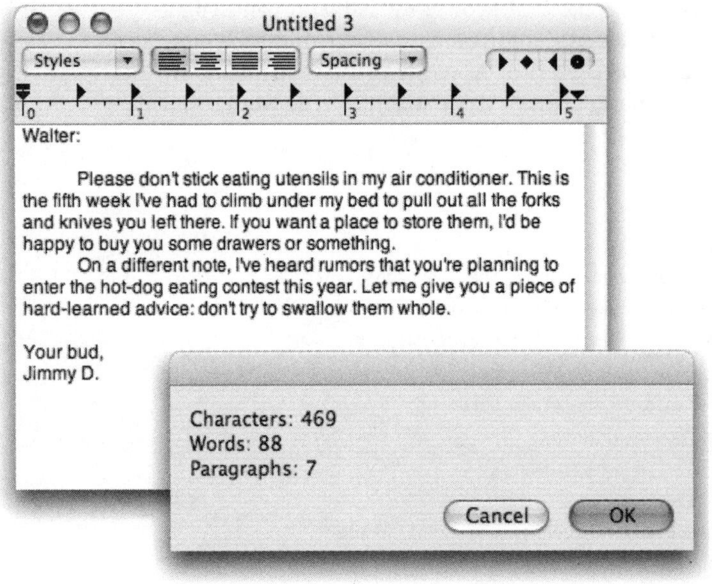

Figure 4-6:
There's no reason to use other programs to count your words when TextEdit and AppleScript can do it for free. For the ultimate in convenience, add your new word-, character-, and paragraph-counting script to the Script Menu (page 15).

Commanding Microsoft Word

If TextEdit were a sardine, Microsoft Word would be a blue whale. Mentioning the two together invites all sorts of comparisons: TextEdit takes up 5 MB, while Word takes up 20; TextEdit has six menus, Word has a dozen. The two programs, in fact, are illustrative of their respective companies' approaches: TextEdit is straightforward and simple, while Word is complex and feature-packed.

Still, Word's AppleScript support puts TextEdit to shame. Word includes the standard Text Suite (page 65) but adds more than *50* commands of its own.

Note: Many of Word's cool AppleScript commands are available only in the most recent release: Word 2004. Therefore, to ensure that the scripts in this chapter—and the rest of this book—work properly for you, you'd be best off upgrading to Word 2004 for the sake of compatibility (page xx in the Introduction).

Adapting a TextEdit Script

On page 65, you created a script that counted the number of characters, words, and paragraphs in an open TextEdit document. Of course, Word already *has* a word count feature (Tools → Word Count). Still, it's a good exercise to adapt your existing TextEdit script for use with Word, to get a feel for the differences in what it's like to script the two programs.

The first step in adapting a TextEdit script is to replace the *tell* statement with one that directs Word instead of TextEdit.

```
tell application "Microsoft Word"
    activate
    . . .
end tell
```

Note: You *must* use the phrase "Microsoft Word" in AppleScript; "Word" won't suffice.

The count Command

In the previous script, you used the *count* command for the first time, to figure out how many words are in a TextEdit document. You'll encounter *count* again in all sorts of scripts, though, so it's important to understand how it works.

In essence, *count* takes a list and returns how many items are inside it. You can take advantage of this command for all sorts of tasks, from counting seashells in a beach-simulation script to counting employees in an employee-management script.

Like the *exists* command (page 47), *count* can come either before or after the object you want to count. That means that both of the following are acceptable commands in AppleScript:

```
count allCharacters --Works
allCharacters count --Also works
```

You'll often see the *count* command used in conjunction with the *every* keyword (page 109), too. This powerful duo lets you get all the objects of a certain type (like all the words in a TextEdit document) and then count them. You can even use this command pair to get the number of items in a folder, like this:

```
tell application "Finder"
    set itemNumber to (count every item ¬
    in the folder "Applications")
    display dialog "You have " & ¬
    itemNumber & " items inside your ¬
    Applications folder."
end tell
```

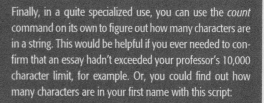

You have 79 files and folders inside your
Applications folder

[Cancel] [OK]

Finally, in a quite specialized use, you can use the *count* command on its own to figure out how many characters are in a string. This would be helpful if you ever needed to confirm that an essay hadn't exceeded your professor's 10,000 character limit, for example. Or, you could find out how many characters are in your first name with this script:

```
set yourName to the text returned of ¬
(display dialog ¬
    "Enter your first name:" default ¬
    answer "Xavier")
set numChars to (count yourName)
display dialog "Your name has " & ¬
    numChars & " characters."
```

If you run the script at this point, you'll get a strange result: both the character and word counts will be 0. This is caused by an odd quirk in Microsoft Word, which requires that you use the *count* and *every* keywords on the same line. To get your script to work properly, therefore, you must merge some of your existing lines to create this new script:

```
tell application "Microsoft Word"
    activate
    --Count the characters:
    set numberOfCharacters to (count every character of the front document)
    set characterText to "Characters: " & numberOfCharacters
    --Count the words:
    set numberOfWords to (count every word of the front document)
    set wordText to "Words: " & numberOfWords
    --Count the paragraphs:
    set numberOfParagraphs to (count every paragraph of the front document)
    set paragraphText to "Paragraphs: " & numberOfParagraphs
    --Assemble the text for the dialog box:
    set dialogText to characterText & return & wordText & return ¬
        & paragraphText
    display dialog dialogText
end tell
```

WORKAROUND WORKSHOP

Word Miscounting

When you run the script on this page, you see a dialog box listing the character, word, and paragraph counts from your frontmost Microsoft Word document. Unfortunately, this word count often conflicts with the results of Word's *included* word count feature (Tools → Word Count).

This problem occurs because AppleScript, when commanding Microsoft Word, considers punctuation marks *their own words*. That means Microsoft Word would see three words in "Don't eat yams!", but AppleScript would see five (the three words, plus two punctuation marks). Of course, this can distort your word counts considerably—especially if you're the type that likes to insert dashes in the middle of your sentences.

Fortunately, you can dodge AppleScript's fuzzy math by communicating with a Microsoft Word *text object*—an abstract AppleScript item that represents the text inside a particular document. Unlike communicating with a document directly (as in the script on page 65), communicating with a *text object* actually produces an accurate word count. So, to remedy your script, you could simply make the following changes:

```
tell application "Microsoft Word"
    set theText to the content of the ¬
        text object of the front document
    set numberOfCharacters to ¬
        (count every character of theText)
    set characterText to "Characters: " ¬
        & numberOfCharacters
    set numberOfWords to ¬
        (count every word of theText)
    set wordText to "Words: " & ¬
        numberOfWords
    set numberOfParagraphs to (count ¬
        every paragraph of theText)
    set paragraphText to "Paragraphs: " ¬
        & numberOfParagraphs
    set dialogText to characterText & ¬
        return & wordText & ¬
        return & paragraphText
    display dialog dialogText
end tell
```

Now when you run your modified script, your word count reflects the *actual* number of words in your document—without counting punctuation.

You'll notice that the two-liners that counted various items—for example, *set allWords to every word of the front document* and *set numberOfWords to (count allWords)*—have been put together into single-line commands. This is enough to satisfy Word's requirement for using *count* and *every* together; when you run the script now, it works properly.

When writing your own scripts for different programs, make sure to try using *count* and *every* together (as used here) and on different lines (as used on page 65). Chances are, the script will work at least *one* of the ways, but the only way to find out is to try both.

Shrinking Documents by a Page

If you write letters or emails—or computer books, for that matter—you've probably experienced the dreaded one-page-too-long problem. It goes like this: you're typing your document, inserting all sorts of different fonts and sizes, but when you come to the end, you realize your document is just one page longer than you want it.

If you're like most people, you'd sigh deeply, and then get to work modifying each individual font in your document, shrinking them in size so the document is one page shorter. The trouble with this approach, of course, is that it can take a *long* time to select blocks of text and change their font sizes, especially if you need to modify multiple fonts on dozens of pages.

Word, conveniently enough, provides an AppleScript command to take care of this whole text-squeezing business for you: *fit to pages*. The trouble is, though, that Word has hundreds of different commands in its dictionary. Does Microsoft really expect you to spend several minutes scanning all the entries in the left pane to find the *fit to pages* command? Yep.

Still, you purchased this book to save you some time, and you can prove Microsoft wrong. Once you've opened Word's dictionary (page 44), simply follow the procedure in Figure 4-7 to find the correct dictionary entry.

The definition of the command (also shown in Figure 4-7) tells you that it's meant to squeeze your fonts "just enough so that the document will fit on one fewer pages." The light blue *document* text, furthermore, indicates that you have to tell *fit to pages* which document you want it to work with.

Armed with this information, you can write your script:

```
tell application "Microsoft Word"
    activate
    display dialog "Shrink document by a page?"
    fit to pages (front document)
end tell
```

Note: When you run this script, make sure you have an open Word file that's more than one page long, so the *fit to page* command has something to perform its magic on.

This script brings Microsoft Word forward and then displays a confirmation dialog box, asking you if you want to shrink the document by a page. Since you haven't defined special buttons for the dialog box (page 60), you're left with only two options:

- If you click OK, the script proceeds with the next statement (*fit to pages*) and squeezes the front document down by one page.

- If you click Cancel, the script ends immediately.

After clicking OK, Word checks what it'll take to knock one page off your document and adjusts the font sizes throughout the document until the mission is complete.

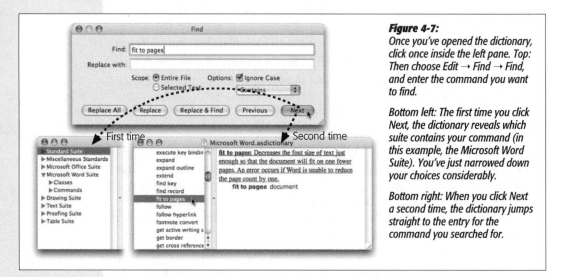

Figure 4-7:
Once you've opened the dictionary, click once inside the left pane. Top: Then choose Edit → Find → Find, and enter the command you want to find.

Bottom left: The first time you click Next, the dictionary reveals which suite contains your command (in this example, the Microsoft Word Suite). You've just narrowed down your choices considerably.

Bottom right: When you click Next a second time, the dictionary jumps straight to the entry for the command you searched for.

Repeating the Shrinking

The script you have so far is convenient, but what if you wanted to shrink your document by *more* than just one page? For example, you might be badgered for writing too much in a business proposal but find it easier to shrink the *size* of your writing than to actually cut text out.

In this situation, of course, you could run your script more than once, returning to Script Editor each time to click Run again. But that would defeat the purpose of using AppleScript in the first place: to automate tasks that you would normally have to do by hand.

Instead, you might as well have AppleScript repeat the *fit to pages* command all by itself, so you can go ride your bike while AppleScript chugs along on its font-shrinking mission.

The key to repeating a command in AppleScript is to use a *repeat* statement. Such statements generally follow this format:

```
repeat <some number> times
    --Commands you want to repeat go here
end repeat
```

When AppleScript encounters a *repeat* statement, it goes through the commands inside—one at a time—and then repeats the entire process however many times you specify. For running the *fit to page* command multiple times, you simply have to add a *repeat* statement to your existing script, as shown here:

```
tell application "Microsoft Word"
    activate
    display dialog "Shrink document by 5 pages?"
    repeat 5 times
        fit to pages (front document)
    end repeat
end tell
```

Now when you run the script, Word tries to shrink the front document by five pages instead of just one. (It accomplishes this, of course, by repeating the *fit to page* command five times.)

Shrinking a Variable Number of Times

Again, the script you have is convenient. However, it still lacks one crucial feature: you can't specify how *many* times you want it to repeat (at least, not without changing the numbers in Script Editor by hand). It would be great if, using a dialog box, you could have the script ask how many times to repeat the *fit to pages* command.

To do so, you simply have to change a few more lines of your script:

```
tell application "Microsoft Word"
    activate
    set theNumber to the text returned of (display dialog ¬
        "Shrink by how many pages?" default answer 3)
    repeat theNumber times
        fit to pages (front document)
    end repeat
end tell
```

Now the *repeat* statement runs however many times you specify in the dialog box. In other words, *you* get to tell Word how many pages you want to shrink the front document by, instead of hard-coding that number into the script. That's the power of AppleScript for you!

There are other instances when you might want to use *repeat* statements, including:

- Renaming multiple files automatically (page 113)

- Repeating a computerized beep at regular intervals to create a virtual metronome (page 152)

- Rating every song in your iTunes library (page 148)

Running Scripts from Text

So far in this chapter, you've created a series of scripts that make new text. In this section, the roles are reversed: you'll create new *text* and have it run scripts for you.

The key to this is the Services menu, which you can find inside any application menu (the bolded menu, directly to the right of the Apple menu in the menu bar). For example, if you're in TextEdit, you access the AppleScript-related commands by choosing TextEdit → Services → Script Editor (Figure 4-8).

Note: Services are a way of accessing one program's features while inside another program. For example, if someone sends you an email containing a short URL (one that doesn't have the *http://* in front of it, like *www.oreilly.com*), you can select the URL with the mouse and then go to Mail → Services → Open URL.

After selecting Open URL from the Services menu, your Web browser jumps into action and opens that Web page for you. Pretty slick, huh?

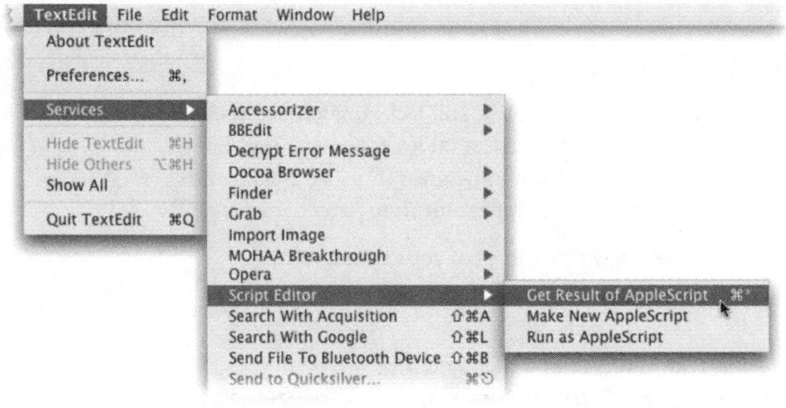

Figure 4-8:
The three AppleScript services. Unfortunately, only one has a keyboard combination, so you'll have to run the other two the old fashioned way: with the mouse.

Running one of these Services commands is a simple process:

1. **Type some AppleScript commands in the current program, then select them.**

   If you're working in TextEdit, for example, you could type *display dialog "Hello!"* and then select it.

2. **Choose the AppleScript service you want to run from the menu bar.**

Note: The Services menu doesn't work properly in certain programs that haven't been completely updated for Mac OS X. Microsoft Word, for example, won't let you use the Services menu. On the other hand, TextEdit—and most other programs written in the last few years—work just fine with Services.

Script Editor has three different Services to offer, as described in the following sections.

Get Result of AppleScript

If you select an AppleScript command (or series of commands) and choose "Get Result of AppleScript" from the Services → Script Editor menu, your commands are run in the background and their result is pasted in place of your commands. Try it out by typing:

```
tell application "Finder"
    count every file in the desktop
end tell
```

Then select your text and choose Services → Script Editor → Get Result of Apple-Script. Script Editor launches in the background, runs your commands, and pastes the result—in this case, the number of files on your desktop—right over your selected text.

Tip: If you don't feel like mousing up to the Services menu, you can also use the convenient keyboard for this Service shortcut instead: Shift-⌘-8. (If your keyboard has a number keypad, you can also press ⌘-*, using the asterisk from the number keypad.)

This command is more useful than it might seem. Since AppleScript can perform mathematical operations, you can use this feature as a quick text-based calculator, straight from TextEdit or Mail, for example. Figure 4-9 shows you how.

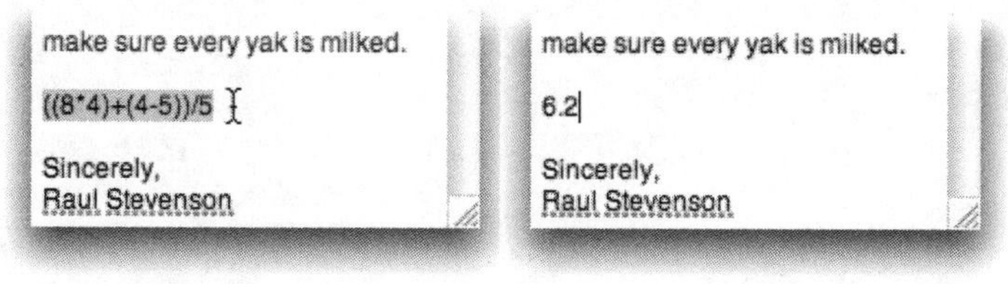

make sure every yak is milked.

((8*4)+(4-5))/5

Sincerely,
Raul Stevenson

make sure every yak is milked.

6.2

Sincerely,
Raul Stevenson

Figure 4-9:
Left: Type out a mathematical expression, then select it.

Right: After you choose Get Result of AppleScript, your text is replaced with the correct answer.

Make New AppleScript

This command takes any text you've selected in the current program and copies it into a new document in Script Editor. This feature is particularly handy if you find some AppleScript code posted on the Web; just select the code and choose Services → Make New Script, and you won't have to copy and paste the code yourself.

This command has another use, although it's much less obvious. You can use the service while *inside* Script Editor to select a portion of an existing script, and then have that code quickly copied into a new script window. That way, if you have a big script, you can copy sections of it to make smaller scripts with more specialized purposes.

Run as AppleScript

This command works almost exactly the same way as "Get Result of AppleScript," with one key difference: it won't replace your commands with their result. That makes this command perfect for quickly running, say, a line or two of code that you entered in an already-open TextEdit document.

Of course, since you can access the Services menu from Script Editor, you can run this command from Script Editor, too. In fact, this command adds a handy feature to Script Editor: you can use it to test only a *few lines* of a script rather than running the entire script at once. Simply select the lines you want to run, choose "Run as AppleScript" from the Services → Script Editor menu, and sit back as Apple-Script runs only your selected lines.

Note: Remember that the Run as AppleScript command—unlike, say, the Get Result of AppleScript command—doesn't return the result of your AppleScript commands. To work around this issue, place *display dialog* commands in your script to show you the status of events in your AppleScript code as they happen.

For even more fun, try running these three services from within Stickies (in your Applications folder). If you prepare a few sticky notes with your favorite Apple-Script code written on them, you can then run the scripts by selecting the Run as AppleScript command. In this way, you can use Stickies as an encyclopedia of your favorite AppleScript code.

POWER USERS' CLINIC

Using Visual Basic from AppleScript

If you come from Windows—or a previous version of Microsoft Office—you might be familiar with Visual Basic, Microsoft's homegrown language for automating Word, PowerPoint, and other Office programs. Visual Basic, while not nearly as English-like as AppleScript, is still used by thousands of people around the world to write *macros*—little Visual Basic scripts. (It's also used to write computer viruses, but that's a story for another sidebar.)

By using the *do Visual Basic* command, you can run a specific Visual Basic command—or series of them—right from within an AppleScript, like this:

```
tell application "Microsoft Word"
    (*Print the front document, but don't
    show a dialog box:*)
    do Visual Basic ¬
```

```
        "ActiveDocument.PrintOut"
    end tell
```

If you have a prerecorded Visual Basic macro stored in one of your documents, you can also run the entire macro with AppleScript's *run VB macro* command. (Keep in mind, however, that these AppleScript commands only work inside a *tell* statement that's targeted at a Microsoft Office program; you can't run Visual Basic scripts targeted at Text-Edit or the Finder, for example.)

For more information on these Visual Basic commands (*do Visual Basic* and *run VB macro*), check out their entries in Microsoft Word's AppleScript dictionary. Or, if you have some time to spare, read Paul Berkowitz's excellent article on the subject at *http://word.mvps.org/MacWordNew/WordAppleScript.htm*.

Controlling Files

Most people have a love-hate relationship with their computer. Sure, your Mac is a great tool for when you want to edit images or video, send and receive email, or play Halo. But your computer also serves as a digital file cabinet: a place where you can create and store files, move them around, organize them in folders, trash them when they're no longer needed, and copy them to another disk or computer on the fly.

Files, of course, are nothing more than individual packages of information that you keep on your hard drive. But for all the filing tasks they perform, most computer users tend to handle files *manually:* drag this file here, create a new folder there, and so on. After a while, these mundane tasks are what make people start to hate their computers.

If you're sick of dealing with your files one at a time—and taking up half your day in the process—there's no better tool in your arsenal than AppleScript. By commanding the Finder, AppleScript lets you:

- Move all the files off your desktop in one fell swoop (page 90)

- Back up an important folder to a separate hard drive, just in case your computer dies (page 93)

- Rename all the files in a folder—without having to type their new names individually (page 113)

For these jobs and more, AppleScript can save you annoyance, tedium, and—most of all—time.

Note: The example scripts from this chapter can be found on the AppleScript Examples CD (see page 24 for instructions).

File Path Boot Camp

The one thing AppleScript *can't* save you from is the fact that files are essentially geeky things. Mac OS X's Unix heritage, while great news for programmers, also means that old Mac fans have to adapt to a few new file conventions—how to name files, what programs to open them with, and so on. Therefore, before you jump head-first into controlling files with AppleScript, there are a few things you should know:

- **In Mac OS X, files should always have a file extension.** A *file extension* is a short abbreviation added after a period in a file name. Microsoft Word files, for example, end in .doc, while sound files often end in .mp3 or .aiff.

  To Mac OS X (and Windows, for that matter) a file extension reveals what kind of information a file holds. In many cases, a file extension also tells Mac OS X which program should open a file: .doc files open in Microsoft Word, while .psd files open in Photoshop. (Of course, certain types of files can open in several different programs; .jpg files, for example, can open in just about any image-viewing program on the planet.)

Note: As a general rule, *folders* should not have file extensions. The exceptions are *bundles*—little folders that masquerade as files (page 34), like the .key files that Keynote produces.

To see what's inside in a bundle, Control-click the bundle in the Finder and select Show Package Contents from the shortcut menu. In the new window that appears, you can sift through the files that comprise the package, discovering, for example, that Keynote "files" are actually made up of dozens of smaller files.

UP TO SPEED

Path Notation

As described on page 77, a *path* is a Unix-esque way of describing where a file or folder resides on your hard drive. When you want to specify the lowest level of your hard drive, you simply specify the Unix path / (a single forward slash). Similarly, when you want to refer to an item *inside* your hard drive, you must *begin* the item's path with a forward slash.

However, when specifying a path, folders must also *end* in a forward slash. That means the path to your Applications folder would be */Applications/* (the first slash to tell Mac OS X to look in your hard drive, and the last slash to tell Mac OS X that Applications refers to a folder).

When you refer to a *file*, however, you omit the trailing slash. The path to your Library → Fonts → Times New Roman file, therefore, would be */Library/Fonts/Times New Roman*, with slashes after Library and Fonts (since they're folders) but no slash after Times New Roman (since it's a file).

When you want to refer to your Home folder, you have two choices. You can specify the folder the normal way, by typing */Users/yourUsername/* (substituting your actual username for *yourUsername*, of course). Or you can use the convenient Unix shortcut (~/), which tells Mac OS X "substitute the actual path to my Home folder here".

If you want to refer to a file on a disk *besides* your startup disk, you have to begin your path with */Volumes/*. Just follow that with the name of the disk and another slash—like */Volumes/Backup Drive/* for a disk named Backup Drive—and the path now refers to your specified disk.

And something to note if you come from the Windows world: in places where you would have formerly used a backslash (\) in a path name—to identify folders, for example—use a forward-slash now. It's just one more instance of how Windows is, well, backward.

Although certain programs don't *require* file extensions, it's still a good idea to use them. That way, if you ever need to send a file to a Windows user, you won't get back an angry email asking you to *resend* the file with an extension so your recipient can actually open it.

- **A *path* is a string that tells you how to get to a certain file or folder.** Each item in path is separated by a forward-slash (/) in Mac OS X—a by-product of your computer's Unix heritage. That means the path to your Home → Desktop folder would be */Users/yourUsername/Desktop/*, while the path to your copy of Text-Edit would be */Applications/TextEdit.app*.

When you want to play with a path in AppleScript, you can use special type of information called a *POSIX* file. (POSIX is nerd lingo for "portable operating system interface," which basically means that file paths can be used anywhere, on any computer that supports the POSIX standard. To learn more about POSIX, you can read up on it online at *www.satimage.fr/software/en/file_paths.html*.) To get the path to your Desktop folder, for instance, you'd write the following, replacing *yourUsername* with your actual one-word username:

```
POSIX file "/Users/yourUsername/Desktop/"
```

Still, you'll find that most commands (like *choose file,* for presenting an Open dialog box [page 97]) use the *alias* type to refer to files. The *alias* format separates each folder in a path with a colon, rather than a forward slash. To get the *alias* to your Desktop folder, for example, you'd write this:

```
alias ":Users:yourUsername:Desktop:"
```

Note: Of course, you should replace *yourUsername* with your actual username. If you don't know what your username is, you can look it up in System Preferences → Accounts; you'll find your username in the Short Name field.

- **You can open any file or folder with the *open* command directed at the Finder.** For example, to open Library → Desktop Pictures → Aqua Blue.jpg (the image that appears behind Mac OS X's login dialog box), you could write:

```
tell application "Finder"
    activate --Bring the Finder forward
    open POSIX file "/Library/Desktop Pictures/Aqua Blue.jpg"
end tell
```

Note: You'll notice a couple of oddities when you run this AppleScript. First off, the *open POSIX file* statement gets changed to *open file*. Then, all the forward slashes are converted to colons, and AppleScript inserts the name of your hard drive at the beginning of the path string. None of these changes affect what your code actually does; AppleScript just makes these changes so it understands what you're asking it to do.

If you prefer to write your code using the more common *alias* type, you could rewrite the previous script as follows:

```
tell application "Finder"
    activate
    open alias ":Library:Desktop Pictures:Aqua Blue.jpg"
end tell
```

Either way you write the script, the Aqua Blue image opens and shows up on your screen.

Displaying Folders

When you're working on a bunch of related documents at once, you might want to jump quickly to their folder in the Finder. Normally, of course, you'd switch to the Finder and navigate through your hard drive to get to the correct folder. Or perhaps, if you're a power user, you've already put the folder in the Finder's Sidebar for easy access. Either way, though, you have to switch to the Finder and open a new window, which is a massive waste of time.

Why go through all those steps when you can get AppleScript to do it for you? Using AppleScript, you can save a folder-opening script as an application (page 33) and place the script on the Dock for easy access. From then on, all you'll need to do is click the script's icon in the Dock, and a Finder window pops open and takes you right to the folder you want.

"But wait," you say, "I could just put the folder's *icon* on the Dock, no script required." You are, of course, correct—and your method is what most people use for accessing commonly used folders. The trouble is, when you click a folder's icon on the Dock, you never know where the folder's window will open onscreen, or whether it'll be in List, Column, or Icon view. Plus, a folder icon on the Dock can open only one *specific* folder, whereas a script can open multiple folders at once—like your Music and Pictures folders—as shown the following example:

```
tell application "Finder"
    activate
    open the folder "Users:yourUsername:Music"
    open the folder "Users:yourUsername:Pictures"
end tell
```

Again, just save this script as an application (page 33), and then drag the script's icon to your Dock. From then on, you'll be just one click away from opening two folders at once.

Tip: Of course, if you have *more* than two folders you'd like to open simultaneously, you can insert extra *open* commands in the previous script for those folders as well.

Opening a Folder with AppleScript (Reprise)

As you've seen on pages 23 and 78, there's more than one way to open a folder from AppleScript. If you want to open your Applications folder, for example, you'd have five separate choices:

```
tell application "Finder"
    activate
    make new Finder window to alias "Macintosh HD:Applications:"   --Option 1
    make new Finder window to POSIX file "/Applications/"          --Option 2
    open alias "Macintosh HD:Applications:"                        --Option 3
    open POSIX file "/Applications/"                               --Option 4
    open the folder "Applications" of the startup disk            --Option 5
end tell
```

If you don't have any Finder windows open and you use one of these commands, the same thing would happen: a new Finder window would appear, taking you right to the Applications folder.

GEM IN THE ROUGH

AppleScript Shortcuts

After using AppleScript for a while, you might be wondering what exactly the word *the* does. The answer? Nothing. Using *the* in your scripts just makes them easier for humans to read—it makes no difference to AppleScript. You can prove it to yourself by running this script, for example:

```
tell application "Finder"
    open the the the folder "Applications"
    of startup disk
end tell
```

The fact that you have three *the's* in a row makes no difference—AppleScript ignores them all.

That's not the only word you can omit in AppleScript, though. If you're writing a series of nested statements (like *if* [page 47], *tell* [page 43], or *repeat* [page 71]) for commanding a program, you can omit the second half of the *end* commands, and AppleScript fills them in for you automatically when you compile the script. For instance, you could write this script:

```
(* This script creates a bunch of new
folders in your Home folder; well, 15 of
them at least. *)
```

```
tell application "Finder"
    repeat 15 times
        if (count every folder in home) ¬
            is less than 15 then
            make new folder at home
        end
    end
end
```

When you compile or run this script (page 24), the last three lines are automatically expanded to include the correct commands (*end if, end repeat,* and *end tell*). You can even shorten the word *application* to *app* (on the fourth line), and AppleScript expands it automatically.

Finally, you can replace the nerdy-sounding word *of* with the more English-like *'s*. For instance, the following script would work just as well as the one shown at the top of this sidebar:

```
tell application "Finder"
    open the startup disk's folder ¬
        "Applications"
    (*Note the apostrophe-S instead of
    the word "of"*)
end tell
```

However, if you *already* have your Applications folder open, the commands behave differently:

- **Options 1 or 2** create *new* windows, each of which drops you off in the Applications folder. Option 1 employs the *alias* data type to do so (page 78), while Option 2 uses the new-age *POSIX file* data type (page 77). The *make* command, used in both Options, is described in detail on page 61.

- **Options 3, 4, or 5** simply bring the existing Applications folder to the front, without opening a new Finder window. Option 3 uses the aforementioned *alias* type, Option 4 uses the *POSIX* file type, and Option 5 uses neither (it simply tells the Finder which disk to look in). That's how *open* works.

The difference between these approaches is pretty small, of course, but it's important to understand: the *make* command always creates a new copy of something (in this case, a window), while the *open* command opens a new copy only if one doesn't already exist.

Changing a Finder Window's View

Why stop with just *opening* a folder when you can change the Finder window's view, too? If you've been using Mac OS X for more than a few days, you probably already know that the Finder has three viewing options (available at the top of the View menu), each of which provides a different, potentially timesaving way of looking at your files:

- **Icon view** shows you the icons for each item in a folder (Figure 5-1, top). That way, if you're browsing a folder full of Photoshop images, for example, you can find the particular image you want just by glancing at its icon.

- **List view** organizes the items in a folder alphabetically, by the dates they were created, or by just about any other criterion you want (Figure 5-1, middle). As an added benefit, list view shows more files in the same space than Icon view does.

- **Column view** gives you a hierarchical view of your hard drive, showing you the order of folders that contain the item you're looking at (Figure 5-1, bottom). This is the most compact way of looking through a folder, so it's worth using if you need to locate a file in a hurry.

But the fun doesn't stop there; each Finder view also has its own *options*. For example, you can change a window's background color from the default white to some other color—or post a picture behind a Finder window. Simply open the Finder's dictionary (page 44) and navigate to the *Finder window* entry (Figure 5-2).

As you can see, there are several useful properties you can set for Finder windows. If you want your script to automatically open the Applications folder in Column view, for example, you could modify your script like this:

```
tell application "Finder"
    activate
    open the folder "Applications" of the startup disk
```

```
        set the current view of the front Finder window to column view
end tell
```

Now when you run your script, the Applications folder comes to the front and then quickly switches into Column view.

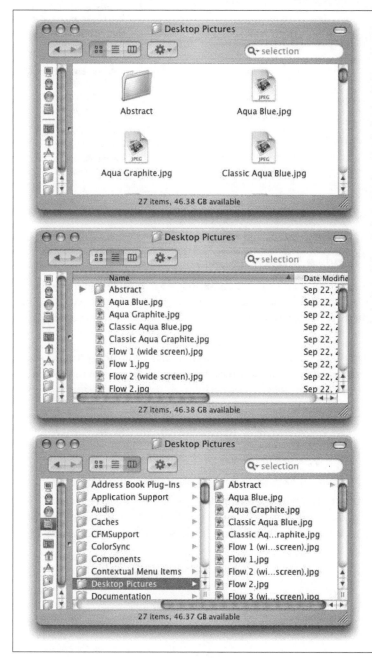

Figure 5-1:
The three ways of looking at your Library → Desktop Pictures folder. Top: Icon view (⌘-1) shows only four items in a window this small, but their icons are quite large. Use this view if you have bad vision.

Middle: List view (⌘-2) shows nine items in a window this small, and lets you sort the items however you'd like. Click the Date Created column to sort your files and folders from newest to oldest, for example, or click the Size column to sort the items from biggest to smallest. (Click either column a second time to reverse the sorting order.)

Bottom: Column view (⌘-3) shows 10 items in a window this small—the most of any of the three views. As a nice side effect, Column view also lets you see where the folder you're looking at is stored (in the left columns).

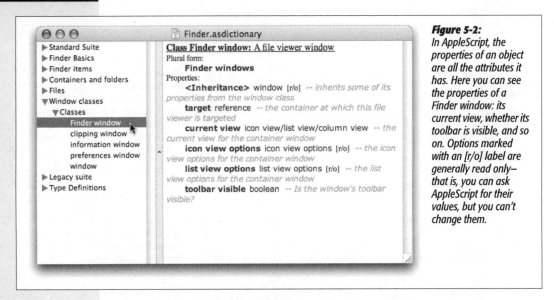

Figure 5-2:
In AppleScript, the properties of an object are all the attributes it has. Here you can see the properties of a Finder window: its current view, whether its toolbar is visible, and so on. Options marked with an [r/o] label are generally read only—that is, you can ask AppleScript for their values, but you can't change them.

More Finder Window Settings

As you can see from the Finder's dictionary, there are a good number of extra properties you can set for Finder windows. You might have noticed with some puzzlement, however, that there's a big bold *<Inheritance>* label inside the entry for *Finder window*.

Your first instinct might be to assume that this property is off-limits to you—after all, it's got the *[r/o]* label, which usually means that you can't change the setting. As it turns out, however, inheritance is a powerful tool in AppleScript that puts even more control at your fingertips.

When you see the *<Inheritance>* label in a dictionary, look at the word immediately to its right. In the entry for *Finder window*, for instance, you'll see *window* next to *<Inheritance>*. That means that a Finder window, along with all its own properties, *also* has all the properties of a regular, everyday AppleScript *window*.

So what's that mean to you when you're up late at night writing scripts? It tells you to look in the dictionary entry for *window* in addition to the entry for *Finder window* (Figure 5-3), essentially doubling the number of commands you can send to a Finder window.

Armed with this information, you can add an extra command to your script:

```
tell application "Finder"
    activate
```

```
      open the folder "Applications" of the startup disk
      set the current view of the front Finder window to column view
      --Minimize the window to the Dock.
      set the collapsed of the front Finder window to true
   end tell
```

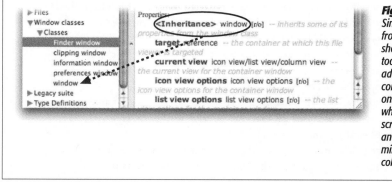

Figure 5-3:
Since Finder windows inherit from plain old windows, you should read the entry for window, too. You'll come across several additional properties you can control: where the window is onscreen (the position property), whether the window is big on the screen (the zoomed property), and even whether the window is minimized to the Dock (the collapsed property).

Working with More than One Window

The current script is great for showing your Applications folder, but it won't save you that much time; you can always just click once on the desktop and use a keyboard shortcut (Shift-⌘-A) to launch the Applications folder instead.

You *really* start saving time when your script opens more than one folder. That way, you can have a quick way to view your Applications, Documents, Music, and Movies folders, for example—all with a single click.

UP TO SPEED

Inheritance

Inheritance is such a simple word. It means you get something for nothing, and when it comes to scripting, you can't get any better than that.

AppleScript's system of *inheritance* is pretty confusing at first, especially if you've never programmed before. The key to understanding it is seeing how similar it is to the real world, where some things have properties of others.

Say you have a Subaru. Now, your Subaru has properties that are different from most other cars: it uses four-wheel drive, for example. However, your Subaru also has properties in *common* with other cars: it has tires, a steering wheel, and brakes (you hope).

Think of it like this: your Subaru is a specific kind of car. In AppleScript, you'd explain the relationship like this: "*Subaru inherits from car.*" Your Subaru has all the properties of a car, plus some extras of its own.

Keep in mind, however, that inheritance is a one-way street. While every Subaru has the properties of a generic car, *not* every generic car has the properties of a Subaru.

Now, applied to AppleScript, this whole scheme just means that an object can use all the properties of the object marked *<Inheritance>*, but not the other way around. That's why you can use the properties from a *window* in your script that controls a *Finder window*, but you wouldn't be able to use the properties from a *Finder window* in a script that controlled a generic *window*.

One approach to opening multiple folders from your script is to simply copy and paste the existing commands repeatedly. (Then you'd insert the names of the folders as appropriate.) Using this method, your final script would look something like this:

```
tell application "Finder"
    activate
    open the folder "Applications" of the startup disk
    set the current view of the front Finder window to column view
    set the collapsed of the front Finder window to true
    open the folder "Documents" of home
    set the current view of the front Finder window to column view
    set the collapsed of the front Finder window to true
    open the folder "Music" of home
    set the current view of the front Finder window to column view
    set the collapsed of the front Finder window to true
    open the folder "Movies" of home
    set the current view of the front Finder window to column view
    set the collapsed of the front Finder window to true
end tell
```

POWER USERS' CLINIC

Moving a Window

Normally, moving a Finder window to a more convenient place on your screen is easy: you just drag any gray area of the window, and the rest of the window follows. This simple task, however, masks the fact that moving a window *precisely* where you want it is an exceptionally difficult task. In fact, getting a window to the exact top-left corner of your screen—so you can see everything on the right side of your monitor—is harder than writing a computer book.

That's why AppleScript's window-placing features are so convenient. By setting a window's *position* property, you can send the window anywhere on (or off) the screen. Here's how:

```
tell application "Finder"
    activate
    open the folder "Applications" ¬
        of the startup disk
    set the current view of the front ¬
        window to column view
    --Move the window where you want it:
```

```
    set the position of the front window ¬
        to {200, 100}
    end tell
```

In that script, you place the Applications window 200 pixels from the left edge of the screen and 100 pixels from the top edge of the screen—a good position if you want to leave room for additional windows at the *bottom* of your screen.

Keep in mind when writing scripts like this, however, that the menu bar is 83 pixels tall. Also, a Finder window needs a 5 pixel "barrier" from the left edge of the screen, so you can see the entire window. Therefore, if you wanted to place a window at *exactly* the top-left pixel on the screen, you would have to substitute the following command in the bold part of the previous script:

```
    set the position of the front window ¬
        to {5, 83}
```

For a more detailed explanation of Mac OS X's odd window-positioning system, see page 124.

This kind of approach, unfortunately, has several downsides:

- **It repeats a lot of commands.** That means your script is longer than it has to be, which can become a problem if you start writing scripts that are hundreds of lines long.

- **It's annoying to use.** Each time you paste the commands again, you have to go back and change the portion of the command that needs modifying. Again, if you're working with a long script, this can be quite a nuisance.

- **If you want to change a command, you have to change it in multiple places.** For instance, if you wanted to change *column view* to *list view,* you'd have to do it four times.

Luckily, there's a solution to these problems: breaking the redundant commands into a separate portion of your script, known as a *subroutine.*

Subroutines

In AppleScript (and in other programming languages), a *subroutine* is a section of code that's meant to be used over and over again. Rather than having to retype a big block of code, a subroutine lets you write that code just once, assign a name *to the code*, and then simply use the subroutine's *name* whenever you want to run the corresponding code. Think of it like using a kitchen appliance: no matter what time of day it is, you can expect the "coffeemaker" appliance to behave the same way. Similarly, no matter what part of your script you run a subroutine from, you can expect the subroutine to run the exact same lines of code.

You can do anything you want in a subroutine: tally the points from a sports game, connect to a Web site, or anything else you're likely to do more than once in your script. (And incidentally, subroutines are sometimes called *handlers,* too.)

Now that you know what subroutines can do, it's time to put them to use in simplifying your Finder window script.

Defining a subroutine

In general, a subroutine looks something like this:

```
on subroutineName( <any variables being passed into the subroutine> )
    --Any commands you want in the subroutine go here
end subroutineName
```

You'll notice that, unlike *repeat, if,* and *tell* statements, subroutines begin with the keyword *on.* That's your way of telling AppleScript, "Hey! There's a subroutine here, and whenever I refer to this name, please run the lines of code that follow."

Note: Some people use the word *to* instead of *on* to introduce their subroutines. Either way is valid.

Running a subroutine

Calling a subroutine from your script couldn't be easier. (*Calling* is just geek-speak for "running the code contained in a subroutine.") You simply type the name of the subroutine, followed by parentheses, like this:

```
subroutineName( <any variables you want to pass into the subroutine> )
```

On the other hand, if your code is inside a *tell* statement, you have to preface your subroutine with the word *my*. That's your way of telling AppleScript, "I know I'm targeting a particular program with my script, but take a break for a second and run my *personal* subroutine, will ya?"

Variables in subroutines

When defining a subroutine, you don't have to put anything between the parentheses on the subroutine's first line. If you *do* choose to put variable names there, however, you'll need to use the same number of values when you *call* the subroutine from your script.

In other words, if you defined your subroutine like this:

```
on displayGreater(a, b) --Note that there are two variables
    if a > b then
        set theResult to a
    else
        set theResult to b
    end if
    display dialog "The greater number is: " & theResult
end displayGreater
```

you'd have to run the subroutine from your code like this:

```
displayGreater(10, 88) --You must provide two values
```

On the other hand, your subroutines don't *have* to accept variables at all. Apple-Script is perfectly happy to run a subroutine defined like this, for example:

```
on displayPi( )
    display dialog pi
end displayPi
```

In that case, since the subroutine doesn't expect any values (indicated by the lack of variables between its parentheses), you'd run this subroutine with this simple command:

```
displayPi( ) --Display a dialog box showing pi
```

Note: *pi* is a special AppleScript keyword, a namesake of the famous irrational number.

Writing the appropriate subroutine

Now that you know how to write and call subroutines, you can eliminate the redundant portions of your Finder-window script (page 84). First, add this subroutine to the bottom of that script:

```
on columnAndMinimize( )
    tell application "Finder"
        set the current view of the front Finder window to column view
        set the collapsed of the front Finder window to true
    end tell
end columnAndMinimize
```

In writing this subroutine, you've isolated your script's redundant code. Now you can *erase* your script's redundant code by calling the *columnAndMinimize* subroutine as follows:

```
tell application "Finder"
    activate
    open the folder "Applications" of the startup disk
    my columnAndMinimize( )
    open the folder "Documents" of home
    my columnAndMinimize( )
    open the folder "Music" of home
    my columnAndMinimize( )
    open the folder "Movies" of home
    my columnAndMinimize( )
end tell

--Here's the subroutine:
on columnAndMinimize ( )
    tell application "Finder"
        set the current view of the front Finder window to column view
        set the collapsed of the front Finder window to true
    end tell
end columnAndMinimize
```

Note: Remember, you must use the word *my* before these subroutine-running commands because you're using those commands inside a *tell* statement.

Now, with this final script, you've not only saved several lines of code, but you've also made it easier to change your script's behavior in the future. If you ever want to modify the code now, it's simply a matter of modifying the subroutine *once*, rather than modifying four separate lines. Here are a few possible tweaks:

- To keep all your newly opened windows from minimizing, delete *set the collapsed of the front Finder window to true* from your subroutine.

- If you'd rather your new windows appear in List view or Icon view (page 80), replace *column view* with either *list view* or *icon view* in your subroutine.

- Finally, if you don't care what view your new windows use, just delete the entire *set the current view of the front Finder window to [whatever]* line from your subroutine.

Moving Files Around

Being able to display your files is useful, but it's only half of what the Finder can do. The other half, of course, is to *move* your files—putting them in a new folder, deleting them, and so on. With AppleScript, you can automate these actions and more.

Transferring Items from One Folder to Another

The simplest action you can perform on a file is dragging it from one folder (or disk) to another. With AppleScript, it's also one of the simplest actions you can control in the Finder.

The key to this trick is the *move* command. It's part of the Finder's Standard Suite (page 45), so it's a pretty common command. And, as the Finder's dictionary explains, the *move* command follows this simple structure:

```
tell application "Finder"
    move someItem to somePlace
end tell
```

Tip: In this example, *someItem* can be either a single item or a list of items. That makes the *move* command perfect for transferring whole clusters of files (or folders) in a single step. (See page 105 for the lowdown on lists.)

And also, if you use the *move* command to transfer files from one *disk* to another, AppleScript (like the Finder) assumes that you mean to *copy* the files. If you want, you can then use the *delete* command (page 94) to erase the files from the original disk.

Now, if you're the sort of person who always saves downloads and email attachments to your desktop, you've probably noticed your desktop getting pretty full. You might have so many icons that you've had to shrink them down (View → Show View Options). Or perhaps your desktop is *so* cluttered that icons have started overlapping each other, obscuring all the important stuff you keep there.

No matter what the issue, AppleScript can help you clean up your desktop. With one fell swoop, a script can sweep up all the files and folders there, and stash them somewhere less intrusive.

Tip: You can use the *move* command for any number of other jobs, too: transferring sounds from an old folder to the Mac OS X–standard Music folder; moving downloaded files to a special Just Downloaded folder; or even sending files to another computer on your network (page 199).

Creating the destination folder

Right out of the box, your computer comes with one Desktop folder—the one you see right now. That won't help much, though, when you want to clear your desktop and sweep all those files into *another* folder.

Thankfully, you can create a new folder to hold everything from your old desktop. (In fact, if you're feeling especially creative, you could even name the folder Old Desktop.) Here's how:

```
tell application "Finder"
    make new folder at home with properties {name:"Old Desktop"}
end tell
```

As you've seen on page 61, the *make* command lets you create a new item (such as a document or folder) straight from AppleScript. The *at* option lets you specify where to create it (in this case, your Home folder). Plus, when you add the *with properties* option, you can specify various extra settings for the new item you create. (In this case, the *name* property gives the new folder a name, which is *Old Desktop.*)

After the *with properties* option, the settings you specify have to follow a special structure: they have to be surrounded by curly brackets, and each setting's name has to be followed by a colon and the value you want to use for it. For instance, to create a folder with the name Old Desktop, you have to use the property *{name: "Old Desktop"}.*

Tip: You can specify as many settings as you want inside the brackets. A more involved *make* command, for instance, could go something like this:

```
make new folder at home with properties ¬
    {name:"Old Desktop", comment:"Old Desktop files and folders"}
```

That creates an Old Desktop folder in your Home folder, but it also adds a *comment* to the folder. Then, at some point in the future, you could see your comment by selecting the folder in the Finder and choosing File → Get Info (⌘-I).

Eliminating the "already an item with that name" error

When you first run your script, it'll silently create a new folder named Old Desktop in your Home folder. The trouble is, if you already *have* an Old Desktop folder when you run the script, you'll see the error message shown in Figure 5-4.

The key to avoiding this problem is placing an *if* statement around the folder-creating command. That way, if the script discovers that there's already an Old Desktop folder, AppleScript just skips over the command for creating the folder and move on to the next command.

To add the *if* statement, just modify the script by adding the lines you see here in bold:

```
tell application "Finder"
    if not (the folder "Old Desktop" of home exists) then
```

```
        make new folder at home with properties {name:"Old Desktop"}
    end if
end tell
```

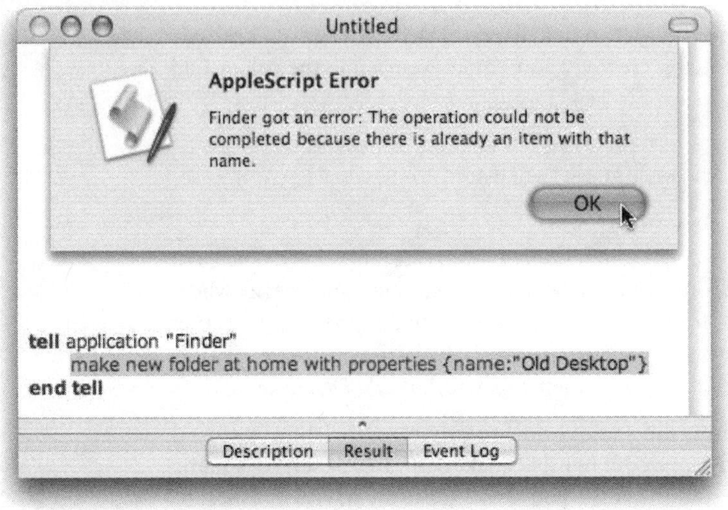

Figure 5-4:
AppleScript isn't very graceful about handling errors with the make command: it stops your entire script and presents a dialog box. Luckily, you can spare it the trouble by enclosing your make command in an if statement.

The new *if* statement looks in your Home folder to see whether you have an Old Desktop folder there already (the *exists* part). If you don't have an Old Desktop folder, the script runs the next command (*make new folder*) and creates one. Now you'll never get that annoying dialog box when you run your script in the future.

Moving the files and folders

Now that your script can tell whether or not there's an Old Desktop folder, you can get down to business: moving the files and folders from your desktop into your Old Desktop folder. Luckily, this is just a matter of adding two *move* commands to your script:

```
tell application "Finder"
    if not (the folder "Old Desktop" of home exists) then
        make new folder at home with properties {name:"Old Desktop"}
    end if
    move every file of the desktop to the folder "Old Desktop" of home
    move every folder of the desktop to the folder "Old Desktop" of home
end tell
```

These *move* commands, as you could probably guess, take all the files and folders that sit on your desktop and deposit them into your Home → Old Desktop folder. In a single click of the Run button, your desktop's clean.

Tip: For the ultimate in convenience, add this script to your Script Menu (page 15). Then you can run it from any program, whenever you want. This can come in really handy when, for example, you're snapping a bunch of screenshots (with either Shift-⌘-3 for a partial-screen picture or Shift-⌘-4 for a full-screen picture) and you want to quickly move the images off your desktop (which is where Mac OS X saves them by default). It's a great trick for Mac book authors, especially.

Backing Up Files

Talk to any computer expert, and you'll be told the same thing: backing up your files is not an option, it's a *must*! Unless you're interested in joining the millions of people who've lost essential files, you should back up your files regularly.

There are plenty of choices for backing up your files; it's only a matter of picking the one with the features and price you like. Here are a few of the options:

- Commercial programs like Dantz's **Retrospect Desktop** (*www.dantz.com/en/ products/mac_desktop/index.dtml;* $130) let you automatically back up important files at intervals you specify.

UP TO SPEED

Boolean Values

One of the cornerstones of all programming languages is the *Boolean* type. This simple kind of information has only two possible states: *true* and *false*. That makes it perfect for simple operations, such as determining whether something exists.

You can set Boolean variables just like any other variable:

```
set finderShouldQuit to true
set scriptDone to false
```

Boolean values also have special *operators* (keywords) you can use. If you ever took a logic course in high school, you'll instantly recognize the three basic operators: *and, or,* and *not.* These keywords let you combine two or more Boolean values in one command, doubling their power. For instance, operators let you check whether two conditions are *both* met in your script, or whether *either* is met. Here's how:

- If both sides of an *and* operator are true, it produces *true.* Otherwise, it produces *false.* For example:

```
display dialog (true and false)
    --That displays "false"
```

```
display dialog (true and true)
    --That displays "true"
```

- An *or* operator, on the other hand, produces *true* if either side is true. The only time it produces a *false* is if both sides are false. For example:

```
display dialog (true or false)
    --That displays "true"
display dialog (false or false)
    --That displays "false"
```

- The *not* operator works with only a single value (either *true* or *false*), and produces its opposite; for example:

```
display dialog (not true)
    --That displays "false"
display dialog (not false)
    --That displays "true"
```

You can use any of these operators in your *if* statements as well. That's why the script for creating the Old Desktop folder works: it checks to see if the Old Desktop folder already exists, and then applies a *not* operator to the result. That means that if the folder *doesn't* exist, the *if* statement is run; if the folder *does* exist, the *if* statement isn't run.

- Apple's own **Backup 2.0** program is a perk for using the .Mac service ($99 per year). You can use it to automatically back up files onto a CD or DVD, to your iPod, or even to your iDisk. See *www.mac.com* for more details about Backup 2.0, a mac.com email address, and all the other benefits of a .Mac membership.

- Shareware programs like Mike Bombich's **Carbon Copy Cloner** (*www.bombich.com/software/ccc.html*; $5) can back up your entire hard drive to another disk, quickly and easily. If you're looking for an inexpensive, simple backup solution, Carbon Copy Cloner is the perfect tool.

- The **Finder** (free, included with Mac OS X) can be used to back up files, too. Unfortunately, every file or folder you want to back up has to be copied—manually—by *you*. Don't use this method if you have lots of important files to back up; it'll take hours.

The problem with all these solutions, of course, is that they either cost money or are too time-consuming to use regularly. That's why AppleScript is a great alternative: you can customize the files you want it to back up, and it's completely free.

The duplicate Command

The *move* command is for transporting an item from one folder to another. The *duplicate* command, on the other hand, is for *copying* an item from one folder to another. The original file stays untouched, and an exact copy of that file is goes anywhere you specify. That location can be another folder, another partition of your hard drive, or another drive altogether (including a USB thumb drive, an external FireWire drive, or your iPod).

The way you use the *duplicate* command is very similar to the way you use the *move* command:

```
tell application "Finder"
    duplicate someItem to somePlace with replacing
end tell
```

Here's how the command breaks down:

- *duplicate* is the command directed at the Finder, to tell it to copy something.

- Everything that follows the *duplicate* command goes by the order of "what you want to duplicate" followed by "where you will save that duplicated copy." You replace the *someItem* variable with the name(s) of the files and/or folders you want to duplicate. Likewise, you replace *somePlace* with the name of the folder or disk where you want those duplicate copies to be saved.

- The *with replacing* bit tells the Finder to erase any older revisions of your files in the backup folder and replace them with the newer version. That way, you won't be stuck with all your month-old backups; you'll just have the newest versions of your files backed up.

Note, however, that the *with replacing* option considers only one thing: file names. If two files have the same name, the file that you're duplicating *always* replaces the one that's already there—even if the file that's already there is bigger, newer, and shinier than the one that you're duplicating.

Note: The *with replacing* option is case insensitive. If you duplicate myllamas.txt to a folder that already has MyLlamas.txt, for instance, Mac OS X considers them the same name, so it would replace the existing file (MyLlamas.txt) with the new file (myllamas.txt).

With that information in hand, you can write a simple backup subroutine, as shown here:

```
on backupFolderToDisk(startFolder, targetDisk)
    tell application "Finder"
        duplicate every file of startFolder to disk targetDisk with replacing
        duplicate every folder of startFolder to disk targetDisk ¬
            with replacing
    end tell
end backupFolderToDisk
```

Say you're a doctor and you want to back up your Patients folder to an external FireWire drive called Medical Backup. While you're at it, you'd also like to back up everything in your Home → Documents folder, just in case your hard drive gets damaged on the flight to your next medical convention.

The good news is that you already have a subroutine for backing up files to a separate disk, so you're halfway to a working script. The bad news is that your script doesn't actually *run* your subroutine anywhere, so your essential files never get copied over to your external drive.

To fix this, you just have to call your existing subroutine from elsewhere in your script. The new subroutine-calling lines (shown next in bold) are what actually tell AppleScript "Please run my backup commands":

```
backupFolderToDisk("Patients", "Medical Backup")
--Replace yourUsername below with your actual username
backupFolderToDisk("Macintosh:Users:yourUsername:Desktop:","Medical Backup")

--Here's the previous subroutine:
on backupFolderToDisk(startFolder, targetDisk)
    tell application "Finder"
        duplicate every file of startFolder to disk targetDisk with replacing
        duplicate every folder of startFolder to disk targetDisk with
replacing
    end tell
end backupFolderToDisk
```

Each time you call the *backupFolderToDisk* subroutine, the Finder whirs into action and copies your requested files to the backup disk (Figure 5-5).

Tip: Be sure to replace "Patients," "Medical Backup," and so on with the actual folders and backup disk you want to use.

And if you'd like to back up additional folders, just insert extra *backupFolderToDisk* calls at the top of your script.

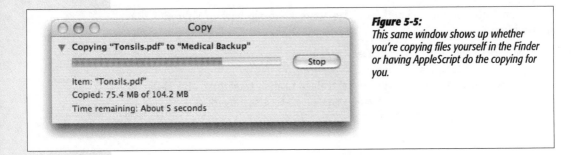

Figure 5-5:
This same window shows up whether you're copying files yourself in the Finder or having AppleScript do the copying for you.

When it's this easy, you have no excuse not to back up your Mac.

Tip: To make it even *easier,* you can schedule your backup script to run on certain days of the week. Page 261 has the details.

Deleting Files

So far, you've moved and copied files in the Finder from one place to another. There are some times, though, when you just want to get rid of a file—and Apple-Script can do that too.

The key here is AppleScript's *delete* command. It works just like *move* or *duplicate,* except you don't have to specify where the deleted files should go (AppleScript automatically knows that deleted files should go in the Trash). Thus, a typical *delete* command would look something like this:

```
tell application "Finder"
    delete the file "Chihuahuas.doc" of the desktop
end tell
```

When you run this command—substituting the name of the actual file you want to delete, of course—you hear a satisfying *clunch* as the Finder wads up your file and deposits it in the Trash can. If you don't hear this sound effect, three things could be wrong:

- **You've muted your speakers.** The fix: press the volume-up key or increase the volume in your System Preferences → Sound → Output tab.

- **You've turned off Mac OS X's sound effects.** To turn them back on, visit System Preferences → Sound → Sound Effects tab and turn on "Play user interface sound effects."

- **You don't have a Chihuahuas.doc file on your desktop.** Either get one, or replace *Chihuahuas.doc of the desktop* with the name of the file you want to delete.

An Example: Clearing Out Safari's Icon Cache

If you use Safari for a few weeks, visiting hundreds or thousands of Web sites, you'll probably notice a significant slowdown each time you load a page. That's caused, in part, by Safari's gigantic database of *favicons*—those little icons you see in Safari's Address bar (Figure 5-6).

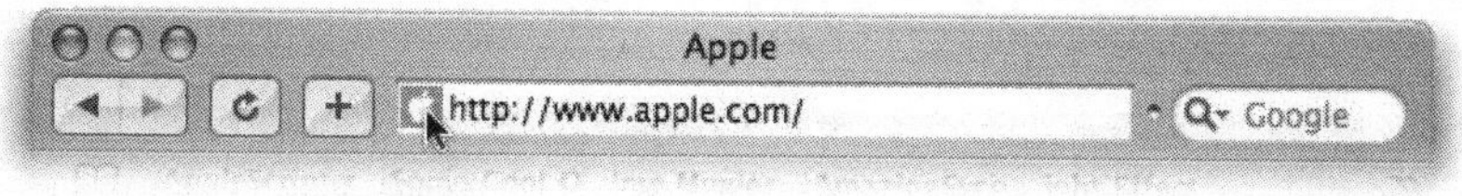

Figure 5-6:
The Apple icon, shown here, is the favicon that goes along with Apple's Web site. If you add this site to your bookmarks (Bookmarks → Add Bookmark), the specialized icon will show up in the Bookmarks menu too.

If you delete Safari's icon cache (which is stored in your Home → Library → Safari → Icons folder), you can give Safari a significant speed boost—and save a few megabytes of space while you're at it. Here's a script to automate the process:

```
tell application "Finder"
    delete folder "Icons" of folder "Safari" of folder "Library" of home
    display dialog "Would you like to empty the trash now?"
    (* If you click Cancel in the dialog box, the script ends here.
       Otherwise, it continues to the next line *)
    empty the trash
end tell
```

When you run the script, the Finder drops the Icons folder in the Trash, and then presents the dialog boxes shown in Figure 5-7.

The only other time you'd really use the *delete* command is when you have a folder that needs to be emptied regularly (like your Decade-old Home Videos folder, for example). Besides that, there's not much use for *delete*, since you can always achieve one-time erasures by choosing File → Move to Trash (or by pressing ⌘-Delete) in the Finder.

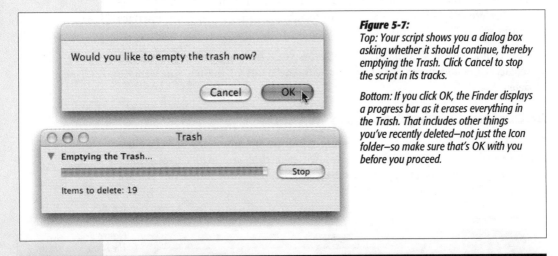

Figure 5-7:
Top: Your script shows you a dialog box asking whether it should continue, thereby emptying the Trash. Click Cancel to stop the script in its tracks.

Bottom: If you click OK, the Finder displays a progress bar as it erases everything in the Trash. That includes other things you've recently deleted—not just the Icon folder—so make sure that's OK with you before you proceed.

GEM IN THE ROUGH

The Reveal Command

As you go about your script-writing business, there might come a time when you want to show a file or folder in the Finder. After you've copied a file from one folder to another, for instance, you might want to display the new location for the file.

AppleScript makes this job easy using the *reveal* command. It works just like the File → Show Song File command in iTunes—that is, it shows you the folder that contains a given file in the Finder. Try this to select your copy of TextEdit in the Applications folder:

```
tell application "Finder"
    activate
    reveal the file "TextEdit.app" ¬
        of the folder "Applications" ¬
        of the startup disk
end tell
```

The *reveal* command is useful for showing folders, too. For example, you could highlight your Home folder (inside the Users folder) with this command:

```
tell application "Finder"
    activate
    reveal home
end tell
```

Picking a File from a Dialog Box

Back on page 60, you learned how to use the *display dialog* command to present information onscreen, and how to give feedback to your scripts while they're running. The trouble with that command, though, is that you can't choose a *file* with it. And when you're using Finder commands, you often *want* to choose a file for your script to work with.

That's where the *choose file* command comes in. Rather than having to specify an actual file name in your script, *choose file* uses Mac OS X's standard Open dialog box, letting you pick the precise file you want to work on (Figure 5-8). That way you can choose a different file for your script to operate on each time it runs.

Figure 5-8:
When you use the choose file command, you see the same Open dialog box that you see in other Mac OS X programs. There's only one difference: the choose file dialog box shows normally hidden files (like .DS_Store), too. There are some benefits to this feature: you can see all the Unix configuration files that Mac OS X uses, for example. However, if it bothers you to have all those hidden files clogging up your Open dialog box, just add the without invisibles option to the end of your choose file command.

In its purest form, the *choose file* command can occupy a line all by itself—displaying an Open dialog box but doing absolutely nothing else:

```
choose file
```

Of course, it won't do much good just to display an Open dialog box on the screen; the *real* power comes when your script can figure out what file you chose. Apple-Script makes this easy, too:

```
set selectedFile to (choose file)
(*The selectedFile variable now stores an "alias" [page 77] of the file you chose*)
```

```
tell application "Finder"
    open selectedFile
end tell
```

When run, this script presents an Open dialog box, and then opens whatever file you chose. It's not going to win any programming awards, but it's a start.

Tip: If you'd like to pick out a folder instead of a file, use the *choose folder* command. For more information on these commands, check out the Standard Additions dictionary (page 50).

Showing When a File was Created

Admit it: you've got folders that you haven't cleaned out in months—or maybe even years. You've let your junk accumulate, putting off the day you have to sort through it. Now, using AppleScript, you can finally tell how long it's been sitting around, so you can brag to your similarly procrastinatory friends.

When you script the Finder, you have access to the *modification date* property for everything on your hard drive. To figure out when a file was modified, therefore, you simply have to tell AppleScript *which* file you want the information for. The *choose file* command provides the perfect opportunity to enlighten AppleScript as to your file of interest:

```
set selectedFile to (choose file)
tell application "Finder"
    set modDate to the modification date of selectedFile
end tell
display dialog "That file was last modified on: " & modDate
```

Still, this script isn't perfect. For one thing, it doesn't give you any perspective, like how many months ago the file was modified. Instead, it just tells you the *date* the file was modified, which isn't as easy to interpret at a glance.

One of AppleScript's nice features, though, is that you can subtract one date from another. It's a great way to figure out how long ago a file was modified—in days, months, or even years. Simply edit your script like this:

```
--Part 1:
set selectedFile to (choose file)
tell application "Finder"
    set modDate to the modification date of selectedFile
    --Part 2:
    set curDate to the current date
    --Part 3:
    if (the year of modDate) ≠ (the year of curDate) then
        set ageInYears to (the year of curDate) - (the year of modDate)
        display dialog "The file was changed " & ageInYears & " years ago."
    --Part 4:
    else
```

```
        if (the month of modDate) ≠ (the month of curDate) then
            set ageInMonths to (the month of curDate) - (the month ¬
                of modDate)
            display dialog "The file was changed " & ageInMonths & ¬
                "months ago."
        --Part 5
        else
            if (the day of modDate) ≠ (the day of curDate) then
                set ageInDays to (the day of curDate) - (the day of modDate)
                display dialog "The file is " & ageInDays & "days old."
            else
                display dialog "The file was changed today."
            end if
        end if
    end if
end tell
```

Note: You can type the ≠ symbol by pressing Option-=. Or, if you'd prefer, you can substitute the plain-English phrase *is not equal to* in place of the ≠ symbol.

This is the most involved script you've written so far. At first it looks pretty complicated, but it actually works fairly simply:

- **Part 1:** The script presents an Open dialog box, and sets *modDate* to the date the selected file was modified.

Tip: If you want to check when a file was created rather than when it was modified, use the *creation date* property instead of *modification date.*

- **Part 2:** The current date, as you're running the script, goes into the *curDate* variable.

- **Part 3:** The script checks if the year the file was modified is the same as the current year. If they're *not* the same, the script sets the *ageInYears* variable to the difference between the two years—and a dialog box tells you how many years ago the file was modified.

On the other hand, if the file *was* modified this year, the script proceeds to the next part.

- **Part 4:** Now the script checks if the *month* the file was modified is the same as the current month. If they're different, the script shows a dialog box with the difference in months. Otherwise, if they're the same month, the script proceeds to the next part.

- **Part 5:** If the script has gotten this far, you know that the file was modified this month of this year. The only thing left to check, then, is whether the file was last modified *today.*

If it wasn't, the script calculates how many days ago the file was modified. It then displays that information in a dialog box.

On the other hand, if the file *was* last modified today, the script presents a dialog box informing you of that. At this point, every possibility has been covered, and the script ends.

As you'll surely notice, the script is full of nested *if* statements, which makes it hard to read. Luckily, AppleScript lets you merge an *else* statement (on one line) with a subsequent *if* statement (on the following line), creating an *else if* statement. Here's what the previous script would look like if you linked your *else* and *if* statements in that way:

```
set selectedFile to (choose file)
tell application "Finder"
    set modDate to the modification date of selectedFile
    set curDate to the current date
    if (the year of modDate) ≠ (the year of curDate) then
        set ageInYears to (the year of curDate) - (the year of modDate)
        display dialog "The file was changed " & ageInYears & " years ago."
    else if (the month of modDate) ≠ (the month of curDate) then
        set ageInMonths to (the month of curDate) - (the month of modDate)
        display dialog "The file was changed " & ageInMonths & "months ago."
    else if (the day of modDate) ≠ (the day of curDate) then
        set ageInDays to (the day of curDate) - (the day of modDate)
        display dialog "The file is" & ageInDays & "days old."
    else
        display dialog "The file was changed today."
    end if
end tell
```

Now the script is much easier to read, and still works exactly the same way.

Note: People use *else if* statements for all sorts of other tasks, too. For example, you can check the file format of a document in this way: *if* it's a Word document…*else if* it's a PowerPoint document…*else if* it's an Excel file, and so on.

You can also use *else if* statements to react to the magnitude of something: *if* there are less than 5 files on the Desktop, leave the files alone…*else if* there are between 5 and 20 files on the Desktop, copy them to a different folder…*else if* there are more than 20 files on the desktop, delete them, for example.

Saving Files

The last piece of the Mac OS X file puzzle is saving documents you already have open. AppleScript makes this simple: the *save* command works the same way as choosing File → Save.

Tip: Similarly, the *save as* command works the same way as choosing File → Save As (that is, when you provide a file path to the *save as* command, Mac OS X saves a *copy* of your current file in the location you specify).

Unfortunately, this trick works only in certain programs (TextEdit, Microsoft Word, and Safari, for example). To see if a particular program supports Apple-Script-based saves, open the program's dictionary and see if the dictionary's Standard Suite (page 45) includes the *save* command.

POWER USERS' CLINIC

You Can't Judge a File by its Extension

Back in the days of Mac OS 9, before you had to put file extensions at the end of documents' names, your Mac knew what kind of files you had by their *type* and *creator codes.* The *type code* told your Mac what kind of information was stored in a file. For example, if a file's type code was "TEXT," that meant the file was just plain text, while a type code of "APPL" meant the file was an application.

The *creator code,* on the other hand, told your Mac which program produced a file. A file created with Photoshop would use the creator code "8BIM," while one created with AppleWorks would use "BOBO"—go figure.

The importance of type and creator codes in Mac OS X is reduced, but they're still around. In fact, if a file has a type and creator code, they *override* any settings for which program should open the file. That's why the help files that come with Photoshop won't open in your default Web browser: Adobe has set their creator code to "MSIE," so they'll always open in Internet Explorer.

Thankfully, AppleScript lets you modify type and creator codes—or get rid of them completely. The following script can help you do it:

```
Current creator code: MSIE. New:
????
              Cancel      OK
```

```
set selectedFile to (choose file)
(* Get the file's current type and creator
codes: *)
tell application "Finder"
    set fType to the file type of ¬
        selectedFile
    set cType to the creator type of ¬
        selectedFile
end tell
(* Get the new type and creator codes you
want to use: *)
set newF to text returned of ¬
    (display dialog "Current type code: " ¬
    & fType & ". New:" default answer "")
set newC to text returned of ¬
    (display dialog "Current creator ¬
    code: " & cType & ". New:" default ¬
    answer "")
--Set the new type and creator codes:
tell application "Finder"
    set the file type of ¬
        selectedFile to newF
    set the creator type of ¬
        selectedFile to newC
end tell
```

If you'd like to banish the type and creator code from a file—so that Mac OS X will judge the file by its extension—enter "????" for both codes (or, if you want the details of erasing such codes, see *http://daringfireball.net/2004/02/setting_empty_file_and_creator_types*). If you'd rather just replace the existing codes with new ones, check out *http://kb.indiana.edu/data/aemh.html* for a list of type and creator codes for different programs and files.

An Example: Saving in TextEdit

As the epitome of Mac-ness, TextEdit does support the *save* command. Thus, if you needed a script to save your current TextEdit document, this one would work well:

```
tell application "TextEdit"
    activate
    save the front document
end tell
```

If you haven't saved your current TextEdit document yet, a Save dialog box appears. (The Save dialog box, as you know, lets you specify a name for the document and where you want it stored.)

Forgoing the Dialog Box

Of course, you could always save your files *without* using AppleScript. The real benefit of scripting Save operations, though, is that you can completely bypass the Save dialog box, saving you several precious seconds:

```
tell application "TextEdit"
    activate
    save the front document in ":Users:yourUsername:Desktop:kiwi.rtf"
    --Remember to replace yourUsername with your actual one-word username
end tell
```

The *in* option lets you specify the colon-separated path of the file into which you want to save your document (in this example, the *kiwi.rtf* file on your desktop). If there's a particular file you often save—say, your personal home page—you might find it useful to run the previous script whenever you want to save a *new* version of the document in the *old* location.

Note: **Make sure you specify a file, not a folder!** If you put a path to a folder after the *in* option, Apple-Script overwrites that folder completely. And if that folder were your desktop, the script would instantly trash your Desktop folder and every file *inside* it, leaving your desktop files as mere memories. Here's what to avoid:

```
    --DO NOT RUN THIS SCRIPT!!
    tell application "TextEdit"
        activate
        --Wanna erase your Desktop? Here's how:
        save the front document in ¬
            "Macintosh HD:Users:yourUsername:Desktop:"
    (* Since you specify the path to your Desktop, Mac OS X overwrites the
    Desktop...permanently! *)
    end tell
```

Instead, specify the actual *file* you want to save the document into. (You can tell you're specifying a file because it won't end in a colon.)

Saving All Documents at Once

There's one more timesaving trick to the *save* command: saving all your documents in one step. This can come in handy for those times when you have multiple files open and want to quickly save all of them—without switching to each document window individually and hitting ⌘-S. Use this script to get the job done:

```
tell application "TextEdit"
    activate
    save every document
end tell
```

When you run this script, TextEdit does the same thing it would do if you chose File → Save All. The nice thing about this script, though, is that it works in many programs that don't even *have* a Save All command, such as Microsoft Word, Safari, and even Script Editor itself. Simply change the *tell* statement to reflect the program you want to command, and run the script again.

For example, here's how that script would look if you wanted to use it with Word:

```
tell application "Microsoft Word"
    activate
    save every document
end tell
```

Now that you know how to open, move, copy, and save documents automatically, you can call yourself a true AppleScript filephile.

CHAPTER 6

Creating Lists

Whether you're a car salesman or a carpenter, you use lists every day. Navigating to your Applications folder, scheduling your events for the day, or just shopping for groceries—all require a list of some sort. And just like those lists you make throughout the day, an *AppleScript* list contains an ordered sequence of items.

AppleScript lists can include just about anything you want—the test scores of several students, for example, or some important to-dos you have to remember. You create lists in AppleScript by surrounding your items in curly brackets—and separating each item with a comma—like this:

```
{"Feed cat", "Eat breakfast", "Clean out earwax"} --Three strings in a list
```

Lists don't have to just store strings, though; you can put numbers, file aliases (page 77), and even *dates* into your lists, like this:

```
{"Dude", 53.87, alias ":Applications:TextEdit.app", current date}
```

Note: There'd rarely be a case when you'd want to store a number, file alias, and date within the *same* list, but you can if you want. A far more common occurrence, though, would be to create a list of *just* numbers (for tracking test scores) or *just* aliases (for keeping track of your favorite folders), for example.

A list may contain only a single item, too. You might create a single-item list if you want to note your accomplishments on a particularly uneventful day, for example:

```
{"Went to sleep"}
```

Or you can have a list with *no* items in it—an "empty list." That's useful if you need to set aside a list for later use—say, a list of birthday presents—but you aren't ready to fill in the list yet (perhaps because you haven't received any presents, for example). In any case, you symbolize an empty list with two curly braces: {}.

Tip: Looking for another list anomaly? Lists can contain *other* lists, making what are called "nested" lists. That's basically what a spreadsheet is: a list of rows, where each row is *itself* a list of cells.

To create a nested list, you'd type something like this:

```
set twoDList to {{"Name:", "Age:", "Home State:"}, ¬
    {"John", 42, "Nebraska"}, ¬
    {"Julie", 12, "South Dakota"}, ¬
    {"Bob", 29, "Virginia"}}
```

This *twoDList* has four items, but each item is *itself* a list with three items. In essence, you've created a four row by three column spreadsheet.

Of course, lists would be all but useless if you couldn't preserve them for later use in your script. Thankfully, you *can* preserve a list in a variable, using the *set* command to store every single one of the list's items. That way, you can keep track of all your favorite cheeses, for instance:

```
set cheeseList to {"Cheddar", "Swiss", "Gorgonzola"}
```

Note: The example scripts from this chapter can be found on the AppleScript Examples CD (see page 24 for instructions).

Common List Commands

Having a list is convenient for storing information, but that won't do much good if you can't *access* the information. Luckily, AppleScript gives you several ways to get to the data in your list:

- You can use the *item* keyword to access a specific item in your list, like this:

```
set lowCarbFoods to {"Lettuce", "Celery", "Water"}
set mySnack to item 2 of lowCarbFoods
```

In this example, *item 2 of lowCarbFoods* would be *"Celery"*—and so would the *mySnack* variable. (The items in a list each get assigned a number, starting with 1 for the first item, so *"Celery"* would be *item 2* in the previous list.)

If you'd prefer, you can specify a certain item in your list by using numerical adjectives: *first, third, eighth,* and so on. For instance, writing *item 2 of lowCarb-Foods* is the same as writing *the second item of lowCarbFoods*.

- You can access multiple items in your list by using the *items* keyword (notice the *s* at the end). Using that keyword, you can create a smaller list that contains a portion of a bigger list, like this:

```
set greetings to {"Hey", "Hello", "Howdy", "Yo", "Hi"}
set myFavorites to items 2 through 4 of greetings
--myFavorites is now {"Hello", "Howdy", "Yo"}
```

Tip: If you're too tired to type out *through,* you can use AppleScript's accepted misspelling: *thru.*

- If you want to create a new list with *non*contiguous items from an old list, you have to surround in curly brackets the specific items that you want to include:

```
set greetings to {"Hey", "Hello", "Howdy", "Yo", "Hi"}
set myFavorites to {item 4 of greetings, item 1 of greetings}
--myFavorites is now {"Yo", "Hey"}
```

- Finally, you can determine how many items are in a list by using the *count* command:

```
set importantFolders to {alias ":Applications:", alias ":System:"}
set numItems to (count importantFolders)
--numItems now contains 2, since there are 2 items in the importantFolders list
```

Tip: For more on the *count* command, see page 67.

Displaying Lists

Once you've created a list, you'll often want to present it onscreen. Just like the *display dialog* command for strings (page 40) and the *choose file* command for files (page 97), AppleScript provides a *choose from list* command for displaying lists in a dialog box. Try running this script:

```
set myWishes to {"A car", "A house", "A vacation", "A spouse", "A life"}
choose from list myWishes
```

You should see a dialog box like Figure 6-1, from which you can choose any item in the list.

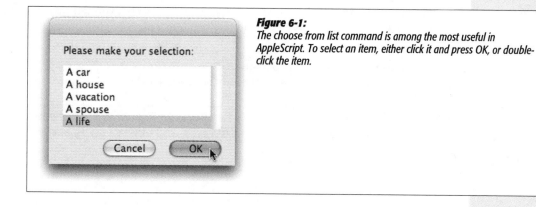

Figure 6-1:
The choose from list command is among the most useful in AppleScript. To select an item, either click it and press OK, or double-click the item.

Getting the Selected Item

When you select something in a *choose from list* dialog box, AppleScript provides your selection back to the script—as another list. Say you modified your previous script, like this:

```
set myWishes to {"A car", "A house", "A vacation", "A spouse", "A life"}
set myChoice to (choose from list myWishes)
```

At the end of the script, the *myChoice* variable would hold a list containing a single item: whatever you selected from the dialog box. If you want to display your choice in a *new* dialog box, however, you have to convert *myChoice* to a string first. That's because the *display dialog* command—unlike *choose from list*—expects to be given a string, not a list.

Luckily, it's easy to convert a list into a string. You simply have to use Apple-Script's *as* keyword, like this:

```
set myWishes to {"A car", "A house", "A vacation", "A spouse", "A life"}
set myChoice to (choose from list myWishes)
display dialog (myChoice as string)
```

This sort of operation, where you turn one type of information into another, is known as a *coercion*.

Tip: You can perform coercions on many types of information. For example:

```
set myString to (10 as string)
--10 gets coerced from a number to a string: "10"

set someNumber to ("57.2" as number)
--"57.2" gets coerced from a string to a number: 57.2

set theString to ({"Pop"} as string)
--{"Pop"} gets coerced from a list to a string: "Pop"
```

Now, since your script coerces *myChoice* into a string, AppleScript can properly display your selection in a dialog box of its own (Figure 6-2).

But that's pretty boring, don't you think? To spice things up a bit, you can alter the script so it takes the value of *myChoice* and inserts it into a plain-English phrase:

```
set myWishes to {"a car", "a house", "a vacation", "a spouse", "a life"}
set myChoice to (choose from list myWishes)
display dialog "Man, I could really use " & myChoice & "."
```

Note: As part of altering this script, you'll need to change the uppercase A's in the *myWishes* list to low-ercase a's. That way, when you run the script, the "a" fits in nicely with the sentence you display in your dialog box.

Now when you select an item from the list's dialog box and click OK, AppleScript inserts your choice (*myChoice*) into the *display dialog* command's string. You'll see a dialog box with a message like "Man, I could really use a vacation" (replacing "a vacation", of course, if you selected something else you're in need of).

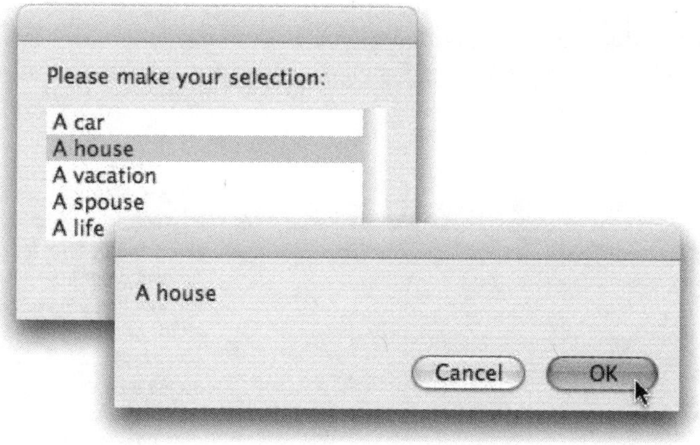

Figure 6-2:
It's a good thing you converted the choose from list command's result into a string. Otherwise, when you ran the display dialog command, you would have ended up with an error dialog box instead of this one.

The Ever-Useful every Keyword

As you've seen on page 67, the *every* keyword is an extremely powerful tool for obtaining a list of items. You can use the Finder to get *every file of the folder "Applications"*, or use TextEdit to get *the name of every document*. No matter how you use it, the *every* keyword is a huge timesaver.

Moreover, when you use the *every* keyword, you're guaranteed to get a list as the result. That makes *every* a perfect companion to use with the *choose from list* command; the combination of these two commands lets you obtain a list and then present the list onscreen.

An Example: Displaying a List of Running Programs

Seeing a list of all your running programs is enormously helpful, because it lets you check what invisible programs are working in the background—and, in some cases, hogging your computer's processing power. You could, of course, use the Activity Monitor program (stored in your Applications → Utilities folder) for this task. But you could also do it with AppleScript, and that's a lot more fun and educational.

To write such a script, you have to command Mac OS X's hidden System Events program, which monitors all the *other* programs running on with your Mac. Proceed like this:

1. **In Script Editor, open System Events's dictionary (File → Open Dictionary, or Shift-⌘-O).**

    Page 48 explains the magic behind AppleScript dictionaries.

2. **Click the Processes Suite flippy triangle, and then click the Classes flippy triangle that appears underneath.**

You get a list of many of System Events's AppleScript nouns (or, in geek-speak, AppleScript *classes*) that you can use in your own scripts.

3. **Select the entry for *process* (Figure 6-3).**

A *process* is just System Events terminology for a "running program." Therefore, by getting a list of *processes* from System Events, you can discover all the programs running on your Mac.

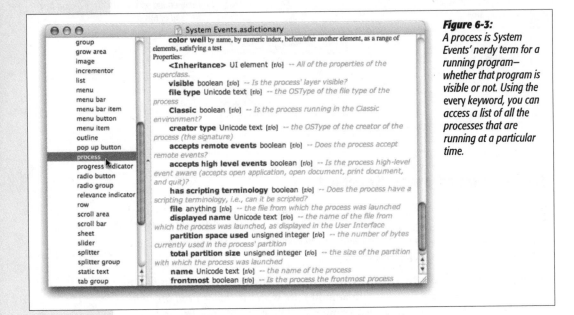

Figure 6-3:
A process is System Events' nerdy term for a running program— whether that program is visible or not. Using the every keyword, you can access a list of all the processes that are running at a particular time.

You can see, in this dictionary, that all processes have a *name* property. Using that, you can display the name of every running program in a dialog box:

```
tell application "System Events"
    set allApps to the name of every process --allApps is a list
end tell
choose from list allApps
```

This four-line script is enough to show you every running program on your Mac—even much of the system-level stuff that you probably didn't know existed. Still, you can't do anything *with* that information—other than brag to your friends about all the hidden programs you have, perhaps.

It would be much more useful if you could double-click a program's name in the list to activate it. And, with a few script modifications, you can:

```
tell application "System Events"
    set allApps to the name of every process --allApps is a list
```

```
end tell
set chosenApp to (choose from list allApps) --chosenApp is also a list
tell application (chosenApp as string) --Convert chosenApp to a string
    activate
end tell
```

These additional lines take whichever program you selected in the *choose from list* dialog box, and send that program the *activate* command. With a quick double-click, therefore, you can bring any open program to the front (Figure 6-4).

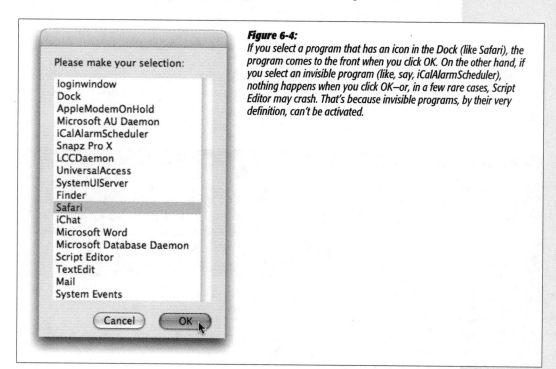

Figure 6-4:
If you select a program that has an icon in the Dock (like Safari), the program comes to the front when you click OK. On the other hand, if you select an invisible program (like, say, iCalAlarmScheduler), nothing happens when you click OK—or, in a few rare cases, Script Editor may crash. That's because invisible programs, by their very definition, can't be activated.

There's only one problem with your current script: if you click Cancel in the dialog box, AppleScript continues running the script. (That's different from the *display dialog* command, where clicking Cancel immediately halts your script.) By the time AppleScript hits the *tell application (chosenApp as string)* line, it's pretty confused: how is your script supposed to know which program to activate if you clicked Cancel in the dialog box?

The fact is, AppleScript doesn't know. If you click Cancel when this script is running, AppleScript considers the result of the dialog box to be *false*—and that's why you get a dialog box asking you to locate the program named "false" (which, of course, you can't, because there is no such program). This is a bug in your script—but, luckily, you can fix it by adding a simple *if* statement:

```
tell application "System Events"
    set allApps to the name of every process --allApps is a list
```

```
    end tell
    set chosenApp to (choose from list allApps) --chosenApp is also a list
    if chosenApp is not false then --In other words, if you didn't click Cancel
        tell application (chosenApp as string)
            activate
        end tell
    end if
```

Now, if you click the Cancel button, your script skips over the *if* statement completely, thereby eliminating the bug.

List Processing

One of the most common operations with a list is *iterating*—that is, going through the list one item at a time. That's what lets you rename all the files in a folder, for example, or search all your open documents, one at a time. No matter what you use it for, iterating can greatly speed up—and simplify—your scripts.

GEM IN THE ROUGH

Choosing from All Applications

In the previous script, you used the *choose from list* command to display a list of all your open programs. But what if you want to display a list of all your *stored* programs—including those that aren't open?

The trick is to use the *choose application* command. When you run that, you'll see a dialog box similar to the one that appears when you choose Script Editor's File → Open Dictionary command. You're presented with a list of every program on your computer—including hidden programs and ones written for Mac OS 9 (if you have that installed on your Mac).

Using the *choose application* command, you can rewrite your program-activating script to let you choose from *any* program on your hard drive:

```
set chosenApp to (choose application)
--chosenApp lists all programs
tell application (chosenApp as string)
    activate
end tell
```

(Incidentally, the reason you have to type *chosenApp as string* is because the *choose application* command returns a *list* of programs you selected. You can't target a *tell* statement at a list of programs, however, so you have to convert your selection to a *string* before you can make Mac OS X activate your selected program.)

For more details on the *choose from list* and *choose application* commands, look in the Standard Additions dictionary (page 50). There, you'll find additional options like *with prompt* (for customizing the message in the dialog box) and *multiple selections allowed* (for letting you select more than one item at once in the dialog box).

To go through all the items in a list, you have to use a specialized kind of *repeat* statement—one where you specify the list to use:

```
set eyeColors to {"Brown", "Black", "Blue"}
repeat with curColor in eyeColors --"repeat with" and "in" are the keywords
    display dialog curColor
end repeat
```

Here's how the script works:

- The *eyeColors* variable is set to a list containing three strings, each representing a different eye color.

- Each time the *repeat with* statement runs, AppleScript sets *curColor* to the next item in your list of eye colors. That means the first time the *repeat* statement runs, *curColor* will be "Brown"; the second time it runs, *curColor* will be "Black"; and the last time the *repeat* statement runs, *curColor* will be "Blue."

Note: *repeat with* statements continue looping until they've reached the very end of your list. Therefore, if your *eyeColors* list had 200 items, your *repeat with* statement would also run 200 times, looping through each eye color until it reached the end of the list.

- The *display dialog* command presents the current item of the list (the *curColor* variable) in a dialog box. By the time the script ends, therefore, you will have seen *each* item in the list appear in a dialog box.

Thus, when you run the script, a dialog box appears with the word Brown in it. Click OK, and a window appears with the word Black. Do this again, and the dialog box displays the word Blue for you. If you hit the Cancel button (or use Cancel's keyboard shortcut, ⌘-period) at any point along the way, the current dialog box closes and you won't see any more dialog boxes from your script.

Batch Renaming

As mentioned earlier, a perfect example of when you'd want to use iteration is for renaming all the files in a folder. AppleScript makes it easy, for instance, to add a certain extension to all the files on your desktop.

The trick is to use a *repeat with* statement, going through the files on your desktop one at a time. By renaming them individually, you can assure that they *all* get renamed, like this:

```
set ext to the text returned of (display dialog ¬
    "Add what extension to all Desktop files?" default answer ".txt")
tell application "Finder"
    set dFiles to every file of the desktop
    repeat with curFile in dFiles
        set the name of curFile to (the name of curFile & ext)
    end repeat
end tell
```

Here's how it works:

- First, the script asks for the file extension you want to add on to the end of each file's name. (The *default answer* option automatically uses .txt if you don't provide an extension yourself.)

- The script sets *dFiles* to the list of every file on the desktop. By going through this list, you can append your extension to each file individually.

- The *repeat* statement, each time it runs, sets *curFile* to the next item in the list. In other words, *curFile* holds the file that needs to be renamed next.

- The script appends the file extension you specified to *curFile*. Since this command is inside the *repeat* statement, *curFile* represents a different file each time. Therefore, by the time the script is finished, every file on the desktop will have your chosen file extension (Figure 6-5).

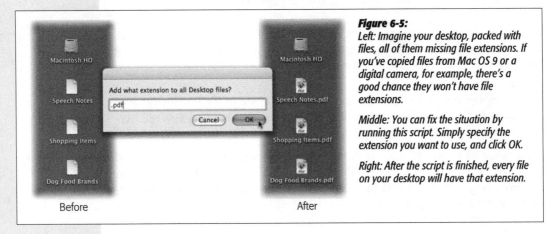

Figure 6-5:
Left: Imagine your desktop, packed with files, all of them missing file extensions. If you've copied files from Mac OS 9 or a digital camera, for example, there's a good chance they won't have file extensions.

Middle: You can fix the situation by running this script. Simply specify the extension you want to use, and click OK.

Right: After the script is finished, every file on your desktop will have that extension.

Before   After

Your script has one problem, though: it blindly appends an extension to every file on your desktop, regardless of whether a file already *has* an extension. For instance, if you have a file called *Geckos.doc*, running this script gives you a file called *Geckos.doc.txt* (or whatever file extension you specified).

Luckily, it's simple to fix this problem. Since every file extension comes after a period, all you need to do is check whether a file name *contains* a period, in order to determine whether it already has an extension:

```
set ext to the text returned of (display dialog ¬
    "Add what extension to all Desktop files?" default answer ".txt")
tell application "Finder"
    set dFiles to every file of the desktop
    repeat with curFile in dFiles
        if the name of curFile does not contain "." then
        (* In other words, if the file being checked doesn't have an
            extension, then *)
```

```
        set the name of curFile to (the name of curFile & ext)
    end if --Otherwise, if the file *does* have an extension, do nothing
  end repeat
end tell
```

Note: Don't worry—any folders or disks you have on your desktop won't be affected by this script. Since the script is specifically checking for *files*, anything else—whether folder, disk, or Frisbee—will not get a file extension.

Now your script works properly, adding extensions only to files that don't have them already.

Tip: If you'd like to change how your script works, just edit what happens to *curFile* in your *repeat with* statement (so that your script *moves* the current file instead of renaming it, for example). Or, if you'd like to see another prewritten example of a Finder-based *repeat with* script, see page 232; there, you'll learn how to automatically delete all new files that enter a folder, to keep that folder permanently clean.

Joining Lists Together

On page 56 you learned how to use ampersands to link strings together (to *concatenate* them, in nerd-ese). You can do the same thing for lists, too, which is a great way to join related items under one virtual roof. For instance:

```
--Example 1:
set combinedList to {"Tomato", "Carrot", "Rutabega"} & {"Broccoli", "Pepper"}
--combinedList is now {"Tomato", "Carrot", "Rutabega", "Broccoli", "Pepper"}

--Example 2:
set bigList to (items 1 thru 3 of combinedList) & ¬
    (items 2 thru 4 of combinedList)
(* bigList is now {"Tomato", "Carrot", "Rutabega", "Carrot", "Rutabega",
    "Broccoli"} *)

--Example 3:
set luckyNumbers to {1, 6, 28} & 496
--luckyNumbers is now {1, 6, 28, 496}
```

These three examples each illustrate an important aspect of concatenating lists:

- **Example 1** shows how you can concatenate two separate lists to create one unified list. That would be useful if you wanted to merge a list of your first-grade and second-grade students, for example, into a single all-student master list.

- **Example 2** demonstrates that you can concatenate different sections of the *same* list. If you wanted to put together a list of only students whose names start with A, E, I, O, and U (for your vowel-themed class party), for instance, you could use concatenation to assemble a new list from these separate subgroups (the list of students whose first names begin with A, concatenated with the list of students whose first names begin with E, and so on).

- **Example 3** shows that you can append a single item to a list, using concatenation as well. If a new student transferred into your class, for example, you could concatenate the student's name directly to your existing class list.

Note: Behind the scenes, the code from Example 3 is actually turning the number 496 into a single-item list. That means AppleScript is actually concatenating this:

```
set luckyNumbers to {1, 6, 28} & {496}
```

Why does that matter? It shows that AppleScript can only concatenate two objects that are the same type (in this case, two lists). If you try to concatenate two objects that are of *different* types (like an alias and a number), AppleScript can't combine the two objects, so it simply throws them in a list together.

As these examples show, list concatenation is a powerful tool in any AppleScripter's toolbox. For further list-concatenating inspiration, though, just read on.

Merging File Lists

If you want to display all the items in a particular folder, you can do it easily with the *choose from list* command:

```
tell application "Finder"
    set allApps to the name of every file in folder "Applications"
end tell
choose from list allApps
```

Or, if you'd like to present a dialog box of all the files in the *frontmost* Finder window, you can modify your script to do that, too:

```
tell application "Finder"
    set allFiles to the name of every file in the front window
end tell
choose from list allFiles
```

Even better, though, would be if your script could summarize all the files in *all* open Finder windows. That way, you wouldn't have to go searching through every window onscreen just to find the one that contains a particular file.

You can pull off this stunt by using the word *every* twice: the first time to locate all open windows, and the second time to get all the files in those windows. Here's how it would look in your script

```
tell application "Finder"
    set allFiles to the name of every file in every Finder window
end tell
choose from list allFiles
```

Now, when you run your script, you'll see something like Figure 6-6.

Unfortunately, the list this script displays is passive—nothing happens if you double-click a file's name. To be truly useful, the dialog box should take the file you select, figure out which window it came from, and open the file for you automatically.

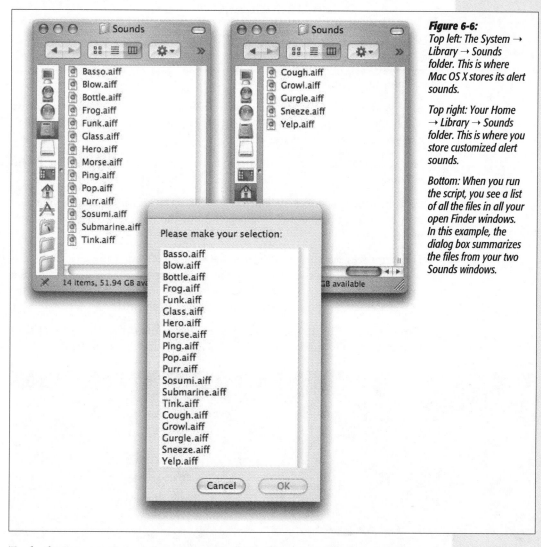

Figure 6-6:
*Top left: The System →
Library → Sounds
folder. This is where
Mac OS X stores its alert
sounds.*

*Top right: Your Home
→ Library → Sounds
folder. This is where you
store customized alert
sounds.*

*Bottom: When you run
the script, you see a list
of all the files in all your
open Finder windows.
In this example, the
dialog box summarizes
the files from your two
Sounds windows.*

To do that, your script needs to iterate through *all* the open Finder windows, and search for the window that contains the file you selected. Here's how:

```
tell application "Finder"
    set allFiles to the name of every file in every Finder window
end tell
set chosenFile to (choose from list allFiles)
tell application "Finder"
    set allWindows to every Finder window
```

```
      repeat with curWindow in allWindows
          if (name of every file in curWindow) contains chosenFile then
              set fileInCorrectLocation to file (chosenFile as string) ¬
                  of curWindow
              open fileInCorrectLocation
          end if
      end repeat
  end tell
```

Here's how these extra lines work:

- After getting a list of every file in every Finder window, the script asks you which file you'd like to open. Whichever you select, the script puts the file's name into the *chosenFile* variable.

- The script gets a list of every open Finder window and stores that list in *allWindows*.

- Each time the *repeat with* statement runs, the script sets *curWindow* to the next item in the list of windows. (See page 113 for more on how *repeat with* statements work.)

- The script sees whether *curWindow* (the window it's currently checking) contains the file you selected. If it does, the script opens the file straight from that window. Otherwise, the script runs the *repeat* statement again, checking the *next* Finder window to see if it contains the file you chose.

By the time the script finishes running, it will have found the window that contains your chosen file and opened the file for you. Mission accomplished!

GEM IN THE ROUGH

Listing Folders and Disks

Like many things in AppleScript, there's more than one way to get a list of the items in a folder. The *list folder* command, from the Standard Additions dictionary (page 50), is perfect if you know exactly what folder you want to get the items from. For example, this command:

```
set systemItems to (list folder ¬
    ":System:Library:")
```

obtains a list of the files and folders inside your System folder and puts that list into the *systemItems* variable.

That command, however, would also include *invisible* files and folders in the list (you can tell because they start with a period). If you'd rather omit such invisible items—because they're too geeky for you, for instance—just specify *without invisibles*:

```
set systemItems to (list folder ¬
    ":System:Library" without invisibles)
```

One nice thing about the *list folder* command is that it's flexible enough to work even outside of a *tell* statement directed at the Finder. The not-so-great thing about *list folder*, though, is that it doesn't give you nearly as much control over which items appear in your list as using the *every* keyword with the Finder (page 116); for example, you can't get a list of week-old files with *list folder*.

However, no matter which of those commands you use to list files and folders, neither one can list the *disks* connected to your computer. For that, you have to use the special *list disks* command, which returns a list of all the CDs, DVDs, floppy disks, and hard drives you can see on your desktop.

Inputting Lists

When you're dealing with lots of information in your AppleScripts, you'll often want to display lists onscreen—and you've already learned how to, using *choose from list*. Just as often, however, you'll want to *input* lists—typing in your list of favorite colors, for example. This section shows you how to create such lists, formed entirely by what you type into dialog boxes.

Adding Items One at a Time

The simplest way to add items to a list is to display a dialog box for each new item. For instance, the following script prompts you to enter 10 of your favorite colors for a list, one dialog box at a time:

```
set favoriteColors to {} --This list will store all the colors you enter
repeat 10 times --You could substitute any number you want here
    set newColor to text returned of (display dialog "Enter a new color:" ¬
        default answer "")
    set the end of favoriteColors to newColor --Append newColor to the list
end repeat
--Display the list of all the colors you've entered
choose from list favoriteColors
```

Each time the *repeat* statement runs, the script prompts you for a new color to add to the list. (Once you input a color and press OK, your script automatically appends the color you entered to the end of the *favoriteColors* list, using the AppleScript command *set the end*.)

Once you've entered 10 colors, the script finishes by presenting a list of them. Now you, too, can astound your friends with your Mac's mastery of your favorite colors!

This method works fine if you want to add just a few items to a list, but you'll get quite annoyed if you have to enter, say, 50 items into separate dialog boxes. Plus, the sight of dialog box after dialog box is known to cause drowsiness in mice.

Adding Multiple Items at Once

A better option, if you want to add lots of things to your list, is to present a *single* dialog box and enter everything there. That method is a little harder to program but a lot easier to use.

The trick is to have your script sweep through your text, picking out the individual items and turning them into a list. You'll enter the items separated by a comma and then a space; your script uses the comma-space pattern as a *delimiter*—something that separates items in a list.

In AppleScript, you have to set delimiters yourself, like this:

```
set AppleScript's text item delimiters to ", "
```

However, *AppleScript's text item delimiters* are a system-wide setting; if you change them in your script, they'll change in all the other scripts running on your Mac as well. That's why it's good practice to store the existing *text item delimiters* before you change them, and then to restore the old *text item delimiters* at the end of your script:

```
set oldDels to AppleScript's text item delimiters
set AppleScript's text item delimiters to ", "
--Do whatever
set AppleScript's text item delimiters to oldDels
```

Having done that, now you can split up a string into a list:

```
set oldDels to AppleScript's text item delimiters
set AppleScript's text item delimiters to ", "
set fruits to (every text item of "Kiwi, Passion, Papaya")
--fruits is now a list: {"Kiwi", "Passion", "Papaya"}
set AppleScript's text item delimiters to oldDels
```

Now that you know how to use text delimiters, you can input multiple list items in a *single* dialog box, like this:

```
set enteredText to the text returned of (display dialog ¬
    "Enter all your favorite shapes, separated by commas and spaces.):" ¬
    default answer "")
--enteredText is now a string, with list items separated by comma-space pairs
set oldDels to AppleScript's text item delimiters
set AppleScript's text item delimiters to ", "
--AppleScript now knows to split strings up at comma-space pairs
set shapeList to (every text item of enteredText)
--shapeList now contains every item from enteredText, stored in a list
choose from list shapeList --Display the list in a dialog box
set AppleScript's text item delimiters to oldDels
```

When you run the script, you'll see something like Figure 6-7.

Getting Lists from Other Programs

When it comes to lists, AppleScript *really* shines when you mix it with other programs. That's because other programs deal with their own unique kinds of information—graphics, formatted text, and sound, for example—which you simply can't create in AppleScript alone.

When commanding programs from AppleScript, you'll find yourself using the *every* keyword all the time. In this chapter alone, for example, you'll use *every* to get a list of all the words in a text document (see the next page), a list of all the open documents in a single program (page 122), and even a list of synonyms for a particular word (see the next page). So don't get listless—you're about to go on a wild list-making ride!

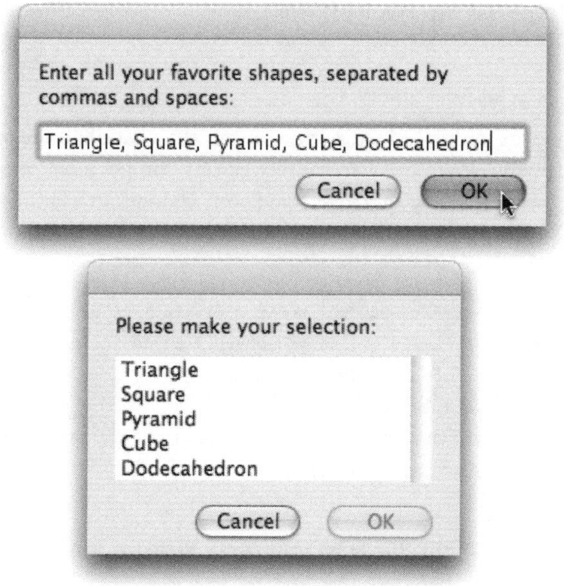

Figure 6-7:
Top: Enter every item you want into the dialog box. If you'd like, you can copy some text from another program, and paste it here using ⌘-V.

Bottom: When you click OK, the script converts your text into a list. In this layout, it's a lot easier to browse.

TextEdit

When you're scripting TextEdit, lists can come in quite handy for breaking your text into smaller chunks. For instance, you can easily get a list of all the words in the frontmost TextEdit document with this script:

```
tell application "TextEdit"
    set wordList to (every word of the front document)
end tell
```

If there's a particular word you're just dying to find—like which word came 2907th in your document—you can tweak your script to let you pinpoint a word by its position. Here's how:

```
tell application "TextEdit"
    set wordList to (every word of the front document)
    set theNumber to the text returned of (display dialog ¬
        "What numbered word would you like to find?" default answer 20)
    display dialog "The word you chose is: " & (item theNumber of wordList)
end tell
```

When you run that script, AppleScript asks you what word you want to find. Simply enter the number of the word (1 for the first word, 2 for the second, and so on), and press OK. In the next dialog box, AppleScript tells you what the word is.

Tip: While this might seem like a useless script, it's actually quite helpful for students. Just create a TextEdit document containing the list of chemical elements, for example, and when you run the script, you can test your knowledge of the periodic table ("What numbered word would you like to find?", in this case, would be the same as asking "What element would you like to find?").

Listing documents

In addition to getting the words within a document, you can get a list of all the *open* TextEdit documents. Narrowing down this list, moreover, lets you get a list of only *modified* documents, which is perfect for quickly saving your changes in TextEdit:

```
tell application "TextEdit"
    activate
    set unsavedNum to (count every document whose modified is true)
    --unsavedNum stores the number of files you haven't saved in TextEdit
    display dialog "You have " & unsavedNum & ¬
    " unsaved documents. Save them?"
    --If you click Cancel, ths script ends before it gets to the next command
    save every document whose modified is true
end tell
```

When you run this script, you'll see the dialog box shown in Figure 6-8.

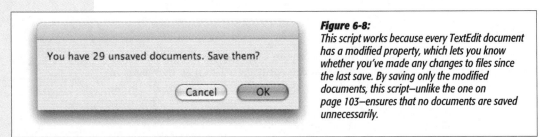

Figure 6-8:
This script works because every TextEdit document has a modified property, which lets you know whether you've made any changes to files since the last save. By saving only the modified documents, this script—unlike the one on page 103—ensures that no documents are saved unnecessarily.

Microsoft Word

As scriptable programs go, Word is among the most useful for creating lists. Not only does it support all the word-, character-, and paragraph-listing features that TextEdit does, but Word also supports many list-creating commands of its own.

Note: Like all the Microsoft Word scripts in this book, you should be using Word 2004 for these scripts. Page xx in the Introduction explains how to get a free demo version if you haven't bought the program.

Among the most useful such commands is the one for getting synonyms of a word. Open Microsoft Word's dictionary (File → Open Dictionary), click in the left pane, and do a search for *synonym* (Edit → Find → Find) and you'll come across the *get synonym info object* command, which you use like this:

```
--Part 1:
set theWord to the text returned of (display dialog ¬
```

```
    "Enter a word to get its synonyms:" default answer "Enter your word here")
--Part 2:
tell application "Microsoft Word"
    set synonymObject to (get synonym info object item to check theWord)
    --Part 3:
    set synonymList to the meanings of synonymObject
end tell
--Part 4:
choose from list synonymList
```

Here's how the commands break down:

- **Part 1:** This command asks for the word to find synonyms for, and stores it in the *theWord* variable.

- **Part 2:** This command gets a *synonym object* for the word you chose—a quirky data type that Word uses to store synonyms. (Nobody ever said Microsoft products were straightforward.)

- **Part 3:** The script tells the *synonymList* variable to store the list of synonyms for your word (in Word's odd universe, synonyms are called *meanings*).

Tip: If you wanted a list of the word's opposites, you'd use the *antonyms* property instead of *meanings*.

- **Part 4:** AppleScript presents a dialog box, displaying the list of synonyms (Figure 6-9).

Figure 6-9:
Top: Enter the word you want the synonyms for.

Bottom: Using Word's built-in thesaurus, AppleScript displays a list of the word's synonyms. If you like to use TextEdit for your everyday word processing but miss Microsoft Word's thesaurus, this script lets you have the best of both worlds: just type any synonym you want from this list directly into TextEdit.

Obviously, it's impossible to go through the zillions of other Microsoft Word commands one at a time in this book. If they interest you, however, spend some more time poking around in Word's dictionary. You'll find lots of list-producing properties—everything from *every footnote of the front document* to *the name of every document.*

POWER USERS' CLINIC

Using Lists for Other Purposes

In this chapter, you've used lists just as you'd expect: for storing ordered sequences of information. However, you can use AppleScript lists for some other, less obvious tasks, too.

For example, when you want refer to a specific pixel somewhere on your screen, you use a list with two numbers:

```
set myPoint to {200, 420}
```

Here, 200 is the *x* coordinate (counting right from the left edge of the screen), and 420 is the *y* coordinate (counting down from the top edge of the screen). You can use points like this to position Finder windows anywhere on the screen; for example, this script:

```
tell application "Finder"
    activate
    set the position of the ¬
        front window to {200, 420}
end tell
```

places the upper-left corner of the front Finder window 200 pixels from the left edge of your screen and 420 pixels down from the top edge of the screen. If you run that script every day before breakfast, you'll come back to find the window in the exact same position as it was the day before—200 pixels down and 420 pixels right.

If you'd like more control over the look of your Finder windows, though, you can create a four-item list to store the position and *size* of a window onscreen, like this:

```
tell application "Finder"
    activate
    set the bounds of the front window to ¬
        {60, 90, 560, 690}
end tell
```

In a list like this, the first two numbers set the position of the upper-left corner of the window—in this case, 90 pixels down and 60 pixels over from the upper-left corner of the *screen.* The last two numbers set the position of the lower-right corner of the window—here, 690 pixels down and 560 pixels over from the upper-left corner of the screen. Therefore, you'd end up with a window that's 500 pixels wide (560–60=500) and 600 pixels tall (690–90=600).

Organizing and Editing Graphics

If there's one thing the Mac is famous for, it's graphics support. After all, it's hard to argue the qualifications of the original platform of Photoshop and QuarkX-Press. And although you *can* use a different platform for graphics work, the Mac is one of the most popular around—and for good reason:

- **Virtually every Mac program lets you convert documents to PDF format (File → Print → Save As PDF), so you can be sure all your Mac- and PC-using friends can open your documents.** The same system-wide PDF support would require Adobe Acrobat ($300) on Windows.

- **Mac OS X comes with Preview, a simple program for opening and converting image files.** Sure, Preview won't replace Photoshop's top-of-the-line image filters—but if you just want to open images in a hurry, Preview's price (free) is hard to beat.

- **Mac OS X supports tons of digital cameras, right out of the box.** With iPhoto (page 126), for example, you can plug your digital camera into your Mac and copy all your pictures with a single click of the Import button.

The best part of being a graphic artist on a Mac, though, is that you can automate most graphics programs from here to the moon. With a single AppleScript, for example, you could perform color correction, work some wild and crazy effects into an image, or even convert a batch of image files to another format—and still have enough time to read the latest edition of *Photoshop User* magazine before dinner.

Note: The example scripts from this chapter can be found on the AppleScript Examples CD (see page 24 for instructions).

Scripting iPhoto

When you're just starting to script graphics programs, iPhoto is a good first step. It's Apple's "digital shoebox" program, the modern-day alternative to keeping thousands of prints in *actual* shoeboxes. Plus, iPhoto comes pre-installed for free on new Macs, and it's available as part of the iLife suite (*www.apple.com/ilife/*) for only $50.

Note: For the scripts in this chapter, you'll want iPhoto 4 or newer.

The key to scripting iPhoto, as usual, is understanding its dictionary. The iPhoto Suite holds the information you need to get started (Figure 7-1).

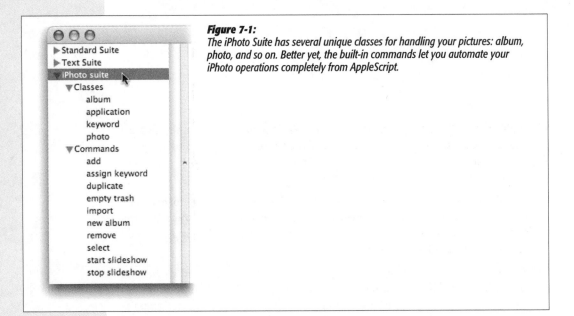

Figure 7-1:
The iPhoto Suite has several unique classes for handling your pictures: album, photo, and so on. Better yet, the built-in commands let you automate your iPhoto operations completely from AppleScript.

Take some time to look over iPhoto's dictionary, to get a feel for what commands and classes are available. Keep the dictionary open as you read on, too, so you can look up commands that you're curious about.

Accessing Pictures by Certain Criteria

Although iPhoto has a few basic features for editing photos, chances are you're going to spend most of your time *organizing* your pictures rather than editing them. That's why the *new album* command is so useful: it lets you create your own albums straight from AppleScript and add whatever pictures you want to them.

Here's how you use this command:

```
tell application "iPhoto"
    new album name "16x12 pics" --Creates a new album called "16x12 pics"
```

```
        add every photo whose dimensions equal {1600, 1200} to album "16x12 pics"
    end tell
```

When you run that script, iPhoto first creates a photo album, called "16x12 pics". Then the script searches through your Photo Library on a quest for any images that are 1600 × 1200 pixels in size. Finally, the script takes every image that matches those dimensions, and uses the helpful *add* command to copy those pictures into your new photo album.

Tip: Feel free to edit the dimensions that the script specifies. If you want to find all pictures that are 1024 × 768 pixels—to use as desktop pictures, for example—simply replace {*1600, 1200*} with {*1024, 768*}.

That's not even scratching the surface of iPhoto's album-handling capabilities, though. Once you've got a set of pictures, you can change their keywords, comments, and so on, using various commands from iPhoto's dictionary. You could add the comment "Dad's birthday party" to every picture you took on your dad's birthday, for example, so you'll never forget where you took that priceless shot of him spilling coffee on himself.

Here's another possibility:

```
    tell application "iPhoto"
        new album name "16x12 pics"
        add every photo whose dimensions equal {1600, 1200} to album "16x12 pics"
        set the comment of every photo of album "16x12 pics" to "Cool snap"
    end tell
```

Adding this line makes sure that every 1600 × 1200 image ends up with the comment "Cool snap."

FREQUENTLY ASKED QUESTION

AppleScript vs. Smart Albums

OK, OK, I've got the script running. I just don't see the point—why would I use AppleScript to sort my pictures when I could do the same thing with Smart Albums from right within iPhoto?

iPhoto's Smart Albums feature is great for creating lists of pictures that match a certain criterion. For instance, you could create a smart album (File → New Smart Album) that listed all 1600 × 1200 pictures; whenever you selected the album from the pane on the left, iPhoto would display an up-to-date list of all pictures with those dimensions.

Smart Albums are fine for everyday use, but AppleScript has one big advantage: power. Once you have a Smart Al-

bum set up, that's just about it—you can't do much but *look* at the album. On the other hand, if you use AppleScript to sort your photos, you can open those pictures in a Web browser, send them to Photoshop for editing, and perform any number of other automatic tasks. To see some of the possibilities, download Apple's iPhoto demo scripts from *www.apple.com/applescript/iphoto.*

There's no reason you can't use *both* methods to organize your photos, however. You could keep Smart Albums for pictures you just want to browse, and write AppleScripts for pictures you want to manipulate.

Tip: To read the comments of your images, select them in iPhoto and click the "i" button in the lower-left corner of the Library window. (You might have to click the button more than once to cycle through iPhoto's various information modes.)

In the Comments field, you can read all the comments that go with the image you're looking at. Or, if you'd like, you can type your very own comments to go with the image—like, "Don't send this picture to Aunt Elizabeth," for example.

Of course, sorting and commenting your images by their *dimensions* is no more useful than sorting your shirts by the number of stains on them. The real power lies in AppleScript's ability to help you sort images by date, keyword, and so on.

Luckily, all you have to do is use the appropriate property—AppleScript handles the rest. In the iPhoto Suite, take a look at the *photo* class's *date*, *keyword*, and *title* properties in particular, and just use whichever property you want to narrow down your list of pictures.

Getting Random Pictures

You've been taking pictures for years—of your dog, your kids, even of your hole-infested hiking socks. By now, you've accumulated more than 10,000 pictures, in dozens of albums. What are you supposed to do if you just want to jump to a few random images—like the iTunes's Shuffle tool, just for pictures?

Program the feature yourself, that's what.

Getting some item

To specify a random element in a list, you use the keywords *some item*. For instance, you could get a random composer by running this command:

```
display dialog (some item of {"Beethoven", "Mozart", "Britney Spears"})
```

To get random items from your list of pictures, though, you have to use *some item* in conjunction with iPhoto's own commands. You'd use a script like this:

```
tell application "iPhoto"
    --Part 1:
    activate
    if not (exists album "Random Pics") then
        new album name "Random Pics"
    end if
    --Part 2:
    set photoList to every photo
    --Part 3:
    set numImages to the text returned of (display dialog ¬
        "Show how many random images?" default answer 10)
```

```
    repeat numImages times
        --Part 4:
        set randomPhoto to (some item of photoList)
        add randomPhoto to album "Random Pics"
    end repeat
    --Part 5:
    select album "Random Pics"
end tell
```

Here's how the script works:

- **Part 1** brings iPhoto to the front and creates a Random Pics album, if there isn't one already. This is the album that will hold your randomly selected images.

- **Part 2** sets the *photoList* variable to a list of every picture in your entire Library. This is the list the script goes through to find random pictures.

- **Part 3** presents a dialog box, asking how many images you want to add to your new Random Pics album (Figure 7-2, top). Your response tells the *repeat* statement how many times to, well, repeat.

- **Part 4** picks out a random picture from your Photo Library, and adds the image to your Random Pics album. Since this code is contained within the *repeat* statement, it runs however many times you specified in the dialog box. Therefore, by the time the *repeat* statement is finished, you'll have exactly the number of random pictures you want in your album.

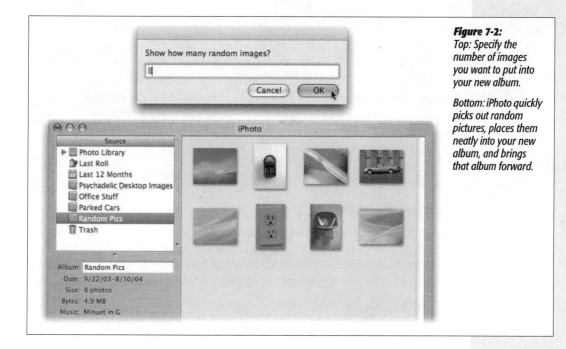

Figure 7-2:
Top: Specify the number of images you want to put into your new album.

Bottom: iPhoto quickly picks out random pictures, places them neatly into your new album, and brings that album forward.

Note: Due to a bug in iPhoto, you may end up with duplicates of some pictures in your Random Pics album. That's because iPhoto doesn't check to see if a picture already *exists* before it adds it to an album; since your script just picks random pictures from the Library, there's a possibility your script could end up picking an image that's *already* in the Random Pics album. Therefore, you might have a little house cleaning to do once the script finishes running, if you want to eliminate all duplicate photos in your new album.

- **Part 5** chooses your new album from the list in iPhoto (Figure 7-2, bottom). You're now shown all your randomly selected images.

Being able to choose random pictures from a list is more than just a cool party trick: it lets you get a feel for your Library without having to scroll through the whole thing.

POWER USERS' CLINIC

Getting Random Numbers

In addition to getting random items in a list, AppleScript lets you get random *numbers*. You might use this feature when creating a dice-rolling or guessing game, for example.

The trick is to use the *random number* command, which when provided with a number, gives you a random number between zero and that number. For instance, this command displays a dialog box with some random number between 0 and 10:

```
display dialog (random number 10)
```

That means that if you run *random number 10*, there will actually be *11* possible results—0, 1, 2, and so on, up to 10. If you run the command again, it displays a new random number.

If you run the *random number* command without *any* number following it, though, you'll get a decimal number between 0 and 1. You might want to use that trick if your script produces a random percentage; for example:

```
set randomDec to (random number)
set randomPerc to (randomDec * 100)
display dialog "You have a ¬
    " & randomPerc & "% chance ¬
    of winning the lottery today."
```

> You have a 31.052100468965% chance of winning the lottery today.
>
> Cancel   OK

As a side note, AppleScript's "random" numbers aren't actually random. Your Mac creates such numbers by performing a series of math operations based on the current time—which, most of the time, is good enough to produce numbers that *seem* random. On the other hand, if you work someplace where true mathematical randomness is a must (say, a graduate math department), you'd be better off using a more advanced programming language, or a Web site like *www.random.org/sform.html*.

Showing Slideshows

One of iPhoto's coolest features—and a trick sure to wow any of your Windows-using friends—is showing a full-screen, cross-fading slideshow of your pictures. When combined with the random-album script from the previous section, you can make AppleScript run a slideshow with any number of random pictures you want.

The first step is to set the preferences you want to use for *all* iPhoto slideshows. (Unfortunately, you have to do this in iPhoto; there's no AppleScript command for setting slideshow preferences.) Just click Organize, click Slideshow, set the image and sound settings you want (choosing crossfades and background music, for example), and click Save Settings. Then click Cancel to close the window.

Now you just have to modify your script to play a slideshow after it creates your random album:

```
tell application "iPhoto"
    activate
    if not (exists album "Random Pics") then
        new album name "Random Pics"
    end if
    set photoList to every photo
    set numImages to the text returned of (display dialog ¬
        "Present how many images in the slideshow?" default answer 10)
    repeat numImages times
        set randomPhoto to (some item of photoList)
        add randomPhoto to album "Random Pics"
    end repeat
    select album "Random Pics"
    start slideshow --This presents your "Random Pics" album full-screen
end tell
```

That's all there is to it! Now your script not only creates a Random Pics album, but it also shows all the pictures onscreen—complete with musical accompaniment, if you so desire.

Controlling Photoshop

As described on page xix, Adobe Photoshop is the standard workhorse program for graphic designers on Mac OS X (and Windows, for that matter—but don't say that out loud). If you've never used Photoshop, you're missing out on a lot of power—and doubly so, because you're missing out on all the AppleScript control. By scripting Photoshop, you can color-correct images automatically (page 133), for example, or make your images look like surrealist paintings (page 135).

Note: The scripts in this chapter require Photoshop CS (or later). If you don't feel like spending several hundred dollars for a new version of Photoshop, check out the fully functional 30-day demo, available at *http://www.adobe.com/products/tryadobe/main.jsp#product=39.*

Recording Actions

Unlike the Finder, Photoshop doesn't support AppleScript *recording* (page 23)—that is, you can't click the Record button in Script Editor and have AppleScript write out all the code for what you're doing in Photoshop. Fortunately, though, Photoshop supports recording of its *own*—you just have to click the appropriate button in Photoshop. And just as AppleScript sequences are called *scripts*, Photoshop's sequences are called *actions*.

Say you want to record a Photoshop action that corrects the color, levels, and contrast of an image, and then saves the file in a format suitable for a Web site. Here's the procedure for recording such an action:

1. **Launch Photoshop CS (it's in your Applications → Adobe Photoshop CS folder).**

   If, contrary to this book's suggestion, you're using Photoshop 7, launch that instead.

2. **Open an image you'd like to modify.**

   This is going to be the guinea pig image—you'll make all your modifications to it now, so that Photoshop knows how to repeat your modifications in the future on other images.

3. **Make sure you see the Actions window.**

   If you don't, choose Window → Actions (Option-F9). This window is where you can record, play back, and otherwise manipulate your Photoshop actions.

4. **In the Actions window, click the button that looks like a folded piece of notebook paper (Figure 7-3, top).**

   This button gets the ball rolling for recording a new action.

5. **In the dialog box that appears, specify the name "Fix Colors and Save for Web" for your new action (Figure 7-3, bottom).**

   If you'd like to run your action from the keyboard, you can specify a keyboard combination from the Function Key pop-up menu, too. (Note, however, that this keystroke works only when you're inside Photoshop.)

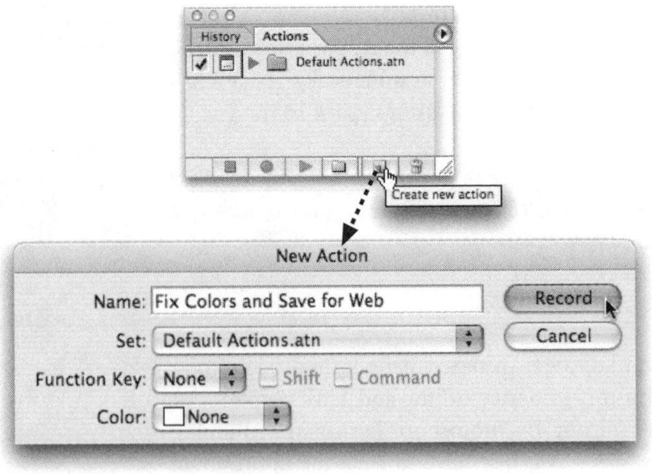

Figure 7-3:
Top: Click this button to create a new Photoshop action.

Bottom: This dialog box lets you name your new action (and give it a keyboard shortcut, if you want). Once you click Record, Photoshop begins "listening" to everything you do, tracking it for future use.

6. **Go through the commands you want to record.**

   From the Image → Adjustments menu, click Auto Levels, Auto Contrast, and finally, Auto Color. Photoshop does its best to fix the coloring of your image.

   Next, choose File → Save for Web. From the right-side Settings pane, pick the type of file compression you want (JPEG Medium, for example, is a good balance between image quality and a small file size). Then save the file on the desktop.

7. **In the Actions window, click the Stop button (Figure 7-4).**

   You should see a list of all the operations you just performed, to let you know that Photoshop recognized them.

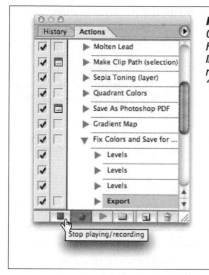

Figure 7-4:
Once you click the Stop button, Photoshop preserves your recorded actions. Here you can see that Photoshop recorded all three commands from the Image → Adjustments menu (they're all classified as "Levels"), and it also recorded your choosing File → Save for Web (in the Actions window, it's called "Export").

Now you've got a full-blown Photoshop action. To test it out, open a new image, select your action from the Actions window, and click the Play button at the bottom of the Actions window (the button that looks like a right-pointing triangle). Photoshop quickly fixes the picture's coloring, then saves the image on your desktop with the compression settings you specified in step 6.

Wrapping Actions in an AppleScript

Of course, nothing you've done thus far has involved AppleScript—you've just recorded a bunch of operations inside Photoshop. The *real* power comes when you wrap your actions in a script, because then you can mix in AppleScript commands as well.

To wrap your action in a script, open Script Editor and enter these commands:

```
--Part 1:
set applyFile to (choose file)
```

```
--Part 2:
tell application "Adobe Photoshop CS"
    open applyFile
    --Part 3:
    do action "Fix Colors and Save for Web" from "Default Actions"
end tell
```

When you run this script, AppleScript applies your Photoshop action to any file you select. Here's how the code works:

- **Part 1** presents a dialog box, letting you choose which file you want to perform the action on. (See page 97 for the intricacies of the *choose file* command.)

- **Part 2** tells Photoshop to open the file you selected.

- **Part 3** runs the Photoshop action you created in the previous section. You're left with a compressed, color-corrected copy of whatever file you selected, right on your desktop.

Since there's no *activate* command in this script, Photoshop stays in the background as it does its work. That means you can continue browsing the Web, reading your email, or composing a letter to Santa while Photoshop tweaks and compresses the image for you.

Tip: For maximum convenience, save your script as an application (page 33) and place it in your Dock for use anytime.

Other Photoshop Commands

So far, you've only used two commands directed at Photoshop: *open* and *do action*. While these commands are certainly powerful for running preassembled Photoshop actions (like the one you created on page 131), there are other AppleScript commands as well, to let you apply various Photoshop effects to your images (Figure 7-5).

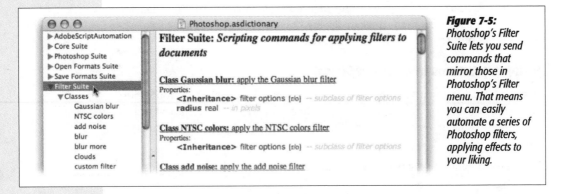

Figure 7-5:
Photoshop's Filter Suite lets you send commands that mirror those in Photoshop's Filter menu. That means you can easily automate a series of Photoshop filters, applying effects to your liking.

Filtering Images

Just about the most powerful Photoshop command is *filter*. That single command gives you access to all Photoshop's powerful image filters (blurs, distortions, lighting effects, and so on), right from the comfort of a wee little AppleScript. To use the *file* command, you'd enter a script like this:

```
tell application "Adobe Photoshop CS"
    filter layer 1 of front document using filterName with options ¬
        {<any options you want to use for the filter>}
end tell
```

You just replace *filterName* with whatever filter you want to use, and specify any particular options (like how strongly to blur your image) after *with options*. And, if you want to distort your image beyond recognition, you can use multiple *filter* commands, one after the other.

An example: Making an image look surreal

If you have aspirations to become the next Miró (the famed Spanish *surrealist* painter, 1893–1983), Photoshop and AppleScript can help you achieve your dreams. By combining three different filters—a glow, a twirl, and a blur—you can make any image look like it came straight out of the surrealist period. Here's how:

1. **Open Photoshop's dictionary, and reveal the Filter Suite → Classes list.**

   This is a comprehensive, alphabetical listing of every filter that Photoshop CS accepts. Take specific note of the *diffuse glow*, *twirl*, and *motion blur* filters.

2. **Assemble your script.**

   Having read the three entries for the filters you want, you can use AppleScript to apply them to a Photoshop image:

```
tell application "Adobe Photoshop CS"
    --Apply a diffuse glow, to make it look artistic:
    filter layer 1 of the front document using ¬
        diffuse glow with options {graininess:5, ¬
        glow amount:10, clear amount:10}
    --Apply a twirl, to make the image look abstract:
    filter layer 1 of the front document using twirl ¬
        with options {angle:150}
    --Apply a blur, to clear out any minor imperfections:
    filter layer 1 of the front document using ¬
        motion blur with options {angle:45, radius:20}
end tell
```

Note: Due to a bug in Photoshop, this script may not work properly on images that have lots of layers. To work around the problem, just choose Layer → Flatten Image before you run the script.

---

3. **Compile and run your script.**

If you entered all the commands properly, you should see your frontmost Photoshop image change right before your eyes (Figure 7-6).

4. **Save your script; you're going to need it later.**

Make sure the format is set to Script, and then save the file as "Surrealify an Image.scpt" in the Library → Scripts folder.

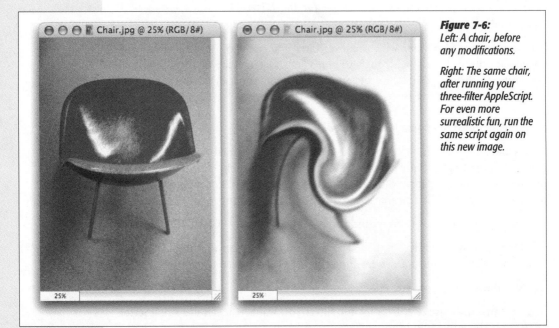

Figure 7-6:
Left: A chair, before any modifications.

Right: The same chair, after running your three-filter AppleScript. For even more surrealistic fun, run the same script again on this new image.

GEM IN THE ROUGH

What Is it?

The Photoshop CS filter script you just wrote on page 135 is great fun if you like imitating 19th-century painters, but it's a big pain to write *layer 1 of the front document* over and over again. Luckily, AppleScript lets you shrink that code mouthful into one word: *it*.

In AppleScript, *it* refers to whatever the nearest *tell* statement is commanding. For example, if you had a *tell application "Finder"* statement, *it* would refer to *application "Finder"*. Therefore, to simplify your Photoshop script, you have to add a new *tell* statement:

```
tell application "Adobe Photoshop CS"
    tell layer 1 of the front document
```

```
        filter it using diffuse glow ¬
            with options {graininess:5, ¬
            glow amount:10, ¬
            clear amount:10}
        filter it using twirl ¬
            with options {angle:150}
        filter it using motion blur ¬
            with options ¬
            {angle:45, radius:20}
    end tell
end tell
```

Your script is now much more compact, since AppleScript automatically substitutes *layer 1 of the front document* for every occurrence of *it*.

Mixing your two Photoshop scripts

The only complaint you might have with your script right now, however, is that the *diffuse glow* filter has a habit of washing out the colors in your images. Of course, you could always insert a few new lines into your script to correct the colors and contrast of your image. But why do that when you've *already* written a script to correct image colors?

Luckily, AppleScript lets you run one script from another—without copying and pasting any code yourself. Using just two commands—*load script* and *run script*—you can integrate several scripts into one.

Open your color-correcting script from page 133, and make the following changes:

```
set applyFile to (choose file)
tell application "Adobe Photoshop CS"
    open applyFile
    set surrealifier to load script ¬
        (alias "Macintosh HD:Library:Scripts:Surrealify an Image.scpt)
    run script surrealifier
    do action "Fix Colors and Save for Web" from "Default Actions"
end tell
```

Now your script loads the **Surrealify an Image** script that you just created and places the contents of that script in the *surrealifier* variable. Then you tell Apple-Script to run the *surrealifier* script, applying your three Miró-esque filters to the image. Finally, AppleScript proceeds with the last command of your color-correcting script, running the Fix Colors and Save for Web action in Photoshop (page 131).

In other words, you wind up with a file on your Desktop that's both surreal looking *and* color corrected.

Note: In this example, you run your **Surrealify** script from your color-correcting script. However, there's no reason you can't do it the other way: running your color-correcting script from your **Surrealify** script, using *load script* and *run script*.

Image Events

Photoshop is the embodiment of pro image editing, but it's a memory and processor *pig*. If you'd like a very simple graphics program—one that works completely in the background—Mac OS X has your ticket. It's called *Image Events*, and AppleScript commands it with ease.

Open the Image Events dictionary (File → Open Dictionary), and browse through the commands in the Image Suite. These commands cover all the manipulations you can make to your images: cropping, scaling, saving in various formats, and so on. The following pages provide just a few examples of what you can do with these commands.

Getting Image Dimensions

One of Image Events's simplest uses is getting the dimensions of any image on your hard drive. You'll find that helpful if you ever need to locate an image that's exactly 1024×768 pixels for your desktop background, for example.

Here's how to script the job:

```
--Part 1:
set selectedFile to (choose file)
--Part 2:
tell application "Image Events"
    set openedFile to open (selectedFile as alias)
    ---Part 3:
    set dimensionList to the dimensions of openedFile
    set fileWidth to the first item of dimensionList
    set fileHeight to the second item of dimensionList
    --Part 4:
    close openedFile
end tell
--Part 5:
display dialog "Width: " & fileWidth & " pixels" & return & "Height: " & ¬
    fileHeight & " pixels"
```

FREQUENTLY ASKED QUESTION

Image Events

What are Image Events, and why do you keep capitalizing their name?

"Image Events" (capitalized like that) is the name of an image-editing program in your System → Library → Core-Services folder. If you double-click Image Events's icon, though, nothing happens. That's because, unlike Photoshop, CorelDraw, and ever other Mac photo program in existence, Image Events is *invisible*—it has no menu bar, windows, or Dock icon.

In fact, Image Events is a kind of counterpart to Preview (in your Applications folder). Preview is an image-editing program that's visible but doesn't accept AppleScript commands, while Image Events is an image-editing program that's invisible but *does* accept AppleScript commands.

Weird. But how can I use a program that I can't even see?

Ah, good question. Since you can't control Image Events with the mouse or keyboard, you have to use AppleScript. That's not a bad thing, though; Image Events supports all sorts of image-editing commands, like *crop* (for cutting off the edges of an image) and *rotate* (for turning an image to the right or left). You can find the full list of Image Events commands by opening its dictionary and looking through the Image Suite.

One thing that trips up many beginners, though, is that Image Events *works* like a visible program, even though it's not. That means you have to *open* images before you can edit them, and *close* images when you're done (using those specific AppleScript commands). Furthermore, it means that none of your image changes get saved until you send Image Events the *save* command. So even though you can't see the image-editing magic that Image Events performs, you still have to send AppleScript commands as if you could.

And here's how it works:

- **Part 1** presents an Open dialog box (page 97), letting you choose which file you want the dimensions for.

Note: Due to an odd bug, Image Events may report the wrong dimensions if you pick a multi-megabyte TIFF file that's saved using *ZIP compression* (an uncommon way of making TIFF files take up less space). To get the correct dimensions, simply open the image in a program like Photoshop, and resave the image in a different format.

- **Part 2** tells Image Events to open the file you've chosen and then assigns the *openedFile* variable to the contents of the file. Keep in mind that you won't *see* anything open, because it's all happening in the background.

Note: As described on page 79 (and demonstrated in the previous script), the *open* command works with *aliases*.

- **Part 3** gets the dimensions of the image you chose and stores them in *dimensionsList*. (In AppleScript, image dimensions are stored as a two-item list.) Then, the script sets the *fileWidth* variable to the image's width and the *fileHeight* variable to the image's height.

- **Part 4** closes the file, telling Image Events that you're done working with it. Note, however, that *fileWidth* and *fileHeight* stay around, because variables aren't lost when a script closes a file.

- **Part 5** displays a dialog box, letting you know the image's exact dimensions (Figure 7-7).

Note: You might be wondering why the *display dialog* command isn't inside the *tell* statement, as it has been for numerous other scripts in this book. The reason is that Image Events is an invisible program; it's incapable of displaying dialog boxes. By putting the *display dialog* command outside the *tell* statement, therefore, you assure that Mac OS X actually presents the dialog box onscreen.

Figure 7-7:
After selecting an image that ends in "(wide screen)" from your Library → Desktop Pictures folder, you'll see a dialog box like this. That's because all Apple's widescreen desktop pictures are the same size: 1280 × 1024 pixels.

Padding an Image

Another convenient use for Image Events is *padding*. That's what you'd use if you wanted to enlarge a picture, for example, but didn't want to stretch out the image itself. Instead, padding the image simply surrounds it with extra black pixels—handy when you want to add a simple frame to an image (Figure 7-8).

Note: Unfortunately, black is the *only* color that Image Events can pad your images with. If you want a hot-pink border around your ice-fishing picture, for example, you'll have to use a program like Photoshop.

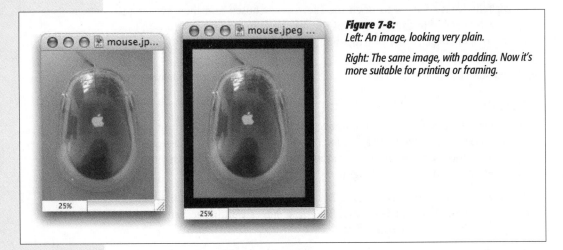

Figure 7-8:
Left: An image, looking very plain.

Right: The same image, with padding. Now it's more suitable for printing or framing.

To add padding to an image, you simply use the *pad* command directed towards Image Events. If you want to add a 50-pixel border, for instance, you would modify your previous script like this:

```
set selectedFile to (choose file)
tell application "Image Events"
    set openedFile to open (selectedFile as alias)
    set dimensionList to the dimensions of openedFile
    set fileWidth to the first item of dimensionList
    set fileHeight to the second item of dimensionList
    set newFileWidth to (fileWidth + 100)
    set newFileHeight to (fileHeight + 100)
    pad openedFile to dimensions {newFileWidth, newFileHeight}
    save openedFile
    close openedFile
end tell
```

Note: Due to a bug in Image Events, this script doesn't work with all types of images. You can safely pad JPEG or TIFF images, for example, but the script may display an error message if you try to use it with a Windows-style BMP image. (Also, Image Events won't pad images that are so small that the padding will be bigger than the image itself.)

These new commands simply calculate how much bigger the image would have to be to have a 50-pixel border. (The 100 extra pixels for the height get split between the top and the bottom of the image, resulting in a 50-pixel border; the same math applies for the width.) Then, using the *pad* command, the script expands the image to the new dimensions, and automatically fills in the new border with black. Finally, the script saves the changes you've made to the image and closes the file.

Creating a Droplet

There's nothing wrong with your script so far—in fact, it works quite well. It would be even better, though, if you could *drag* images onto the script's icon and have your script pad them automatically.

To implement this drag-and-drop behavior, you have to add two *handlers* (subroutines) to your script. These handlers turn your unsuspecting script into a *droplet:* an AppleScript that performs its operations when you drag and drop files on its icon.

The two handlers you're concerned with are *open* and *run*. Your script calls the *open* handler when you drag and drop files onto the script's icon. On the other hand, your script calls the *run* handler if you just double-click the script's icon, without dropping any files.

Note: Technically, the *run* handler isn't required. However, if your droplet doesn't have a *run* handler and you double-click its icon, nothing happens. A droplet without a *run* handler, therefore, can *only* accept drag-and-dropped files.

Here's what the two handlers look like:

```
on run --Called when you double-click the script's icon without dropping stuff
    --Your commands go here
end run


on open draggedItems --draggedItems is a list of the items that were dropped
    --Your commands go here
end open
```

As you can tell, these handlers look slightly different than normal subroutines. A typical subroutine (like the one on page 86) always has parentheses after its name, and you put any variable names in those parentheses. A handler like *run* or *open*, on the other hand, has no parentheses after its name; you put a variable's name (like *draggedItems*) directly after the name of the handler.

Why the two ways of doing things? In AppleScript, you use a variables-in-parentheses subroutine when you're writing your *own* shortcut functions, but you use a variables-without-parentheses handler when you're implementing one of Apple's predefined functions (like *run* and *open*). Other than that, the two kinds of subroutines work exactly the same way.

Adapting your script

To turn your existing script into a full-fledged droplet, you have to adapt its code to use the new handlers. Luckily, this is fairly simple to do:

```
on run
    display dialog ¬
        "To use this script, please drag files onto its Finder icon"
end run


on open draggedItems
    repeat with currentFile in draggedItems
        tell application "Image Events"
            set openedFile to open (currentFile as alias)
            set dimensionList to the dimensions of openedFile
            set fileWidth to the first item of dimensionList
            set fileHeight to the second item of dimensionList
            set newFileWidth to (fileWidth + 100)
            set newFileHeight to (fileHeight + 100)
            pad openedFile to dimensions {newFileWidth, newFileHeight}
            save openedFile
            close openedFile
        end tell
    end repeat
end open
```

Your new *run* handler displays a dialog box if you try to run the droplet without dragging any files to it. If you *do* drag files to the script, however, the *open* handler takes over and goes through the dragged files, one at a time, until they're all padded. (That's why there's a *repeat with* statement, like the one seen on page 113: to make sure every image gets padded.)

Your work isn't done, though. If you click the Run button in Script Editor, you'll simply get the dialog box from the *run* handler, which isn't very helpful. Instead, you have to save your script as a self-sufficient icon to which you can drag files. Here's how:

1. **Choose File → Save, and set the File Format pop-up menu to Application.**

   Droplets won't work properly if you save them in Script format (page 31).

2. **Make sure all the Options checkboxes are turned *off*.**

   Page 33 has a breakdown of what these options do.

3. **Give the droplet a memorable name (such as Drag-and-Drop Padding.app), and save it wherever you want.**

   Your desktop might be a good place.

Tip: No matter where you save the droplet, it'll be even more convenient if you drag it to your Dock. From then on, you can simply drag a bunch of images to the droplet's Dock icon and have them all padded automatically.

4. **Find the unique-looking droplet icon wherever you saved the script (Figure 7-9, right).**

Drag any group of image files to this icon, wait a few seconds while the script does its work, and check out your newly padded images!

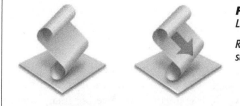

Figure 7-9:
Left: A normal script icon, if you save it as an application.

Right: A droplet, if you save it as an application. The gray arrow is supposed to suggest, "Drag files here!"

Converting Images from One Format to Another

If you take pictures on a digital camera—or use a scanner—you've probably run into the dreaded image format problem. That's what happens when you set your camera or scanner to use its highest quality, and you end up with a bunch of bloated TIFF files far too big to email or post on a Web page. Of course, you have no interest in retaking or rescanning all those pictures at a lower quality. So what should you do?

Convert your files using AppleScript!

In previous scripts, you've used Image Events's *save* command to finalize changes you've made to an image. If you look in Image Events's dictionary, though, you'll find that the *save* command is far more powerful, because you can specify exactly what *format* to save an image in. Here, then, is a script you can use to convert any image files—whether TIFFs, GIFs, or PDFs—to space-saving JPEGs:

```
--Part 1:
on run
    display dialog "Please drag image files to this script to turn them into
JPEGs"
end run
```

```
--Part 2:
on open draggeditems
    repeat with currentFile in draggeditems
        tell application "Image Events"
            set openedFile to open (currentFile as alias)
```

```
--Part 3:
set fileLocation to the location of openedFile
set fileName to the name of openedFile
--Part 4:
save openedFile as JPEG
close openedFile
        end tell
        --Part 5:
        tell application "Finder"
            set the name of file fileName of fileLocation to ¬
                (fileName & "->.jpg")
        end tell
    end repeat
end open
```

Save this script as an Application, and give it a memorable name (such as *Convert2JPEG.app*), as described on page 142. Then, when you drag a bunch of files onto the droplet's Finder icon, you'll transform your once-big image images into compact JPEGs (Figure 7-10).

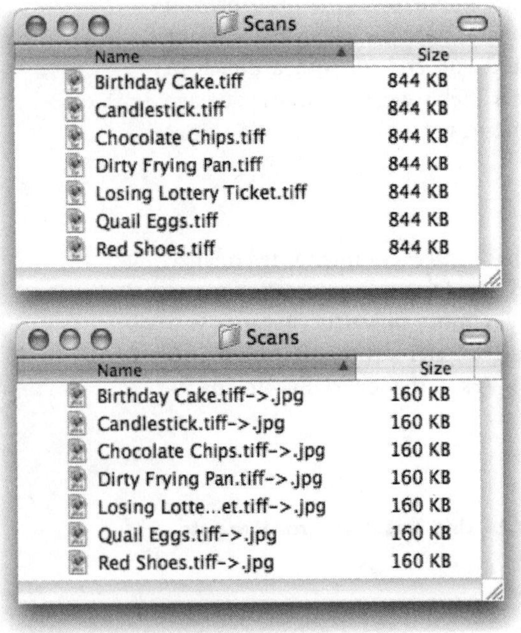

Figure 7-10:
Top: A folder of large TIFF files, each taken from a scanner.

Bottom: The same folder, after dragging the images onto your droplet. They now take up about one-fifth of the space.

Here's how the script works its magic:

- **Part 1** handles what happens if you simply double-click the droplet: the script presents a dialog box telling you to drag and drop files instead.

- **Part 2** is an exact duplicate of the commands from the script on page 142. These commands simply tell AppleScript to iterate through the files you dropped, one at a time, and to set the *openedFile* variable to the currently open file.

- **Part 3** sets two other important variables: *fileLocation* (the folder that contains the current image) and *fileName* (the name of the current image itself).

- **Part 4** converts the current image to a JPEG and saves it.

Tip: Mac OS X also supports the newer, higher-quality JPEG2 format. (You can specify it by substituting *as JPEG2* for *as JPEG*.) Not all other computers support JPEG2, though, so you'd be better off sticking with the standard JPEG format if you're going to be distributing your images online or by email. (Another option would be to use *as PNG,* to save your images in the even newer, even *higher*-quality Portable Network Graphics [PNG] format.)

Unfortunately, Image Events isn't smart enough to rename your file with a .jpg extension. That means that if your original file was called horses.tiff, your new JPEG file will *still* be called horses.tiff. This is a recipe for massive confusion when you try to open the file in Photoshop or Preview, since your image's extension (.tiff) won't match the format of the actual image (JPEG).

- **Part 5,** therefore, tells the Finder to rename your file with the correct .jpg extension. It does this by finding the file you want to rename (*fileName* in *fileLocation*), then appending "->.jpg" to the end of the file name, producing a fully working JPEG file with the correct extension.

Now you've got three convenient Image Events scripts, all of *I*which work without any tedious work in a graphics program like Photoshop CS.

CHAPTER 8

Playing Sound and Video

Turn on your radio. Go ahead, flip to that Top 40 station your kids listen to. Yes, now listen for a few minutes.

Chances are, you've just been listening to music that passed through a Mac on its way to your eardrums. And that voice-over you hear in the commercial? Probably done on a Mac, too. Macs are the standard for audio work, doing everything from sound correction to CD mastering. And with the iTunes Music Store, you can even *buy* music with your Mac, right from the comfort of your living room sofa.

The fun doesn't stop at music, however. With QuickTime built-in, your Mac supports all sorts of multimedia formats—including sharp, full-screen video.

If you're a power user, though, you're craving more. You want to batch-convert music files, unlock secret QuickTime features, and make your Mac talk to you. You want to make a computerized metronome, rotate your movies 90°, and make your computer *listen* to you. And when the day is over, you want to make yourself some popcorn, lie in bed, and watch a DVD on your laptop.

In other words, you want the precise multimedia features that AppleScript can unlock.

Note: The example scripts from this chapter can be found on the AppleScript Examples CD (see page 24 for instructions).

Scripting iTunes

Unless you've been living underwater for the past three years, you've probably heard of iTunes. It's Apple's free digital jukebox program, which ships with every

Mac sold. And just in case you can't find iTunes on your Mac (it should be in your Applications folder), you can download the most recent version—for free—from *www.apple.com/itunes/download/*.

In fact, since the scripts in this chapter will work best with the most recent version of iTunes, you might as well download a new copy right now.

Note: You can download iTunes for Windows, too, but only the Mac version supports AppleScript.

Playing Tracks

The simplest task that iTunes can perform—and the one you're most likely to use it for—is playing music. But the fact is, AppleScript can do far more with iTunes playback than you can do yourself (playing only sections of songs, say, or skipping songs automatically). For that reason, it's a good idea to get acquainted with the *play* command; it'll be your best friend when you script iTunes.

You use the *play* command like this:

```
tell application "iTunes"
    (* Substitute any song for TrackName. Substitute the name of any playlist
        for PlaylistName, or just use "Library". *)
    play track "TrackName" of playlist "PlaylistName"
end tell
```

For example, if you've got U2's latest killer track, "Vertigo," here's how that script would look:

```
tell application "iTunes"
    play track "Vertigo (Single Version)" of playlist "Library"
end tell
```

One thing to remember is that if you're going to play a specific track, you need to place the entire track name in quotes; the same applies to the playlist name. On the other hand, if you simply want to play the first song that iTunes finds, just type this:

```
tell application "iTunes"
    play
end tell
```

Tip: A similar command, *playpause,* toggles whether the music is playing. Run it once, a song starts; run it twice, the music stops.

Now that you know the basics, you can start mixing things up a bit.

Rating Songs

In iTunes, ratings are what you use to specify your favorite songs—and your not-so-favorite ones. Think of them like Favorites in Safari: they're there to let you set aside your most visited songs.

APPLESCRIPT: THE MISSING MANUAL

The thing is, ratings don't help much until you've *set* them. Sure, you could go through your 10,000-song Library and find your unrated songs—it'll just take a month of your life.

If you'd rather let AppleScript take care of finding your unrated songs, though, the following script is just for you:

```
--Part 1:
tell application "iTunes"
    activate
    set unratedSongs to every track of playlist "Library" whose rating is 0
    --Part 2:
    repeat with currentSong in unratedSongs
        --Part 3:
        play currentSong
        --Part 4:
        set currentName to the name of currentSong
        set currentArtist to the artist of currentSong
        --Part 5:
        set newRating to the text returned of (display dialog ¬
            "Current song: " & currentName & return & "Artist: " & ¬
            currentArtist & return & "Enter your rating (1-5):" ¬
            default answer 3)
        --Part 6:
        set newRating to (newRating * 20)
        set the rating of currentSong to newRating
    --Part 7:
    end repeat
    display dialog "All your songs are now rated."
end tell
```

When you run the script, AppleScript opens iTunes and finds all your unrated songs. Then it plays each song, letting you rate it on a scale from 1 to 5 stars, just as you would if you were clicking the little rating stars in iTunes itself. Pretty slick, huh?

Here's how the magic works:

- **Part 1** finds every unrated song in your iTunes Library and places that list in the *unratedSongs* variable. In iTunes, songs are rated on a scale from 0 to 100, with each star taking a value of 20. So all your one-star songs have a rating of 20, two-star songs have a rating of 40, and five-star songs have a rating of 100, for example.

  In this script, your list, named *unratedSongs*, holds all your songs that have a rating of 0. In other words *unratedSongs* is a list of every song that hasn't been rated yet.

Note: While it might seem strange, this 0 to 100 scale is pretty common in programming. When a programmer wants to rate, rank, or check the progress of something, she'll often use a scale of 0 to 100 *percent.* That's all that's going on here: your songs with a rank of 0 stars are at 0 percent, while songs with a 5-star rating are at 100 percent.

- **Part 2** starts a *repeat* loop, setting the *currentSong* variable to the next unrated song each time the *repeat* statement runs. This part is what makes sure your script goes through *all* the unrated songs, without skipping any.

- **Part 3** starts playing the current song. That way, you'll be able to hear the song you're rating.

- **Part 4** gets the name and artist of the *currentSong* and places them into the *currentName* and *currentArtist* variables. This information can come in handy if you've got several covers of the "Star Spangled Banner" in your Library, for example; by checking the song's name *and* artist, you won't have to guess which version you're currently listening to.

- **Part 5** displays a dialog box that shows you the name (*currentName*) and artist (*currentArtist*) of the currently playing song, and asks you to give the song a rating (Figure 8-1).

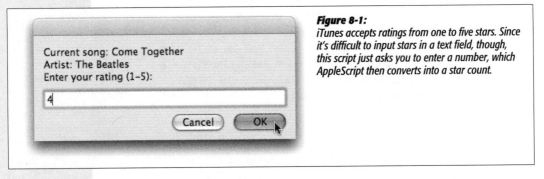

Figure 8-1:
iTunes accepts ratings from one to five stars. Since it's difficult to input stars in a text field, though, this script just asks you to enter a number, which AppleScript then converts into a star count.

- **Part 6** multiplies the rating you entered by 20. As described in part 1, by multiplying the number you enter by 20, your script can command iTunes to set the correct rating for the song.

- **Part 7** marks the end of the *repeat* statement. Once every song has been processed, the script finally displays a dialog box to let you know.

Now run the script, and rate all your songs. Once finished, you can organize your Library by rating: Simply choose File → New Smart Playlist (Option-⌘-N), and fill in the settings like Figure 8-2.

Note: In iTunes, a *smart playlist* is a playlist that updates itself with songs that match certain criteria. It's like a *smart album* in iPhoto (page 127), just for music.

Skipping Tracks

OK, you like music, but enough is enough. You don't have to listen to *all* of Chameleon by Herbie Hancock to get the picture (er, sound). Instead, wouldn't it be convenient if you could listen to bite-sized, 10-second snippets of every song in your whole Library? That way, you could play a sampling of your Classical-heavy Library to your friends, for instance, without them getting bored out of their minds.

With a new script, this job is a piece of cake. Run the following in Script Editor, and sit back as your ears fill with song samples:

```
--Part 1:
tell application "iTunes"
    play
    --Part 2:
    repeat until the player state is stopped
        --Part 3:
        delay 10
        --Part 4:
        next track
    end repeat
end tell
```

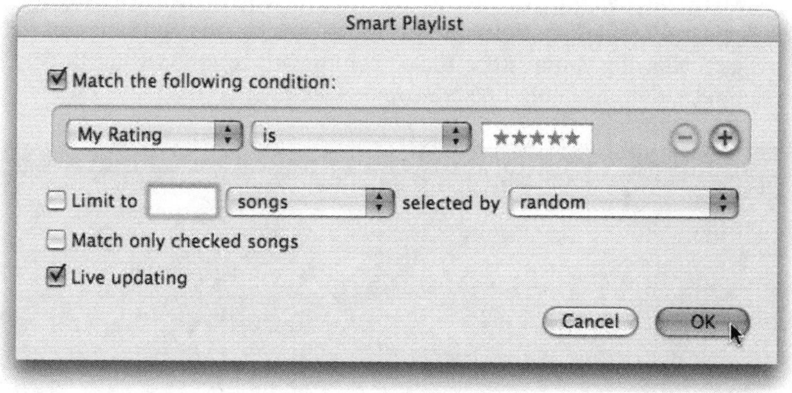

Figure 8-2:
Here's what you'd use to create a "Five Star Favorites" smart playlist. Then, when you selected this playlist from iTunes' left pane, you'd see a list of all the songs you've rated with five stars. (If you'd like, you can create an album for four-star tracks, too—or even a "Masochist Music" playlist for all your one-star hits.)

Here's how the parts break down:

- **Part 1** starts playing the first song in your iTunes Library.

- **Part 2** uses a special kind of statement—*repeat until*—that keeps running until a condition is met.

  In this case, the *repeat* statement keeps running until iTunes's *player state* is stopped (in other words, iTunes isn't playing anything at that moment). Once the last song is played, iTunes's player state *will* be stopped—and therefore, the *repeat* statement will stop as well.

- **Part 3** holds up the script for 10 seconds. (That's the only thing the *delay* command is good for: pausing your script's next command.) By doing this, you assure that the song will have 10 full seconds to play.

- **Part 4** skips to the *next* song in your Library, looping back to part 2 afterward.

Now you can listen to your whole Library in a few hours, rather than a few days. And if you encounter a song that you want to play *all* of, simply click Cancel in the dialog box; iTunes continues playing the whole song.

Converting Song Files

When you buy a music CD, you're essentially buying a disc full of AIFF-formatted music files. Record companies can fit 80 minutes of music on a 700 MB CD because each minute of AIFF music takes up about 9 MB.

Of course, if you're from the era of floppy disks, you're probably thinking "9 MB? That's sinful! I couldn't even fit 9 MB on my Mac Classic's hard drive!"—and you'd be right. Even today, in the era of 500 GB hard drives half the size of the latest *Harry Potter* book and 60 GB iPods that fit in your pocket, you can quickly fill up your computer if you use uncompressed (AIFF-format) music.

That's why iTunes supports a number of space-saving, *compressed* song formats. These formats let you fit up to 10 times as much music in the same amount of hard drive space, allowing you to store 10,000 compressed songs on your 40 GB iPod, for example, rather than only 1,000 uncompressed songs.

GEM IN THE ROUGH

Beeping

It's great to be able to play songs with iTunes, but sometimes you might just want your script to play back a quick noise—a chirp, a squeak, or a ding, for example—to get your attention. AppleScript provides the simple *beep* command for just this purpose:

```
display dialog ¬
    "Do not click the OK button!"
display dialog "I warned you!"
display dialog "This is your last chance!"
beep
```

When your script runs the *beep* command, it plays back the sound you've selected in the System Preferences → Sound → Sound Effects tab. You can even specify a number after the command, to tell AppleScript how many times to beep. Try this command as an April Fools prank on your boss's computer, for example:

```
beep 1000 --Beeps 1000 times
```

There are benevolent uses for beeps, too. For instance, you can create a simple metronome with AppleScript by having your computer beep at regular intervals:

```
display dialog ¬
    "Welcome to the AppleScript Metronome"
set bpm to the text returned of ¬
    (display dialog ¬
    "How many beats per minute?" ¬
    default answer 60)
set pauseBetweenBeeps to (60 / bpm)
repeat
    beep
    delay pauseBetweenBeeps
end repeat
```

That script calculates what fraction of a second it has to pause between beeps, and then just continues beeping. Since you don't specify any number of times after the *repeat* command, though, your Mac continues beeping forever—or at least until you press the Stop button in Script Editor.

If simply an *auditory* beep isn't enough for you, though, visit System Preferences → Universal Access → Hearing tab and turn on "Flash the screen whenever an alert sound occurs." Now, whenever a script runs the *beep* command, it'll flash the screen, too—perfect for a visual metronome.

Of course, you have to give up some sound quality in exchange for these smaller files—but iTunes gives you a choice of formats, so you can choose the space/quality trade-off that you like best. To get started converting your music, just choose iTunes → Preferences → Importing, and look at the Import Using pop-up menu. You have five format possibilities to choose from, as shown in Table 8-1.

Table 8-1. *iTunes audio formats*

Format abbreviation	Full name	What is it?	How much smaller than AIFF?
AAC	Advanced Audio Codec	AAC is the newest really-small music format, where each minute of music takes up only about 1 MB of space. AAC's sound quality is quite good—almost as good as a CD—and that's why it's the format used by the iTunes Music Store.	About 10x smaller
AIFF	Audio Interchange File Format	As described on page 152, AIFF is a space-hogging, uncompressed music format. When you hear people refer to "CD quality," this is the format they're talking about. (In fact, AIFF *is* the sound format used by commercial audio CDs.)	N/A
Apple Lossless	N/A	This is a new, proprietary format that Apple developed for music aficionados. As its name suggests, this format doesn't lose any of your music's quality. What it *does* lose, though, is about half of a song's file size.	About 2x smaller
MP3	MPEG Layer 3	This is the original really-small music format, developed by the Moving Pictures Experts Group (MPEG) for playing music on computers. MP3's size makes it perfect for storing on small hard drives—or even sharing over the Internet. And although MP3's quality isn't quite as good as AAC's, MP3 are supported by virtually every operating system in existence. (Plus, many modern CD players can play *MP3 CDs*—music mixes you burn yourself, which can hold about 10 times as much music as normal audio CDs.)	About 10x smaller
WAV	Waveform Audio	Unless you're a Windows die-hard, avoid this format. WAV takes up just as much space as AIFF, but has no better sound quality. In fact, WAV's only advantage—if you can call it that—is that it's the format of choice for Microsoft Windows audio files.	Not smaller at all

Once you pick a format that's small enough for your sound-quality tastes, you can drag a bunch of songs into your iTunes Library. Then, once iTunes has finished importing the songs, just select them and choose Advanced → "Convert Selection to *[Whatever format you chose]*". In a few minutes, iTunes converts all your songs into the format you selected the Preferences window.

Tip: Once iTunes is done converting your music, you can delete the old, unconverted music files to save hard drive space.

There are a few downsides to this whole procedure, though. For one thing, your converted files end up buried deep inside your Home → Music → iTunes → iTunes Music folder—not exactly the easiest place to access from the Finder (if you want to email a song to a friend, for example). For another thing, any songs you convert using this method end up with entries in your iTunes Library—a minor annoyance if you're the type who likes to keep your files organized in folders, not programs. Finally, the whole procedure is far too complicated; you shouldn't have to add songs to your Library and *then* convert them.

Thankfully, there's another choice. Using an AppleScript, you can convert your songs to a new format, move the song files to the desktop, and erase the songs' entries from your iTunes Library, automatically. It's a clean, simple alternative to paying big bucks for a commercial music-converting program—or suffering through iTunes's infuriating multistep conversion process.

Your new script is a *droplet,* an icon to which you can drag and drop files (page 141). Here's how you code it:

```
--Part 1:
on run
    display dialog "Drag files to this script to convert them with iTunes"
end run


--Part 2
on open selectedItems
    tell application "iTunes"
        set convertedTracks to (convert selectedItems)
    end tell
    --Part 3:
    repeat with currentTrack in convertedTracks
        tell application "iTunes"
            set trackLocation to (location of currentTrack)
            --Part 4:
            delete currentTrack
        end tell
        --Part 5:
        tell application "Finder"
            move trackLocation to the desktop
        end tell
    end repeat
end open
```

Here's how it works:

- **Part 1:** The *run* handler defines what happens if you simply double-click this script in the Finder. In this case, AppleScript presents a dialog box telling you to *drag* files to the script instead.

- **Part 2:** The *open* handler defines what happens if you drag and drop files onto the script's icon. In this script, you send iTunes the *convert* command, giving it a list of all the files you want to convert. iTunes automatically returns a list of the newly converted files; that list then goes into the *convertedTracks* variable.

Tip: iTunes not only supports converting *music* to other music formats, it also supports converting *video* to music formats. For example, if you drag almost any QuickTime movie onto this script, iTunes strips out the audio and converts the movie's soundtrack to your preferred sound format. It's a great way to extract the Led Zeppelin music from Cadillac commercials—or the hip-hop songs from iPod commercials.

- **Part 3:** The *repeat* statement tells AppleScript to go through your newly converted files, one at a time. For each converted song, AppleScript sets the *trackLocation* variable to the place the song is stored on your hard drive. (You'll use this information later to move the song file to your desktop.)

- **Part 4:** Using the *delete* command (page 94), the script removes your converted song from iTunes's Library. Keep in mind, though, that this code doesn't remove the song file *itself*; it only removes the song's entry in iTunes.

- **Part 5:** Like the script on page 90, this part uses the *move* command, directed at the Finder. Here, *move* pulls the song file out of its original location (*trackLocation*) and places the file on the desktop for easy access.

Note: This script does *not* erase your original audio files; it simply moves the newly converted files to the desktop.

Save this script as an Application (page 33) to create a working droplet. Now, whenever you drag a few music files to the droplet's icon, they'll quickly be converted into your preferred music format and placed on your desktop. From there, you can email the song files to a friend, listen to them in a program besides iTunes (like QuickTime Player [page 164]), or move the song files to a more convenient folder on your hard drive (like your Music folder, for example).

Speaking and Listening

Just like HAL from *2001: A Space Odyssey*, your Mac can talk to you. Granted, it sounds more like a Norwegian struggling to learn English than Douglas Rain, but it's still unmistakably cool.

You don't need AppleScript to make your Mac speak, though. If you just type some words in TextEdit, choose Edit → Select All, and then choose Edit → Speech → Start Speaking, you'll get a sample of what it's like to have your Mac talk to you.

This can come in handy, for example, if you've written a long paper, since it's often easier to *hear* typos than to find them with your eyes.

Tip: If you don't like the voice you hear, go to System Preferences → Speech → Default Voice and select a different one. (The easiest voices to understand are Bruce, Vicki, and Victoria.) You can even set how fast they speak with the Rate slider.

Having *AppleScript* speak, though, is much more powerful than using TextEdit's dinky speech features. You can make an AppleScript assemble the sentences you want it to speak on-the-fly, for example, or even have AppleScript listen to your spoken commands. But best of all, you can have AppleScript speak *into a file,* so you can take its prerecorded speech with you on a CD or iPod.

Speaking from a Script

To make AppleScript speak to you, use the *say* command. Here's a simple example:

```
say "Hello there"
```

When you run that script, you'll hear "Heh-lo thay-er"—the Mac's valiant attempt at speaking English. Feel free to type whatever you want after the *say* command, though—you're not restricted to dull two-word phrases.

If you want to override the default computer voice, you can even specify a different voice with the *using* option:

```
say "lah lah lah lah lah lah lah lah lah lah lah" using "Bad News"
```

If you enjoy entertaining voices, be sure to try out Bells (the voice of ringing instruments), Princess (a high-pitched girl), and Zarvox (an alien voice) as well. And if you want even *more* of a selection, there are 21 voices waiting for you in the System Preferences → Speech → Default Voice tab, as described earlier. Once you find a voice you like, just specify the voice's name after the *using* option of the *say* command.

Note: Unlike most things in AppleScript, the text after the *using* option *is* case-sensitive. That means typing "bad news" for the voice's name (instead of "Bad News") would result in an AppleScript error.

You can specify nontext items for AppleScript to speak, too, as long as you use *as string* (page 108) to convert them to text first. For instance, this simple script would speak the current date and time:

```
say (current date as string)
```

Note: When you run that script, Script Editor surrounds the *current date* command in an extra set of parentheses. Don't worry about it, though–that's just an AppleScript quirk, and it doesn't affect how your script runs.

Linking your script to a keyboard shortcut

Now that you have a script that tells you the date and time, you can do away with that space-wasting menu bar clock (Figure 8-3). That'll free up more space for, say, the Script Menu (page 4).

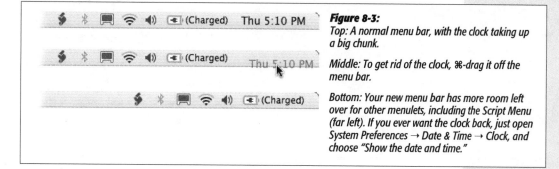

Figure 8-3:
Top: A normal menu bar, with the clock taking up a big chunk.

Middle: To get rid of the clock, ⌘-drag it off the menu bar.

Bottom: Your new menu bar has more room left over for other menulets, including the Script Menu (far left). If you ever want the clock back, just open System Preferences → Date & Time → Clock, and choose "Show the date and time."

Your script is a convenient way to get the current date and time, but rather than storing the script in your Dock (page 33), it would be even *more* convenient if you could link the script to a keyboard shortcut. That way, you could press Shift-Control-T, for example, to make your computer speak the time to you. There'd be no clutter in your Dock, and no clutter in your menu bar—a power user's dream.

Here's how to give your script a keyboard shortcut:

1. **In Script Editor, choose File → Save for your date- and time-speaking script. Make sure the File Format is set to Script.**

   You can save the script wherever you want, but your Library → Scripts → Info Scripts folder is as good a place as any. (Remember, if you put your script there, it'll also appear in the Script Menu for convenience.)

   Name the file something creative (like "Say the Time and Date"), and click Save.

2. **Download Keyboard Maestro from *www.keyboardmaestro.com.***

   Keyboard Maestro is a shareware program for programming keyboard shortcuts. It's perfect for running your AppleScript.

Note: There are oceans of other keyboard shortcut programs, each with their own features. If you'd prefer to use one besides Keyboard Maestro, check out *http://www.macdevcenter.com/pub/a/mac/2004/04/09/launchers.html* for a comparison of your options.

---

3. **Copy Keyboard Maestro to your Applications folder, and launch it.**

   In the main window, click the New Macro button (Figure 8-4).

4. **Type a name for your shortcut in the Macro Name field.**

   "Speak the Date and Time" is as good a name as any.

5. Click Triggers, click New Trigger, and choose Hot Key.

In the dialog box that appears, turn on the checkboxes for the keys that you want to trigger your script (Figure 8-5, top). Then click Save.

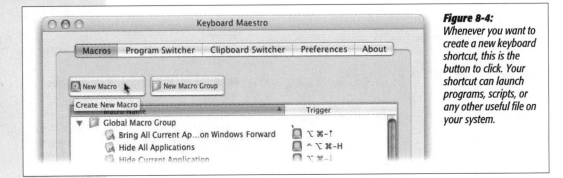

Figure 8-4:
Whenever you want to create a new keyboard shortcut, this is the button to click. Your shortcut can launch programs, scripts, or any other useful file on your system.

6. Click Actions, click New Action, and choose Execute → Execute AppleScript. Then click Set File, and select the script you saved in step 1.

Once you click Save, you're left with a window that looks like the bottom of Figure 8-5.

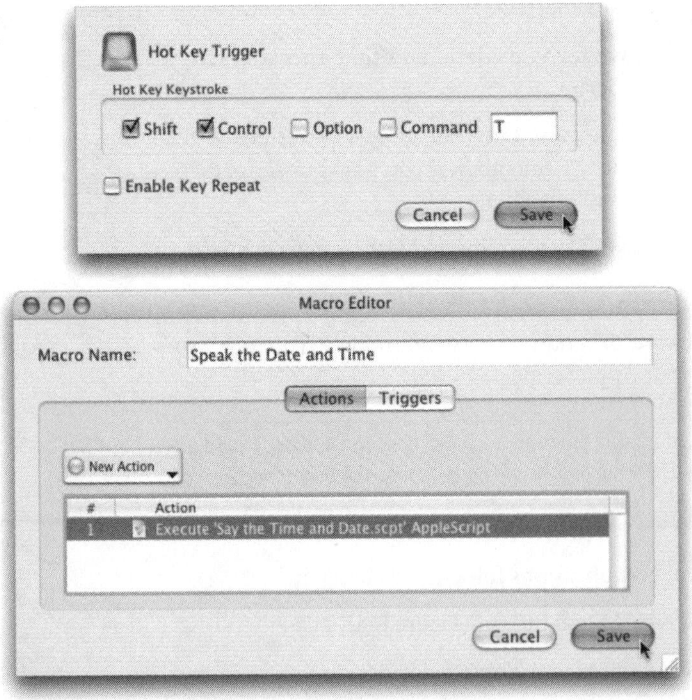

Figure 8-5:
Top: Turn on the checkboxes for Shift and Control, and type T in the text box, so you'll be able to run your script by pressing Shift-Control-T in any program.

Bottom: The Macro Editor, where you set up what happens when you press a particular key combination. If you'd like, for example, you can run additional scripts when you press Shift-Control-T, by choosing additional actions from the New Action pop-up menu.

7. **Click Save again, and quit Keyboard Maestro.**

Now you can listen to the time and date whenever you want by simply pressing the shortcut you set in step 5.

Having a script at your fingertips is a powerful addition to any AppleScripter's toolbox. If there are any other scripts you find especially useful (like, say, the color-correcting script from page 133), give them shortcuts, too, for even more time savings.

Making a File Speak

Among commuters, books on tape are a popular way to listen to long books in a car or on a train. The digital equivalents are commercial audiobooks from the iTunes Music Store or *www.audible.com,* which you can listen to on an iPod.

Still, the selection of these recordings is pretty small: a few classic novels, bestsellers, and maybe an interview here or there. If you want to listen to your *own* files on the road—say, your email or TextEdit documents spoken out loud—you can employ the help of AppleScript to speak your personalized text into an audio file. Best of all, *this* service is free.

To make AppleScript speak into a sound file instead of through your speakers, you have to use the *say* command's *saving to* option. You must also specify the name of an AIFF file, which is where the command saves your sound.

So, put it all together and what do you get? The following script, that's what:

```
say "Norwegian Wood" using "Bruce" saving to ¬
    ":Users:yourUsername:Music:wood.aiff"
```

Note: Make sure to replace *yourUsername* with your actual, one-word user name.

When you run that script, you'll end up with a two-second file, named wood.aiff, in your Home → Music folder. You can listen to that file in QuickTime Player or iTunes, hypnotized by the sounds of your Mac saying "Norwegian Wood."

Converting Clipboard text into audio

Having AppleScript speak two-word phrases into audio files is a great way to spend a blustery afternoon, but it's not going to help you convert your email messages for listening on your iPod, for example. Instead, you need to adapt your script so it takes any text from the *Clipboard* (which contains something you've copied with either Edit → Copy, or ⌘-C) and speaks that text into a file. Then, you can run the script regardless of whether you've copied text from your word processor, email program, or Web browser.

Note: Unfortunately, the newest version of Microsoft Word copies text to the Clipboard in a nonstandard format. If you want to save a spoken version of a Word document, therefore, you should first paste the Word document's text in *TextEdit,* then copy the text from TextEdit, and finally run the script.

The trick is to use the keywords *the clipboard,* which represent the information currently stored on the Clipboard (page 41):

```
--Part 1:
set soundLocation to (choose file name default name "clipboard.aiff")
--Part 2:
set theText to (the clipboard as string)
say theText saving to soundLocation
```

Here's how the script works:

- **Part 1** presents a dialog box, letting you choose where to save the audio file (Figure 8-6, top). The *default name* option simply tells your script what file name should be used if you don't specify one manually in the dialog box—kind of like the *default answer* option for *display dialog* commands (page 55).

  Once you click Save in the dialog box, the script puts the name and location of the file you chose into the *soundLocation* variable.

- **Part 2** gets the contents of the Clipboard, converts it to text, and places that text in the variable *theText.* AppleScript then speaks this text (*the clipboard*) into the file you chose in part 1.

Note: AppleScript won't read text into compressed MP3 or AAC files—only into uncompressed AIFF files. So if you're tight on hard drive space, be sure to compress your sound files afterward using the instructions on page 152.

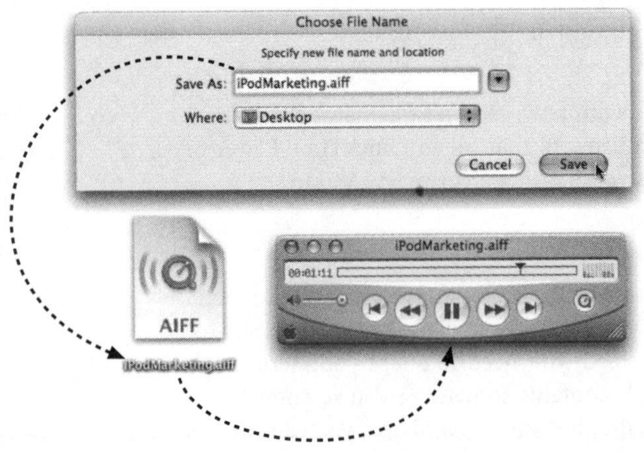

Figure 8-6:
Say you've selected and copied some text from www.apple.com/ipod. Top: The script asks you to choose where you'd like to save the spoken text and what you'd like to name the file.

Lower left: Unless you've changed the program that opens AIFF files automatically, you'll see an icon like this, named whatever you specified in the dialog box on top.

Lower right: Double-click the icon, and it'll open in QuickTime Player. Click the play button to get the computer speaking.

Reading multiple emails into a file

For ultra convenience, you can even use this script to read the contents of *several* emails into a single file. That way, on your ride to work, you could listen to every email your boss has sent you, and catch up on the day's upcoming events.

Here's how:

1. **Launch Mail (it's in your Applications folder).**

   As described on page 186, Mail is the free email program that comes with every copy of Mac OS X.

2. **Select all the messages that you want to include in your audio file.**

   For example, if you wanted to include every message from Steve Jobs, you would click the little magnifying-glass icon in the upper-right corner of the Mail window; choose In All Mailboxes → From; type "Steve Jobs"; and finally select every message in the list (Edit → Select All, or ⌘-A).

3. **Press the Forward button.**

   This trick forces Mail to open a New Message window, incorporating the contents of every email message you selected into a single window.

4. **Delete the line "Begin forwarded message."**

   That way, you won't have to hear your Mac say "Begin forwarded message" at the beginning of your audio file.

5. **Select all the text in the New Message window.**

   As mentioned earlier, you can choose either Edit → Select All, or press ⌘-A.

6. **Copy the text to the Clipboard.**

   Use Edit → Copy or ⌘-C.

7. **Close the New Message window.**

   Click Don't Save, since you don't need to preserve this compilation message.

8. **Switch to Script Editor, and run the script from page 160.**

   AppleScript asks you where you want to save the audio file and then proceeds to read *every* message you copied to the Clipboard into that single file.

This process is a huge timesaver over the alternative method: converting individual email messages to audio files, one at a time. Now you have no excuse not to read—or listen to—the email that your boss sends you!

Speaking to a Script

OK, now you've got your computer talking to you. But what if you want to talk back? Unfortunately, your computer won't respond when you say, "No! Don't crash without saving my thesis!"

Still, your Mac *can* respond to certain verbal commands, with a little help from AppleScript.

The trick is to use the *listen for* command. You give this command a list of phrases to be on the alert for, and once you say one into your Mac's microphone (or iSight camera), the script figures out which one you said and does whatever it's supposed to. In that way, your script can respond to verbal commands—plus, it's a great way to show off your Mac's superiority to all those self-righteous PC users out there.

Note: AppleScript's speech processing is nowhere near a full-blown speech recognition package, at least for Mac OS X Panther (version 10.3.x).

For one thing, AppleScript doesn't always hear accurately with the Mac's built-in microphone (a third-party headset microphone can help, though). For another thing, AppleScript can be quite slow in recognizing what you say—as long as 10 seconds, in some cases. Finally, you have to tell AppleScript *beforehand* which things you might say—your Mac doesn't have a built-in dictionary with tens of thousands of words, like IBM's ViaVoice ($130, *www.scansoft.com/viavoice/osx/*).

Here's how you'd use AppleScript's basic speech recognition:

```
--Part 1:
tell application "SpeechRecognitionServer"
    --Part 2:
    set heardPhrase to listen for ¬
        {"One fish", "Two fish", "Red fish", "Blue fish"}
end tell
--Part 3:
display dialog "You said " & heardPhrase
```

And here's how the script works:

- **Part 1** invokes the invisible SpeechRecognitionServer program, which is in charge of listening to you speak. The first time you run the script, Mac OS X may ask you, "Where is SpeechRecognitionServer?" The solution: Click the Browse button and navigate to System → Library → Frameworks → Carbon.framework → Versions → A → Frameworks → SpeechRecognition.framework → Resources → SpeechRecognitionServer (phew!). Once you click Choose, the script works just fine.

- **Part 2** starts listening for four possible phrases. To let you know that Mac OS X is all ears, it shows you the microphone window for Apple's Speakable Items (Figure 8-7).

Tip: If you find the Speakable Items microphone window distracting, you can double-click its upper half to minimize it to the Dock.

Figure 8-7:
The Speakable Items microphone. The word Esc indicates what key you have to hold down while talking to Mac OS X (in this case, Escape). If you want to customize this key, visit System Preferences → Speech → Speech Recognition tab → Listening mini-tab, and click Change Key.

Once you say "One fish," "Two fish," "Red fish," or "Blue fish," the script places your response in the *heardPhrase* variable.

- **Part 3** displays a dialog box of what you said, using the *heardPhrase* variable from part 2.

Now, this is simply a demonstration of speech *recognition*. If you want true power, you have to mix it with a dose of speech *generation*. For instance, you can create a script that listens for a verbal command—like "Tell me what date it is"—and responds verbally, too. Here's how:

```
--Part 1:
tell application "SpeechRecognitionServer"
    set heardPhrase to listen for {"Tell me what date it is", ¬
        "Tell me how many programs are open"}
end tell
--Part 2:
if heardPhrase is "Tell me what date it is" then
    say (current date as string)
--Part 3:
else if heardPhrase is "Tell me how many programs are open" then
    tell application "System Events"
        set programCount to (count every process)
    end tell
    say "There are " & programCount & " programs running."
end if
```

When you run this script, the Speech Recognition Blob appears and waits for you to say either "Tell me what date it is" or "Tell me how many programs are open." No matter which one you ask for, the script generates the appropriate response and speaks it out loud. Here's how:

- **Part 1** gives the SpeechRecognitionServer a list of two possible phrases you might say. Once you say one (while holding down the key specified in the Speech Recognition Blob), the script puts the one you said in the *heardPhrase* variable.

- If you ask for the date, **part 2** says it out loud. This *say* command is an exact copy of the script on page 156.

- If you ask for the number of open programs, **part 3** speaks, "There are [however many] programs running." It does this by counting the number of System Events *processes* (page 110)—in other words, open programs.

With this script in place, you can now talk to your computer without sounding like a total geek.

Tip: For more on AppleScript's speech support, visit *http://developer.apple.com/ue/speech/applescript.html*. Or, if you're a speech-recognition freak, visit *http://auc.uow.edu.au/conf/conf00/papers/AUC2000_Woo.pdf* to read an ultra-detailed paper on the intricacies of AppleScript's speech features.

Scripting QuickTime

Once you're tired of still graphics, music, and voice, you've got one multimedia medium left to cover: video. Apple's powerful video technology, QuickTime, comes preinstalled on Mac OS X, and you can access all its power with QuickTime Player (stored in your Applications folder). Double-click just about any movie on your hard drive, and QuickTime Player promptly launches.

Tip: QuickTime Player can open more than just movies. For example, you can use QuickTime Player with music files, still pictures, and even plain text files. Still, QuickTime Player isn't the best program for handling those formats—that's why you've got iTunes, iPhoto, and TextEdit, for example.

Even beyond the capabilities of QuickTime Player, you can use AppleScript to unlock *additional* multimedia features. For example, AppleScript lets you play videos full-screen (see below)—a stunt that's normally reserved for the $30 QuickTime Pro.

Getting Started

As a budding AppleScripter, you should take some time to meet QuickTime Player—in part, because there are more than 100 million copies of QuickTime in the world! QuickTime is available for both Macs and Windows PCs—even though the AppleScript features work only with the Mac version.

If you want to play with QuickTime Player, though, you first need a movie to use. Chances are you've got a few lying around on your hard drive—just do a search in the Finder for files that have an extension of .mov. Or, if you'd prefer, you can download a folder of QuickTime demo scripts from *www.apple.com/applescript/quicktime/*, and included with those scripts are a few demo movies.

Once you've got a movie you like, double-click to open it in QuickTime Player, and then read on.

Presenting a Movie Full-Screen

One of the neatest tricks QuickTime Player can perform is showing you a movie full-screen. Yes, the movie might appear a little grainy from being enlarged, but it still turns your computer into a mini-cinema. And after a while, it almost makes you feel guilty for not keeping a popcorn maker next to your computer.

Once you've got a movie open, the only command you have to use is *present*. That's what turns an unsuspecting QuickTime movie file into a full-screen theater imitation (Figure 8-8).

Here's how you use *present*:

```
tell application "QuickTime Player"
    activate
    present the front movie --This is the important line
end tell
```

As soon as you click Run, AppleScript brings QuickTime Player forward and presents the front-most movie in full-screen mode. Unfortunately, you lose access to the menu bar and Dock while the movie's playing. Therefore, Table 8-2 shows you how to use the keyboard to navigate a movie while it's in this mode.

Table 8-2. Useful QuickTime keystrokes

Keystroke	What it does
Space bar or Return key	Pauses the movie (press it a second time to resume)
Right arrow/Left arrow	When paused, moves the movie one frame forward/back
⌘-Right arrow/⌘-Left arrow	Plays the movie in forward/reverse
Option-Right arrow/Option-Left arrow	Jumps to the end/beginning of the movie
Up arrow/Down arrow	Increases/decreases the movie's volume
Escape key	Exits full-screen mode and pauses the movie

Tip: If you'd like, you can play movies in other modes too—like half-size or double-size. Simply add the *scale* option to the end of your *present* command, like this:

```
tell application "QuickTime Player"
    activate
    present the front movie scale half
end tell
```

Mac OS X still darkens your screen with a black border; the difference is, your movie won't appear as grainy, since you're not stretching the image to fill your entire monitor. (You can replace *half* with *normal, double,* or *current,* too, to adjust the scale at which your movie plays.)

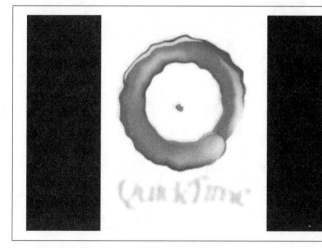

Figure 8-8:
A movie, playing full-screen. If the movie is too wide or narrow for your screen, QuickTime automatically places black bars around the sides.

Including a Movie with Your Script

If you're writing a script that involves playing a specific movie, it'll work great on your computer. The trouble is, the script won't work on *other* people's computers unless they, too, have the same movie stored in the same place on their hard drive.

Luckily, AppleScript lets you include a movie with your script. Then, when you send your script to your aunt in Beijing, the movie file goes along for the ride, too—guaranteeing that the script can find and play the movie. Here's how to pull of this stunt:

1. **Find the movie you want to include with your script, and keep its folder open.**

   For the purposes of this example, suppose the movie is called Poodles.mov and it's saved in your Movies folder (Home → Movies).

2. **Create a new script in Script Editor (File → New, or ⌘-N), and immediately save the script (File → Save, or ⌘-S).**

   For the File Format, make sure you choose Application Bundle—a special script format that lets you package files with your script (page 34). Keep all the Options turned off, name the script whatever you want, and save it anywhere you want.

3. **In the Finder, navigate to the script you just saved. Control-click the script's icon, and from the shortcut menu, choose Show Package Contents.**

   A new window opens, letting you navigate into the guts of your script's application bundle.

4. **Inside the new window, open the Contents → Resources folder.**

   This is where you can store any files you want distributed with your script.

5. **Copy Poodles.mov into this new window.**

   The movie is now stored *inside* your script.

6. **Back in Script Editor, write out the code that incorporates the movie into your script. Use the keywords *path to me* so your script can locate the file inside your application bundle.**

   Here's one possibility for a script (it'll play Poodles.mov full-screen):

   ```
   set locOfMovie to (path to me as string) & "Contents:Resources:Poodles.mov"
   --locOfMovie is now the file path (page 77) to your Poodles.mov file
   tell application "QuickTime Player"
       activate --Bring QuickTime forward
       open file locOfMovie --Open Poodles.mov
       present the front movie --Play the movie full-screen
   end tell
   ```

7. **Save your script again.**

   If you try to run your script from Script Editor, you'll get an error message, because AppleScript thinks *path to me* is referring to Script Editor *itself*, not your specific script. To get around this problem, simply close your Script Editor window and run your script by double-clicking its icon in the Finder.

Rotating a Movie

In addition to simply showing movies at a different size, QuickTime can *rotate* a movie—and it'll play just fine in its rotated state. It's the perfect solution if you accidentally videotaped your sister's wedding at a 90-degree angle.

Here's a script that rotates whatever movie you drag to the script's icon by 90 degrees—and then starts the footage rolling:

```
--Part 1:
on run
    display dialog "Drag a movie onto my icon to rotate and play it"
end run

--Part 2:
on open selectedItem
    if (selectedItem count) > 1 then
        display dialog "Sorry, you dragged more than one movie onto my icon."
    --Part 3:
    else
        tell application "QuickTime Player"
            activate
            open selectedItem
            --Part 4:
            rotate the front movie by 90
            play front movie
        end tell
    end if
end open
```

Note: Just like the script on page 141, this script is a *droplet*. That means you have to save it as an Application before the script will work properly.

Here's how the code works:

- **Part 1** runs only if you double-click the script without dragging a movie to it. In that case, you'll see a dialog box with instructions for what to do—namely, "drag a movie onto my icon to rotate or play it."

- **Part 2** (and all the subsequent parts) runs if you *do* drag a movie to the script's icon. First, the script checks whether you dragged more than one movie—if you did, it presents an error dialog box.

Note: This script chooses to work with only one movie because QuickTime Player can become jerky when playing several movies at once. If you want to do away with this one-movie limitation, though, just erase the *if* statement.

And if you'd like to be able to watch multiple *unrotated* movies with this script–say, so you can see several views of your sister's wedding simultaneously–delete both the *if* statement and the *rotate the front movie by 90* line..

- **Part 3** brings QuickTime Player forward, and opens a new window for the movie you dropped on top of the script's icon.

• **Part 4,** finally, rotates your movie clockwise by 90 degrees and starts playing it (Figure 8-9).

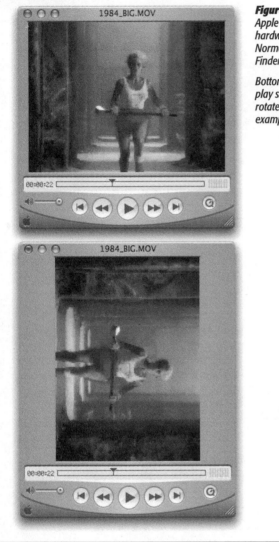

Figure 8-9:
Apple's famous 1984 commercial (http://www.apple.com/ hardware/ads/1984/), playing in two different modes. Top: Normally, if you simply double-clicked the movie's icon in the Finder, this is what you'd see.

Bottom: However, if you run this script, you'll see your movie play sideways, like this. (For even more fun, use AppleScript to rotate your movies by irregular numbers of degrees—96.7, for example.)

Tip: To rotate your movie counterclockwise, you can use a negative number with the *rotate* command (for instance, *rotate the front movie by –45*). Alternatively, you can simply use a positive number greater than 180 (*rotate front movie by 315,* for example, would accomplish the same thing).

Beyond these features, QuickTime Player has many other capabilities, too. Download Apple's well-commented sample scripts from *www.apple.com/applescript/ quicktime/* for more scripting inspiration, and don't forget to check out QuickTime

Player's dictionary (File → Open Dictionary, Shift-⌘-O) for a list of additional AppleScript commands

---

POWER USERS' CLINIC

DVD Player

If you're one of the lucky Mac owners with a DVD drive, you've got a whole set of extra AppleScript commands at your service. The DVD Player program (in your Applications folder) has a dictionary that includes such useful commands as *step DVD* (for skipping ahead one movie frame at a time) and *go* (for quickly jumping to the DVD's main menu or title screen).

The truth is, though, Apple's done most of the hard work for you. DVD Player includes its own Script menu (page 12), where you can access a bunch of useful, built-in scripts to control all facets of your DVD watching. Here's what they do:

- **Open Script Folder** takes you to your Home → Library → Application Support → DVD Player Scripts folder, which is where Mac OS X stores the files that appear in DVD Player's Script menu. You can add or remove any scripts you want from here; ones that end in "-.scpt" appear as divider bars in the menu. (If you'd like your DVD Player scripts to appear in the *global* Script Menu as well [page 12], Option-⌘-drag the files from this folder into your Library → Scripts folder to create aliases there.)

- **Go to Chapter** lets you choose what segment of a DVD you want to jump to. It's a lot easier than flipping back to the DVD's Chapter Selection screen, that's for sure.

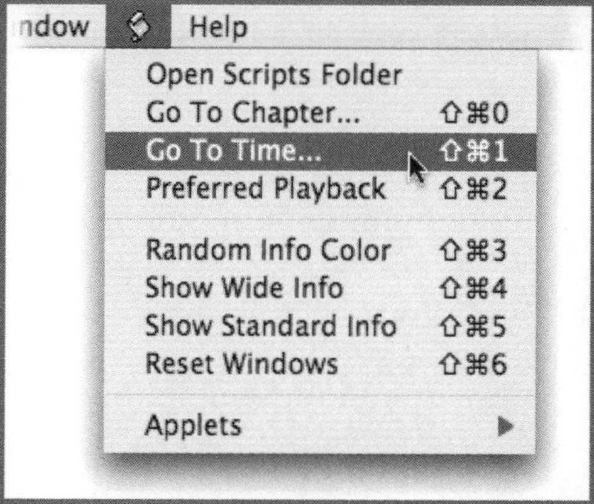

(menu screenshot showing:)
ndow | Help
Open Scripts Folder
Go To Chapter...   ⇧⌘0
Go To Time...   ⇧⌘1
Preferred Playback   ⇧⌘2
Random Info Color   ⇧⌘3
Show Wide Info   ⇧⌘4
Show Standard Info   ⇧⌘5
Reset Windows   ⇧⌘6
Applets   ▶

- **Go to Time** lets you pick a specific time in the movie to jump to. If you remember that an action sequence starts exactly 23 minutes and 42 seconds into a movie, for instance, this command can get you there in a snap.

- **Preferred Playback** is a shortcut for using Apple's optimum DVD Player settings. That involves a full-screen DVD window and a horizontal Controller window, among other minor preferences.

- **Random Info Color**, an utterly useless script, uses randomly colored text for the Info window, which shows the title and chapter of the movie you're watching.

- **Show Wide Info** and **Show Standard Info** let you switch between the two display modes of the Info window: either square with big text (Standard) or rectangular with small text (Wide).

- **Reset Windows** sets your DVD Player windows to their factory-fresh size and position.

Finally, the Applets submenu has three extra scripts:

- **Changing Info Color** continuously changes the text color in the Info window. It's totally useless but kinda fun to watch.

- **Loop Movie** plays your movie—and then plays it over and over again from the beginning when it finishes playing. You could use this if you'd made a corporate DVD for a trade show, for example, but didn't want to hover over your computer and keep restarting the DVD by hand

- **Preview Movie** plays the first few seconds of each scene, much like the script on page 151 does for iTunes music. If you need to prepare a next-day movie review for a newspaper article, this trick lets you watch a DVD in only a fraction of the time that it takes to watch the entire thing.

Internet and Network Scripting

Of all the operating systems available today, Mac OS X is by far the easiest to network. All Macs include not only a modem (for dial-up Internet access) but also an Ethernet port (for high-speed Internet access, computer-to-computer networking, or both). Today's Mac laptops even come with a built-in AirPort card for *wireless* networking—and you can install such a card for less than $100 in any other Mac made in the past few years.

The point of this chapter, however, isn't to show you how to network computers together, or even how to get connected to the Internet. If that's what you're interested in, switch to the Finder, choose Help → Mac Help and search for *networking*.

What this chapter *is* for is to introduce you to AppleScript's powerful control of Internet and networking programs. You'll learn how to script Safari (Apple's Web browser), Mail (Apple's email program), and iChat (Apple's instant-messaging program). And along the way, you'll get a deeper look into AppleScript's powerful interaction with all facets of the Web.

Note: The example scripts from this chapter can be found on the AppleScript Examples CD (see page 24 for instructions).

Internet Connect

If you connect to the Internet using a dial-up modem or an AirPort wireless card, Internet Connect is your best friend. Located in your Applications folder, Internet Connect lets you connect and disconnect to the Internet at will. And if you're having connection problems, Internet Connect can help by showing you how strong your wireless signal is.

Even better, Internet Connect is 100% scriptable. If you want to automate your connecting, the Internet Connect/AppleScript combo makes it a cinch.

Dialing Up to the Internet

Dial-up connections, while only a fraction the speed of DSL or cable, have a number of unique advantages. For one thing, dial-up is much cheaper—about 20% the cost of a high-speed connection, in many areas. For another, dial-up connections are available *everywhere*—a major advantage if you happen to live in Guam. Plus, you can access a dial-up connection even when traveling, as long as there's a phone jack where you're going.

The best part about a dial-up connection, however, is that you can create an AppleScript to automatically connect you to the Internet, wherever and whenever you want. Here's how:

Note: If you connect to the Internet using a high-speed connection, turn off your connection before trying this dial-up script.

```
set thePhoneNumber to the text returned of (display dialog ¬
    "Please enter the phone number to connect to:" default answer "")
set theUsername to the text returned of (display dialog ¬
    "Please enter your username:" default answer "")
set thePassword to the text returned of (display dialog ¬      \
    "Please enter your password:" default answer "")
tell application "Internet Connect"
    --This is the part that actually connects:
    connect to telephone number thePhoneNumber as user theUsername ¬
        with password thePassword
end tell
```

Using a series of three dialog boxes (Figure 9-1), that script is all you need to dial up to the Internet.

Tip: If you regularly connect to the same phone number, you might as well preprogram your connection information into Internet Connect → Internal Modem. On the other hand, if you just want to test out a new dial-up phone number *once,* the previous script is a quick, painless way to go about it.

Finding AirPort Signal Strength

Surfing the Internet wirelessly is great, but it's got some annoying requirements. First, you need a wireless card to insert into your Mac. Next, you need a wireless *base station*—a small device that broadcasts your Internet connection throughout your house or apartment. Finally, you have to be within range of the base station— usually a few hundred feet—to pick up the wireless signal on your Mac.

The trouble is, if you have a laptop, the signal strength changes as you move around. Taking the computer from your kitchen to your basement, for example, could make the signal twice as weak. Of course, the weaker your signal is, the slower you'll be able to connect to the Internet, so you should find the part of your house that has the best signal.

Like so many other tasks, AppleScript makes this quite easy. Simply run the following script, and you'll get a dialog box whenever your signal is exceptionally strong—or exceptionally weak—as you walk around your house:

```
--Part 1:
tell application "Internet Connect"
    set strongestSignalSoFar to the signal level of AirPort configuration 1
    set weakestSignalSoFar to the signal level of AirPort configuration 1
end tell
--Part 2:
repeat
    delay 3
    --Part 3:
    tell application "Internet Connect"
        set currentSignal to the signal level of AirPort configuration 1
    end tell
    --Part 4:
    if currentSignal > strongestSignalSoFar then
```

Figure 9-1:
Top: Type the phone number that your ISP (Internet Service Provider) gave you to connect to the Internet. (Unfortunately, if you use AOL, this won't work.)

Middle: Type your Internet account's user name; capitalization matters.

Bottom: Type your password (capitalization still matters). Make sure no one's looking over your shoulder, though, because AppleScript shows your password in plain text.

```
        display dialog "You're getting the strongest signal so far: " ¬
            & currentSignal & "%"
        set strongestSignalSoFar to currentSignal
    --Part 5:
    else if currentSignal < weakestSignalSoFar then
        display dialog "You're getting the weakest signal so far: " &
currentSignal & "%"
        set weakestSignalSoFar to currentSignal
    end if
end repeat
```

Here's how the script works:

- **Part 1** gets the current strength of your AirPort connection, on a scale from 0 (no signal at all) to 100 (standing right next to your base station). The script then places the signal strength in both the *strongestSignalSoFar* and *weakestSignalSoFar* variables. Later in the script, you'll refer back to these variables to check if your signal is at its highest or lowest level yet.

Note: When scripting Internet Connect, you have to refer to *AirPort configuration 1* rather than just *the AirPort configuration* (which would make more sense). That's because, in theory, you could have more than one AirPort card connected to your Mac, and Internet Connect needs to know which one you're referring to.

- **Part 2** starts a *repeat* loop, pausing for 3 seconds each time before it proceeds. Since you don't include a specific number right after the *repeat* statement, your script will repeat its signal-checking code until you either click Cancel in a dialog box or click Stop in Script Editor.

- **Part 3** gets AirPort's signal strength at the moment and puts it into the *currentStrength* variable.

- **Part 4** compares the current signal to your previously strongest signal. If the current signal is stronger, you see a dialog box telling you that you're getting exceptionally good reception (the script then updates the *strongestSignalSoFar* variable to reflect your new, stronger signal).

- **Part 5** on the other hand, shows you a different dialog box (Figure 9-2), if your signal is the *weakest* it's been so far. That's a sure sign that you should avoid using your wireless connection in that part of your house.

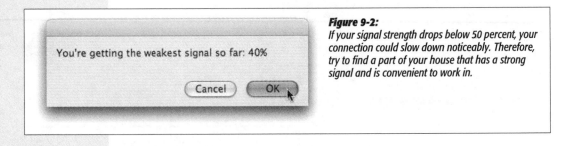

Figure 9-2:
If your signal strength drops below 50 percent, your connection could slow down noticeably. Therefore, try to find a part of your house that has a strong signal and is convenient to work in.

Run the script, and then start walking around your house. As you go from room to room, you'll notice your signal strength fluctuate. Once you find a room with a strong signal (ideally 60% or higher), you can sit down and surf the Web, confident that you're not losing speed to poor reception.

Tip: Don't forget to walk *outside* with your laptop, too. You might get a strong signal on your front porch, for example, which would let you browse outside in your rocking chair on a nice summer day.

Safari

For years, Microsoft was the dominant company in Mac Internet programs. Internet Explorer (IE), Microsoft's Netscape-devouring Web browser, came preinstalled on all Macs, and with good reason: for a while, IE was the fastest, least crash-prone Web browser available on the Mac.

However, as time went on, Microsoft slowed down development on Internet Explorer for Mac. Other Web browsers began to join the crowd: OmniWeb, Mozilla, Camino (formerly known as Chimera), Opera, and other similarly strange-named programs. Soon Apple decided to join the party, with its own browser named Safari. With emphasis on speed and simplicity, Safari quickly eclipsed Internet Explorer as a favorite of Mac fans worldwide. In fact, more than a million people downloaded Safari within the first *two weeks* of its existence.

Opening Web Sites

The simplest thing you can do with any Web browser is, of course, load a Web site. Thanks to AppleScript, however, you can load *multiple* Web sites, automatically and without fuss, by commanding Safari. That way, you can use AppleScript to load all your favorite Web sites as you're eating breakfast and come back to find all your pages just waiting to be read.

Here's how:

```
tell application "Safari"
    activate
    open location "http://www.apple.com/"
    open location "http://www.apricot.com/"
    open location "http://www.banana.com/"
end tell
```

The *open location* command lets you tell Safari what sites to load; if you have multiple *open location* commands, Safari will load multiple pages for you. (As described on page 199, *open location* has a number of other Internet-related uses as well.)

Opening Web sites within the same window

The trouble with your current script is that Safari loads each Web site in a separate window—a recipe for massive screen clutter. The problem gets even worse if you add extra *open location* commands to the script, since Safari will have to open even *more* windows to load your Web sites.

Luckily, Safari has a helpful feature, called *tabbed browsing*, to cut down on this window overload. When you turn on tabbed browsing (in Safari → Preferences → Tabs), you get to open multiple Web sites within the *same* window, with each site getting its very own "tab" at the top of the window. That way, you can browse your favorite 10 Web sites without opening 10 separate windows.

FREQUENTLY ASKED QUESTION

Scripting Other Browsers

I use a Web browser besides Safari. Am I left out of the AppleScript party?

If you visit banking or gaming Web sites a lot, you might prefer to use a more widely compatible browser than Safari. Or, if you're just the power-user type, Safari might not give you the features you crave. Either way, there are plenty of alternative Web browsers.

Depending on the browser you choose, though, you'll get a much different dose of AppleScript control. Every Web browser supports the *open location* command (page 199), but beyond that, the differences are huge. Here are your options:

*   **OmniWeb** (*www.omnigroup.com/applications/omniweb/*) is just about the most powerful Web browser money ($30) can buy. Its powerful *workspaces* feature, for instance, lets you cluster your favorite Web sites into specific windows. Even better, OmniWeb has the sort of AppleScript control that would make even Safari blush: the *check* command (for seeing if one of your Favorites has changed since the last time you visited the page) and the *bookmark* class (for creating your own Favorites from AppleScript) are just a couple examples.

*   **Internet Explorer** (*www.microsoft.com/mac/ie/*) is Microsoft's Web browser. Since it hasn't been updated in a few years (and won't be updated ever again for the Mac), it's missing a lot of Safari's features: pop-up blocking, tabs for different sites within one window, and so on. Still, if you use Internet Explorer for compatibility with certain Web sites, you'll be happy to know that it has its own complete scripting dictionary to rival Safari's.

*   **iCab** (*www.icab.de*) is a sort of souped-up Internet Explorer. In other words, it supports all the AppleScript commands that Internet Explorer does—and a few more. If scriptability is important to you, you'll be glad to know that iCab supports such useful commands as *cancel progress* (for stopping downloads) and *enter kiosk mode* (for browsing the Web full-screen).

*   **Mozilla** (*www.mozilla.org/products/mozilla1.x/*) is a complete Web-browsing, email-reading, carpet-cleaning program—the Microsoft Office of Web browsers. Unfortunately, its complete feature set doesn't extend to its AppleScript support; its abysmal dictionary supports only *four* commands—and unhelpful ones at that.

*   **Netscape** (*www.apple.com/downloads/macosx/internet_utilities/netscape.html*) is essentially a copy of Mozilla with a different look. Its AppleScript support is also identical to Mozilla's—that is to say, terrible.

*   **Camino** (*www.mozilla.org/products/camino/*), another spin-off of the Mozilla project, has impressed thousands of Mac fans with its friendly, Mac-like interface. Unfortunately, Camino has no AppleScript dictionary whatsoever.

*   **Firefox** (*www.mozilla.org/products/firefox/*) is yet another spin-off of the Mozilla project. Unlike Mozilla and Netscape, however, Firefox is *only* a Web browser—and a fast, customizable one at that. However, Firefox sadly lacks a powerful dictionary.

*   **Opera** (*www.opera.com/download/*) is a speedy, powerful, and expensive ($40) Web browser. If you're looking for AppleScript support, stay far away; Opera has none either.

Normally, you create additional tabs inside a window with the File → New Tab command (⌘-N). Then you type the URL of the page you want to open into the Address bar, and press Return to load the page. (By repeating this process, you can create additional tabs inside the same window.)

There's another timesaving way to use tabs, though. If you choose Safari → Preferences → General and pick "Open links from applications: in a new tab in the current window," your existing script will not only open multiple Web sites for you, but the script will open all the Web sites *inside the same window*. That way, when you run the script in the morning, you can come back from breakfast to find all your favorite Web sites open—but with only a single Safari window on the screen.

Tip: For even more usefulness, have Mac OS X run your favorite Web site script *automatically* when you log in to your Mac (page 33 has the directions).

Viewing a Site's Code

Whenever you type a URL in the Address bar and press Return, Safari goes out and fetches that site's *HTML code*—the instructions that tell your Web browser how to present the Web site onscreen. If you're a budding Web designer, this code (also called *source*) can help you understand how to build Web pages.

For example, by looking at a Web site's HTML source, you can see precisely how the Web designer laid out the page. Sometimes, you'll even find hidden notes that the Web designer embedded in the code, to remind himself why he coded something a particular way. If you have an interest in learning HTML, you ought to spend at least a little time browsing Web pages' source.

Once you've opened a page in Safari, you can examine the page's source by choosing View → View Source (Option-⌘-V). The trouble is, the code is uneditable in Safari; you can page through the commands, but you can't experiment by changing them.

That's where AppleScript comes in.

If you open Safari's AppleScript dictionary and look at the Safari Suite, you'll notice that every Safari document has a *source* property. With this information in hand, you can write a script that copies a Web page's source to a new TextEdit document, where you *can* edit the code:

Note: Of course, when you edit a Web page's source in this manner, you're actually editing a *copy* of the Web site; changes you make on your own computer won't take effect on the actual Web site that people visit.

```
--Part 1:
tell application "Safari"
    set pageSource to the source of the front document
end tell
```

```
--Part 2:
tell application "TextEdit"
    activate
    make new document at the front
    set the text of the front document to pageSource
end tell
```

Here's how your new script works:

- **Part 1** gets the HTML source of your frontmost Safari document (Figure 9-3, top). This part of the script then puts that information into the *pageSource* variable.

- **Part 2** activates TextEdit, creates a new document, and places the *pageSource* text into it (Figure 9-3, bottom). You're left with fully editable HTML code.

Tip: If you're interested in Web design and programming, check out a Web site like *www.htmlgoodies. com* to learn HTML. Once you're a little more experienced, look at a book like *Learning Web Design* or *HTML & XHTML: The Definitive Guide* (both from O'Reilly) for a more thorough explanation of the various display commands that make Web sites work.

Viewing a Site Without Formatting

There's a time for blinking Web ads, animated corporate logos, and flashy multimedia Web pages, but there's also a time for good old text. For instance, if you're looking at a page on a small screen, all the graphics can leave you with no room to read the actual content. Therefore, when you just want to get some quick information, it can be more helpful to have just a Web site's text than to have all the visual distractions that come along with it.

That's the logic behind the following script, at least. When you run the script, Safari extracts just the *text* from the front-most window, and places that text into a new TextEdit document. You'll end up with a simple, uncluttered window—no buttons, no links, and most importantly, no flashy banner ads:

```
tell application "Safari"
    set textVersion to (the text of the front document) --Gets just the text
end tell
tell application "TextEdit"
    activate
    make new document at the front
    --Put the text in TextEdit
    set the text of the front document to textVersion
end tell
```

Once you've got a plain-text version of a Web site with this script, it's easier to use AppleScript with the site, too. You can run the script from page 160, for example, to speak your text-only Web site out loud. Another option would be to use AppleScript to print out that text document for you, using the *print the front document* command directed at TextEdit. Then, on your train ride to work, you could catch up on the day's news without any of the annoying graphical fluff that usually gets printed.

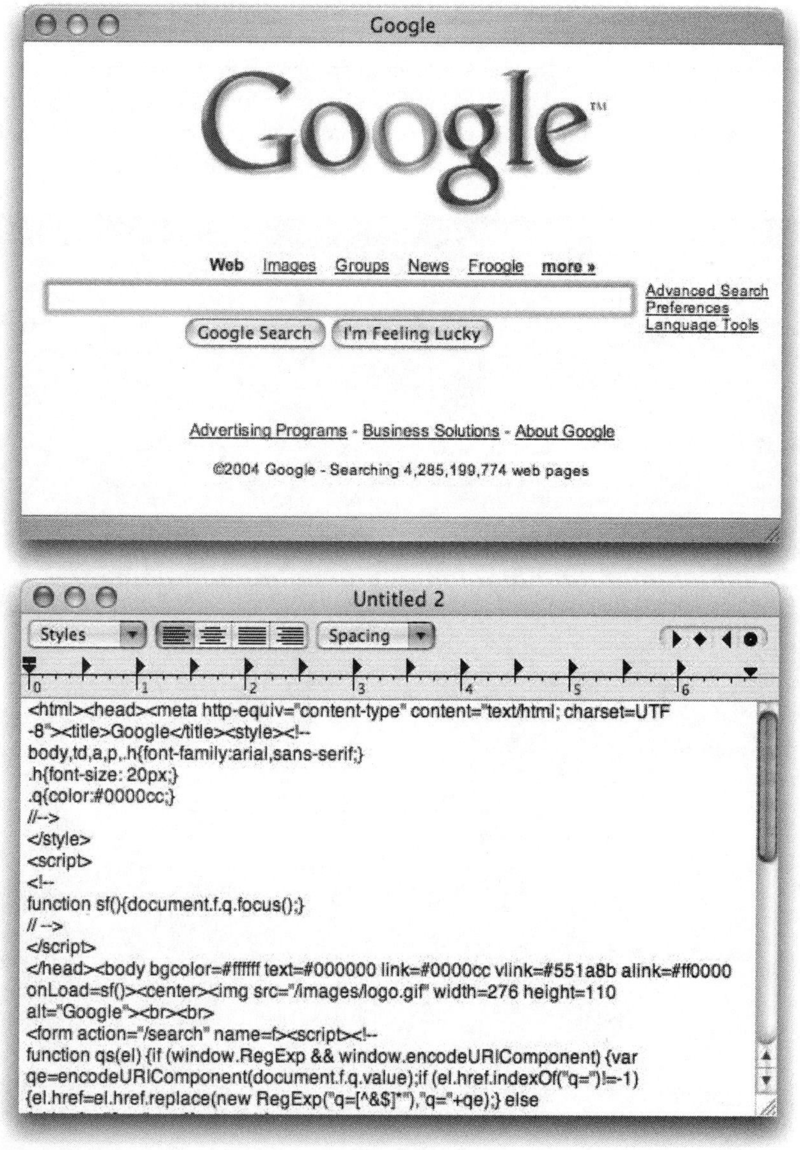

Figure 9-3:
Top: An open window in Safari. As it turns out, this document is no more than a series of HTML (HyperText Markup Language) commands.

Bottom: Run the script and you'll be able to see—and change—your copy of the site's source in TextEdit. Once you've modified the code to your liking, choose Format → Make Plain Text, and then choose File → Save. Make sure the file name ends in .html (otherwise, Mac OS X won't know that you're saving a Web page). When the Append dialog box appears, click Don't Append. Finally, navigate to your newly saved file in the Finder, and double-click it to see your changes in Safari.

Running AppleScripts from Safari

Script Editor is a great place to run your scripts, but you probably spend a lot more time in *Safari* every day than you do in Script Editor. Luckily, Safari has several different ways to run AppleScripts—some straightforward and some totally hidden.

Using these convenient tricks, you won't have to flip back to Script Editor every time you feel the proverbial "tug of the AppleScript."

Scripts that appear on Web pages

If you're browsing AppleScript Web sites (like those mentioned on page 309), you can simply select the AppleScript code you see on a Web page and choose Safari → Services → Script Editor → Run as AppleScript (page 74). In the background, Script Editor runs your script, and displays any dialog boxes along the way. That's a heck of a lot faster than selecting the script on the Web page, copying it from Safari, pasting the code in Script Editor, and then running the script from there.

POWER USERS' CLINIC

Running JavaScript Code in Safari

As described on page 44, JavaScript is an alternative language for controlling your Mac. More importantly, however, JavaScript is a language for automating the *Web*. It's what makes a Web site's buttons change color when you move your mouse over them, for example, and what lets you click the Print link on Mapquest.com to automatically bring up a Print dialog box. Even if you never write a line of JavaScript code yourself, you still use it dozens of times a day while browsing the Web.

Understanding this, Safari's programmers decided to include a special AppleScript command in Safari's dictionary: *do JavaScript*. When you provide that command with a line of JavaScript code (or even a few lines in a row) Safari obediently runs them—even if you haven't installed Late Night Software's (*www.latenightsoftware.com*) version of JavaScript for your entire Mac.

Now, a lot of what JavaScript can do in Safari is the same stuff you can do with AppleScript. For instance, if you wanted to print the current Web page, you could write either this (in pure AppleScript):

```
tell application "Safari"
    print the front document
end tell
```

or this (as an AppleScript/JavaScript hybrid):

```
tell application "Safari"
    do JavaScript "window.print( )" in the
front document
end tell
```

On the other hand, there are plenty of things in Safari that you can *only* do with JavaScript. For instance, the following script would display a dialog box that lists every link on the current Web page—something impossible to do with just AppleScript:

```
tell application "Safari"
    set theCode to "var links = document."¬
    & "links;"for(var i=0;i<DEFANGED_"¬
    & "links.length;i++){alert(\"Link#\"+"¬
    & "(i+1)+\":\"+links[i].href);}
    do JavaScript theCode in the front
document
end tell
```

If that code looks foreign to you, you're in good company; JavaScript is significantly uglier than AppleScript. If you're interested in pursuing JavaScript further, though, you can start out with something like *Designing with JavaScript* before moving on to a more reference-y book like *JavaScript: The Definitive Guide* (both books from O'Reilly).

And if you're just interested in some more code (without necessarily understanding how it works), Apple's written a number of JavaScripts just for Safari. Check out *www.apple.com/applescript/safari/bookmarks.html*, for example, for some useful JavaScripts that integrate Safari's features with Sherlock and iTunes.

If you want to *modify* a script you see on a Web page, though, you have no choice but to copy the code into Script Editor (Safari won't let you edit the text on Web pages). And while that might sound tedious, Safari's Services menu helps you out here, too. All you need to do is select the AppleScript code on the Web page and then choose Safari → Services → Script Editor → Make New AppleScript. That command copies the AppleScript code and then pastes it into a new Script Editor window for you automatically.

From there, all you need to do is compile and run the script to test it on your Mac and then make any code tweaks as you see fit. If the script runs to your satisfaction, just save it in your favorite location (like the Library → Scripts folder).

Mini-scripts in the Address bar

If there's a quick script you want to whip up—say, a single-line *display dialog* command—you can type it straight into Safari's Address bar, using this format:

```
applescript://com.apple.scripteditor?action=new&script=yourScriptCommands
```

In this special kind of URL, everything before *yourScriptCommands* is always the same. To substitute your own code, you simply replace *yourScriptCommands* with whatever commands you want, like this (type it all on one line):

```
applescript://com.apple.scripteditor?action=new&script=display dialog "My oh
my"
```

When you press Return in Safari's Address bar, a new Script Editor opens with your commands all written out for you. All you have to do is click Run, since Safari doesn't do that automatically (Figure 9-4).

Of course, that doesn't seem too earth-shattering. "Why don't I just type the commands directly into Script Editor?" you wonder.

As it turns out, you can use URLs in this format on your own Web pages. If you happen to maintain an online journal (or *Weblog*), for example, you can place an AppleScript URL like this right on a page, so that any viewers can click the link and see *your* code in Script Editor. In other words, the biggest benefit of AppleScript URLs isn't that you can use them on your own computer—it's that you can put them on the Internet so you can share your code with other people.

If you don't feel like memorizing that complicated URL format, though, you can simply type *applescript://* and press Enter to jump right to Script Editor from Safari.

Better yet, type *applescript://* and *don't* press Enter—instead, drag the globe icon from the Address bar to your Bookmarks bar. Safari asks you to name your new bookmark (call it something creative, like "Launch Script Editor"). From then on, you can simply click your bookmark in *Safari* to jump right to Script Editor.

Tip: For more information about AppleScript's special URL format—including a script to *create* URLs in this format—see *www.apple.com/applescript/scripteditor/12.html*.

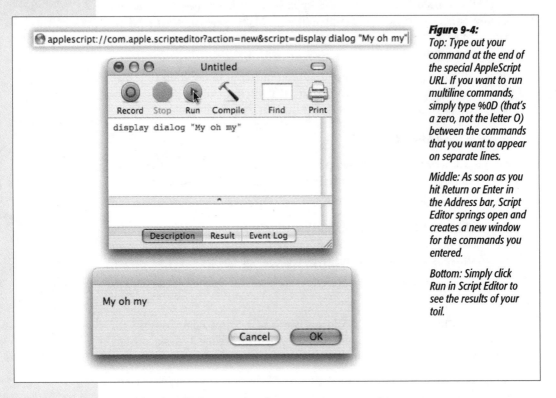

Figure 9-4:
Top: Type out your command at the end of the special AppleScript URL. If you want to run multiline commands, simply type %0D (that's a zero, not the letter O) between the commands that you want to appear on separate lines.

Middle: As soon as you hit Return or Enter in the Address bar, Script Editor springs open and creates a new window for the commands you entered.

Bottom: Simply click Run in Script Editor to see the results of your toil.

Saved scripts in the Favorites bar

If you've saved a script as an Application (page 33), you can run it from Safari's Favorites bar with ease. Here's how:

1. **Find the path to the application.**

   If you saved a script called **Hyena** as an application in your Library → Scripts folder, for example, the path would be */Library/Scripts/Hyena.app*.

2. **Type the path to the file into Safari's Address bar.**

   To get Safari to open a file for you, use *file:///* (yes, that's three forward slashes, not the two you normally see after *http:*), followed by the path to where the file lives on your Mac. For example, the file path for the Hyena.app script would look like this:

   ```
   file:///Library/Scripts/Hyena.app
   ```

   At this point, you could press Return to open the file (and, as a result, run the script). Or you could wait a few steps, to make that script a permanent fixture of Safari's Bookmarks bar.

3. Drag the mini-icon from Safari's Address bar into the Bookmarks bar (Figure 9-5, top).

This is a quick way to create a new bookmark.

4. **Enter a name for your bookmark (Figure 9-5, middle).**

This is the name that will appear in your Bookmarks bar, so try not to make it too long.

Now, whenever you want to run your script from Safari, simply click the script's name in the Bookmarks bar (Figure 9-5, bottom).

Tip: If the Safari scripts in this book don't leave you satisfied, visit *www.apple.com/applescript/safari/*. There, you'll find many more scripts, including a script for placing browser windows side-by-side and a script for sending a link to the current Web page in a new email message.

Figure 9-5:
Top: Using Mac OS X's special URL format, you can specify any file or folder on your hard drive. In this case, you enter the path to an AppleScript on your system.

Middle: When you drag the URL into your Bookmarks bar, you see this dialog box. (If you'd rather the bookmark appear in your Bookmarks menu, choose Bookmarks → Add Bookmark instead of dragging the URL to your Bookmarks bar.)

Bottom: Now, whenever you want to run your script, simply click it once in the Bookmarks bar. Or, if you prefer, you can use the key combination listed in the Bookmarks → Bookmarks Bar menu.

Address Book

In the same spirit of standardization that inspired Apple to create Safari, Mac OS X includes the Address Book program built-in. As *PIMs* (Personal Information Managers) go, Address Book is hardly the most advanced. Still, Address Book works wonderfully with Mail, synchronizes with other Macs (if you've paid for the $99-a-year .Mac service [page 92]), and, of course, Address Book is free.

What makes Address Book the darling of power users, however, is its AppleScript support. By sending simple commands to Address Book, you can:

• Find every one of your friends who's employed by a particular company (page 185).

- Create your very own *Smart Groups*, to sort your contacts by certain criteria (page 185).

- Write your own Address Book plug-ins, to add extra features to Address Book's shortcut menus (see below).

Writing Address Book Plug-ins

Try this: In Address Book, choose a contact and click the word "home" or "work" next to his phone number. You'll see a pop-up menu listing a few actions Address Book can perform on the phone number—Large Type (to display the number in monstrous digits) and Dial with Cell Phone (to automatically connect to the number using a Bluetooth-enabled cellphone), for example. This menu is a very powerful tool, but one overlooked by many beginners.

Even more powerful, however, is adding your own, customized actions. Address Book supports a special kind of plug-in for these menus, requiring no more than a few lines of AppleScript to create. Here's how you'd write a generic Address Book plug-in:

```
using terms from application ¬
    "Address Book"
    on action property
        return phone
    end action property

    on action title for thePerson ¬
        with phoneNumber
        return [whatever you want to
appear in the menu]
    end action title

    on should enable action for ¬
        thePerson with phoneNumber
        return true
    end action title

    on perform action for thePerson ¬
        with phoneNumber
        --this runs whenever you select
the menu item
    end perform action
end using terms from
```

To make the script actually *do* something, you can replace the italicized part of the *action title* handler with, for exam-

ple, "Copy Phone Number to Clipboard." Then you can replace the italicized comment in the *perform action* handler with a command like this:

```
set the clipboard to (the value of ¬
    phoneNumber) as string
```

Save the script (with the File Format set to Script) in your Library → Address Book Plug-Ins folder. Or, if you don't want other people who use your computer to run the script, save it in your *Home* → Library → Address Book Plug-Ins folder. (In either case, if the folder doesn't already exist, create it yourself.)

Once you restart Address Book, you'll see your new plug-in appear in every phone number's "home" or "work" menu. Simply click the Copy Phone Number to Clipboard command, and you'll automatically run your script's *perform action* handler. In other words, when you click the shortcut menu next to a phone number, the Copy Phone Number to Clipboard command does the same thing as selecting the phone number and choosing Edit → Copy.

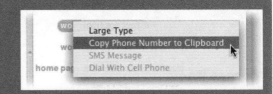

But feel free to replace the comment in the *perform action* handler with any AppleScript commands you want, to change how the plug-in works. And if you ever tire of writing Address Book plug-ins that simply work with phone numbers, *www.macosxhints.com/article.php?story=2003110614140491* (at the bottom of the page) has an example of a more complex AppleScript plug-in that displays a map for a particular *street address*.

And of course, you can always link Address Book commands with those of other programs, to create powerful workflow-automation scripts like the one on page 212.

Finding Contacts

At heart, Address Book is a database program. It's is great for storing contact information for your friends and business associates, and for keeping track of their birthdays, anniversaries, and more. When you add a new contact to your Address Book, that person's information gets stored in a simple database file. And when you click on someone's name, Address Book goes back into the database file, finds that person, and displays her information in Address Book's window—all without your ever seeing what's happening in the background.

If you use AppleScript, though, you can take this person-finding to a whole new level. For instance, if you want to display all your Address Book buddies who work for Umlaut Enterprises, you could use this script:

```
tell application "Address Book"
    set thePeople to (the name of every person whose organization is ¬
        "Umlaut Enterprises") --thePeople is now a list of employees' names
end tell
set selectedPerson to (choose from list thePeople) --Presents that list
```

On the other hand, that script is pretty strict; if one of your friends works for Umlaut Enterprises, *LLC,* your script won't find her, since her company isn't precisely "Umlaut Enterprises." To work around that problem, you can simply make this small tweak:

```
tell application "Address Book"
    set thePeople to (the name of every person whose organization contains ¬
        "Umlaut")
end tell
set selectedPerson to (choose from list thePeople)
```

Now your script will find all your friends who work for *any* company with the word "Umlaut" in its name. (Of course, you should replace "Umlaut" with the name of any company whose employees are in your Address Book.)

Tip: You can narrow down your list of contacts using other criteria, too: email address (to find all contacts with *apple.com* addresses), phone number (to find contacts only within your area code), or instant-messaging screen name (to get all contacts who use AOL Instant Messenger), for example. For a complete list of the possibilities, open Address Book's dictionary in Script Editor, and select Address Book Script Suite → Classes.

Adding Contacts to a Group

Of course, the previous script gives you the same ability as Address Book's built-in search field (Edit → Find → Find, or ⌘-F). For true power, you can create the equivalent of iPhoto's smart albums feature (page 127), making entirely new *groups* to list contacts that match certain criteria. That way, you can keep a permanent list of all your friends who work for Umlaut Enterprises, for example, so you can email them as a group.

To create a new Address Book group from the result of your previous script, simply make the following tweaks:

```
tell application "Address Book"
    --Part 1:
    make new group with properties {name:"Umlauters"}
    --Part 2:
    add (every person whose organization contains "Umlaut") ¬
        to group "Umlauters"
    --Part 3:
    save addressbook
end tell
```

Here's how the script works:

- **Part 1** creates a new Address Book group named "Umlauters." Just like iTunes and iPhoto, Address Book lists groups in its left pane. (If you don't see a left pane, choose View → Card and Columns, or press ⌘-1.)

Tip: For a refresher on the *with properties* option, see page 89.

- **Part 2** finds all the employees of Umlaut Enterprises you have in your Address Book and then adds them to the group you created in part 1.

- **Part 3** is an unusual command, and one that's needed only in Address Book. If you left out this command, you wouldn't see any changes when you switched back to Address Book—at least, not until you restarted the program. However, since you *do* include this command, Address Book knows to update its window to show you the new group from part 1.

Now, if you wanted to send an email message to everyone who works for Umlaut Enterprises, you could simply create a new message in Mail and address it to "Umlauters". Then, Mail would take a look in Address Book, see that you have a group entitled Umlauters, and automatically substitute the email addresses of everyone who works for Umlaut Enterprises in the email message's "To:" field.

Mail

Back in the days of Mac OS 9, every Mac came with a copy of Microsoft's Outlook Express for handling email. But even though Outlook Express worked fine, many Mac users resorted to using third-party, more powerful mailers like Eudora and Netscape Communicator. Nowadays, though, Mac OS X comes with Apple's homegrown email program, simply named Mail. (How many engineers does it take to name an email application? Knowing Apple, probably a dozen or so.)

Mail has plenty of convenient features—too many, in fact, to list individually in this book. If you enjoy bragging to your friends about your email client (you know who you are), see *www.apple.com/macosx/features/mail/* for a list of talking points.

Otherwise, read on to learn how AppleScript can simplify your emailing life.

Checking for New Messages

If there's one thing Mail's good at, it's checking for new messages. In fact, if that's the sort of thing you find exciting, you can use any of these four different methods:

- **Choose Mailbox → Get New Mail → In All Accounts (Shift-⌘-N).** Or, if you'd only like to check mail in a *specific* account, choose Mailbox → Get New Mail → [Whatever account you want to check].

- **Click the Get Mail button in Mail's toolbar.** Of course, if you've chosen View → Hide Toolbar (to save screen space, for example), this method isn't an option.

- **Control-click Mail's icon in the Dock, and then choose Get New Mail from the shortcut menu.** This trick works as long as Mail is open—even if it's not the frontmost program.

- Use AppleScript's *check for new mail* **command.** You can either send the command alone, to check all your mailboxes:

```
tell application "Mail"
    check for new mail --Checks all mailboxes
end tell
```

or add the *for* option, to check only a specific mailbox:

```
tell application "Mail"
    check for new mail for account "Mac.com"
end tell
```

Note: The previous script only works if you've subscribed to Apple's .Mac service (page 92). Otherwise, simply substitute the name of one of your *own* accounts for "Mac.com".

For total convenience, save either of these scripts as an application (page 92), and drop it onto your Dock. Then, even if Mail isn't already open, clicking your script will launch Mail and force it to check for new messages.

Mailboxes, Etc.

Mail has an unusual way of thinking about your email. In Mail's world, every message you have is stored inside a *mailbox*, and every mailbox you have is stored inside of an *account*. For instance, you might have a message that says "Cheese Soufflé" in its subject line, which you've neatly tucked inside a mailbox called Cooking Recipes. That mailbox, in turn, might be stored inside your Mac.com account (Figure 9-6).

Once you understand this hierarchy, it's easy to understand why Mail scripts seem so complicated at first glance.

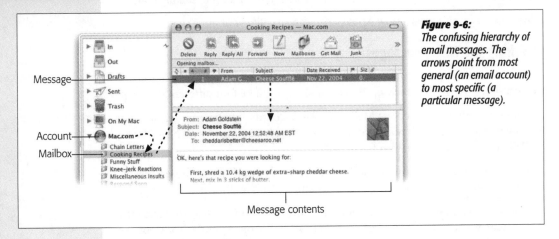

Message

Account

Mailbox

Message contents

Figure 9-6:
The confusing hierarchy of email messages. The arrows point from most general (an email account) to most specific (a particular message).

Finding mailboxes with unread messages

Open Mail, and take a look at its Dock icon. If you have any new mail, you see a red circle with a number inside; this number tells you how many new unread messages you have. The trouble is, the icon doesn't tell you which *mailbox* the new mail is in. That extra piece of information could go a long way, for example, toward telling you whether you should read the mail right away (if it's in your Personal account) or whether you can put it off until later (if it's in your Business account).

As you'd expect by now, AppleScript can help. When you run the following script, you'll see a dialog box listing the particular mailboxes that have new email. From there, you can double-click a mailbox's name to open it in Mail and read your new messages:

```
--Part 1:
set boxesWithUnreads to {}
--Part 2:
tell application "Mail"
    set allAccounts to every account
    --Part 3:
    repeat with currentAccount in allAccounts
        set allMailboxes to every mailbox of currentAccount
        --Part 4:
        repeat with currentMailbox in allMailboxes
            if the unread count of currentMailbox is not equal to 0 then
                --Part 5:
                set boxesWithUnreads to (boxesWithUnreads & ¬
                    the name of currentMailbox)
            end if
        end repeat
```

```
        end repeat
    end repeat
end tell
--Part 6:
set chosenBox to (choose from list boxesWithUnreads)
--Part 7:
tell application "Mail"
    activate
    repeat with currentAccount in allAccounts
        --Part 8:
        if exists mailbox (chosenBox as string) of currentAccount then
            set the selected mailboxes of the front message viewer to ¬
                {mailbox (chosenBox as string) of currentAccount}
        end if
    end repeat
end tell
```

Now, this script is the most complex you've seen so far. Don't run away, though—it can teach you loads about scripting Mail.

Tip: Since there are a bunch of new commands and classes in this script, it's a good idea to follow along in Mail's dictionary (page 44).

- **Part 1** sets the *boxesWithUnreads* variable to a plain, empty list. This list holds the names of all mailboxes with unread messages.

- **Part 2** gets a list of every account you use with Mail. If you've got a business email address and a Mac.com email address, for instance, they'll both be stored as separate items in the *allAccounts* variable.

- **Part 3** goes through the list of your accounts, one at a time, and finds all the mailboxes inside the current account. You might have an Inbox, Trash, and Sent folder within a single account, for example.

- **Part 4** goes through the list of mailboxes from Part 3 to see if any have unread messages. (In Mail, the *unread count* property lets you check how many messages are unread in a mailbox; therefore, any mailbox whose *unread count* isn't zero has messages waiting to be read.)

- **Part 5** only runs if the mailbox the script is checking has unread messages. This part simply adds the mailbox's name to the *boxesWithUnreads* list. In essence, this part ensures that *boxesWithUnreads* will hold a complete list of every mailbox with unread messages by the time the script hits part 6.

- **Part 6** presents a dialog box listing every mailbox with unread messages (in other words, the *boxesWithUnreads* list). Figure 9-7 shows one possibility.

Note: If you've deleted email but not erased Mail's Trash can yet (Mailboxes → Erase Deleted Messages → In All Accounts, or ⌘-K), you may see an extra mailbox in this dialog box: Deleted Messages.

Whatever mailbox you select, the *chosenBox* variable holds it. That variable is how Mail knows which mailbox to show you.

Figure 9-7:
When you run this script, you'll see a dialog box listing all the mailboxes with unread messages. Select one and click OK, and you'll jump straight to the mailbox. Or, if you've had enough new Chain Letters for the day, click Cancel to return to your work.

- **Part 7** brings Mail forward and then proceeds to search all your accounts again. This time around, however, it's searching for the account that contains the mailbox *you* selected in part 6.

- **Part 8** checks whether the current account does, in fact, contain the mailbox you selected in part 6. Here's where things get tricky. First, your script needs to

---

POWER USERS' CLINIC

Mail Rules!

On page 188, you wrote a script to display which mailboxes have new messages. The trouble is, *you* have to run this script. Even if you put the script in the Dock or your Script Menu to save time, you still have to run the script by hand.

That's where Mail's special *rules* feature comes in. A rule, in Mail's mind, is a set of criteria and actions: if a message that arrives matches the criteria, Mail runs the actions. Luckily for you, the actions you specify can include running an AppleScript. That means Mail can run a script *automatically* whenever a certain kind of message arrives. (Of course, before you can continue, you need to make sure you've saved the script you want to use.)

Simply visit Mail → Preferences → Rules, and click Add Rule. In the new dialog box, Mail lets you specify any criteria you want in the upper blue box. If you only want to run your script when an email arrives from an Apple employee, for example, you could specify "From" "Contains" "apple. com". On the other hand, if you want your script to run whenever *any* new email arrives, just choose "Every Message" from the upper blue box.

Now under the heading that says "Perform the following actions," select Run AppleScript. Click Choose, navigate to your saved script, and then click Choose File. Finally, click OK to eliminate the Rules dialog box, and drag your new rule to the very top of the list (to ensure your rule runs before any of the others). Now, whenever you receive a new message, Mail automatically runs your AppleScript!

That's only the beginning, though. If you have power-user aspirations, you can use Mail rules to create automatic email replies while you're on vacation (using the Apple-Script *reply* command), or even send messages onto another email address (using the *forward* command). No matter what your emailing goals, rules are an invaluable tool—especially when you link them with AppleScripts.

find the current *message viewer,* which is AppleScript's way of symbolizing the list of mailboxes and messages you see onscreen.

Next, your script must set the *selected mailboxes* property. This single property is what makes the difference between seeing your Inbox and the contents of your Trash can, for example.

Finally, your script has to convert the *chosenBox* variable from part 6 into a string because of a quirk in the *choose from list* command (page 108). Only then can the script select the mailbox you chose in part 6.

Note: You have to put the mailbox inside curly brackets because the *selected mailboxes* property expects to receive a *list* of the mailboxes you want selected.

That's it. Congratulations on making it through your first big script!

iChat Control

Instant messaging, a sort of real-time email system, is one of the most popular developments of the Internet age. You can chat with your grandma in Washington D.C., your dad in Wichita, or your sister in Walla Walla—all for free. In fact, instant messaging has become so popular that Apple developed its very own chat program: iChat.

Tip: If you've never signed up for an instant messaging account, visit *www.aim.com* and click Starting Out → Registration on the left side. Follow the online procedure, and in a few minutes, you'll end up with a free *screen name* (online identity) that you can use with iChat.

Now, iChat isn't just any chat program; it supports voice and video chats, too (assuming you have a microphone or video camera). Unfortunately, iChat's *AppleScript* support reaches only into the realm of text messaging—you can't automatically snap pictures with your Webcam, for example.

Still, if you're an AppleScript addict, there are several opportunities to sharpen your skills on iChat's text features. For example, you can let your online buddies know you're not available when your screen saver's running, or keep your buddies entertained with an endless parade of pithy quotes. Read on for the secrets.

Notifying iChat when the Screensaver's On

One of iChat's coolest features is that it lets you notify your friends as to whether you're around or not. When you're at your computer, you set your iChat status to *available;* when you're out, you set your status to *away* (and if, for some unthinkable reason, you actually disconnect from the Internet for once, you set your status to *offline*). Conveniently for you, AppleScript can do the same thing:

```
tell application "iChat"
    set the status to available --Or you can use away, or offline
end tell
```

Of course, that's nothing really unique. To add real power, you can have your script set your status to away only if your *screen saver* is running.

Tip: To enable your screen saver, visit System Preferences → Desktop & Screen Saver.

Here's how:

```
--Part 1:
on idle
    --Part 2:
    tell application "System Events"
        if (the name of every process) contains "ScreenSaverEngine" then
            --Part 3:
            tell application "iChat"
                set the status to away
            end tell
        end if
    end tell
    --Part 4:
    return 10
end idle
```

Now, before your script will run properly, you have to select File → Save. For the File Format, choose Application, and turn on the Stay Open checkbox, so your script continues running in the background all the time. Save the file wherever you want—but try to make it somewhere that's easy to access, because you can only run the script by double-clicking its icon in the Finder.

Here's how the code works:

- **Part 1** is an *idle* handler. To AppleScript, that means, "run the following code whenever this script isn't busy doing something else." To you, it means the script will run constantly—unlike most of your other scripts, which run and then quit themselves.

Note: *idle* handlers only work if you've turned on "Stay Open" in a script's Save dialog box.

- **Part 2** tells System Events (page 109) to get a list of all currently running programs on your system. Then the script checks whether that list contains Screen-SaverEngine—Mac OS X's program in charge of running screen savers.

  In other words, part 2 checks if your screen saver is running at the moment. If it is, the script proceeds to part 3.

- **Part 3** sets your iChat status to *away* if your screen saver is running. That way, your friends won't try to chat with you when your screen saver is blocking your chat windows.

- **Part 4** tells the *idle* handler to check back again in 10 seconds. The end result is that your script checks every 10 seconds whether your screen saver is running—and, if it is running, the script sets your iChat status to *away*.

Note: Once you turn your screen saver off, set your status back to *available* so your friends know that you're ready to chat again.

When your screen saver isn't playing, the only indication you'll have that your script is running is its icon in the Dock. Since you turned on Stay Open for the script, your code continues checking your screen saver forever (or at least until you Control-click its icon in the Dock and choose Quit from the shortcut menu).

Displaying a Random Status Message

In addition to telling your buddies what your status is, you can post a special message to your buddies, using iChat's *status message* setting. You might post some information on how to reach you while you're away, a pithy quote, or a link to a Web site you find particularly interesting.

Normally, you set your status message by clicking the small pop-up button at the top of iChat's Buddy List window (Figure 9-8). However, using AppleScript, you can set your status message automatically.

Figure 9-8:
Click this button to bring up a menu of status messages. If you don't like any of the built-in choices, choose Custom. (Status messages with green circles indicate that you're available; status messages with red squares indicate that you're away.)

Try a script like this:

```
tell application "iChat"
    set the status to away
    set the status message to ¬
        "I don't want to talk to you right now. Go away."
end tell
```

Of course, if you run that script and don't change your status message for a while, your buddies will get both bored *and* annoyed at your rudeness. Nowadays, not changing your status message regularly is the equivalent of not changing your bedsheets.

That's why changing the script to rotate among a few status messages is such a convenient modification. Edit the script as follows, and your witty, rotating status messages will entertain your friends even when you don't have time to:

```
--Part 1:
global messageList
```

```
--Part 2:
on run
    set messageList to {"Don't leave your seat, 'cause I'll be back soon", ¬
        "Stay Tuned!", ¬
        "The stuff I'm doing right now is more important than talking to you"}
end run

--Part 3:
on idle
    tell application "iChat"
        set the status to away
        set the status message to (some item of messageList)
    end tell
    --Part 4:
    return 600
end idle
```

Since your script uses the *idle* handler, you have to save it as an application, using the procedure from page 192. Once you've done that, you can run the script by double-clicking its icon in the Finder.

Here's how the parts breaks down:

- **Part 1** is what's known as a *declaration*. Essentially, the *global* keyword tells AppleScript, "The variable name that follows should be accessible anywhere in this script." If you left out this part, AppleScript would get confused when you used the *messageList* variable down in part 3, because it wouldn't know that you were referring to the same variable as in part 2.

- **Part 2** uses AppleScript's *run* handler (page 141) to define what happens when you double-click the script's icon in the Finder. In this case, the script simply prepares the *messageList* variable with a list of possible status messages, in anticipation of the list being used in part 3.

Tip: Feel free to customize *messageList* with any number of messages you want.

- **Part 3** uses an *idle* hander, just like the iChat script on page 192. In this case, however, your script picks a random message from *messageList* each time the *idle* handler runs, and then posts that random message in iChat. Think of it like a Magic 8 Ball, on a timer, for iChat.

- **Part 4** simply tells AppleScript to check back with your *idle* handler in 10 minutes (or, since AppleScript can only think in seconds, 600 seconds). At that point, your script starts at part 2 all over again, rotating in a new status message.

Note: Your script runs the *idle* handler every 10 minutes until you physically quit the script. You can do that in one of two ways: click the script's icon in the Dock and choose [Script's Name] → Quit from the menu bar, or Control-click (or right-click) the script's icon in the Dock and choose Quit from the shortcut menu.

If you like to keep your buddies posted on what you're doing, scripting iChat's status message is definitely the easiest way. Luckily, other people have already created some more scripts for you; the free iChat Script Collection (*http://cocoaobjects.com/applescript/ics/index.php*), for example, includes several scripts for posting a status message based on your currently playing iTunes track.

URL Access Scripting

Quick: Your friend just emailed you a link to a file on the Web. What do you do now?

If you're like most people, you open Safari (or some other Web browser), paste the URL in, press Return, and wait for the file to download. Life's too short to download files that way, though.

The easier approach is using *URL Access Scripting*, a built-in Mac program for downloading (and uploading) files in the *background*. As a simple, fast, invisible program, you can think of URL Access Scripting kind of like Image Events (page 137), just for the Web.

Downloading a File Quickly

When you want a file downloaded right this minute, the following script can help:

```
--Part 1:
set theURL to the text returned of (display dialog ¬
    "Enter the URL to download:" default answer "http://")
--Part 2:
set theFile to (choose file name)
--Part 3:
tell application "URL Access Scripting"
    download theURL to theFile
end tell
display dialog "Your download is complete"
```

Once you run that script, you'll see a series of three dialog boxes:

• The first asks what you want to download.

• The second asks you where you want to save the downloaded file.

• The third tells you that the file's been downloaded. (Figure 9-9 has the details.)

Lest the script confuse you, here's how it works:

• **Part 1** uses the standard *display dialog* command to ask you what file to download. You can specify a Web site, a specific page on a Web site, an online picture, or just about anything else you can get to using a Web browser or FTP program.

Note: An *FTP server* is simply a Web site whose purpose is to transfer *files*. That distinguishes it from a *Web server*, whose job it is to transfer actual Web pages.

- **Part 2** uses the *choose file name* command (page 97) to ask where you want to save the file. Your desktop is as good a place as any.

- **Part 3** uses URL Access Scripting to download the file you specified in part 1 and save the file in the location you specified in part 2. Once the download's finished, you see the final informative dialog box.

Note: Due to a bug in AppleScript, the Mac OS 9 version of URL Access Scripting might launch when you run this script. If that happens, pop open a Finder window and navigate your way to Mac OS 9's System Folder (the folder named "System Folder," *not* "System"). Then go to the Scripting Additions → URL Access Scripting subfolder, drag the URL Access Scripting file to the Trash, and empty the Trash can (Finder → Empty Trash).

From now on, your scripts will always use the new, Mac OS X version of URL Access Scripting instead of the obsolete, Mac OS 9 version.

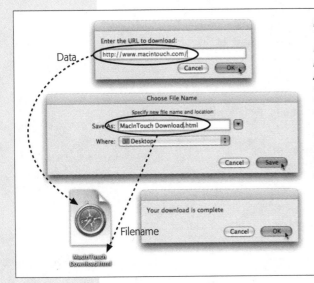

Figure 9-9:
Top: Enter the URL of the file you want to download. If you want a file from a Web site, make sure you preface the URL with http://. You're not limited to just Web sites, though—you can download files from FTP servers (preface the URL with ftp://) or even other Macs on your network (preface the URL with afp://).

Middle: Choose where you want to save the file, and give the file a name. Also, make sure you give the file an appropriate extension (.html for Web pages, .mov for QuickTime movies, and so on), or else Mac OS X won't know what program should open the file.

Bottom: Once the download is finished, two things happen. First, an icon appears in whatever location you specified (left). Soon after, you see a dialog box telling you the download is complete (right).

Uploading a File

While URL Access Scripting is convenient for downloading files, it can be even *more* convenient for uploading them. That way, you don't have to go through all the Finder's red tape (Go → Connect to Server, then type out the URL, choose the file to upload, drag the file to the server, and disconnect) when you want to upload a file. True, if you use URL Access Scripting, you won't get the full-fledged progress indicator that the Finder shows you as a file's being copied. Still, this AppleScript is just about the *fastest* way to upload something to the Internet:

```
--Part 1:
set theFile to (choose file)
--Part 2:
set theServer to (choose URL)
```

```
--Part 3:
tell application "URL Access Scripting"
    upload theFile to theServer with authentication without binhexing
end tell
display dialog "Your upload is complete"
```

Here's how the script works:

- **Part 1** uses the *choose file* command to let you pick the file you want to upload (Figure 9-10, top).

- **Part 2** uses *choose URL* (a command for locating computer servers on your network or the Internet) to ask you where you want to upload the file (Figure 9-10, middle).

Tip: If you have your own home page as part of the $99-per-year .Mac service (page 92), you can use that dialog box to upload files directly to your Web site. Simply type this URL:

> http://idisk.mac.com/*yourMemberName*/Sites/

but replace *yourMemberName* with your actual .Mac member name (which you can find in System Preferences → .Mac). In a snap, AppleScript uploads the file to your Web site, saving you the annoyance of having to load your iDisk (your virtual Web-storage disk) in the Finder with the Go → iDisk → My iDisk command.

Note, however, that due to a bug in the *upload* command, this script can only copy files *that don't have spaces in their names* to your .Mac Web site. If you need to upload files that have spaces in their names, you either have to rename the files to get rid of the spaces or load your iDisk in the Finder and copy the files by hand.

- **Part 3** does the actual deed, using URL Access Scripting to upload the file to the server. The *with authentication* bit tells AppleScript to present a password dialog box (Figure 9-10, bottom), and the *without binhexing* option tells Mac OS X not to use any special file encoding when uploading the file. In other words, this part simply copies the file you selected in part 1 to the server you selected in part 2, safely and securely.

Finally, the script presents a dialog box once the uploading is finished.

Congratulations: you just saved a small fortune on commercial Web-updating software.

Recalling Passwords

If there's one downside to this whole Internet concept, it's the sheer number of passwords you have to remember. You've got a password for your email address, one for your banking Web site, a bunch for connecting to computers on your network, one for eBay, Amazon.com, .Mac, PayPal—the list goes on and on. How on earth are you supposed to remember all of them?

Well, if you're like many people, you try to use the same password for everything—thereby sparing yourself the trouble of remembering several hundred different pass-

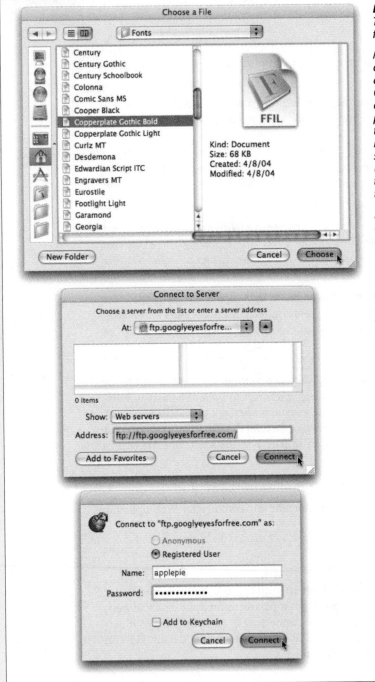

Figure 9-10:
Top: The script asks you to pick a file to upload.

Middle: Using AppleScript's special choose URL command (basically, a simplified version of the Finder's Go → Connect to Server command), the script asks you to pick the server you want to upload to. It can be a computer on your network, your Web site's FTP server, or even a Unix mainframe. (To make AppleScript remember the server in the future, click Add to Favorites.)

Bottom: The script asks for your user name and password. If you want to connect anonymously, try entering "anonymous" in the Name field and your email address in the password field. And, if you want AppleScript to remember your name and password in the future, turn on Add to Keychain.

words. Or perhaps you've realized that that method is very insecure (since if hackers get one of your passwords, they have access to *everything*), and you've decided to use a bunch of different passwords instead. Either way, you're risking something: either forgetting a password and locking yourself out, or inadvertently exposing your whole life to a malicious hacker.

That's why Mac OS X comes with a feature called *Keychains*—special clusters of passwords that you have access to simply by logging into your Mac. Introduced with Mac OS 9, Keychains are the perfect compromise: you only have to remember one password (your account's Keychain password) to automatically unlock all the other passwords you use. And no hacker can get access to your passwords unless they're sitting right in front of your Mac—a fairly remote possibility.

Of course, this book wouldn't even mention Keychains if you couldn't AppleScript them. Here's a simple example to list all the passwords being saved in your Keychain:

```
tell application "Keychain Scripting"
    set allKeys to the name of every key of keychain 1
end tell
choose from list allKeys --Lists all the keys for you
```

GEM IN THE ROUGH

Open Location

You've got Safari for opening Web sites, Mail for creating email messages, the Finder for connecting to Web severs, and any number of other programs for handling your other Internet jobs. The problem is, there's no single command for handling *any* Internet job—or so you might think.

Luckily, AppleScript includes the helpful *open location* command, which comes pretty close. For instance, you can use this command to open a Web page, without even using a *tell* statement:

```
open location "www.apple.com"
```

Of course, as shown on page 175, you *can* direct an *open location* command at a particular Web browser, if you want a particular browser to load the page. However, if you omit a *tell* statement, AppleScript locates your default Web browser (the one you set in Safari → Preferences → General) and opens the Web page in that browser.

Perhaps even more conveniently, though, you can use *open location* to create a new email message in your preferred email program. Here are a few possibilities:

```
--Create a blank email message:
open location "mailto:"
--Create a message addressed to someone:
open location "mailto:stevejobs@apple.com"

(* Create a message with an address and a
subject: *)
open location ¬
    "mailto:stevejobs@apple.com?subject:G6 Mac"
```

(For even more fun with *mailto* links, take a look at *http://www.ianr.unl.edu/internet/mailto.html*.)

Finally, you can use *open location* to connect to servers—both on the Internet and on your own network. If there were a Mac in your house named Santa, for example, you could open it over your network with a command like this:

```
open location "afp://Santa.local/"
```

Whether you want to open a Web page, email message, or network server, therefore, your first AppleScript instinct should always be to try the *open location* command.

This script searches through your Keychain and displays every *key* (or password-protected item) your Mac is set to remember. If you have a lot of passwords in your Keychain, this script could take a few seconds to run—and display a hugely long dialog box. If you've never used the Keychain Access utility before (Applications → Utilities), chances are you'll be amazed when you see how big this list is.

Note: As with the script on page 195, this script may not work properly if you have Mac OS 9 installed on your computer. To work around this problem, delete Keychain Scripting from Mac OS 9's System Folder → Scripting Additions folder, and then empty the Trash can.

One thing you'll notice, however, is that when you select one of the keys in the dialog box and click OK, nothing happens. And while seeing a plain list of your keys is useful for geek bragging privileges, that won't do much if you forget a password.

Luckily, you can modify your script to tell you the password to a key if you happen to forget it, like this:

```
tell application "Keychain Scripting"
    set allKeys to the name of every key of keychain 1
end tell
--Part 1:
set keyName to (choose from list allKeys)
--Part 2:
tell application "Keychain Scripting"
    tell keychain 1
        set chosenKey to the first key whose name is (keyName as string)
```

POWER USERS' CLINIC

Using Web Services with SOAP and XML-RPC

If you've spent some time picking around in your computer's built-in scripts, you may have noticed that the ones in your Library → Scripts → Internet Services folder are pretty unique. Not only do those scripts connect to the Internet to get information for you (a stock quote, for example), but they do it without ever opening Safari, Mail, or any other Internet programs. To an everyday AppleScripter, this seems like magic. To you, intrepid scripter, this is simply an obstacle on your quest to complete AppleScript enlightenment.

The trick to these scripts is a special kind of Internet communication, commonly referred to as *Web services*. AppleScript can use two types of Web services—*SOAP* (Simple Object Access Protocol) and *XML-RPC* (Extensible Markup Language Remote Procedure Call)—but both types are essentially just a way to communicate between your computer and various online databases.

In AppleScript, you use either of two commands to interact with Web services: *call soap* or *call xmlrpc*. And to locate Web services on the Internet that you can use with AppleScript—from global thermometers to foreign-language dictionaries—browse a site like *www.xmethods.com*.

Unfortunately, the complex AppleScript syntax for Web services is far too involved to explain in this book (just take a look at your Internet Services scripts for proof). Thankfully, Apple has written an online book that explains everything you need to know to make AppleScript work with Web services; the document is available from *http://developer.apple.com/documentation/AppleScript/InternetWeb-date.html*.

```
        set chosenPassword to the password of chosenKey
    end tell
end tell
--Part 3:
display dialog "The password to the key you chose is " & chosenPassword
```

Here's how the new code works:

• **Part 1** lets you choose one of the keys, and then puts your choice into the *key-Name* variable.

• **Part 2** locates the key you chose (all your keys are stored in *keychain 1*, in AppleScript's mind), and then finds the key's password (*chosenPassword*). While this part of the script is running, AppleScript asks you to authorize Script Editor—just to make sure some remote hacker isn't trying to get a password without your permission (Figure 9-11).

• **Part 3**, finally, displays a dialog box with the password for the key you chose.

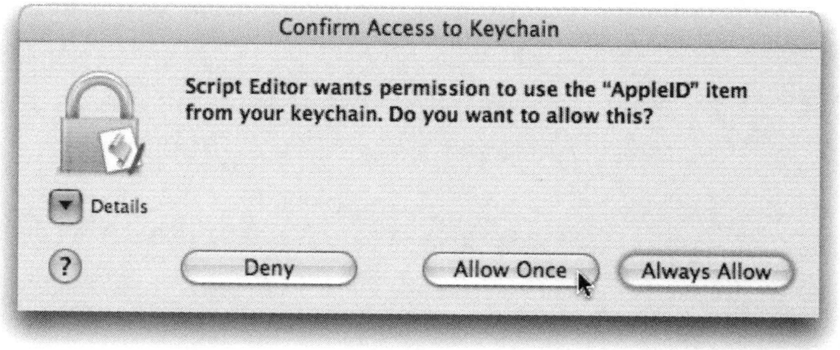

Figure 9-11:
Whenever you try to access a password from your Keychain, you see this dialog box. In fact, if you run the script from Script Editor, you actually see this dialog box twice (don't worry—it's just Mac OS X being its typical safety-freak self). If you want to proceed with the script, press Allow Once (to authorize Script Editor to display a password just this once—the most secure method). Or, if you're into convenience, click Always Allow, and Script Editor will never ask you to authorize it again. Of course, to prevent AppleScript from displaying your password at all, just click Deny.

Now that you know how convenient Keychains are, make sure to click Add to Keychain in *any* program's dialog box that has a password you want Mac OS X to remember. Then, if you forget that password in the future, you can run this script to retrieve it

Organizing Information in Databases

It might seem geeky, but databases are a cornerstone of computing. They're absolutely *everywhere*—from iTunes's jukebox feature to Amazon.com's book listings. Even if you haven't bought a dedicated database program like FileMaker Pro (page 209), you encounter databases every day in your regular computer work.

"But what *is* a database?" you're probably wondering. A database is a computerized information table—a spreadsheet, in essence. If you imagine turning an Excel document into a database, for example, each row in the spreadsheet would correspond to a *record* (entry) in the database, while each column in the spreadsheet would correspond to a *field* (specific information in an entry) of the database. Group a bunch of records together, and voila! You have a database.

Note: The example scripts from this chapter can be found on the AppleScript Examples CD (see page 24 for instructions).

Record Notation

In AppleScript, you use the special *record* data type to store database information, much like how you use the *list* data type (page 105) to store ordered sets of information. To create a record in AppleScript, you use this format:

```
set recordName to {fieldName:fieldData, otherFieldName:otherFieldData, ...}
```

You've already used this notation, although perhaps without knowing it, for the *make* command's *with properties* option (page 89). Record notation is useful for far more than just AppleScript commands, though; records are also convenient for storing clusters of information.

Say you wanted to create a database entry for a chicken (storing its nickname, weight, and height). You could use this code to do the deed:

```
set myChicken to {nickname:"Matthew", weightInPounds:20, heightInInches:26.5}
```

Then, if you wanted to access a specific piece of information from the record, you would use the ubiquitous *of* keyword:

```
set myChicken to {nickname:"Matthew", weightInPounds:20, heightInInches:26.5}
display dialog (nickname of myChicken) --Gets the data from myChicken record
```

But just seeing the *name* of the chicken probably seems pretty boring to you. By changing that script around a little, you can use AppleScript to pull information out of the record and string it together in an amusing dialog box message:

```
set myChicken to {nickname:"Matthew", weightInPounds:20,
    heightInInches:26.5}
display dialog (nickname of myChicken) & " the chicken weighs " & ¬
    (weightInPounds of myChicken) & " pounds. Man, that's one ¬
    big chicken!"
```

Now when you run the script, a dialog box appears to display the *nickname of myChicken* (Matthew) and the *weightInPounds of myChicken* (20). The result is a message that says: "Matthew the chicken weighs 20 pounds. Man, that's one big chicken!"

Note: Just like other AppleScript variables, you can also *set* the values inside a record using the *of* keyword. For instance, this script:

```
set myWardrobe to {shirts:7, pants:2}
set the shirts of myWardrobe to 6
```

updates the *shirts* value inside the *myWardrobe* record with 6 instead of 7.

Making a Simple AppleScript Database

AppleScript records can store just about any type of information you want. In the previous scripts, for example, you stored numbers and strings of text. But suppose you had the information from Table 10-1 and wanted to create a database from that.

Table 10-1. A sample of information you can put in a database

Name	Weight (in pounds)	Height (in inches)	Rooster?
Matthew	20	26.5	Yes
Colonel	15	22.3	Yes
Little	3	10.9	No

Here's how you'd encode that information in AppleScript:

```
set myChicken to {nickname:"Matthew", weightInPounds:20, ¬
    heightInInches:26.5, rooster:true}
set kfcChicken to {nickname:"Colonel", weightInPounds:15, ¬
    heightInInches:22.3, rooster:true}
set chickenLittle to {nickname:"Little", weightInPounds:3, ¬
    heightInInches:10.9, rooster:false}
set myDatabase to {myChicken, kfcChicken, chickenLittle} --Creates a database
```

As you can see, a simple AppleScript database is no more than a list of individual records. (In fact, even when you work with commercial database programs, you'll find that *they're* really just clusters of records, too.)

This script stores three separate kinds of data in *myDatabase:* strings for a chicken's *nickname,* numbers for a chicken's *weightInPounds* and *heightInInches,* and Boolean values (page 91) to specify whether the chick is a *rooster.* AppleScript keeps each type of information separate, so it won't get confused if you use three, four, or even more kinds of information in your database records.

Searching an AppleScript Database

For most things in AppleScript, you can use the *every* keyword to narrow down a list of items to a few that match certain criteria (page 109). Unfortunately, this neat trick doesn't work for finding records within an AppleScript database.

To work around this limitation, you have to iterate (page 112) through the database, checking each record *individually* to see if it matches your criteria. Obviously this is an annoying, slower way of searching, but it's unfortunately your only choice for AppleScript databases.

Here, for example, is how you'd search through that chicken database to find the chickens that weigh more than 10 pounds:

```
set myChicken to {nickname:"Matthew", weightInPounds:20, ¬
    heightInInches:26.5, rooster:true}
set kfcChicken to {nickname:"Colonel", weightInPounds:15, ¬
    heightInInches:22.3, rooster:true}
set chickenLittle to {nickname:"Little", weightInPounds:3, ¬
    heightInInches:10.9, rooster:false}
set myDatabase to {myChicken, kfcChicken, chickenLittle}
--Part 1:
set heavyChickens to {}
--Part 2:
repeat with currentRecord in myDatabase
    --Part 3:
    if the weightInPounds of currentRecord is greater than 10 then
        set heavyChickens to (heavyChickens & the nickname of currentRecord)
    end if
end repeat
```

```
--Part 4:
choose from list heavyChickens with prompt ¬
    "Chickens weighing more than 10 pounds:"
```

Here's how the new code works:

- **Part 1** creates a new list, *heavyChickens,* which holds the names of the matching, heavier-than-10-pound chickens later in your script.

- **Part 2** starts a *repeat* statement, assigning *currentRecord* to the next record in *myDatabase* each time the loop repeats. In other words, this section ensures that the script will process every chicken by the time the script is finished.

- **Part 3** checks the current chicken to see if it weighs more than 10 pounds. If the chicken does, the script adds that chicken's nickname to the *heavyChickens* list. If the chicken weighs less than 10 pounds, though, the *repeat* statement simply proceeds to examine the next chicken.

- **Part 4** displays a list of all the chickens weighing more than 10 pounds (Figure 10-1), thereby completing your search.

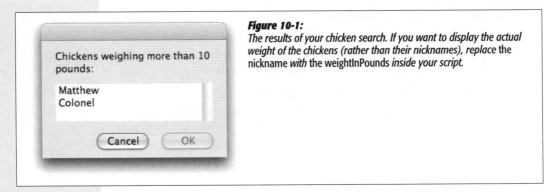

Figure 10-1:
The results of your chicken search. If you want to display the actual weight of the chickens (rather than their nicknames), replace the nickname with the weightInPounds inside your script.

Now that you know how to create, modify, and search databases, you can get down to real business: making databases out of *useful* information.

Getting File Information

Back in Chapter 5, you learned how to use the Finder to gather information about a file—like its *modification date,* for example (page 98). As it turns out, however, there's a much more powerful command for gathering file information: *info for.* This command has a number of advantages over scripting the Finder:

- *Info for* **provides a more complete analysis of files.** In addition to telling you a file's name, modification date, and size (all things you can get by commanding the Finder), the *info for* command lets you get a file's *displayed name* (how the file name actually looks in the Finder) and *name extension* (the short string that comes after the period in a file's name), among other useful properties.

Note: Lest you think the *info for* command can access everything about a file, there are actually a few pieces of information you can get *only* by commanding the Finder. These include a file's *comment* (its Finder note, as described on page 89) and a file's *owner* (the person who created it). Therefore, until Apple updates the *info for* command to access the same information as the Finder, you'll have to live with using a combination of *both* methods to access complete file information.

- The *info for* command doesn't require a *tell* statement directed at the Finder. You'll save two lines of code automatically: *tell* and *end tell*.

- The *info for* command returns its information as a record. Among other things, this means you can use the *info for* command on a *list* of files and end up with a database of all those files' information.

Running the *info for* command is simple enough. You just tell AppleScript where to find the file in question, and let it rip:

```
info for alias ":Library:User Pictures:Animals:Butterfly.tif"
```

That script locates your Library → User Pictures → Animals → Butterfly.tif image and gets the file information about it. AppleScript doesn't have a built-in command for displaying records, though, so you'll have to be satisfied with reading the information in Script Editor's Result pane (Figure 10-2).

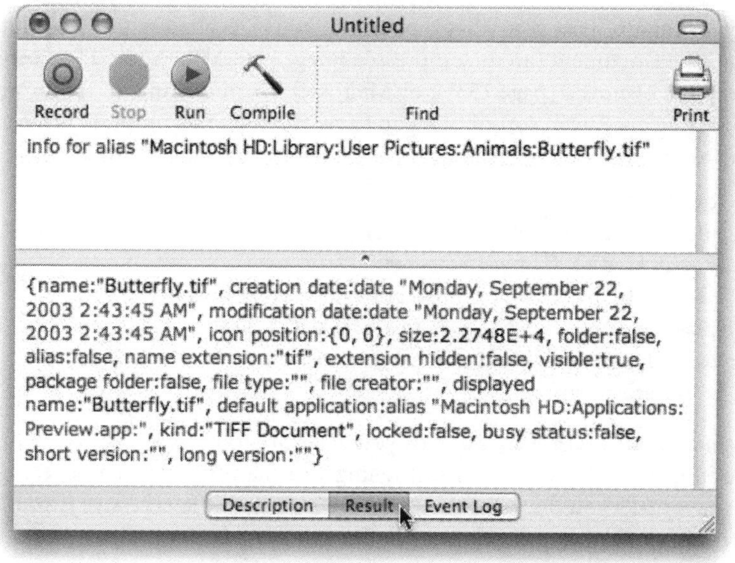

Figure 10-2:
Since AppleScript doesn't have a choose from record command (or something similar for displaying records in a dialog box), you have to read your records inside Script Editor's Result pane. If you don't see this pane, you can either click the Result button at the bottom of your script's window or press ⌘-2.

Useful Properties

You could collect information records for the rest of your life using *info for,* but it wouldn't do you much good. That's because records are only useful for the information *inside* them—and that's especially true for the *info for* command, which provides a range of unique file statistics.

Tip: Although this chapter mainly explores using *info for* with *files* you can just as easily use the command with folders.

Here are some of the most useful properties in an *info for* record:

- A file's ***name*** property is, of course, the name that would appear if you selected an item in the Finder and chose File → Get Info (⌘-I). It's a useful property to use with files you pick in Open dialog boxes, for example, so you can store the file's name for later use in your script—or just display the name in a dialog box:

```
--Show an Open dialog box:
set selectedFile to (choose file)
--Get an information record for the selected file:
set infoRecord to (info for selectedFile)
--Get the name of the selected file:
set fileName to the name of infoRecord
--Display the file's name in a dialog box:
display dialog "The name of the file you chose was " ¬
    & fileName --Display a dialog box with the filename
```

- The ***kind*** property tells you what type of file you're dealing with. Possibilities include TIFF Document (an uncompressed image file), MP3 Audio File (a compressed piece of music [page 153]), or Microsoft Word document. If you want to know at a glance what sort of files you have, checking this property is the easiest way to find out:

```
set selectedFile to (choose file)
set infoRecord to (info for selectedFile)
--Find what kind of file you selected:
set fileType to the kind of infoRecord --The file's kind
--Display the file's kind in a dialog box:
display dialog "Congratulations! You just chose a " ¬
    & fileType
```

- The ***default application*** property tells you what program is designated to open the file in question. Rather than just telling you the program's name, though, this property tells you the program's *path*—which is a little excessive if you just want to know whether your Peanut.txt file will open in TextEdit or Microsoft Word, for example.

Still, if you want to find out just the *name* of the program that's designated to open a particular file, you can use this script:

```
set selectedFile to (choose file)
set infoRecord to (info for selectedFile)
--Find the program that's supposed to open selectedFile:
set defApp to the default application of infoRecord
--Get an information record for that program:
set programInfoRecord to (info for defApp)
--Get the name of that program:
set programName to the name of programInfoRecord
--Display that program's name in a dialog box:
display dialog ¬
    "The default program to open that file is " ¬
    & programName
```

For a complete list of information record properties, open the Standard Additions dictionary (page 50) and examine File Commands → Classes → File Information.

Note: Although there are tons of file properties AppleScript can access, you can only *check* these properties—you can't change them. If you want to edit a file's name, for example, you can't use the *info for* command; instead, you'd have to command the Finder directly (page 113).

Scripting FileMaker Pro

Although AppleScript databases are convenient for managing small batches of related information, they have some serious limitations. For one thing, any time you want to change an AppleScript database, you have to do so *in code*—a big annoyance for anyone used to the graphical comfort of Mac OS X. For another thing, you can't very easily display an AppleScript database in a dialog box; you have to settle for displaying individual *properties* from the database. Finally, AppleScript databases become unwieldy when they hold more than a few hundred items, since AppleScript was never really meant to do super-fast data processing.

The solution to these annoyances, of course, is to use a *graphical* database program. That way, you won't have to deal with convoluted AppleScript commands just to hold your information (although you're free to use AppleScripts to *filter* database information once it's already entered). And when it comes time to display your information, you won't have resort to AppleScript hackery to see your database onscreen.

If you feel the tug of the graphical database program, FileMaker Pro is your best choice for Mac OS X. It's easy to use—at least, as far as database programs are concerned—and full of helpful features, including powerful searching and predesigned databases for common tasks, such as cataloging a movie collection. But best

---

of all, FileMaker Pro has a comprehensive AppleScript dictionary for automatically entering, filtering, and sorting your database entries.

Tip: If you don't feel like spending $300 on a full version of FileMaker Pro, you can download a free, fully functioning 30-day trial from *https://www.filemaker.com/downloads/trial_download.html.*

Creating a New FileMaker Database

People use databases for an enormous number of things, but one fairly common use is storing employee information. Rather than keeping physical files on each employee, for example, a FileMaker Pro database lets you store all that information on your *computer*—which is easier to search, email to hiring managers, or destroy if the government comes after you. This section, therefore, helps you create such a database, and then shows you how to write the scripts you'll need to automate sorting the database's information.

In FileMaker Pro, you create a new database by choosing the File → New Database command. At that point, you see a dialog box where you can pick one of the pre-designed databases layouts (Product Catalog, Movie Library, To Do List, and so on). However, since you're going to build a *customized* database, you'd be better off starting from scratch, so just select "Create a new empty file." Once you've turned that option on, click OK to jump to the next dialog box, where you can specify the location to save the database on your hard drive. (You can save the database in your Documents folder, or anywhere else that it's convenient.)

Now, after you click Save in the dialog box, you see yet *another* dialog box (Figure 10-3). This is where you specify the individual fields to appear in your database entries: an employee's name, tenure, and résumé, for example.

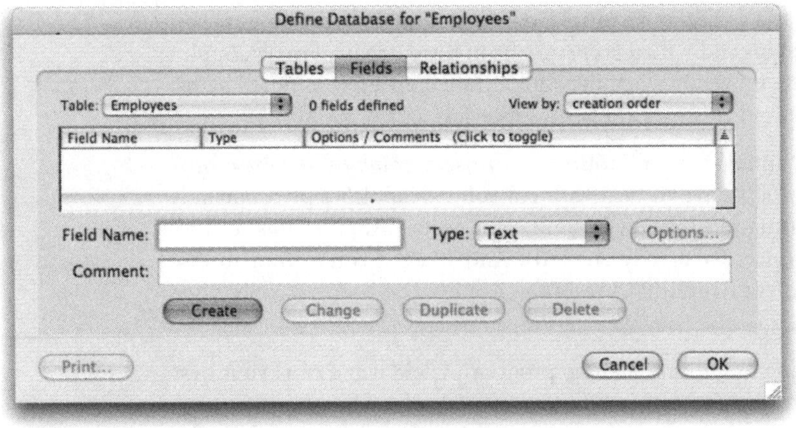

Figure 10-3:
This complicated dialog box is what lets you name the individual fields for your database. In essence, it lets you take care of all the database setup before you start entering information. If, at some later point, you want to change your database's fields, simply choose View → Layout Mode and add or delete fields as you please.

Here's the procedure for setting up the dialog box with the necessary field information:

1. **Enter "First Name" for the Field Name; in the Type pop-up menu, make sure Text is selected, and click Create.**

   You just added a First Name field to your employee database.

2. **Repeat step 1, but add a new text field named Last Name.**

   The reason for using two separate fields is that, later on, you can sort by either first name *or* last name. If you only had a single Name field (containing both first and last names), you wouldn't have the option of sorting them separately.

3. **For the Field Name, type Tenure; from the Type pop-up menu, select Number (⌘-N); then click Create.**

   You've just created a third field in your database. This one lets you specify how many years you've employed someone.

4. **Add another field to your database, naming it Picture, and choosing Container (⌘-R) for its Type.**

   This field lets you store a headshot, mug shot, or other embarrassing photograph of each employee. (Make sure you've clicked Create to add the field to your database before proceeding.)

5. **For your last field's Name, type Résumé; for the Type, select Container; then click Create.**

Tip: To create the accented é character, type Option-E, release both keys, and then press E again.

This field allows you to include your employees' résumés right inside your database, making it easy to check up on their college degrees when you feel the need.

6. **Click OK to exit the dialog box. You now see a single record in your new database, just waiting for you to fill out (Figure 10-4).**

Tip: If you'd like to see the record in a more compact way, choose View → View as Table.

Entering Information into a FileMaker Database

Now that you've got a database with all the fields you want, it's time to enter your employees' actual information. FileMaker Pro allows you to do this in two different ways: by typing the information yourself or by having AppleScript enter it for you.

Enter your information manually

This is the approach most people use when they fill out a database: type the current employee's information in, insert the images and files you want, and move on to the next employee. (You create a new, blank employee record by choosing Records → New Record, or by pressing ⌘-N.)

Needless to say, this method is slow, tedious, and error-prone. Use it only if you're retired—or an insomniac.

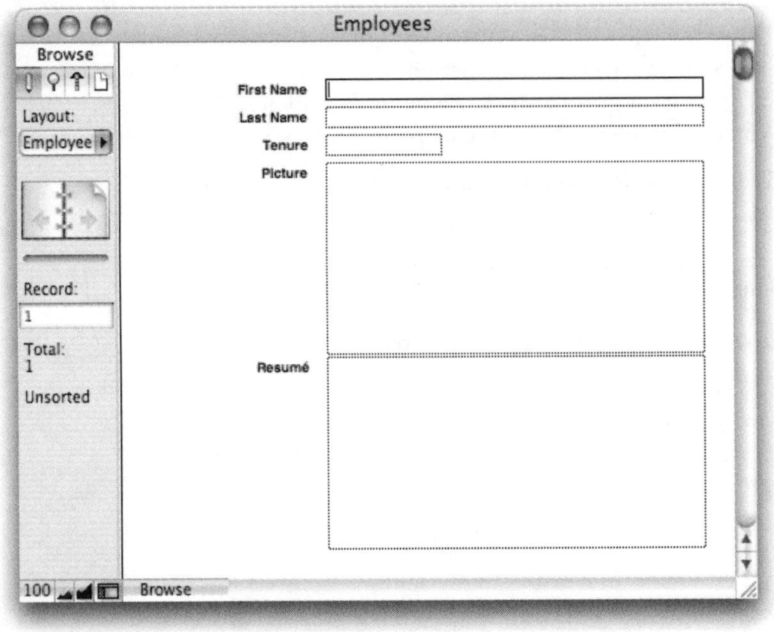

Figure 10-4:
You can type an employee's information straight into the First Name, Last Name, and Tenure fields. For the Picture field, however, Control-click the box, choose Insert Picture from the shortcut menu, and choose the image that you want to appear in the database. Similarly, for the Résumé field, Control-click the box next to it, choose Insert File, and navigate to the résumé file you want to add to your database.

Use an AppleScript to enter your information

If you're short on time, AppleScript can help you copy your employees' information out of your Address Book (page 183) and into your new FileMaker database. Not only does this method take only a fraction of the work, it also cuts down on any typos that might occur if you tried to transfer the information by hand.

The following script shows you how to integrate your Address Book with FileMaker Pro, illustrating a wide variety of powerful commands. By the time the script is finished, your database will contain the names of your employees (picked out of your Address Book), their tenures (which you enter in a dialog box), their pictures (copied from Photoshop), and their résumés (chosen from within FileMaker). This script truly illustrates AppleScript's power at controlling different programs:

Note: If you have more than one copy of FileMaker Pro on your computer—say, an old version for Mac OS 9 and a new version for Mac OS X—you have to change the phrase "FileMaker Pro" to include the newest version's full name—for instance, "FileMaker Pro 7."

```
--Part 1:
tell application "Address Book"
    activate
    set myCompany to the text returned of (display dialog ¬
        "Enter your company's name:" default answer "")
    --Part 2:
    set theEmployees to every person whose organization is myCompany
end tell
--Part 3:
repeat with currentEmployee in theEmployees
    --Part 4:
    tell application "Address Book"
        set employeeFirstName to the first name of currentEmployee
        set employeeLastName to the last name of currentEmployee
    end tell
    --Part 5:
    tell application "FileMaker Pro"
        activate
        set employeeTenure to the text returned of (display dialog ¬
            "How many years has " & employeeFirstName & space & ¬
            employeeLastName & " been working for you?" default answer 2)
        --Part 6:
        set employeePicture to (choose file with prompt ¬
            "Choose " & employeeFirstName & "'s picture:")
        --Part 7:
        create new record at the end
        go to the last record
        --Part 8:
        set the contents of field "First Name" of the current record ¬
            to employeeFirstName
        set the contents of field "Last Name" of the current record ¬
            to employeeLastName
        set the contents of field "Tenure" of the current record to ¬
            employeeTenure
    end tell
    --Part 9:
    tell application "Adobe Photoshop CS"
        activate
        open employeePicture
        --Part 10:
        tell the front document
            select all
            copy
            close
        end tell
    end tell
```

```
    --Part 11:
    tell application "FileMaker Pro"
        activate
        go to field "Picture" of the current record
        paste
        --Part 12:
        go to field "Resumé" of the current record
        do menu (menu item "File..." of menu "Insert")
    end tell
end repeat
```

Note: You enter the ... character on the third-to-last line by pressing Option-; (*not* by pressing the period key three times).

Here's how this mega-script works:

- **Part 1** asks for your company's name (Figure 10-5). Make sure you spell it exactly as it appears in Address Book, or else the script won't be able to locate your employees.

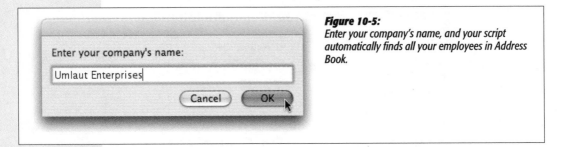

Figure 10-5:
Enter your company's name, and your script automatically finds all your employees in Address Book.

- **Part 2** gets every contact in your Address Book whose *organization* property matches your company. In other words, this part puts a list of your employees into the variable *theEmployees*.

- **Part 3** starts a loop to go through each of your employees. Each time the *repeat* statement runs, it sets *currentEmployee* to the next employee in the list.

- **Part 4** sets *employeeFirstName* and *employeeLastName* to the current employee's first and last names, respectively, from Address Book. Later, your script inserts this information into the appropriate fields in your database.

- **Part 5** brings FileMaker Pro forward and asks you how long the current employee has served for (Figure 10-6). Later in the script, this information also gets inserted into the appropriate database field.

- **Part 6** asks you to select the current employee's picture on your hard drive and then puts the file you choose into the *employeePicture* variable.

Tip: FileMaker Pro can accept most standard graphics formats for pictures (TIFF, GIF, JPEG, and so on).

- **Part 7** creates a new record in your FileMaker database to store the current employee. Then, since FileMaker Pro automatically creates new records at the *end* of the current records, this part navigates to the last record in your database before proceeding.

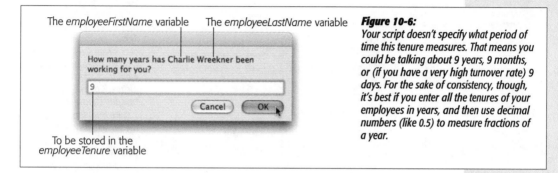

The *employeeFirstName* variable   The *employeeLastName* variable

To be stored in the
employeeTenure variable

Figure 10-6:
Your script doesn't specify what period of time this tenure measures. That means you could be talking about 9 years, 9 months, or (if you have a very high turnover rate) 9 days. For the sake of consistency, though, it's best if you enter all the tenures of your employees in years, and then use decimal numbers (like 0.5) to measure fractions of a year.

- **Part 8** enters the current employee's first name, last name, and tenure into the new record—with no human intervention.

- **Part 9** opens the picture from part 6 in Photoshop.

Note: Since FileMaker Pro can't open images on its own (it can only accept them when pasted from other programs or chosen from a dialog box), you have to open the image in another program first, and then copy it into FileMaker. You could use a different graphics program if you wanted, but Photoshop is as good as any.

- **Part 10** takes the frontmost window in Photoshop (the one you opened in the previous step), selects the image inside, copies it, and closes the window. Your Clipboard now holds the current employee's picture.

Note: Photoshop won't let you copy images (using the *copy* command) unless Photoshop is the frontmost program at the time. In this script, that's accomplished with the *activate* command in part 9.

- **Part 11** takes you back to FileMaker Pro, where the script selects the Picture field and pastes your employee's picture. At this point, four out of five of your record's fields are filled in.

- **Part 12** selects the Résumé field. Then, using FileMaker's special *do menu* command, the script runs the Insert → File command from FileMaker's menu bar. This is what lets you pick a résumé to insert into the current employee's record.

Tip: To see other unique AppleScript commands for FileMaker Pro, don't forget to examine its dictionary from within Script Editor (File → Open Dictionary → FileMaker Pro).

Figure 10-7 shows what a single record might look like after part 12 is done. Then, once you've finished inputting one record, the script jumps back to part 3 to deal with your next employee.

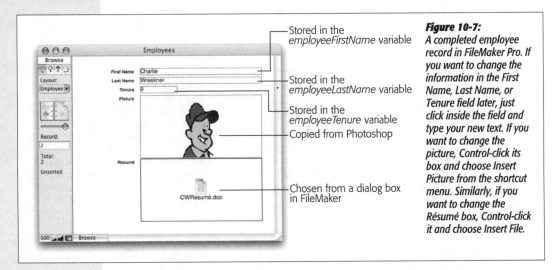

Stored in the *employeeFirstName* variable

Stored in the *employeeLastName* variable

Stored in the *employeeTenure* variable
Copied from Photoshop

Chosen from a dialog box in FileMaker

Figure 10-7:
A completed employee record in FileMaker Pro. If you want to change the information in the First Name, Last Name, or Tenure field later, just click inside the field and type your new text. If you want to change the picture, Control-click its box and choose Insert Picture from the shortcut menu. Similarly, if you want to change the Résumé box, Control-click it and choose Insert File.

Congratulations! Once you run the script, all your employees from Address Book will sit happily in FileMaker Pro.

Sorting FileMaker Records

You've got several dozen employees entered in FileMaker Pro, all with pictures and résumés. But what if you want to sort your employees—say, by last name, or from newest to oldest?

As with most things in FileMaker Pro, you can sort your database's records by using FileMaker's graphical interface *or* by commanding the program with AppleScript.

The advantage of sorting graphically (by choosing Records → Sort Records, and then selecting the criteria to sort by) is that you have greater control. For example, you can sort by last name, and then sort people who have the *same* last name by their first name. This kind of multilayered sort lets you break a "tie" between employees who would otherwise be sorted the same way.

On the other hand, using AppleScript to sort your records has advantages of its own. For one thing, it's faster; once you have a script that sorts the way you want, you never have to re-enter your sort again (as you would if you used the Records → Sort Records dialog box). For another thing, an AppleScript can incorporate commands *beyond* sorting (so that, after sorting, you can jump to the first or last record in your database, for example). Finally, you can save an AppleScript as an application, so you can run it from the menu bar or Dock whenever you want (page 33).

Here's a script to sort your database by employee tenure, for instance:

```
tell application "FileMaker Pro"
    tell the front layout
        sort by field "Tenure" in order descending
    end tell
end tell
```

FREQUENTLY ASKED QUESTION

Scripts Inside FileMaker

I was poking around in FileMaker's menus, and I noticed this thing called ScriptMaker. What's it for, and how's it different from AppleScript?

You've just stumbled upon FileMaker Pro's personal script bakery. When you choose Scripts → ScriptMaker, you see a dialog box, where you can create special, FileMaker-only scripts without writing a line of code yourself.

Unfortunately, the scripts you create in ScriptMaker are *not* AppleScripts. They're stored in a special FileMaker-specific format, which means you can't open them in Script Editor, save them in the Dock, nor perform any of the other cool tricks described in Chapter 2 with them.

That's not to say that ScriptMaker isn't useful, however. It has a number of advantages over AppleScript, despite the fact that ScriptMaker works only within FileMaker Pro:

- **With ScriptMaker, you don't have to type any commands yourself.** Of course, it can be *quicker* to type commands than to navigate a series of ScriptMaker dialog boxes in FileMaker Pro. Still, it's *easier* to use the dialog box approach, because you don't have to look commands up in FileMaker Pro's AppleScript dictionary.

- **ScriptMaker gives you a choice of more commands than AppleScript does.** For instance, you can perform automatic database spell checking with ScriptMaker's Correct Word command, even though there's no command to do this with AppleScript.

- **Any scripts you create with ScriptMaker are automatically listed in FileMaker's Scripts menu.** ScriptMaker scripts are also given keyboard shortcuts automatically—⌘-1 for the first script, ⌘-2

for the second, and so on. That makes ScriptMaker scripts a lot easier to run than AppleScripts, which you have to either put in the global Script Menu or the Dock (neither of which uses keyboard shortcuts for its items).

- **ScriptMaker works on both Macs and Windows PCs.** That's different from AppleScript commands, which only work on the Mac version of FileMaker Pro.

To construct a script with ScriptMaker, click New in the Define Script dialog box. Then choose the commands you want to use from the pane on the left, and click Move to add the commands to your script's list (the pane on the right).

If there's a command that has extra options—say, Perform Find/Replace, for changing occurrences of certain text in your database—a Specify button appears at the bottom of the window to let you fine-tune the command.

If you absolutely *must* control other programs from your ScriptMaker scripts, you can do it—but you have to be sneaky. Scroll all the way down to the bottom of the Edit Script dialog box, and double-click Perform AppleScript. When you click the Specify button, FileMaker Pro lets you paste in AppleScript code from Script Editor—even if that code controls other programs.

(Similarly, you can run ScriptMaker scripts from *AppleScript* using FileMaker Pro's *do script* command. That way, you can access the internal features available to ScriptMaker from a hand-coded AppleScript.)

Finally, once you're done inputting ScriptMaker commands, click OK to save your script for future use. Note, however, that your ScriptMaker scripts will work only within the *current* database.

It might seem strange to tell a *layout* to sort itself, but in fact, that's how you have to command FileMaker Pro. That's because, in theory, you could have *multiple* layouts for a database—each sorted independently—and you have to tell File-Maker which one to perform the sort on.

Just sorting your records, however, isn't going to win any programming awards. That's why the following script not only *sorts* your employees by last name, but also brings FileMaker Pro forward and jumps to the first record alphabetically:

```
tell application "FileMaker Pro"
    activate --Bring FileMaker Pro forward
    tell the front layout
        sort by field "Last Name" in order ascending
        go to the first record --Jump to the first person, alphabetically
    end tell
end tell
```

As you can see, a few simple commands in AppleScript can make it much easier to navigate your records in FileMaker Pro. Note, however, that you can only sort your records by text fields (First Name, Last Name, or Tenure); the ability to sort your employees in order of their pictures' attractiveness isn't expected until File-Maker 9.

Part Three:
Power-User Features

3

Chapter 11, *Linking Scripts to Folders with Folder Actions*

Chapter 12, *Scripting Programs That Don't Have Dictionaries*

Chapter 13, *Mixing AppleScript and Unix*

Chapter 14, *Testing and Debugging Scripts*

Chapter 15, *AppleScript Studio*

Linking Scripts to Folders with Folder Actions

Imagine: your Mac reminds you to clean the sink whenever you open your Applications folder. You automatically see a dialog box whenever someone on your network drops a file in your Public folder. And your desktop automatically cleans itself up when you fill it with too many icons.

Now stop dreaming. Everything you just imagined is only a script away, thanks to the special *folder actions* feature you get with AppleScript and Mac OS X.

Note: If you've used Mail rules before (page 190), you'll instantly understand the power of folder actions. That's because Mail rules and folder actions are based on the same idea: triggering scripts *automatically* when something happens on your Mac.

A folder action is an AppleScript like any other. The difference is that you can attach a folder action to a *specific folder*—and have the script run automatically when you do something to that folder. You can trigger a folder action when you open a folder, close a folder, or copy items into a folder, for example. With triggers like these, the scripting possibilities are truly limitless.

Note: The example scripts from this chapter can be found on the AppleScript Examples CD (see page 24 for instructions).

Enabling Folder Actions

Don't lose sleep imagining the possibilities—yet. Before you start linking up scripts to your folders, you first have to turn on folder actions on a system-wide level. Luckily, that's a simple procedure: just Control-click anywhere on the desktop, and choose Enable Folder Actions from the shortcut menu. That tells your Mac to start paying attention to all the folder changes you make, and to trigger scripts accordingly.

Tip: If you'd like to turn on folder actions *without* switching to the Finder first, open the Script Menu (page 4) and choose Folder Actions → Enable Folder Actions.

You won't see anything different in the Finder, but folder actions are now available for any folder on your Mac.

Built-in Actions

To get you started on your folder actions journey, Apple included 13 predesigned scripts for you to attach to any folders you'd like. You can find these scripts in your Library → Scripts → Folder Action Scripts folder, and you can open them in Script Editor if you'd like to read their code.

Note: Don't get confused between the Folder Action Scripts folder and the *Folder Actions* folder. Both are in your Library → Scripts folder; the difference is that Folder Action Scripts contains *actual* folder actions you can attach to folders on your computer, whereas the Folder Actions folder contains Apple-Scripts for enabling, disabling, and otherwise manipulating folder actions on a *system-wide* level. (Also, only the Folder Actions folder appears in the global Script Menu.)

Attaching a Folder Action

If you're a control freak, you might want to use the **add - new item alert** script with your Documents folder. That script automatically shows you a dialog box when you add new files to the Documents folder, making it easy to keep an eye on your documents without impulsively switching to the Finder every 5 minutes. Here's how you'd pull off the folder-attaching trick:

1. **In the Finder, open your Home folder.**

   You'll see your Documents folder inside. Whenever you want to attach an action to a folder (in this case, the Documents folder), you must first open that folder's *parent folder* (in this case, your Home folder).

Tip: The Finder doesn't restrict you to attaching folder actions to just *folders*—you can attach them to hard drives, CD-ROMs, disk images, and anything else that can contain a file. Note, however, that if you attach a folder action to a removable disk (such as a CD or DVD), Mac OS X will forget all about the action when you eject and reinsert the disk.

2. **Control-click the Documents folder (or right-click it, if you have a two-button mouse). Then choose "Attach a Folder Action" from the shortcut menu (Figure 11-1).**

Note: You must Control-click the Documents folder *itself;* if you happen to keep your Documents folder in the Finder's Sidebar or in the Dock, you can't Control-click it there.

An Open dialog box appears, taking you straight to the Library → Scripts → Folder Action Scripts folder.

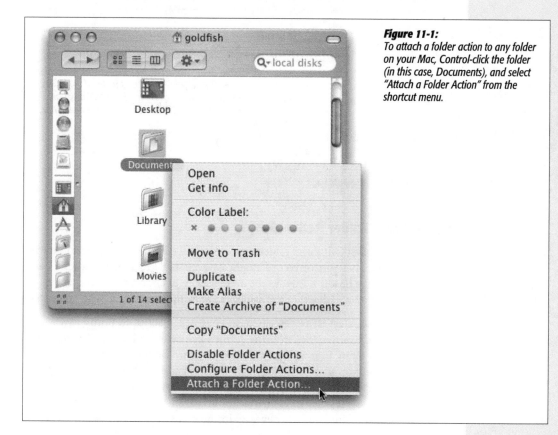

Figure 11-1:
To attach a folder action to any folder on your Mac, Control-click the folder (in this case, Documents), and select "Attach a Folder Action" from the shortcut menu.

3. Select "add - new item alert.scpt" (this should be right at the top of the Open dialog box), and click Choose to attach the script to the Documents folder.

If you'd rather associate a different folder action with your Documents folder, simply select a different script.

Tip: You can associate *more than one* folder action with a single folder. That way, one script could run when the folder opens, and one could run when the folder closes, for example. Mac OS X would know which script to run by the *handlers* inside the scripts; for instance, a folder action script with an *opening* handler (page 229) would run when you opened the folder, but a folder action script with an *adding* handler (page 232) would run when you copied new files into the folder.

To attach multiple folder actions to a folder, simply Control-click the folder you have in mind, choose Attach a Folder Action from the shortcut menu, and select any *additional* scripts you want to attach from the dialog box.

Now whenever you—or anyone on your network—adds a new item to your Documents folder, a dialog box appears on your screen to let you know (Figure 11-2).

Tip: If you're interested in keeping closer tabs on your network activity, attach the same script to your Home → Public → Drop Box folder. On a network, that's the only folder people can copy files to (unless they know your password, in which case they can copy files *anywhere* on your hard drive.)

Figure 11-2:
If this dialog box appears out of nowhere, there's a good chance someone on your network just copied three files to your Documents folder. If you'd like to see the files in question, click Yes. Otherwise, click No or press Return to dismiss the dialog box.

The Included Folder Action Scripts

So far, you've played with one folder action script—out of the 13 that come with your computer. That sort of record might be acceptable to a minor-league baseball player, but it's hardly a way for a power user to live. To satisfy your curiosity, therefore, here's a breakdown of the folder action scripts that come with your Mac:

- **add - new item alert** is, as described on page 222, a script to notify you whenever somebody moves files into the script's associated folder. This script's got just about as many uses as duct tape: attach it to the folder where you download files, and you'll see a dialog box whenever a download starts; attach the script to your Public folder, and you'll get a notification whenever someone on your network copies files to your Mac; or attach the script to your Applications folder, and you'll find out whenever an installer copies a new program there.

Tip: There's nothing to keep you from attaching the same folder action to *multiple* folders. For maximum convenience, then, attach the **add - new item alert** script to all three of the folders mentioned previously.

- **close - close sub-folders** is a script for reducing window clutter. When attached to a folder, this script automatically closes any of that folder's *subfolders* when you close the attached folder itself.

  For example, say you attached this script to your Home folder and then opened up three separate windows: one for your Home folder, one for your Home → Music folder, and one for your Home → Pictures folder. When you closed your

Home folder, the other two windows would close automatically, because they're subfolders of your Home folder. If you hadn't attached this script to your Home folder in the first place, you'd be left closing up the other two windows by hand.

- **convert - PostScript to PDF** is mainly useful for graphics professionals and other geeks who deal with PostScript files (raw graphics and layout information) every day. The script converts any PostScript files you drop in its attached folder into PDFs—for sending off to a print shop, for example. The script then places the converted documents into a PDF Files subfolder, and moves the original PostScript documents to an Original Files subfolder.

  In other words, you're left with a fresh new PDF file, suitable for emailing to your friends, posting on a Web site, or printing out to post on your wall.

- **Image - Add Icon** takes any image files you drop onto its associated folder (in JPEG, TIFF, or PNG format) and automatically changes the files' icons to display the images themselves. That scheme can save you a lot of time, since you can see at a glance what each image contains without actually opening it. For maximum convenience, attach this script to your desktop, so that any images you download from the Internet *to* your desktop automatically receive preview icons of their own.

Note: This script automatically moves the icon-added images to an Original Files subfolder, which can be slightly confusing if you were expecting to find the images in the exact place you saved them.

WORKAROUND WORKSHOP

Using Folder Actions with Subfolders

If you spend a lot of time with folder actions, one thing will strike you as quite odd: actions work fine with the folder to which they're attached but don't work at all with any *subfolders* in them. That means that the script you attached to your Documents folder (page 222) takes effect only when you drop files *directly* into your Home → Documents folder; the folder action doesn't run at all when you drop files into your Home → Documents → Shopping Lists folder, for example.

Of course, there are some times when this one-folder-deep behavior is exactly what you want. If the Finder *didn't* have this safeguard in place, for instance, you'd run into problems if you attached an action to your hard drive, because the same action would trickle down to every folder on your Mac.

Still, there are plenty of circumstances when it *would* be better to have a folder action apply to all subfolders. If you wanted to see a dialog box whenever somebody added a file to your Home folder *or* any folder inside it, for example, an *apply to all subfolders* command would be quite helpful.

Unfortunately, there is no such command. To attach a folder action to subfolders, you must Control-click each subfolder one at a time, and select Attach a Folder Action from the shortcut menu.

The only relief you get from this painful process is that Mac OS X automatically shows you the Library → Scripts → Folder Action Scripts folder in each Open dialog box. That way, you don't have to locate the same script on your hard drive every time you want to attach the same folder action to a different subfolder.

CHAPTER 11: LINKING SCRIPTS TO FOLDERS WITH FOLDER ACTIONS

• **Image - Duplicate as JPEG/PNG/TIFF** are three scripts for converting image files into JPEG, PNG, or TIFF image formats. Simply drag an image—or a group of images—onto the folder associated with one of these scripts, and watch in amazement as Mac OS X creates a new folder (called JPEG Images, PNG Images, or TIFF Images, as appropriate) for your converted images.

Note: Unfortunately, due to a bug in the underlying graphics features of Mac OS X, you may not be able to convert EPS files using these scripts.

• **Image - Flip Horizontal/Vertical** are two scripts for reversing your pictures horizontally or vertically. For example, if you had a picture of the front of an ambulance, you could drop it into a folder with the **Flip Horizontal** script attached, so you could read the word "Ambulance" from left to right. (In the U.S., most ambulances have the word "Ambulance" in reverse on their hoods, so the drivers in front can see that they have an ambulance behind them when they look in their rear-view mirror.)

Note: To make your flipped images easier to find, Mac OS X moves them to a subfolder named, appropriately enough, Flipped Images.

Also note that these Flip scripts are only designed to work with TIFF, JPEG, and PNG images.

• **Image - Info to Comment** is meant to take any information from a graphics file—its width, height, number of colors, and so on—and automatically copy that information to the file's Comment field, which you can see by selecting the image in the Finder and choosing File → Get Info. Then, whatever folder you attach this script to creates a Processed Images subfolder to hold all the newly commented pictures.

• **Image - Rotate Left/Right** takes any images you drop into the associated folder—at least, those images in TIFF, JPEG, or PNG format—and automatically rotates the images either left or right by 90 degrees (depending on which script you use). If you often take portrait-oriented pictures (where you rotated your camera 90 degrees to fit more of the image vertically than horizontally), this script can come in handy, since you won't have to rotate your *head* sideways to see the images as you originally intended.

Note: The just-rotated pictures are placed in a Rotated Images folder, for your browsing pleasure.

• **open - show comments in dialog** is a script for viewing a folder's Comments field (page 89) without having to choose File → Get Info. Whenever you double-click a folder to which this script is attached, a dialog box appears, telling you that folder's comments—and letting you change or delete them, if you so desire.

Although it's not very obvious, you can also use this script to create a daily to-do list. For instance, after attaching this script to your Applications folder, you

---

could enter a reminder in the folder's Comments field—like, say, "Remember to walk the dog." Then, whenever you double-clicked the Applications folder in the Finder, you'd see a dialog box reminding you of whatever you typed into the Comments field (Figure 11-3). It's a simple, free to-do reminder that shows up whenever you double-click that most useful of folders: Applications.

Figure 11-3:
If you attached the open - show comments in dialog script to your Applications folder and then added a comment to the Applications folder, you'd see a dialog box like this whenever you opened the folder. Click Open Comments to edit the comments associated with the folder (to add a different reminder, for example). Click Clear Comments to delete the reminder entirely. Or, to leave the comment as is, simply click OK.

Viewing and Changing an Action's Code

Maybe you're curious how the **PostScript to PDF** script actually works. Or maybe you'd like to tweak the **Show Comments in Dialog** script, so the buttons in the dialog box have shorter names. Either way, it would sure be helpful if you could open your folder action scripts in Script Editor, so you could tweak the scripts to suit your particular needs. After all, your Mac does belong to *you,* so why settle for Apple's choices?

Luckily, you can tweak folder action scripts to your heart's content. Mac OS X gives you two ways to view (or edit) a folder action script's code in Script Editor:

- **Navigate to your Library → Scripts → Folder Action Scripts folder, and double-click the script you'd like to open.** You can browse the code at your leisure, or make changes to it, and choose File → Save to modify the folder action's behavior.

- **If the script you want to edit is already *attached* to a folder, Control-click the folder and choose the script from the Edit a Folder Action submenu.** Script Editor springs to life, opening the script attached to that folder.

An example: shortening button names in a folder action's dialog box

As explained on page 226, the **Show Comments in Dialog** script is a handy tool for reminding yourself to do chores whenever you double-click a folder. As shown in Figure 11-3, however, the buttons in the dialog box are absolutely enormous. Not only do they look ugly and un-Mac-like, the buttons also make the dialog box *itself* twice as wide as it has to be, obscuring windows underneath.

Luckily, there's an easy fix; since Mac OS X lets you modify the built-in folder actions, you simply have to locate the **Show Comments in Dialog** script and tweak the button sizes yourself. Here's how:

1. **In the Finder, open Library → Scripts → Folder Action Scripts, and double-click "open - show comments in dialog.scpt."**

   Alternatively, Control-click a folder that *already* has the **Show Comments in Dialog** script attached, and choose the script's name from the Edit a Folder Action submenu.

2. **Edit the script as you see fit.**

   For example, to get rid of the oversized buttons, edit this command:

   ```
   display dialog alert_message buttons {"Open Comments", ¬
       "Clear Comments", "OK"} default button 3 giving ¬
       up after dialog_timeout
   ```

   so it says this:

   ```
   display dialog alert_message buttons {"Open", ¬
       "Clear", "OK"} default button 3 giving ¬
       up after dialog_timeout
   ```

   Then edit these lines:

   ```
   if the user_choice is "Clear Comments" then
       set comment of this_folder to ""
   else if the user_choice is "Open Comments" then
   ```

   so they read like this:

   ```
   if the user_choice is "Clear" then
       set comment of this_folder to ""
   else if the user_choice is "Open" then
   ```

   Those simple tweaks are all it takes to shorten the button names.

3. **Save the script (File → Save, or ⌘-S).**

   Now, when you double-click any folder with this script attached, you'll see the much leaner dialog box shown in Figure 11-4.

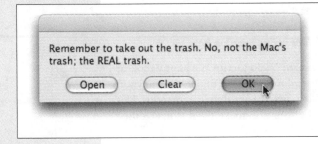

Figure 11-4:
Your new, smaller dialog box. In exchange for shorter button names, unfortunately, the buttons are a little harder to understand. In case you forget: Open takes the place of the Open Comments button (for editing the reminder that appears at the top of the dialog box). Along the same lines, Clear takes the place of Clear Comments (for deleting that reminder altogether).

Removing an Action

If you're getting tired of seeing the dialog box from Figure 11-4 whenever you double-click your Applications folder, it's time to turn off the folder action you attached back on page 222. To remove the action, simply Control-click the Applications folder, and pick the script out of the Remove a Folder Action submenu. Your Applications folder now behaves as it would on a fresh new Mac—that is, the folder doesn't display a dialog box when you double-click it.

Note: Of course, if you want to remove a script attached to a folder *besides* your Applications folder, Control-click that other folder instead.

Removing all actions

If you'd like to turn off *all* folder actions at once—because the constant dialog boxes are starting to get to you, for example—Control-click anywhere in the Finder and choose Disable Folder Actions.

Note: If you decide to turn folder actions back on later (by Control-clicking in the Finder and choosing Enable Folder Actions), all the scripts you've previously set will be automatically reattached to the appropriate folders.

If you'd prefer not to switch to the Finder to disable all folder actions, you can simply open the Script Menu (page 4) and choose the exact same menu command from the Folder Actions submenu.

Running Your Own Actions

You can use any of the folder actions that come with Mac OS X, or you can tweak them to your liking (page 227). But after a while, you'll probably want to write your *own* folder actions from scratch, to truly customize what your folders do.

Luckily, writing a folder action isn't much harder than writing a normal AppleScript. As usual, you open Script Editor, create a new document (by choosing File → New, or pressing ⌘-N), and enter your script's code in the big text box. The only difference, of course, is that you have to surround folder action commands in a special AppleScript handler, so the Finder recognizes your script as a bona fide folder action.

When a Folder Opens

The easiest kind of folder action to create is one that runs when you double-click a folder in the Finder—just like the Show Comments in Dialog script from page 226. The following script, for example, automatically displays whatever folder it's attached to in Column view, whenever you open that folder in the Finder:

```
--Part 1:
on opening folder theFolder
```

```
    --Part 2:
    tell application "Finder"
        set windowName to the name of theFolder
        --Part 3
        set the current view of Finder window windowName to column view
    end tell
end opening folder
```

Here's how the folder action works:

- **Part 1**, and the *on opening folder* handler in particular, is what lets the Finder know to run your script when you open a folder (as opposed to closing or adding icons to the folder, for example). The variable name following the handler—in this case, *theFolder*—stores the path of the folder you just opened.

- **Part 2** gets the name of the folder this script is attached to, using the *name* property described on page 113. With the folder's name in hand, you can command the Finder to adjust the view for that folder's window.

- **Part 3** locates the window that goes with the folder you just opened, and displays the folder's file list in Column view. To round out the script, this part also includes the appropriate *end* statements.

At this point, you've got a series of clever commands—but nothing more. If you click the Run button in Script Editor, for example, none of the commands will run because they're all contained within an *opening folder* handler. A folder action runs only when it's attached to a folder—and even then, only when something *happens* to that folder (such as double-clicking it).

To make any use of your script (besides admiring Script Editor's code coloring), you have to follow these steps:

1. **Choose File → Save (⌘-S), and give your folder action a descriptive name. Don't click Save yet, though.**

   Typical names for folder actions incorporate what your action's triggered by (in this case, opening a folder) and a brief description of what the script does when it runs (here, displaying a window in Column view.) A good name for this script, therefore, might be **open - display in column view.scpt**.

Note: Make sure you choose Script for the File Format, since that's the format the Finder expects for all folder actions.

---

2. **For the script's location, navigate to Library → Scripts → Folder Action Scripts.**

   It's very important that you deposit your script in the Folder Action Scripts subfolder. *Now* you can click Save (Figure 11-5).

3. **In the Finder, select any folder or disk, and attach your new script to it (page 222).**

Now, whenever you double-click that folder, its window automatically adjusts to Column view for your navigating pleasure.

Tip: Attach this script to *all* your most-often-used folders for even more Column view convenience.

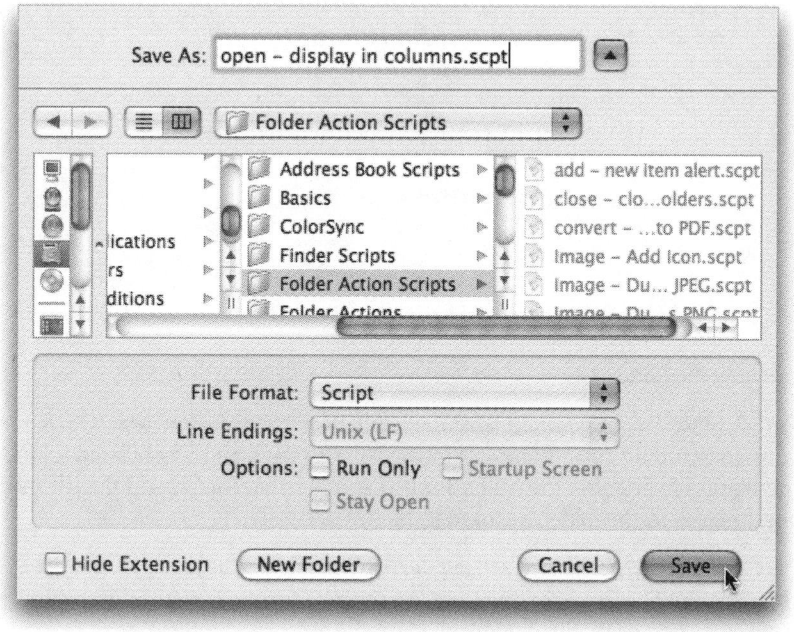

Figure 11-5:
The Save dialog box for your first homemade folder action. Once you click Save, you get a full-fledged folder action script, which you can attach to any folder you want.

When You Add Files to a Folder

Far more useful than running a script when you *open* a folder, however, is running a script when you add new items to a folder. That way, you can filter the incoming files as you see fit—organizing them by name, for instance, or forwarding them to another folder.

An example: Sending files to the Trash can

One of the biggest shocks to people coming from Mac OS 9 is the lack of a Trash can icon on the desktop. And even if you're not an old Mac hand, it probably comes as a surprise that you can't put a Trash can icon in the Finder's toolbar or Sidebar for easy access.

Of course, all those problems could be eliminated if you just had an alias of the Trash folder. Then, you could deposit your *alias* wherever you wanted, and when you dragged files there, they'd be sent straight to the Trash can.

Unfortunately, you can't create an alias of the Trash can the usual way (by choosing File → Make Alias), because Apple cleverly buried the actual Trash folder deep in your Mac's invisible files. (Technically, you *can* access the actual Trash folder, with the info at *www.macosxhints.com/article.php?story=20031222122301840,* but it's not a lot of fun.) That's why the following script is so helpful: whatever folder you attach the script to instantly becomes a trash-forwarding machine.

```
--Part 1:
on adding folder items to theFolder after receiving theItems
    --Part 2:
    repeat with currentItem in theItems
        tell application "Finder"
            --Part 3:
            if the name of currentItem is not ".DS_Store" then
                --Part 4:
                delete currentItem
            end if
        end tell
    end repeat
end adding folder items to
```

Here's how the folder action works:

- **Part 1** (and the *on adding folder items* bit in particular) lets Mac OS X know your code should run whenever you add files to the script's associated folder. In the world of variables, the folder itself is stored in *theFolder,* and the list of files you dragged to the folder is stored in *theItems.*

- **Part 2** starts a *repeat* loop, setting *currentItem* to the next file in the list every time it runs. Therefore, by the time the script is finished, your folder action will have processed every file you dropped on the associated folder.

- **Part 3** checks to make sure the current item isn't named .DS_Store—an invisible file stored in just about every Mac OS X folder. Deleting a .DS_Store file can bring up nasty error messages, so your script skips over such files. Otherwise, if the current file *isn't* named .DS_Store, the script proceeds to the next part.

- **Part 4** deletes the current item, forwarding it to the Trash can. (You hear a satisfying ka-clunk to let you know the deed's been done.)

Now simply save your script and attach it to a new, empty folder; this folder becomes the trash-forwarding machine. For total convenience, name your folder Trash, put it on the desktop, and drag a copy of the folder to your Finder's toolbar or Sidebar. You've just created a poser Trash folder, which sends all the files you drag there to the *real* Trash can.

Tip: If you're really into the details, you can even copy the Trash's *icon* to your new trash-forwarding folder. To do so, click the Trash in the Dock, choose File → Get Info (⌘-I), and select the icon in the Info window. Then choose Edit → Copy (⌘-C), select your *new* Trash folder, choose File → Get Info, select its generic icon, and choose Edit → Paste (⌘-V).

Moving old desktop files

If you're old, nearsighted, or you just like to see images in all their glory, you may have increased the size of your desktop icons by choosing View → Show View Options (⌘-J) in the Finder. The trouble is, when your icons get bigger, you can fit fewer of them on your screen at once. And if you're the type who stashes hundreds or thousands of files on your desktop—or if you just happen to have a small screen—this arrangement a recipe for stacked-icon soufflé.

Luckily, you can employ the help of folder actions in cleaning up your desktop. By attaching the following script to your desktop, any files beyond the number you specify will automatically get thrown into an Old Desktop folder:

```
--Part 1:
on adding folder items to theFolder after receiving theItems
    set maxItems to 5
    --Part 2:
    tell application "Finder"
        if not (exists folder "Old Desktop" of home) then
            make new folder at home with properties {name:"Old Desktop"}
        end if
        --Part 3:
        set desktopFiles to every item of the desktop
        --Part 4:
        if (count desktopFiles) > maxItems then
            move items (maxItems + 1) through (count desktopFiles) ¬
                of desktopFiles to folder "Old Desktop" of home
        end if
    end tell
end adding folder items to
```

Here's how this script works its magic:

- **Part 1** sets the *maxItems* variable to the maximum number of icons you're willing to tolerate on the desktop. Specify any number you want.

- **Part 2** checks to see if you already have a Home → Old Desktop folder. If you *don't*, the script creates one for you (this is where your superfluous desktop icons will be sent).

- **Part 3** gets a list of all the items on your desktop—files, folders, and disks.

Note: Your folder action runs *after* you've moved files to the desktop, so this list will also include the files you just moved.

Folder Actions Setup

After you use folder actions for a while, you might lose track of which folders you've attached scripts to. And if you've attached more than one script to a *single* folder (page 223), folder action relationships can be even harder to remember.

Luckily, Mac OS X comes with a tool specially designed for organizing, tracking, and editing your folder actions from one central location. It's called Folder Actions Setup, and you can find it in your Script Menu by selecting Script Menu → Folder Actions → Folder Actions Setup. Here are the key features to this powerful program:

- **To turn Folder Actions off for your entire Mac, turn off the Enable Folder Actions checkbox.** In an instant, all the scripts you've attached to various folders on your Mac are disabled. The scripts aren't *deleted*, though; if you'd like, you can re-enable them later by simply turning this checkbox back on.

- **The left list shows every folder on your Mac that has a Folder Action attached.** If a folder's *name* isn't enough to identify it (say, if you're not sure which Library folder you've attached a script to), click Show Folder to reveal the selected folder in the Finder.

- **If you'd like to detach *all* the scripts from a folder, select the folder in the left list and click the – button in the lower-left portion of the window.** A dialog box asks you to confirm the deletion before proceeding.

- **To add a new folder to the left list, click the + button in the lower-left corner of the window.** A standard Open sheet appears, allowing you to select the folder you'd like to attach scripts to. In the next dialog box, Folder Actions Setup lets you choose the actual scripts you want to attach to the folder; to attach more than one, ⌘-click each script individually.

- **Select a folder from the left pane to see a list of all its attached scripts in the right pane.** To remove some of the attached scripts from that folder, select them and click the – button in the lower-middle of the window.

- **To attach a new script to the currently selected folder, click the + button in the lower-middle section of the window.** A dialog box appears, letting you attach any of the currently available folder action scripts to the folder you chose.

- **To see the code that goes with a particular folder action, select the script from the right pane, and click Edit Script.** Just like the methods described on page 227, this button opens the selected folder action script in Script Editor.

You can always launch Folder Actions Setup by double-clicking its icon in the Finder (found in Applications → AppleScript), but that's the old-fashioned way. Instead, Control-click anything in the Finder and choose Configure Folder Actions from the shortcut menu. Or, if the Finder is hidden, open the Script Menu and choose Folder Actions → Folder Actions Setup. No matter which method you use, Folder Actions Setup springs to life, letting you organize your sprawling collection of folder actions.

- **Part 4** checks whether your desktop is full, based on whether it has more items than you specified in part 1. If there *are* too many items, the script finds all the ones after the cutoff point and sends them to your Home → Old Desktop folder. For example, if you had 15 icons on your desktop but decided in part 1 that there could be a maximum of 10, the last 5 icons would get moved to your Old Desktop folder when the script ran.

All you have to do now is save your script and attach it to the desktop (Control-click the desktop background and choose Attach a Folder Action). Now, when your desktop gets too full, don't fret—just sit back and relax as your Mac cleans it up for you!

Tip: For additional timesaving folder actions, visit *http://www.apple.com/applescript/folderactions/05.html.*

Scripting Programs That Don't Have Dictionaries

In every script since Chapter 1, you've used AppleScript commands that come from programs' dictionaries. Dictionaries are the cornerstone of application control (page 44), and they're great for discovering new commands. The only problem is, not every program *has* as a dictionary.

Some programs, like Chess, are too unimportant for Apple to create a dictionary. Others, like System Preferences, have such limited dictionaries that they're almost not worth mentioning. Still other programs are written by overworked third-party programmers, who might not fully comprehend the benefits of making their application AppleScriptable. And programs like Final Cut Pro and GarageBand really *ought* to have AppleScript dictionaries, but Apple hasn't gotten around to writing them. If you want to script such programs, you're left out in the cold—or so you might think.

The fact is, *every* program—even one without dictionaries—supports three universal commands. They're not particularly powerful, but they form the backbone of most scripts. Table 12-1 has the low-down.

Table 12-1. Commands you can send to any program

Command	What it does
activate	Brings the target program forward, launching it if necessary (page 19).
launch	Opens the target program but doesn't bring it forward.
quit	Closes the target program, asking you to save any unsaved documents in the process.

If you only used those three commands, however, you'd be left with some pretty dinky scripts. Of course, if the program you're controlling has a dictionary, the commands from that dictionary are likely to make up the vast majority of your script.

Still, even if a program *doesn't* have a dictionary, you can control the program with AppleScript; it's just a little harder than usual. The trick is to use Mac OS X's *GUI Scripting* feature, through which you can control a program's interface (*GUI*, in fact, stands for *Graphical User Interface*). In essence, you use GUI Scripting to automate the clicking of buttons or the typing of keys, rather than directing programs with special commands like *make* or *count*.

Note: Even though you can control any program with GUI Scripting, you should use it only if the program you want to control doesn't have an AppleScript dictionary. That's because GUI Scripting is *always* slower and less reliable than scripting a program with direct AppleScript commands (as you've done in the last 11 chapters).

GEM IN THE ROUGH

Checking Whether a Program Has a Dictionary

When deciding how to script a program, it's important to know whether that program has a dictionary. If the program does, you can use any of the commands *from* that dictionary, automating your Mac with ease. On the other hand, if a program lacks a dictionary, you have to use GUI Scripting if you want to control the program with AppleScript.

But you already knew all that. To figure out whether a program has a dictionary, you can make an educated guess—or you can use the Finder's *has scripting terminology* property. You give that command a file alias, and you get back a Boolean value: *true* if the program has a dictionary or *false* if it doesn't. For example, you can use the following script to check whether TextEdit has a dictionary:

```
tell application "Finder"
    if has scripting terminology of alias ¬
        "Macintosh HD:Applications:¬
    TextEdit.app:" then
        display dialog "Yes, TextEdit has ¬
            a dictionary."
    else
        display dialog ¬
            "TextEdit has no dictionary."
    end if
end tell
```

To prove that the Chess program *doesn't* have a dictionary, simply replace the word "TextEdit" with "Chess" everywhere in the previous script. Or, if you'd like to check another program, substitute that program's name in the script instead.

At a certain point, however, you'll get tired of editing your entire script just to check a different program. By making the following changes, however, you you'll be able to pick the program you want to check right from a dialog box:

```
set selectedProgram to (choose file)
tell application "Finder"
    if has scripting terminology of
selectedProgram then
        display dialog ¬
            "Yes, that program has a
dictionary."
    else
        display dialog ¬
            "That program does not have a
dictionary."
    end if
end tell
```

Incidentally, the benefit of this script over the File → Open Dictionary command is that it lets you pinpoint a *particular* program to check for a dictionary. If you used the Open Dictionary dialog box, you'd have to sort through dozens of programs just to find the one you want.

Note: The example scripts from this chapter can be found on the AppleScript Examples CD (see page 24 for instructions).

Enabling GUI Scripting

In a fresh installation of Mac OS X, GUI Scripting is turned off. It's easy to turn it on, though—and you *have* to do that before running any of the scripts in this chapter.

Here's how to enable GUI Scripting:

1. **Open System Preferences → Universal Access.**

   This System Preference pane is where you can turn on various accessibility features of Mac OS X. It also happens to be where you can turn on GUI Scripting.

2. **Click "Enable access for assistive devices."**

   This is the master switch for GUI Scripting on your Mac (Figure 12-1).

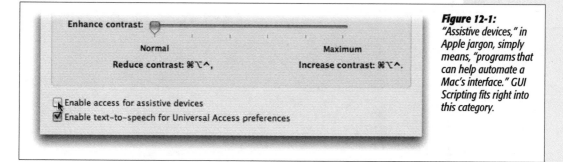

Figure 12-1:
"Assistive devices," in Apple jargon, simply means, "programs that can help automate a Mac's interface." GUI Scripting fits right into this category.

3. **If your Mac presents an Authenticate dialog box, enter your user name and password.**

   Click OK to dismiss the dialog box.

Now you're free to use GUI Scripting to your heart's content.

GUI Scripting Basics

The cornerstone of GUI Scripting is the invisible program named System Events. Back on page 110, you used System Events to get a list of all the *processes* (or running programs) on your Mac. But even more powerfully, you can use System Events to *control* these processes, clicking buttons and typing keystrokes from AppleScript.

The first step, then, is to open System Events's AppleScript dictionary in Script Editor (File → Open Dictionary → System Events). Since you want to learn how you can control processes, take a look specifically at the Processes Suite (Figure 12-2). Inside, you'll find:

- **Classes.** Here, you can discover all the different kinds of interface elements you can control with your scripts: windows, menu items, buttons, text fields, and more. Later, when you write a script, you'll specify individual interface elements (like *window "Universal Access"*) to direct your script to click or type in a certain part of the screen.

- **Commands.** These are what do the real work of GUI Scripting: clicking and typing. You send commands like *click* (see the next page) and *keystroke* (page 248) to particular processes, and Mac OS X pretends that you *yourself* clicked or typed into those programs.

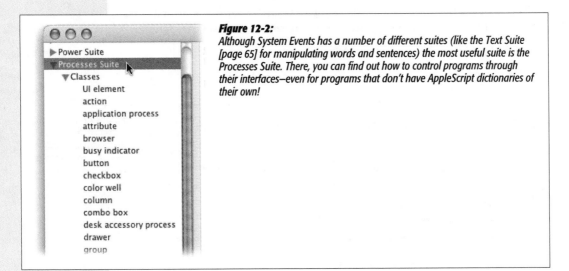

Figure 12-2:
Although System Events has a number of different suites (like the Text Suite [page 65] for manipulating words and sentences) the most useful suite is the Processes Suite. There, you can find out how to control programs through their interfaces—even for programs that don't have AppleScript dictionaries of their own!

Keep this dictionary open as you proceed through this chapter. That way, if there's a command you're not familiar with, you can look it up in the Processes Suite.

Controlling Menus

Back on page 214, you used FileMaker Pro's *do menu* command to run an action from the menu bar. Unfortunately, that command is specific to FileMaker Pro; *do menu* won't work in TextEdit, Photoshop, the Finder, and so on.

Luckily, you can use GUI Scripting to extend AppleScript's menu control to *any* program. If you're sick of Web site pop-up windows, for example, the following script will choose the Safari → Block Pop-up Windows command from the menu bar, all automatically:

```
--Part 1:
tell application "Safari"
```

```
        activate
    end tell
    --Part 2:
    tell application "System Events"
        --Part 3:
        tell process "Safari"
            --Part 4:
            click the menu item "Block Pop-Up Windows" of the menu "Safari" ¬
                of menu bar 1
        end tell
    end tell
```

Here's how the script works:

- **Part 1** brings Safari forward, allowing you to command its menu bar.

Note: Bringing a program forward is the necessary first step in *any* script that employs GUI Scripting.

- **Part 2** invokes System Events, the invisible program in charge of your other programs (page 109).

Note: When you're using GUI Scripting, every AppleScript command must go through System Events. The exception, of course, is *activate,* which you should send directly to the program you want to bring forward.

- **Part 3** directs your GUI Scripting commands at Safari. The keyword *process*, as described on page 110, is simply the way that System Events refers to a currently running program.

- **Part 4** is the meat of the script. Here, you specify the menu command you want to run (Block Pop-Up Windows) and the menu that it's inside of (Safari). In other words, this command is just a fancy way of telling AppleScript to run the Safari → Block Pop-Up Windows command.

Note: Whenever you're commanding a menu with GUI Scripting, you always have to append *of menu bar 1* to the end of the command. That's because, in theory, programs could have *more than one* menu bar, and AppleScript needs to know which one you're talking about. (In reality, of course, programs on the Mac never have more than one menu bar, so you'll always refer to *menu bar 1.*)

Clicking Buttons

Another useful feature of GUI Scripting is the ability to automate button clicks. In fact, if a program doesn't have a dictionary, this ability is often the *only* way you can use AppleScript with that program.

System Preferences (the control panel hub of Mac OS X), for example, has such a measly dictionary that it's a common target for GUI-scripted button clicks. Plus,

System Preference panes are chock full o' buttons, leaving you plenty of targets for your GUI scripts.

For example, you can change your computer's network name by visiting System Preferences → Sharing and clicking Edit. Or, if you change your computer's network name *often*—say, to throw off your nosy spouse downstairs—you can automate the process with this script:

```
tell application "System Preferences"
    activate
end tell
tell application "System Events"
    --Part 1:
    tell process "System Preferences"
        --Part 2:
        click the menu item "Sharing" of the menu "View" of menu bar 1
        --Part 3:
        delay 4
        --Part 4:
        click the button "Edit..." of window "Sharing"
    end tell
end tell
```

Note: To type the three dots after "Edit" in part 3, press Option-semicolon. *Don't* simply press the period key three times.

When you run that script, System Preferences springs forward and happily opens its Sharing pane. The script then performs a virtual click on the Edit button, displaying a dialog sheet to let you change your Mac's network name.

Here's how the script works its magic:

- **Part 1** tells System Events that you're interesting in scripting the interface of System Preferences (not Safari, like you did in the previous script).

- **Part 2** performs a virtual click on the View → Sharing menu command. This part opens the Sharing pane of System Preferences.

- **Part 3** pauses for 4 seconds as System Preferences loads and displays your pane.

Note: If you have a fast computer, your System Preference panes load quickly, so you can pause for a shorter period of time than 4 seconds. Similarly, if you have an absolutely ancient Mac, you'd be better off making your script pause for slightly *more* than 4 seconds while your preference pane loads.

- **Part 3** performs a virtual click on the Edit button in your Sharing pane. You'll see the dialog sheet shown in Figure 12-3, which lets you give your Mac a new network name.

From now on, you don't have to remember how to change your Mac's network name; you can just run your script instead.

Use this name to reach this computer from machines on your local subnet.

Local Hostname: Cool-Mac-Upstairs.local

Cancel   OK

Figure 12-3:
You can enter letters, numbers, and hyphens in your Mac's network name, but no other symbols. The .local ending is common to all network names, so you can't delete it.

Clicking Tab Buttons

Some System Preference panes have all their options laid out in one screen (Appearance and Exposé, for example). Other preference panes, however, have multiple *different* screens, and you have to access each screen by clicking on different tabs (Figure 12-4). Therefore, before you can script such preference panes as International and Universal Access (which have multiple tabs) you need to know how to script the tabs themselves.

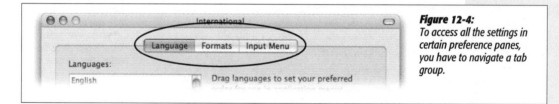

International

Language   Formats   Input Menu

Languages:

English   Drag languages to set your preferred

Figure 12-4:
To access all the settings in certain preference panes, you have to navigate a tab group.

Fortunately, it's easy to use GUI Scripting for selecting a tab in a tab group. Say you wanted to open System Preferences → Universal Access → Keyboard tab:

```
tell application "System Preferences"
    activate
end tell
tell application "System Events"
    tell process "System Preferences"
        --Part 1:
        click the menu item "Universal Access" of the menu "View" of menu bar 1
        --Part 2:
        delay 4
        --Part 3:
        click the radio button "Keyboard" of the first tab group ¬
            of window "Universal Access"
    end tell
end tell
```

Here's how the script breaks down:

- **Part 1** selects the View → Universal Access command from System Preferences's menu, bringing forward the Universal Access pane.

- **Part 2** pauses as System Preferences loads and displays the pane.

- **Part 3** performs a virtual click on the Keyboard tab, bringing its options forward for you to see (Figure 12-5). Note how System Events refers to individual tabs: they're called *radio buttons,* in memory of old car radios that let you select only one button at a time.

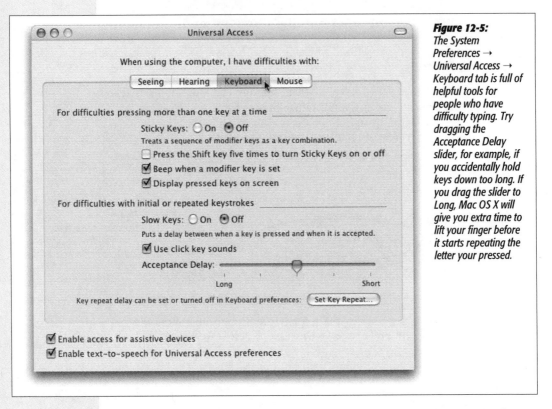

Figure 12-5:
The System Preferences → Universal Access → Keyboard tab is full of helpful tools for people who have difficulty typing. Try dragging the Acceptance Delay slider, for example, if you accidentally hold keys down too long. If you drag the slider to Long, Mac OS X will give you extra time to lift your finger before it starts repeating the letter your pressed.

Of course, simply opening a tab in System Preferences is something a trained monkey could do. To get some *real* use out of your script, you should have it turn on Mac OS X's Sticky Keys feature, so you can press a special key (Command, Option, Control, or Shift) and have that key "stick" in place while you press other keys.

That feature is convenient if you have pains in your fingers, for example, and can't hold down the keystroke ⌘-S comfortably (to select File → Save). Using Sticky Keys, if you first pressed the ⌘ key (and lifted your finger), you would see the cloverleaf symbol appear on your screen—and then if you pressed the S key (and lifted your finger), you'd complete the keystroke. In other words, if Sticky Keys is turned on, you only have to type keystrokes in *sequence*—you don't have to hold down all the keys at once.

The only problem is, the Sticky Keys radio button is stuck deep inside your System Preferences pane—*too* deep, in fact, to figure out how to AppleScript the button on your own. All hope isn't lost, though; you can still use GUI Scripting to enable Sticky Keys—provided you read on.

Deciphering Interface Hierarchies

Whenever there's an interface element (like the Sticky Keys radio button) that's deep inside a window, your best bet is to use Apple's UIElementInspector tool. This powerful program, available from *www.apple.com/applescript/uiscripting/downloads/uiinspector.dmg,* gladly reveals the hierarchy of your windows, so you can figure out precisely how to script an interface element.

Once you've downloaded the program, copy it into your Applications folder. From there, follow these simple steps to script the Sticky Keys radio button:

1. **Double-click UIElementInspector in the Finder.**

   The program opens but without a menu bar or Dock icon. You deal with UIElementInspector *entirely* through its mini–title-barred windows.

2. **Hover your mouse over the Sticky Keys "On" radio button in System Preferences.**

   UIElementInspector displays bits of geeky information, telling you the radio button's name, size, position, and so on.

Tip: If you want to inspect a different interface element—say, a text field or a checkbox—simply hover your cursor over *that* element instead.

---

3. **Press ⌘-F10 to lock UIElementInspector's current display (Figure 12-6).**

   That'll allow you to move the mouse around without worrying about changing what's in the Inspector window.

Tip: For a more thorough explanation of UIElementInspector's features, check out *www.apple.com/applescript/uiscripting/02.html.*

---

4. **Examine the top lines of the Inspector window to discover the interface hierarchy for the button.**

   You should see an indented list, like this:

```
<AXApplication: "System Preferences">
<AXWindow: "Universal Access">
 <AXTabGroup>
  <AXRadioGroup>
   <AXRadioButton: "On">
```

In plain English, that means that the "On" radio button (*<AXRadioButton>*) is stored inside a group of radio buttons (*<AXRadioGroup>*), which *itself* is stored inside a tab group (*<AXTabGroup>*) inside the Universal Access window (*<AXWindow>*) of System Preferences.

Note: The "AX" prefix stands for "accessibility," Apple's term for features that make it possible to control your Mac without the keyboard and mouse.

Figure 12-6:
After you press ⌘-F10, UIElementInspector turns its text red to indicate that it's locked onto the current interface element. To unlock the program—so you can inspect other interface elements—simply press ⌘-F10 again.

5. **Quit UIElementInspector.**

   Since the program doesn't have a menu bar or Dock icon, just click the Inspector's upper-left close box instead.

6. **Using your newly discovered interface information, incorporate the appropriate GUI Scripting command into your script.**

   In this example, the final script would look like the following:

   ```
   tell application "System Preferences"
       activate
   end tell
   tell application "System Events"
       tell process "System Preferences"
           click menu item ¬
               "Universal Access" of menu "View" of menu bar 1
   ```

```
delay 4
click the radio button "Keyboard" of the ¬
    first tab group of window "Universal Access"
--This is it:
click the radio button "On" of the first ¬
    radio group of the first tab group of ¬
    the window "Universal Access"
        end tell
    end tell
```

POWER USERS' CLINIC

PreFab UI Browser

UIElementInspector is a powerful tool for discovering how your windows are laid out, but it's certainly not the most user-friendly program Apple ever made. If you use UIElementInspector to decipher the organization of windows with, say, a dozen nested interface elements, you may find yourself going crazy trying to transcribe all the "AX" terms to an AppleScript.

Luckily, there's another choice for discovering how to script interface elements. PreFab UI Browser (*www.prefab.com/uibrowser/*) has tons of power-user GUI Scripting features, but still manages to stay user-friendly. Here's just a sampling of what UI Browser can do:

* **Navigate deep into the menus of your programs, without you actually opening the menus.** UI Browser has the almost spooky ability to inspect the interfaces of programs that aren't in front at the moment—and to tell you how to script them.

* **Find the order of interface elements onscreen.** For instance, some programs have several different tab groups within the same window. If you wanted to script a particular tab group, you'd have to direct the commands at *the first tab group, the second tab group,* and so on—and UI Browser can tell you which tab group is which.

* **Write GUI Scripting code automatically.** Using the AppleScript pop-up menu, you can have UI Browser write code that clicks, selects, and otherwise plays with your interface elements—all without typing a single command yourself. That's a welcome

break from Apple's own UIElementInspector, which wouldn't write you a line of code even if you got down on your knees and begged.

* **Highlight interface elements onscreen.** While UIElementInspector can do this too, there's no comparison between the two programs. For one thing, Prefab UI Browser can highlight interface elements of programs that are hidden, displaying where elements *would* be if the programs were visible at the moment. Plus, UI Browser can list interface elements you didn't even know existed—like invisible buttons—and reveal them to you onscreen. Taken together, these features let you not only discover new interface elements in your existing programs, but also *control* these interface elements from AppleScript.

Unfortunately, all this power comes at a cost—$55, to be exact. If you make GUI Scripting you life's work, that's well worth the price. However, if you're just a casual scripter, it might make more sense to stick with the free UIElementInspector.

And on the subject of PreFab Software: take a look at Pre-Fab's UI Actions technology (*www.prefab.com/uiactions/*). UI Actions are based on the same idea as folder actions (page 221); however, instead of running scripts when you add files to a folder or disk, a UI Action runs a script whenever you visit a particular Web site or bring a new TextEdit window forward (in other words, any time a program's interface changes). If you're a hard-core AppleScripter, the ability to trigger scripts straight from programs' interfaces is not to be missed.

As shown here, you simply translate the hierarchy you discovered back in part 4 into an AppleScript command. Then, when you run your script, System Preferences comes forward, opens Universal Access, and turns on Sticky Keys.

Tip: If you'd like to learn more about Sticky Keys and other keyboard-assisting features, visit *www.apple.com/accessibility/physical/*.

And don't forget: a *radio button* isn't the only kind of interface element you can click. If there were a push-style button you wanted to click (like the reload button in Safari) you would simply call it a plain old *button* in your script.

Fake Typing

Even though you turned on Sticky Keys in the last script, the script *itself* only impersonated mouse clicks—clicking a menu item and then clicking a few radio buttons. As you know, however, a mouse is only half of your computer's input.

The other half, of course, is the keyboard. If you want to do any serious work with GUI Scripting, you have to emulate keystrokes as well. Thanks to the *keystroke* command, this task is quite easy:

```
tell application "System Events"
    keystroke "Q"
end tell
```

When you run that script, you should notice the letter Q magically typed into your Script Editor window. Behind the scenes, your script convinces Mac OS X that *you* just typed the letter Q on your keyboard.

Of course, you probably want to type keystrokes in *other* programs, too—and thankfully, that's just as convenient:

```
tell application "TextEdit"
    activate
end tell
--Now the keystroke "Q" will appear in TextEdit
tell application "System Events"
    keystroke "Q"
end tell
```

You can even specify more than *one* key to press, in sequence:

```
tell application "TextEdit"
    activate
end tell
tell application "System Events"
    keystroke "Quack" --This types "Q", "u", "a", "c", "k"
end tell
```

Zooming In and Out

In the script on page 246, you turned on Mac OS X's Sticky Keys feature. Even more useful to everyday Mac users, though, is Mac OS X's *screen zooming* feature, which lets you focus in on a small section of your screen for detailed graphics work.

Note: You enable screen zooming by opening System Preferences → Universal Access → Seeing tab and clicking "Turn on Zoom."

Normally, you zoom in on the screen by pressing Option-⌘-+, and zoom out by holding Option-⌘-minus sign.

That process, however, is imprecise. Unless you can hold the keys down for *exactly* the same amount of time each time you press them, the magnification factor will differ each time you zoom in on your screen. You might be looking at an image of your kids' hair at 5× magnification one time you zoom in, and 15× the next.

That's where GUI Scripts can come in handy. Each time you run the following script, the screen zooms in and out a *consistent* amount, giving you an up-close view of your screen that's exactly the same magnification each time:

```
tell application "System Events"
    --Part 1:
    key down option
    key down command
    --Part 2:
    key down "+"
    delay 2
    key up "+"
    --Part 3:
    delay 5
    key down "-"
    delay 2
    key up "-"
    --Part 4:
    key up option
    key up command
end tell
```

Here's how the new commands work:

- **Part 1** holds down the ⌘ and Option keys, a prerequisite to zooming in (⌘-Option-+) or out (⌘-Option-minus sign).

Note: The *key down* command is an extension of the *keystroke* command. However, instead of simply typing the specified key, the *key down* command holds *down* the key you specify—at least until the script encounters a *key up* command.

- **Part 2** holds the + key down, thereby completing the ⌘-Option-+ keystroke—and zooming in on your screen. Two seconds later, the script releases the + key (using *key up*), stopping your screen from zooming in any further.

- **Part 3** pauses 5 seconds, letting you get a good view of your zoomed-in screen. Then the script zooms out, by holding ⌘-Option-minus sign for 2 seconds.

- **Part 4** lifts up the ⌘ and Option keys, because your script is done pressing key combinations.

Note: It is *very* important that every *key down* command be paired with a matching *key up* command later in your script. If you forget *key up,* the keys you specified will remain held down—even after your script is finished running!

That's all there is to it. Now, whenever you want to examine a blown-up version of your screen for a few seconds, simply run your script.

FREQUENTLY ASKED QUESTION

Typing Function Keys

I'm really digging the GUI-scripted typing feature, but it seems kind of limited. Is there any way I can automate typing function keys from my scripts?

Function keys, like many features in Mac OS X, offer shortcuts to various parts of your Mac world. For example, you can use the function keys (F1–F12 on most keyboards) to manage your windows with Exposé, or have function keys trigger special AppleScripts (page 158). No matter what you use function keys for, however, it would sure be useful if you could have GUI scripts press function keys *for* you, to save you the finger movement.

If you wanted to make a script press F9, your first instinct might be to use a command like this:

```
tell application "System Events"
    key down "F9"
end tell
```

As it turns out, though, that script would merely type the keys "F," then "9," in sequence. To type an actual function key, you have to know its *key code*—Mac OS X's secret identification number for every key on your keyboard. The key code for F9 happens to be 101, so the proper script would look like this:

```
tell application "System Events"
    key code 101
end tell
```

Of course, unless you're a Mac Genius, you probably don't know the key code for every function key on your Mac. Luckily, if you download a program like Full Key Codes (*www.bajram.com/_downloads/?server=01&file=Full_Key_Codes.sit*), you can discover the key code for just about any key on your Mac—function key or otherwise. Just keep in mind that you want the *decimal* key code (not the *hex* key code) for use in your GUI scripts.

For more addiction-satisfying GUI scripts, examine Script Menu → UI Element Scripts. Or visit *www.apple.com/applescript/uiscripting/03.html* for a series of helpful GUI-controlling subroutines and extra scripts.

CHAPTER 13

Mixing AppleScript and Unix

Although Mac OS X is one of the nicest looking operating systems around, its Unix core is decidedly ugly. In Unix, you run programs by typing their names, not by double-clicking their icons. And not only that, if you misspell a Unix program's name—or even mis-*capitalize* it—the program simply won't run.

Still, Unix is the foundation of Mac OS X, and it's got a few benefits to its name. For one, Unix is much older than Mac OS X, and it's been refined by generations of programmers. As a result, it's efficient, secure, and crash-resistant to its core.

As if that weren't enough, Unix is a power user's dream. Often-used programs have quick, short names (*ls, cp,* and *mv,* for example), and you can redirect the results of one program into a completely separate program with the pipe symbol, a simple vertical bar (|). And since Unix was invented in the days before graphical operating systems, it's got *tons* of timesaving keyboard shortcuts—like pressing the up arrow key to run a previous Unix program.

Finally, there are some things you can *only* do with Unix. To tweak hidden Mac OS X settings, for example, you have to use a special Unix program called *defaults.* Or, if you want to admire how long your computer's been running, the *uptime* program comes in handy. Either way, you're getting information you can't find anywhere else.

Note: The example scripts from this chapter can be found on the AppleScript Examples CD (see page 24 for instructions).

Terminal

To interact with Mac OS X's Unix core, you use the Terminal program, located in your Applications → Utilities folder. When you launch that program, you see a pretty meager window, with a line of text and a cursor for you to enter programs' names (Figure 13-1).

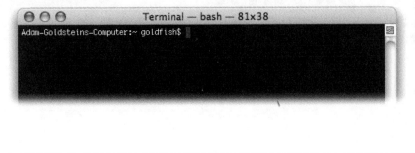

Figure 13-1:
A Terminal window. To change the window's coloring, visit Terminal → Window Settings, choose Color from the pop-up menu at the top, and pick out any colors you want for the window's text and background.

This line of text is known as a *command prompt*—or, in casual geeky conversation, just a *prompt.* You type the name of a program here and press Enter (or Return) to run that program. When a new prompt appears, Unix is ready to accept a new program's name.

Note: Depending on your Mac's name, your user name, and various other settings, your prompt may look different than the one shown here.

If you wanted to run the *uptime* program, for example, you'd type this:

```
Adam-Goldsteins-Computer:~ goldfish$ uptime
```

Once you pressed Enter, you'd see a result like this:

```
11:27  up 27 days, 17:50, 1 user, load averages: 0.50 0.45 0.43
```

That information tells you: what time it is; how long your computer's been running without restarting; how many users are on your computer right now; and how hard your processor is working (on a scale from 0 to 2).

Of course, if you want to check that information *often*—say, so you can brag to your friends that your Mac's been running for a month straight—it's kind of annoying to enter *uptime* in Terminal every time you want to check your Mac's status. Luckily, Terminal supports a special AppleScript command, *do script,* that can greatly automate the process of running Unix programs. Here, for example, is a script to run *uptime* from AppleScript:

```
tell application "Terminal"
    activate
```

```
    do script "uptime" --Here's where you specify the Unix program
end tell
```

When you run that AppleScript, Terminal comes forward and runs the Unix *uptime* command for you.

Tip: By default, the *do script* command creates a whole new Terminal window to run your Unix program. If you'd rather run *uptime* in the *current* Terminal window, though, simply modify your script like this:

```
tell application "Terminal"
    activate
    do script "uptime" in the front window
end tell
```

Changing System Settings

There are far more sophisticated programs you can run in Terminal, too. For instance, you can display a floating blue Exposé button (Figure 13-2) by running the following command in Terminal:

```
defaults write com.apple.dock wvous-floater -bool true
```

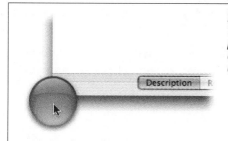

Figure 13-2:
The Exposé blob. Click it once to display all the windows of the current program (the equivalent of pressing F10 on your keyboard), or Option-click the blob to display all the windows in all visible programs (the equivalent of F9 on your keyboard).

You won't see the blob, however, until you quit and restart the Dock. You can do that in one of two ways:

- **Use Applications → Utilities → Activity Monitor.** Select the entry named Dock, click Quit Process, and choose Quit from the dialog box.

- **Log out and log back in.** Or, if that's too dainty for you, restart your entire Mac.

Once the Dock restarts, your blob appears onscreen, ready for action.

Note: The *defaults* Unix command is meant for tweaking all sorts of system settings. For more information about *defaults,* run this in Terminal:

```
man defaults
```

Incidentally, the *man* program gives you help with other Unix programs. For more about the *man* command, run *man man*.

Of course, you can package your blob-creating Unix command in an AppleScript—so you can share the blobby convenience with all your friends, for example:

```
tell application "Terminal"
    activate
    do script "defaults write com.apple.dock wvous-floater -bool true"
end tell
tell application "Dock"
    quit --Restart the Dock
end tell
```

Tip: If you get bored with the Exposé blob, you can turn it off by running that same script, just replacing *true* with *false.*

And if this example doesn't satisfy your thirst for system tweaks, examine a site like *www.macosxhints.com* for dozens more uses of the Unix *defaults* command.

Unix Text Editing

If you come from the graphical world of Mac OS X, the idea of a *Unix text editor* probably strikes you as pretty odd. In a Unix text editor, you can't use the menu bar or mouse to edit text, you can't drag-and-drop sentences to different places, and perhaps worst of all, you can't spell check your writing. Why on earth would people subject themselves to this?

Power, that's why. For people who spend their days writing computer programs, Web pages, and the like, Unix text editors offer all sorts of power-user features: simple looks, extreme customizability, and tons of keyboard shortcuts, for example. Even non-geeks might want to use Unix text editors on occasion—so they can edit system files, for example.

Unfortunately, there's no simple way to open a text file from the *graphical* side of Mac OS X in the Unix side. The best you can do is type the name of the text editor in Terminal, followed by the path to file you want to open, like this:

```
pico ~/Desktop/CheeseDoodles.txt
```

That, of course, would open your Home → Desktop → CheeseDoodles.txt file in the Unix text editor named *pico.*

Note: In Unix, the ~ symbol simply means, "in my Home folder." Additionally, forward slashes (/) are used to separate folder names. (In the Unix world, folders are also known as *directories.*)

Luckily, you can use AppleScript to simplify the process of opening a file in *pico* (or any other Unix text editor, for that matter). That way, you can edit your text files the old-fashioned way—in the Terminal—which many power users prefer for its total reliance on the keyboard (and total avoidance of the mouse). This script gets you started:

```
--Part 1:
on run
    display dialog "Drag files to my icon to open them in pico."
end run

--Part 2:
on open draggedItems
    --Part 3:
    repeat with currentItem in draggedItems
        --Part 4:
        set unixPath to the POSIX path of currentItem
        --Part 5:
        set unixString to ("pico " & unixPath)
        --Part 6:
        tell application "Terminal"
            activate
            do script unixString
        end tell
    end repeat
end open
```

Note: As you can tell from the *on open* line in part 2, this script is a droplet, so it works when you drag files onto the script's icon. See page 142 for instructions on how to save your script as a droplet.

Here's how the script works:

- **Part 1** tells you to drag files onto the script's Finder icon to open them in Terminal. Of course, part 1 only runs if you *don't* drag files onto the script's icon in the first place.

- **Part 2** runs if you *do* drag files onto the script's icon. This part puts a list of the files you dragged into *draggedItems*.

- **Part 3** starts a *repeat* loop so the script can process every file you dropped. The file currently being operated on goes in *currentItem*.

- **Part 4** gets the *POSIX path* of the current file—basically, its Unix-compatible path. (Page 77 has more information on POSIX.)

- **Part 5** creates a new variable, *unixString*, to hold the command you're going to send to Terminal. For example, if you dragged your Documents → Quesadillas.txt file onto the script's icon, *unixString* would hold "pico /Documents/Quesadillas.txt" after this part of the script.

- **Part 6** brings Terminal forward and runs your Unix program, *pico*. Since you don't specify what window to run the program in (page 253), Terminal automatically spawns a *new* window for each file you dragged.

Tip: Although *pico* is the easiest Unix text editor to use, there are plenty of others that pack more features (*vi* and *emacs,* for example, are popular among programmers).

If you'd rather make your AppleScript open text files in a *different* Unix program, simply replace the word *pico* with *vi, emacs,* or the name of whatever text editor you'd like to use. And if you're confused by all the choices of Unix text editors, visit *www.reallylinux.com/docs/editors/editor.shtml* for some guidance.

Now, if you ever feel the need to open some text files in Terminal, just drag the files to your script's icon. For easy access, you can even store your script in the Dock, so *pico* is never more than a file-drag away.

Unix Without Terminal

After using the Terminal for a while, you're bound to get bored. That's because, despite all the window settings you can tweak, Terminal is still a holdover from the days of mainframes. At some point, you'll probably wonder, "Why can't I just run Unix programs *straight* from AppleScript, without going through an ugly Terminal window?"

As it turns out, you can. AppleScript includes a special command, *do shell script,* for running Unix programs without Terminal's assistance. For instance, if you wanted to run the *defaults* program from page 253, you could use the following commands instead of invoking Terminal:

```
do shell script "defaults write com.apple.dock wvous-floater -bool true"
tell application "Dock"
    quit
end tell
```

When you run that script, AppleScript runs the Unix *defaults* program, silently and in the background. If there's a problem while running the Unix program, Apple-Script displays an error dialog box. Otherwise, if there aren't any problems, your script proceeds to restart the Dock—and, in doing so, displays the blue Exposé blob.

Of course, this background-only *do shell script* command has its limitations. For example, you can't run *pico* with *do shell script,* because you wouldn't get to see a Unix text-editing window. And certain Unix programs, like *top,* run forever—or at least until you force them to quit—and therefore aren't very well suited for using in the middle of an AppleScript.

Note: The Unix *top* program is meant for checking the status of all your *other* programs—kind of like a text-only Activity Viewer (in your Applications → Utilities folder). For more information about *top,* type *man top* in Terminal.

Getting Program Results Back

Still, there *are* some Unix programs that give you back information—and don't take forever to finish running. The *cal* program, for instance, presents a nicely formatted calendar of the current month when you run it in Terminal.

Now, suppose you wanted to run *cal* from AppleScript. If you were of the page 252 mindset, your first instinct would be to write a script that asked *Terminal* to run the *cal* command for you. However, there's a much simpler way to do it, using *do shell script:*

```
--Part 1:
set theResult to (do shell script "cal")
--Part 2:
display dialog theResult
```

Here's how the script works:

- **Part 1** runs *cal*—in the background, of course, because you opted to use *do shell script* rather than commanding Terminal directly. The result of your Unix program (in this case, a text representation of the current month) gets stored in *theResult.*

- **Part 2** displays a dialog box with the result of your Unix program (Figure 13-3).

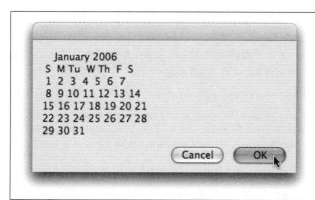

Figure 13-3:
The output of the cal program. The reason some of the numbers don't line up quite right is that Terminal uses fixed-width fonts (that is, every letter, number, and space takes up the same amount of room), whereas AppleScript uses varying-width fonts (so spaces appear narrower than letters and numbers).

Now, whenever you want a calendar of the current month—so you can check whether New Year's day falls on a weekend, for example—just run your script.

Tip: If you want the calendar for some month *besides* the current month, just use *cal* like this:

```
cal 3 2006
```

That would get you a calendar for March (month 3) of 2006.

Running Superuser Commands

In the world of Mac OS X, there are three kinds of people: *standard* account hold-ers, *administrators,* and *superusers.* The kind of account you have determines what kind of changes you can make to your Mac (Table 13-1).

Table 13-1. Different kinds of accounts and the powers they wield

Type of account	Can change account-specific preferences	Can change other accounts' preferences	Can open and delete other people's files	Can open and delete *system* files
Standard	Yes	No	No	No
Administrator	Yes	Yes	Yes	No
Superuser	Yes	Yes	Yes	Yes

Note: In a fresh installation of Mac OS X, the first account you create is automatically an administrator account. From then on, you can create additional accounts (either standard or administrator) by opening System Preferences → Accounts and clicking the lower-left + button.

Say you wanted to edit some files in the System → Library → CoreServices folder, where Mac OS X stores all its private settings and programs. Naturally, if you were a standard or administrator account holder, the files there would be off-limits. However, by posing as a *superuser,* you can convince Mac OS X to let you modify those system files.

Since the *chown* Unix program transfers control of a folder from Mac OS X to you, your first instinct would probably be to write an AppleScript like this:

```
do shell script "chown user /System/Library/CoreServices/"
```

Note: Replace *user* with your own user name. Otherwise, Mac OS X will try to transfer ownership of the folder to a nonexistent account on your Mac—unless, of course, you happen to have an account named *user.*

In essence, that single-line script tells Mac OS X, "Run the *chown* program, and tell it to transfer ownership of the System → Library → CoreServices folder to me." Unfortunately, you'll encounter a roadblock when you run the script, as described in Figure 13-4.

The solution? Add *with administrator privileges* to the end of your command:

```
do shell script "chown user /System/Library/CoreServices/" ¬
    with administrator privileges
```

Now, rather than seeing an error message when you run your script, you see a password dialog box, as shown in Figure 13-5.

Once you enter your password, your script successfully runs *chown*, making you the new owner of the CoreServices folder. Be careful what you do with your newfound powers, though; if you feel like deleting a system program (say, the Finder), nothing will stop you now.

Tip: If this folder-mangling power becomes too overwhelming for you, you can reverse the effects of your previous script by running this one:

```
do shell script "chown root /System/Library/CoreServices"
```

with administrator privileges. The term *root* describes Mac OS X itself. Therefore, when you run this script (and enter your administrator password), you surrender control of System → Library → CoreServices back to Mac OS X.

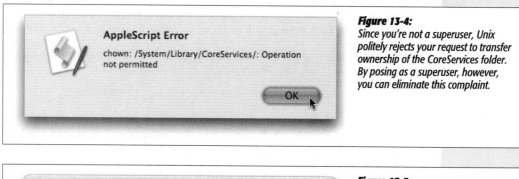

Figure 13-4:
Since you're not a superuser, Unix politely rejects your request to transfer ownership of the CoreServices folder. By posing as a superuser, however, you can eliminate this complaint.

Figure 13-5:
Enter your administrator password, and your Unix command proceeds with superuser powers.

Running AppleScripts from Unix

So far in this chapter, you've spent a lot of time running Unix programs from AppleScript. You've commanded Terminal directly, and even run Unix programs in the background with *do shell script*. What you haven't done, however, is run *AppleScript* commands from *Unix*.

If you're new to the world of Unix, you might not understand how useful this feature can be. Nevertheless, this AppleScript-from-Unix bridge can save you time in several ways:

- **If you run an AppleScript in Terminal, you don't have to launch Script Editor.** Speed freaks, take note.

- **You can mix your AppleScript commands with other Unix programs very easily.** For instance, you could present a dialog box (using AppleScript), and then—depending on what you typed in the dialog box—run one of several Unix programs.

- **You can send AppleScript commands over a network.** Using a "Secure Shell" with the *ssh* command, Unix lets you run programs on other computers on your network—or anywhere in the world. You can also take advantage of this feature to send AppleScript commands to remote computers. See *www.macdevcenter.com/pub/a/mac/2004/07/09/inside_ssh_pt1.html* for details on using *ssh*.

The key to all these tricks is the Unix program *osascript*. You provide it the path of a script to run, and Unix obediently runs that script, like so:

```
osascript "/Library/Scripts/Finder Scripts/Switch to Finder.scpt"
```

That, of course, would run the script from Library → Scripts → Finder Scripts → Switch to Finder.scpt (which brings the Finder forward and hides the windows from other programs).

You're not limited to just running script *files*, however; you can run individual script *commands* as well. All you have to do is append *–e* to *osascript*, and follow up with the AppleScript command you want to run. For example, you could type this in Terminal if you wanted to display a dialog box in the Finder:

```
osascript -e 'tell application "Finder" to display dialog "Quail Eggs"'
```

Note: When using *osascript*, you should surround the entire AppleScript command in single-quotes, but all the AppleScript *strings* should be in double-quotes, as shown in the previous code.

You can even string together several AppleScript commands with *osascript*, by using more than one *–e* flag (make sure you type the following text all on one line):

```
osascript -e 'tell application "TextEdit"' -e 'activate' -e 'make new window
at front' -e 'end tell'
```

That, of course, would be the equivalent of running this script in Script Editor:

```
tell application "TextEdit"
    activate
    make new window at front
end tell
```

A big advantage to running your AppleScript commands in Terminal, of course, is that you don't have to launch Script Editor. But that's only the beginning; you can integrate *osascript* with *other* Unix programs, as explained on the following pages.

Scheduling AppleScript Commands

If there's one annoyance in AppleScript, it's that scripts are finicky to run. Sure, you can double-click them, or trigger them with folder actions (page 221) or Mail rules (page 190). But in all these situations, it's *you* who decides what should trigger the script.

Thankfully, if you're feeling lazy, you can set repeating schedules for your scripts. At whatever days and times you specify, Mac OS X will whir into action and run your scripts—without even being asked.

Note: Your scheduled scripts will only run if your computer is on *and awake* at the moment they're scheduled to run. If your Mac is off or asleep, AppleScript can't wake up your computer just to run your scripts.

The key to this feature is the *cron* program from Unix. *cron* lets you specify Unix programs you want to run at certain times—or, with the help of *osascript*, you can even specify *AppleScripts* you want to run at certain times.

Here, for example, is how you'd tell *cron* to run a Desktop-cleaning AppleScript every day at 10:15 PM:

1. **Enter your script in Script Editor.**

   This is the script that will run regularly, so make sure it does something useful. The folder action from page 233, for example, is the inspiration for this desktop-cleaning script:

   ```
   set maxItems to 5
   tell application "Finder"
       if not (exists folder "Old Desktop" of home) then
           make new folder at home with properties {name:"Old Desktop"}
       end if
       set desktopFiles to every item of the desktop
       if (count desktopFiles) > maxItems then
           move items (maxItems + 1) through (count desktopFiles) of ¬
               desktopFiles to folder "Old Desktop" of home
       end if
   end tell
   ```

2. **Save your script somewhere handy.**

   Your Library → Scripts folder would be as good a place as any. Give the script a creative name, like Clean.scpt, and make sure the File Format is set to Script.

3. **Open Terminal, and type this:**

```
sudo pico /etc/crontab
```

pico, as described on page 254, is a simple Unix text editor. */etc/crontab* speci-fies the path of the file you want to open; this so-called *crontab* file is what dic-tates what day and time recurring events should occur. Finally, the *sudo* bit tells Unix you mean business: you need to run *pico* as the superuser (page 258), because you're editing a system file.

4. **When prompted, type your administrator password.**

This gives you the authority to edit the *crontab* file, and actually runs *pico*.

GEM IN THE ROUGH

Scheduling Scripts with iCal

Although the Unix-based script scheduler from page 261 is a geek's dream, it's not very friendly to novices. Thankfully, you don't *have* to use Unix to schedule your scripts; if you can accept a little less control, iCal serves as a perfectly accept-able alternative. Here's how to schedule a script in iCal:

1. **First, make sure your script is saved as an Application (page 33).** This'll prevent problems later on, because iCal can trigger only *programs,* not raw scripts.

2. **Choose File → New Calendar (Option-⌘-N), and name your new calendar Scripts.** Obvi-ously, if you already have a Scripts calendar, there's no need to create a new one.

3. **Choose File → New Event (⌘-N), and give your event a name.** This event will trigger your script, so make sure you place the event on the date and time you want the script to run.

4. **In the Alarm section of the Info pane, choose "Open file."** This lets you pick a file that should run when the event is approaching. Select the Apple-Script from step 1, and adjust the schedule using the lower pop-up menu.

5. **Adjust any other settings you want.** For example, if you want iCal to trigger the script at regular intervals, choose an interval from the "repeat" pop-up menu.

That's it—your script is now scheduled to run on the date and time you specified. Of course, you didn't have the precise minute-by-minute control you would have had with *cron*—but just think of all the Unix nerdiness you avoided.

Adjust Screen
home

all-day	☐
from	10/26/05 at 1:00 PM
to	10/26/05 at 2:00 PM
attendees	None
status	None ⬍
repeat	every week ⬍
end	Never ⬍
alarm	Open file ⬍
	Mimic PC monitor ⬍
	2 minutes after ⬍
calendar	■ Scripts ⬍
url	None

Notes

---

5. **Use the arrow keys to navigate to the bottom of the *pico* window, and add this line:**

```
15 22 * * * user osascript "/Library/Scripts/Clean.scpt"
```

Note: Make sure you replace *user* with your actual user name, as that is the person that Mac OS X will impersonate when it runs your script. Also, replace */Library/Scripts/Clean.scpt* with the path to the script you want to run.

This geeky list presents tons of information to *cron*. First, the number 15 on the left tells *cron*, "Run my program 15 minutes after the hour." The 22 indicates that your command should run 22 hours after midnight—in other words, at 10:00 PM. Taken together, these two settings tell *cron*, "Run my program at 10:15 PM."

Next, there are three asterisks. To *cron*, an asterisk means, "Ignore this setting." For instance, the leftmost asterisk tells *cron*, "Run the program regardless of what day of the month it is." The middle asterisk implies, "Run the program regardless of what month it is." Finally, the right asterisk tells *cron* to run the program no matter what day of the *week* it is. Had you replaced these asterisks with specific numbers, *cron* would have limited your program to running on only certain days, or only in certain months.

Tip: If you're ever confused about which setting controls which periods of time, just look at the line near the top of the */etc/crontab* file that begins #minute hour mday month wday. By looking down from these table headings, you can discern, for example, that the second column from the left controls which hours your program will run.

The rightmost portion of the line tells *cron* what Unix program you want to run. In this case, you specify *osascript*, along with the actual script file you want to run.

At this point, your Terminal window should look something like Figure 13-6.

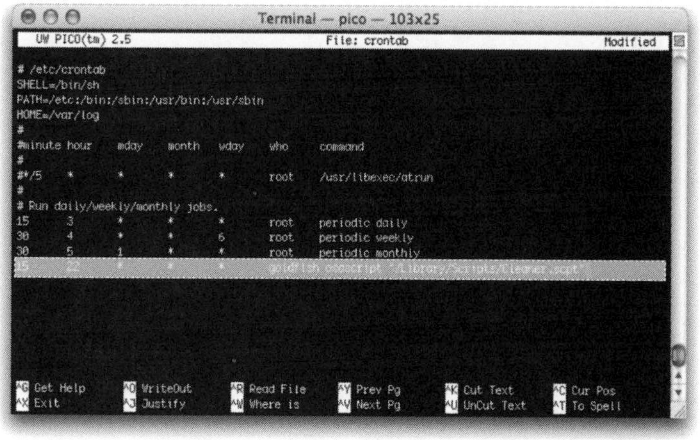

Figure 13-6:
Your crontab file after editing. If you wanted to schedule more than one script, you could add additional lines beyond this one.

6. **Press Control-X to exit** *pico*.

Confirm your changes by pressing *y*, and press Enter when *pico* asks you whether you want to resave the file as *crontab*.

7. **Wait patiently.**

Every night at 10:15, your script will spring into action and clean up your desktop. You don't even have to trigger it yourself!

Tip: If this chapter whetted your appetite for Unix, check out a dedicated book like *Learning Unix for Mac OS X* (O'Reilly). With several hundred pages of Unix information, you're bound to get more out of a book like that than this single chapter.

CHAPTER 14

Testing and Debugging Scripts

At some point, you're bound to write a script that misbehaves. Maybe you'll forget to press Return after a line of code, or you'll accidentally use *if* when you mean to use *repeat*. Either way, your script won't work the way you want it to, and you'll waste several minutes—or longer—trying to track down the problem.

Fortunately, AppleScript has several tools for fixing scripts. Some, like the Apple-Script compiler (see below), make sure that your script works *before* you try to run it. Other tools, like the Xcode debugger (page 275), let you track down errors *while* your script is running. No matter what tool you use, you're never left to hunt for errors alone.

Note: The example scripts from this chapter can be found on the AppleScript Examples CD (see page 24 for instructions).

First Line of Defense: The Compiler

When you click the Run button in Script Editor, the first thing that happens is your script gets *compiled*. That's AppleScript's way of finding typos, misplaced punctuation, and so on. If AppleScript finds an error, you'll see a dialog box like the one in Figure 14-1. Otherwise, your script proceeds to its regularly scheduled commands.

Unfortunately, AppleScript compiler errors are notoriously hard to decipher. Unless you have a Ph.D. in programmer-ese, therefore, Table 14-1 will be of great assistance in your compiling adventures.

Table 14-1. Common AppleScript compiler errors

Error message	Code that would produce it	What's the problem?

A class name can't go after this identifier.	`tel application "iCal"`
	    `activate`
	`end tell`
		Misspelling a command

Expected end of line but found ".	`tell aplcaton "iCal"`
	    `activate`
	`end tell`
		Misspelling the word before a string

Where is iCa?	`tell application "iCa"`
	    `activate`
	`end tell`
		Misspelling a program's name

Expected "'"' " but found end of script.	`tell application "iCal`
	    `activate`
	`end tell`
		Missing a quotation mark

Expected end of line but found identifier.	`tell application "iCal"`
	    `activat e`
	`end tell`
		Space in the middle of a command

Expected end of line, etc. but found "tell".	`tell application "iCal"`
	    `activate`
	`en tell`
		Misspelling the first part of an *end* statement

Expected "tell", etc. but found "if".	`tell application "iCal"`
	    `activate`
	`end if`
		Mismatch between the kind of statement (*tell*) and the end of the statement (*if*)

Of course, the compiler can only catch superficial errors (typos, missing quotations marks, and so on). If you *misprogram* your script—but spell everything correctly—the compiler won't catch your mistakes. That's why it's important to track what your scripts are *doing* as well; that way, you can narrow any problems down to a few lines of code.

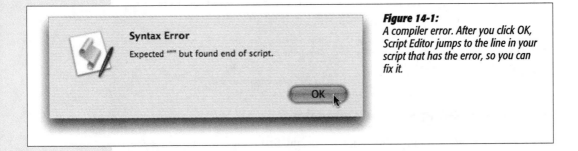

Figure 14-1:
A compiler error. After you click OK, Script Editor jumps to the line in your script that has the error, so you can fix it.

Noting Important Events

If you want a notification when something important in your script happens, the *display dialog* command (page 60) is always a good choice. In a script like the following, for example, careful use of *display dialog* can let you figure out how many times a *repeat* statement is running:

```
set currentIteration to 1 --How many times the repeat statement has run
repeat 10 times
    tell application "Finder"
        make new Finder window
    end tell
    display dialog "Made new Finder window #" & currentIteration
    set currentIteration to currentIteration + 1
end repeat
```

Each time that script creates a new Finder window, you'll see a dialog box like the one in Figure 14-2. That way, you can keep track of how many times your *repeat* statement has run so far—and stop your script if you've seen too many Finder windows appear.

Figure 14-2:
This dialog box lets you know that your script has just created a seventh Finder window. And that information, along with $130, will buy you a retail copy of Mac OS X.

Of course, there's one big disadvantage to using *display dialog:* it interrupts your script's progress. You have to stick around while your script is running, so you can click away each dialog box. And if your *display dialog* command is inside a long *repeat* statement, you could be spending the rest of the week just clicking OK.

The Event Log

Luckily, you don't have to use bothersome dialog boxes to track your script's progress. AppleScript's *log* command lets your script take silent note of events while they're happening—and lets you read the notes when the script is done. This is the perfect arrangement if you want to know what your script is doing but don't mind finding out *after* everything has happened.

Here's how to use the AppleScript log:

1. **Incorporate the *log* command into your script.**

   Anywhere you can use *display dialog,* you can use *log.* For example, the following tweaks would modify the previous script to *log* notifications instead of displaying them in dialog boxes:

   ```
   set currentIteration to 1
   repeat 10 times
       tell application "Finder"
           make new Finder window
       end tell
   ```

```
log "Made new Finder window #" & currentIteration
    set currentIteration to currentIteration + 1
end repeat
```

2. **Click the Event Log tab at the bottom of the Script Editor window (or press ⌘-3).**

   By switching to this tab before you click Run, you tell Script Editor, "Please show me everything that gets logged while my script is running."

3. **Click Run, and watch as your Event Log fills up with notifications (Figure 14-3).**

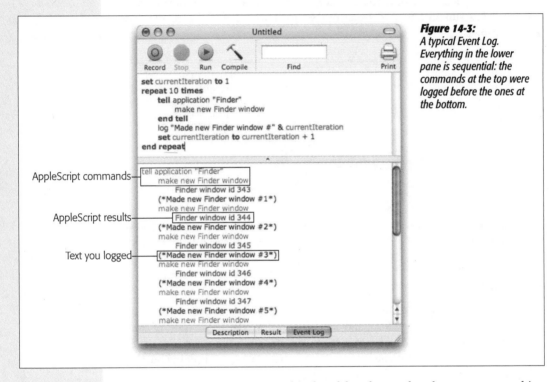

Figure 14-3:
A typical Event Log. Everything in the lower pane is sequential: the commands at the top were logged before the ones at the bottom.

It may surprise you to see a multicolored log, but each color means something special:

- **Blue text** indicates a verbatim AppleScript command. When your script comes upon *tell application "Finder"* or *make new Finder window,* for example, Apple-Script automatically logs them in blue. That way, when your script is finished, you can look in Event Log and discover the order in which your commands ran.

- **Purple text** indicates the *result* of an AppleScript command. After logging each *make new Finder window* command, for example, you'll notice that Script Editor puts purple text like "Finder window id 314." That's AppleScript's way of telling you, "I just ran the *make new Finder window* command, and once it was finished, there was a new Finder window hanging around. (By the way, in case you want to refer to that window in your script, the window's *id* number is 314.)"

- Finally, **black text** (surrounded in parentheses and asterisks) is text that *you* logged. When you run this example, you'll notice black text like "(*Made new Finder window #7*)", which corresponds exactly to what you'd see in a dialog box like Figure 14-2.

The Event Log History

The Event Log (described in the previous section) is a great tool for seeing how your scripts run, but it's hardly perfect. For one thing, you have to switch to the Event Log *before* you run your script, or else AppleScript won't log your events. For another thing, you don't have much control of what AppleScript actually logs (commands, results, and so on). Finally, every time you run a script, AppleScript overwrites the script's existing Event Log, making it impossible to see what the script has done in the past.

Luckily, there's a tool that avoids all these problems: the Event Log *History*. This self-standing window logs the events from *all* your scripts and lets you browse the logs at your leisure. You can even see the logs from scripts you've already closed.

Before you can pull off any of those tricks, though, you first have to *open* the Event Log History. You can do this in either of two ways: by choosing Window → Event Log History or by pressing Option-⌘-L. Whichever way you choose, Script Editor displays a window like Figure 14-4.

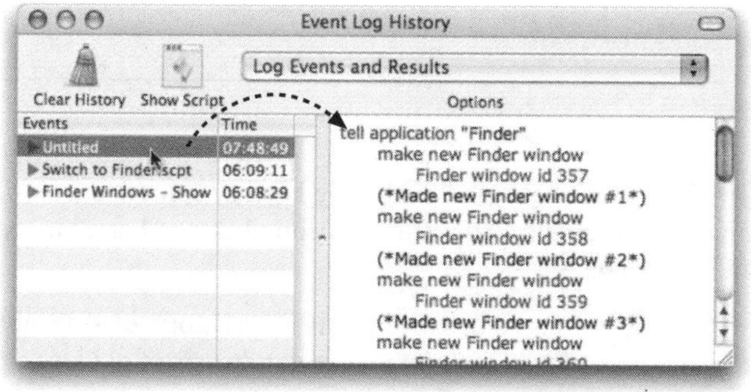

Figure 14-4:
The Event Log History. Click an entry in the left pane to display that script's log in the right pane. Or, if you just want to browse the left list, double-click the vertical divider bar in the middle of the window to hide the right pane entirely.

Navigating logs

At first glance, the Event Log History might seem pretty self-explanatory: the left list shows you the most recently run scripts (and when you ran them), and to read a script's log, you simply click its entry. However, if that's all you do with the Event Log History, you're missing out on a whole lot of tricks.

For one thing, you can Shift- or ⌘-click *multiple* items in the left list, so you can see the logs of several scripts simultaneously. This trick can save you time when, for example, you want to see how the Event Logs of two similar scripts compare to each other. (You can even use this trick to select several occurrences of the *same* script in the left list, so you can compare how a script ran yesterday to how it ran 5 minutes ago.)

Note: Unfortunately, the Event Log History displays multiple scripts one above the other—not side by side—so it's hard to compare logs directly.

If those features aren't exciting enough, though, you can even narrow down a *single* log into its various components. Figure 14-5 shows you how.

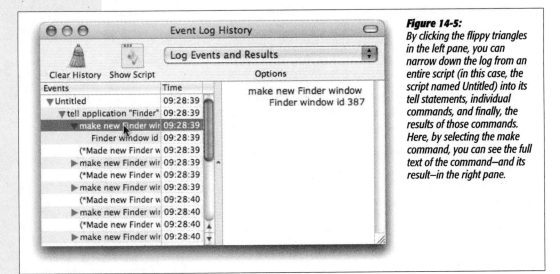

Figure 14-5:
By clicking the flippy triangles in the left pane, you can narrow down the log from an entire script (in this case, the script named Untitled) into its tell statements, individual commands, and finally, the results of those commands. Here, by selecting the make command, you can see the full text of the command—and its result—in the right pane.

The toolbar

Just like normal Script Editor windows, the Event Log History comes with its own set of toolbar buttons. You won't find any Run or Debug buttons here, however; instead, you'll see the following:

- **Clear History** lets you wipe clean your entire Event Log History, erasing all the entries in the left pane. This trick is useful if you've got dozens of old logs clogging your History and you don't need to read them anymore.

Note: Of course, this Event Log History–purging happens automatically when you quit and restart Script Editor. But, if you'd just like to *cap* the number of entries in your Event Log (rather than erasing all the entries), visit Script Editor → Preferences → History and turn on "Maximum entries" for the Event Log History.

- **Show Script** finds the script that's selected in the left pane, and opens that script in its own window. This can save you time when a log is confusing, for example, and you want to figure out which commands produced which lines.

  This feature works for scripts you've already *closed,* too; as long as a script's log remains in the History window, you can reincarnate the script's code by clicking Show Script.

Tip: If mousing up to the toolbar to click Show Script is too slow for you, you can simply double-click a script's name in the left pane to bring that script back to life.

- The **Options** pop-up menu lets you choose how specific you want your logs to be. The default setting, Log Events and Results, is meant for verbose people: it shows you AppleScript commands, command results, and your own *log* statements, too. The less talkative setting, Log Events, shows you everything *except* your commands' results. And the simplest setting, Log Nothing, is perfect if your scripts work so flawlessly that you never need to read their logs.

  Note, however, that no matter what setting you choose, it won't take effect on your *existing* logs.

Tip: You can use all the toolbar tricks from page 25 with the Event Log History window, too.

Preventing Errors

There's no sure-fire way to keep your scripts from misbehaving, but there *are* a few problems that happen more often than others. By keeping an eye out for these pitfalls, you can greatly reduce the chance of your script crashing, hanging, or otherwise misbehaving:

- **Stop infinite loops.** Page 152 has a tempting proposition: letting a *repeat* statement run forever. Unfortunately, if you do that, you won't be able to quit your script without clicking the Stop button in Script Editor—an unduly harsh way to halt your code.

  The fix? Insert an *exit repeat* command somewhere in your *repeat* statement. That way, there'll always be something to trigger your loop to stop.

- **Make sure an item exists before you try to use it.** Using the *exists* command (page 47), you can verify that an item does, well, exist. Whenever you're scripting tentative items—say, a specific Finder window that might not be around tomorrow, or a particular TextEdit document—it's always a good idea to put your commands inside an *if/exists* statement, so your script doesn't end up sending commands to nonexistent items.

- **Don't convert between incompatible data types.** As described on page 108, the *as* command lets you turn one kind of information into another—say, a number into a string. This is a powerful tool for type-specific commands (like *choose* *from list,* which won't accept anything but a list), but be warned: some kinds of data don't respond well to being coerced. Table 14-2 shows the results of the most common coercions.

Table 14-2. *What happens when you coerce different data types*

Coerce	To string	To number	To list	To record	To alias
From string	No change.	Works fine if you're coercing a quoted number (like "2.5") into an AppleScript number. On the other hand, your script will crash if you try to turn any *other* string (like "Welp") into a number.	Encases the string in curly braces, creating a single-item list. For example, "Goat hut" would become {*"Goat hut"*}.	*Error*	Works fine if you're coercing a string in colon-separated path form (like "Macintosh HD:Applications:") into an alias. However, if you try to convert a nonpath string (like "airplane") into an alias, you'll be left with an error.
From number	Puts the number in quotation marks. 4 would become "4", for example.	No change.	Encases the number in curly brackets, creating a single-item list. For example, 7.2 would become {*7.2*}.	*Error*	*Error*
From list	Concatenates each item from the list, inserting *AppleScript's text item delimiters* (page 119) in between. For instance, if the text item delimiters were set to a hyphen, and you converted {*"pizza", 4, "me"*} into a string, you'd end up with "pizza-4-me".	Works correctly if the list is only one item long, and that item is a number (for example, {5} would become 5. On the other hand, if you try to convert a multi-item list into a number, you'll get an error.	No change.	*Error*	Works correctly if the list is a single item long, and that item is a colon-separated path (see above). However, if your list is more than one item long—or the items aren't file paths—you'll get an error.
From record	*Error*	*Error*	Returns a list of just the *values* from the record (page 204). For instance, {*name:"José", age: 33*} would become simply {*"José", 33*}.	No change.	*Error*
From alias	Returns a string of the alias, in colon-separated form. For example, an alias to your System folder would become the string "Macintosh HD:System:".	*Error*	Encases the alias in curly braces, much like for strings (see above).	*Error*	No change.

Isolating and Handling Errors

Although logs (page 267) are a great way to track a script's progress, they suffer from one major flaw: you can't *correct* code errors with them. Sure, you can always go back to your script—once you've read its log—and try to make your corrections by hand. But that's a hit-and-miss endeavor; if your script continues misbehaving, you have to continue tweaking it over and over again until you fix the problem.

Suppose you had the following script, for example:

```
tell application "Finder"
    close Finder window "Macintosh HD"
end tell
```

Now, if you had a Finder window open to Macintosh HD when you ran that script, everything would work just fine. The trouble comes if you *don't* have a Finder window open to Macintosh HD. In that case, since AppleScript can't locate a matching Finder window, you get the unhelpful dialog box shown in Figure 14-6.

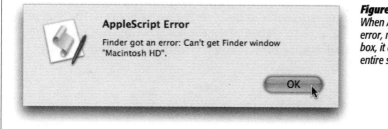

AppleScript Error

Finder got an error: Can't get Finder window "Macintosh HD".

OK

Figure 14-6:
When AppleScript encounters an error, not only does it display a dialog box, it also stops the progress of your entire script. Not fun.

Using try

Luckily, AppleScript provides a special statement for isolating such errors: *try*. When you surround a section of code in a *try* statement, you're telling AppleScript, "run this code, but if there's an error with it, just ignore it and carry on." To make your previous script error-proof, therefore, you'd make these changes:

```
tell application "Finder"
    try
        close Finder window "Macintosh HD"
    end try
end tell
```

When you run *that* script, everything works as it should. If there's a Finder window named Macintosh HD, the script closes it; if there isn't a matching Finder window, your script simply remains silent. That way, you get error handling *and* a functioning script, all in one.

Multiple commands in a try statement

On the other hand, if you use a *try* statement that surrounds more than one line of code, AppleScript will jump to the *end* of the *try* statement if an error occurs. That means that in the following script:

```
try
    display dialog ("hello" as number)
    display dialog "goodbye"
end try
tell application "Finder" to activate
```

AppleScript never gets to your second *display dialog* command, because there's an error with the first. But AppleScript *will* get to your *activate* command, because it's outside of the error-afflicted *try* statement.

Discovering Errors

Unfortunately, even using a *try* statement isn't perfect. Sure, your script will continue to run without showing any errors, but you'll never know if a problem actually occurred.

That's why an *error* statement is so useful: it lets you not only isolate bugs in your script but also run a *special* section of code if a bug occurs. For example, the following script will silently log a message to your Event Log if an error occurs:

```
tell application "Finder"
    try
        close Finder window "Macintosh HD"
    on error
        log "An error occurred while your script was running."
    end try
end tell
```

Now when an error occurs, the script jumps to the *error* statement and runs your *log* command (page 267). You get both error protection (with *try*) and error notification (with *on error*), all without bringing your script to a halt.

Tip: If you'd like to know the *specific* error that stopped your *try* statement, simply append a variable to your *error* handler, like this:

```
tell application "Finder"
    try
        close Finder window "Macintosh HD"
    on error theMessage
        --The error message is now held in theMessage
        log "This error occurred:" & theMessage
    end try
end tell
```

For more *error* statement tricks, visit *http://developer.apple.com/documentation/AppleScript/Conceptual/ AppleScriptLangGuide/AppleScript.c4.html.*

The Xcode Debugger

If Script Editor is the hamburger of AppleScript, Xcode is the two-pound steak. It's fatter, heavier, and more tender in the middle than the humble Script Editor.

In all seriousness, though, Xcode is a power user's *dream* compared to Script Editor. Although most people use Xcode for writing full-fledged programs (page 283), there's nothing to keep you from using Xcode to write and debug your scripts. In fact, Xcode has a number of features that simply aren't available in Script Editor—features that can save you time, trouble, and tons of repetitive debugging.

First, however, you have to install Xcode.

Tip: If you're a feature fiend, be sure to check out third-party AppleScript editors like Smile and Script Debugger. Those programs include even *more* debugging features than Xcode, as detailed on page 38.

Obtaining and Installing the Developer Tools

Xcode is part of a powerful package for programmers (say *that* five times fast). Depending on whom you ask, this package is known as either the Developer Tools or the Xcode Tools. Either way, you have to install these tools to use Xcode.

GEM IN THE ROUGH

The error Command

When you want to handle an error in your script, *try* and *error* statements are your best friends. Sometimes, however, you want to *create* an error message—when your script encounters an unknown file, for example. In these situations, you'll be glad to have the *error* command, which lets you create (or, in nerd-ese, *raise*) your own error messages.

The *error* command (not to be confused with error *statements*, which are meant to handle errors) works very similarly to the *log* command. Unlike *log*, however, the *error* command displays an error dialog box and interrupts your script. Therefore, the *error* command's use is mainly limited to critical sections of code, like the following:

```
tell application "Finder"
    if not (exists the folder ¬
        "Applications" ¬
        of the startup disk) then error ¬
        "Your Applications folder is gone!"
    end if
end tell
```

When you run that script, AppleScript checks whether you have an Applications folder. If you *don't*, the script presents the dialog box shown here, and stops your script in its tracks.

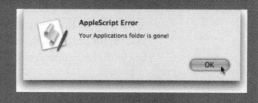

Of course, you can use error *statements* (page 274) in conjunction with the *error* command. That way, you can trap problems that would otherwise interrupt your script, and instead log a message, or have your script do nothing at all. The power of these two debugging tools—*error* commands for *creating* error messages and *error* statements for *suppressing* them—opens up a world of opportunity for any scripter with buggy code.

If you bought the retail, boxed version of Mac OS X, the Xcode Tools came on a special CD of their very own. If so, you have it easy: simply insert the CD and follow the instructions in the included help document.

On the other hand, if Mac OS X *came* with your Mac, you may not have received the Xcode Tools on a disc. In that case, you have it harder:

1. **Visit *http://connect.apple.com/,* and click Join ADC.**

   The ADC (or, as geeks would have it, Apple Developer Connection) is a club for Mac programmers. Once you've joined (the simplest membership—"Online"—is free), you can download various programs and sample code.

2. **Click Agree to accept Apple's terms of membership.**

   Basically, the agreement boils down to two parts: you are who you say you are, and you won't go telling people trade secrets.

3. **Provide all the information Apple requests, and click Continue when you're done.**

   You should receive a welcome email after you've set up your account.

4. **Once your account is active, return to *http://connect.apple.com/,* and log in.**

   If you're using a Web browser like Safari, you can even have Mac OS X remember your user name and password for future use.

5. **Click Download Software. In the submenu that appears, click Mac OS X.**

   You see a list of updates to the Xcode Tools.

6. **Download the most recent revision of the tools.**

   Be patient, though: the download can be more than 350 MB, so it may take several hours to download, even over a high-speed Internet connection.

7. **Install the Xcode Tools from the disk image you just downloaded.**

   A *disk image* is a virtual recreation of a disk. With the tools you just downloaded, for example, the disk image contains what you'd see if you had an *actual* CD with the Xcode Tools on it.

Once you install the tools successfully (and restart your Mac), you're ready to go. Launch Xcode from your Developer → Applications folder.

Creating a New Project

Unlike Script Editor, Xcode creates new files as *projects*. A project is, in essence, a cluster of related files meant to be edited and run as a group. To use Xcode's powerful AppleScript tools, therefore, you have to create a new project.

Luckily, that's a pretty simple procedure:

1. **Choose File → New Project, or press Shift-⌘-N.**

   You'll see the dialog box shown at the top of Figure 14-7.

2. **Choose AppleScript Droplet and click Next.**

An AppleScript Droplet automatically comes with *run* and *open* handlers, which you can fill in with any code you please (page 141).

Tip: If you don't need either of these handlers in your project, you can choose AppleScript Application instead. Still, for the purposes of this example, you *will* use the *idle* handler, so be sure to choose Apple-Script Droplet.

---

3. **Give your project a name, such as Debugaroo, and click Choose to specify where you want to save the project.**

Click Finish to create the project in the location you specified (Figure 14-7, bottom).

Now you have a full-fledged Xcode project, just awaiting some of your code.

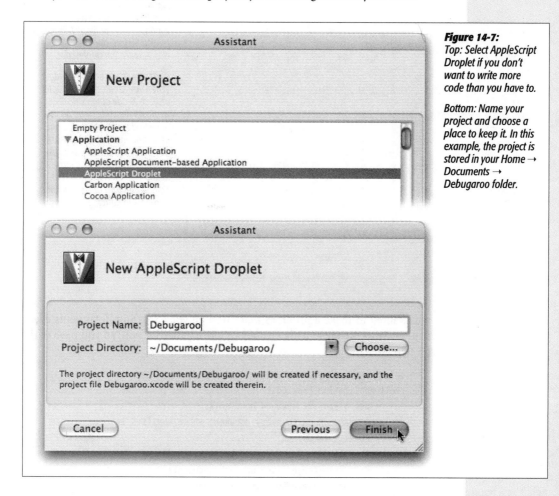

Figure 14-7:
Top: Select AppleScript Droplet if you don't want to write more code than you have to.

Bottom: Name your project and choose a place to keep it. In this example, the project is stored in your Home → Documents → Debugaroo folder.

Note: Technically, what you just created was an AppleScript *Studio* project. That means, if you wanted to, you could create a full-fledged graphical interface for your script (page 285).

Still, if all you want to do is *debug* a script, all these graphical capabilities are downright distracting. For the rest of this chapter, therefore, you'll stick with the nongraphical side of AppleScript. (But if you *do* want to learn more about creating graphical interfaces for your scripts, just skip ahead to Chapter 15.)

Changing the Script

Of the myriad folders in the project before you, only the Scripts folder contains an AppleScript file. To add code to your project, you have to open this file—named, creatively enough, Application.applescript, and make your modifications there (Figure 14-8).

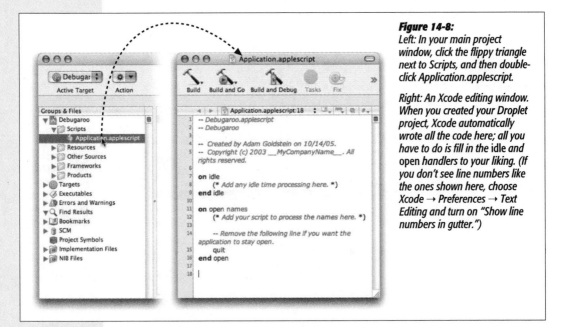

Figure 14-8:
Left: In your main project window, click the flippy triangle next to Scripts, and then double-click Application.applescript.

Right: An Xcode editing window. When you created your Droplet project, Xcode automatically wrote all the code here; all you have to do is fill in the idle and open handlers to your liking. (If you don't see line numbers like the ones shown here, choose Xcode → Preferences → Text Editing and turn on "Show line numbers in gutter.")

Say you wanted to make a program that saved all your TextEdit documents every 10 minutes. Since Xcode already created an *idle* handler for you, all you have to do is fill it in:

```
on idle
    tell application "TextEdit"
        --Get a list of unsaved documents:
        set unsavedDocs to every document whose modified is true
        --Count them up:
        set numberOfUnsavedDocs to (count unsavedDocs)
        --Make sure there *are* unsaved documents
        if numberOfUnsavedDocs is not 0 then
            --Save the documents one at a time:
```

```
                repeat with currentDoc in unsavedDocs
                    save currentDoc
                end repeat
            end if
        end tell
        --Come back and check if there are any unsaved documents in ten minutes
        return 600
    end idle
```

Note: Although your Xcode project also includes an *open* handler, there's no need to fill it in with any code. For this script, only the *idle* handler is of any use (although some scripts, like the one on page 142, do use *open* handlers for operating on a group of files).

Stepping Through the Code

Now, all the commands from that script are pretty straightforward. The only problem is, you have no way of knowing *when* the script is running each command. This, unfortunately, is a problem with all AppleScripts: there's no way of stepping through a script command by command.

At least, that would be your feeling if you were trained on Script Editor. Don't despair, though—Xcode can take over the job where Script Editor left off: by letting you step through your code.

Before you can do that, though, you have to set *breakpoints* in your script. Basically, breakpoints tell Xcode, "When you run my script and hit one of these lines, pause the script." To set breakpoints, simply click in the left gutter of your script window (Figure 14-9).

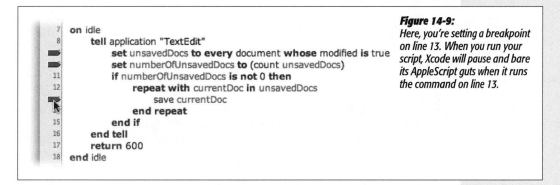

Figure 14-9:
Here, you're setting a breakpoint on line 13. When you run your script, Xcode will pause and bare its AppleScript guts when it runs the command on line 13.

Once you've set breakpoints on the lines that interest you, choose Build → Build and Debug (⌘-Y) to get your script cooking. Xcode prompts you to save your project first, so just go ahead and click Save All.

Tip: Normally, if you just wanted to *run* your script—without making Xcode pause at breakpoints—you'd select Build → "Build and Run" (⌘-R) instead.

As soon as Xcode encounters a line for which you've set a breakpoint, it stops. As an added bonus, Xcode displays all sorts of technical information: the values of your variables, the handler that's currently running, and other statistics that only a geek could love (Figure 14-10).

Tip: Amazingly, you can actually *change* the values of your variables while your script is running! Simply double-click in the Value column and enter the new value you want to use.

You might find this trick useful if, for example, you accidentally misspell a response in a dialog box. Rather than restarting your entire script, you could simply open the Debugger, double-click the variable that stores your response, correct the typo, and let your script continue running.

On the other hand, don't get *too* carried away with the ability to change variables while your script is running. Since the Debugger won't stop you from replacing a number with a string, for example, there's nothing to keep you from seriously messing up your variables. In the *worst* case, tweaking your variables could lead your entire script to crash.

Variables and their values

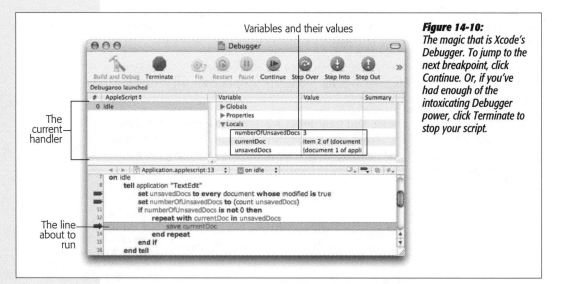

Figure 14-10:
The magic that is Xcode's Debugger. To jump to the next breakpoint, click Continue. Or, if you've had enough of the intoxicating Debugger power, click Terminate to stop your script.

This script is but one example of debugging in action. For *real* fun, try taking a big, complicated script—like the one on page 213—and copying it into an Xcode project. Set a few breakpoints, get the Debugger going, and—Voila!—your script pauses for inspection at each breakpoint.

Tip: If you want to know what a script is doing at the moment—even if it isn't at a breakpoint—click the Pause button in the Debugger. Xcode locates the command that's currently running, and highlights it for your inspecting pleasure.

Finally, if none of the tricks in this chapter can fix a certain problem, be sure to check out Appendix C. There, you'll find a list of books, Web sites, and email lists for people with scripting problems.

AppleScript Studio

281 pages into this book, you're probably pretty sick of dinky scripts that simply command programs and display dialog boxes. What would *really* be cool is if you could create full-fledged programs of your own, complete with text fields, buttons, windows, and other staples of the Mac interface.

"But of course," you say, "that's what advanced programming languages like Objective-C, C++, and Java are for!" You're right, but those aren't the only options. Thanks to AppleScript Studio, a beginner-friendly programming tool, you can write your own graphical Mac OS X programs with nothing but AppleScript as the underlying code.

Note: The example scripts from this chapter can be found on the AppleScript Examples CD (see page 24 for instructions).

What Is AppleScript Studio?

Contrary to popular opinion, AppleScript Studio is not a chic art gallery tucked away in Building 5 of Apple's campus in Cupertino. Instead, it's the name Apple gave to the integration of two programs—Xcode and Interface Builder—with AppleScript. When you use AppleScript Studio, you design your program's look and feel in Interface Builder and write the AppleScript code that makes the program tick in Xcode. By the time you're done, you've got a slick-looking Mac OS X program, coded entirely with AppleScript.

Now, this arrangement might seem pretty ridiculous to a seasoned programmer— after all, AppleScript is one of the slowest programming languages around. Still, if you're coming from the world of simple AppleScripts, there are plenty of good reasons to write your programs in AppleScript Studio:

- **You already know the language!** There's no need to spend time learning Cocoa, Carbon, or any of Apple's other geeky programming technologies.

- **You can split your code into multiple scripts.** You could have one script that handles button presses, for example, and a separate script that handles menu clicks. This arrangement makes it much easier to keep your code organized, since you can customize each script for a specific task.

- **You have total control of your program's interface.** With normal AppleScripts, you can display three-button dialog boxes—and that's about it. But when you use AppleScript *Studio,* your programs can display all the interface elements you'd see in a professional program, including pop-up menus, text boxes, tables, QuickTime movies, and more.

- **You can mix more advanced programming languages into your AppleScripts if you have to.** That means that, unlike normal scripts, AppleScript Studio programs can handle complex networking tasks, display Web pages, and perform other tasks normally reserved for Java or C++.

Note: If you want to do advanced programming jobs, you'll still have to *use* a more advanced programming language. The difference, if you use AppleScript Studio, is that you won't have to write your *entire* program in a more complicated language; you can simply write the tough parts in another language and continue to use AppleScript for the basic programming jobs.

- **It's easy to write working programs quickly.** Since you already know AppleScript—and you create a program's interface with drag-and-drop—you can make a simple, working program in less than an hour. That's why some people use AppleScript Studio for *prototyping* their programs—creating programs with AppleScript Studio to prove that they work, and then reprogramming them in a more advanced language later to improve their speed.

On the other hand, you don't always *need* all the power that AppleScript Studio offers. For instance, if you just want to create a script that launches TextEdit, AppleScript Studio is overkill. There are other disadvantages to AppleScript Studio programs, too:

- **They take longer to start up than normal scripts.** Since AppleScript Studio projects are full-fledged *programs,* Mac OS X has to load all their interface elements, Dock icons, and menu bar commands before you can run any of the AppleScript code. (Normal AppleScripts don't have this problem, because they *can't* have interface elements, Dock icons, or menu bar commands.)

- **Programs you create with AppleScript Studio can't be used as folder actions (page 221) or Mail rules (page 190).** Again, that's because AppleScript Studio creates programs, not scripts.

Tip: You *can* still use AppleScript Studio programs in the Script Menu (page 15).

- **AppleScript Studio programs only work in Mac OS X.** In fact, they work only in Mac OS *10.1.2* or later. Linux and Windows fans (and even people who use earlier versions of the Mac OS) are left out in the cold.

- **Your code is there for the whole world to see.** Unlike programs written in C, C++, or Java, AppleScript Studio programs don't hide your code very well. That means that sneaky Mac fans can crack your program open, examine your code, and copy it into their own programs, if they so desire. (This is one of the reasons you won't find many commercial Mac programs written in AppleScript Studio.)

If, on balance, AppleScript Studio fits your program-writing needs, read on. Otherwise, see page xix for alternative—albeit more complicated—programming tools that may do what you want.

Making a Program

In this section, you'll create a simple program to speak text out loud. In doing so, you'll learn how to design a program's look in Interface Builder and how to write the associated AppleScript commands in Xcode. Once you're done, you'll have a fully functioning Mac OS X application, ready to email to your friends or post online.

Before you can do *any* of this, however, you have to install the Xcode Tools. Luckily, if you don't have them, you can get them for free. Page 275 has the details.

Tip: If you're not sure whether you've installed the Xcode Tools already, double-click your hard drive in the Finder. If you have a Developer folder, you're good to go. Otherwise, you have to install the tools.

Creating a Project

Once you've installed the Xcode Tools, it's pretty easy to create a new, basic AppleScript Studio program. Here's how:

1. **Open your Developer → Applications folder, and double-click Xcode.**

   This program is where you'll write your AppleScript code (page 276). Since Xcode is such an essential program, power users often keep a copy in their Dock for easy access.

2. **Choose File → New Project (Shift-⌘-N).**

   Xcode presents a list of new-program templates, ranging from Tools (Unix programs) to Address Book plug-ins.

3. **Select AppleScript Application and click Next.**

You've just selected the simplest template for an AppleScript Studio program. If you wanted to write a more complicated program, you could choose Apple-Script Droplet (for making a program that can open files) or AppleScript Document-based Application (for making a program that can open and *save* files). For writing a plain old program that doesn't deal with files, however, Apple-Script Application fits the bill nicely.

4. **Enter a name for your new program in the Project Name field.**

Not only will this be the name of your *project* (the Xcode folder than contains your program's code), it'll also be the name of your AppleScript Studio program. You can name the project whatever you want, but SpeakToMe would be as good a name as any.

5. **Click Choose to tell Xcode where to save your project.**

Alternatively, type the Mac OS X–style folder path in the Project Directory field (Figure 15-1).

Figure 15-1:
Xcode makes you give your project a name before you can start writing a line of code. For the Project Directory (where Mac OS X saves your project), you can either navigate to a folder with the Choose button or type a folder path yourself.

6. **Click Finish.**

After a few seconds, Xcode opens the project window for your new AppleScript Studio application.

At this point, your project has everything it needs to work. To prove it, choose Build → Build and Run (⌘-R), and wait for Xcode to assemble your program. After a short wait, your program opens, displaying a simple window and menu bar (Figure 15-2). Not bad for not writing a single line of code!

When you're done being impressed with your bare-bones program, choose Speak-ToMe → Quit. You return to Xcode, where you can start building a program that actually *does* something.

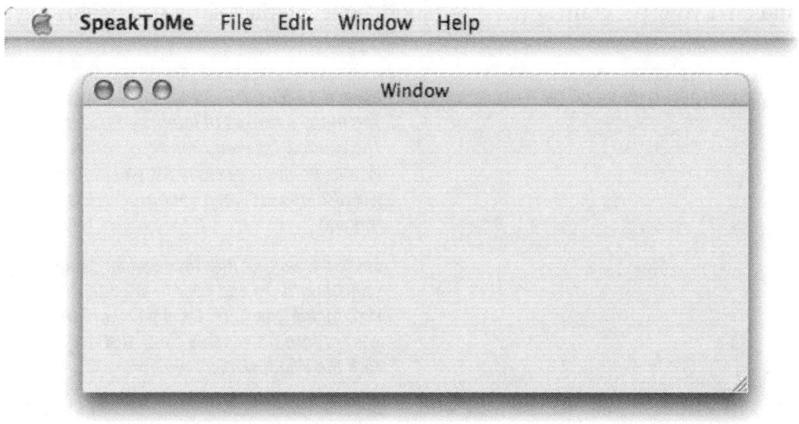

Figure 15-2:
Your program's generic interface. You get a plain old window and a plain old menu bar. As an added convenience, many of the menu items work automatically: Quit, Close, and Minimize, for example.

Designing the Interface

Before you start writing any code, you must first design your program's interface. (OK, technically your program already *has* an interface—a blank window—but it's hardly something to email home about.) What you really need are interface elements.

To edit your program's interface, you use Interface Builder, a program included with the Xcode Tools. Rather than double-click Interface Builder in the Finder, however, it's much easier to simply double-click MainMenu.nib in Xcode. (MainMenu.nib is the file in charge of your program's interface.)

FREQUENTLY ASKED QUESTIONS

Interfacing Like a Pro

I don't know a thing about graphic design or user interaction. How am I supposed to design a decent interface for my programs?

To a typical Mac user, the idea of creating a program's interface conjures up thoughts of geeks working at graphics workstations late into the night. As it turns out, though, it's remarkably easy to create a good interface, provided you follow a few simple guidelines—the Apple Human Interface Guidelines, to be exact.

The Apple Human Interface Guidelines (or HIG, as they're known by geeks) are put together in an online book, available from:

http://developer.apple.com/documentation/
UserExperience/Conceptual/OSXHIGuidelines/
OSXHIGuidelines.pdf.

Divided into 11 separate chapters, the Human Interface Guidelines detail everything from how far apart your buttons should be to which fonts you should use in dialog boxes.

Still, you don't have to follow the HIG to the *letter*. As long as you stick to its basic usability suggestions—like making sure your program has a Quit item in its File menu—your interfaces should come out fine. And don't lose too much sleep about interface design—even *Apple* doesn't follow its own guidelines all the time.

Once you do that, Interface Builder pops open, displaying four different windows (Figure 15-3).

Before you jump headlong into building your interface, however, you should have some idea of what your program should look like. Since you want to be able to enter text and have your program speak it out loud, your interface should probably have:

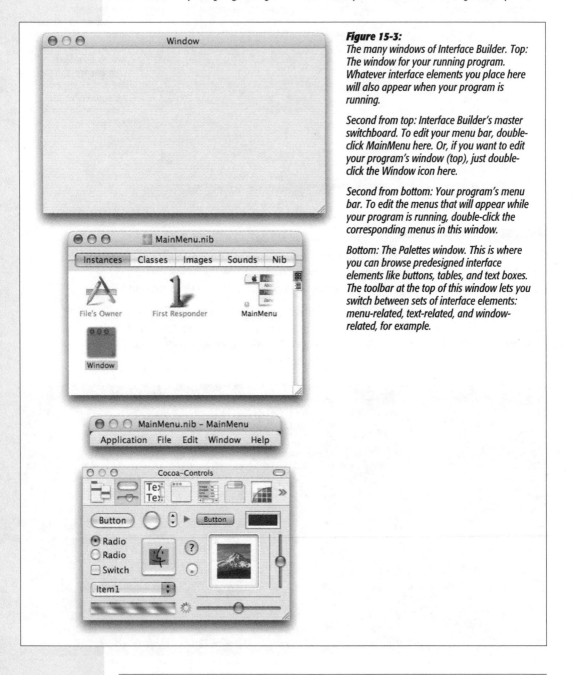

Figure 15-3:
The many windows of Interface Builder. Top: The window for your running program. Whatever interface elements you place here will also appear when your program is running.

Second from top: Interface Builder's master switchboard. To edit your menu bar, double-click MainMenu here. Or, if you want to edit your program's window (top), just double-click the Window icon here.

Second from bottom: Your program's menu bar. To edit the menus that will appear while your program is running, double-click the corresponding menus in this window.

Bottom: The Palettes window. This is where you can browse predesigned interface elements like buttons, tables, and text boxes. The toolbar at the top of this window lets you switch between sets of interface elements: menu-related, text-related, and window-related, for example.

- **A text field,** where you'll enter what you want the program to speak.

- **A pop-up menu,** to choose the voice you want to hear.

- **A button,** to trigger your program to start speaking.

Now that you know what interface elements you need, you can put your window together. Here's how:

1. **Switch to the Cocoa-Text pane of the Palette window (Figure 15-4, top).**

   To do so, click the third toolbar button from the left.

2. **Drag the text field from the upper-left corner of the Palette window into the upper-left corner of your main program window (Figure 15-4, bottom).**

   If you drag the button into *just* the right spot, you'll see blue dashed lines. That's Interface Builder's way of telling you, "let go of the text field here, and I'll automatically snap it 20 pixels from both sides of the window."

Tip: If you'd rather the text field *not* snap like this, hold down ⌘ before you let go of the text field.

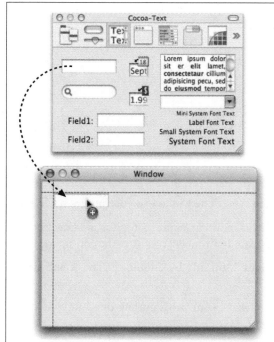

Figure 15-4:
Top: The Cocoa-Text pane, a list of every text-related interface item known to humanity.

Bottom: Drag the text field near the corner of the window, and Interface Builder will display its "drop-to-snap" dashed lines. Or, if you're a nonconformist, drag the text field somewhere else in the window.

3. **Drag the right-edge dot of the text field until it snaps near the right edge of the window.**

   Once you release the mouse, your text field will be centered at the top of the window.

---

4. **Switch to the Cocoa-Controls pane of the Palette window (Figure 15-5, top).**

   That's the second toolbar button from the left.

5. **Drag the pop-up menu (labeled "Item1") from the Palette window to the left edge of your program window, below the text field (Figure 15-5, bottom).**

   Again, blue dashed lines indicate that the pop-up menu will snap 20 pixels from the left edge of the window when you release the mouse.

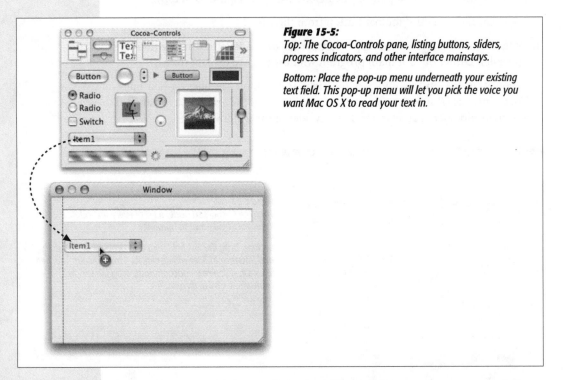

Figure 15-5:
Top: The Cocoa-Controls pane, listing buttons, sliders, progress indicators, and other interface mainstays.

Bottom: Place the pop-up menu underneath your existing text field. This pop-up menu will let you pick the voice you want Mac OS X to read your text in.

6. **Drag the upper-left button from the Palette window to your program window.**

   If you place the button just right (as shown in Figure 15-6), it snaps away from the right side of the window, *and* it snaps horizontally even with the pop-up menu.

7. **Give the button a name (besides "Button") by double-clicking it and typing your new name.**

   Since you'll click this button to make your program talk out loud, you could name it Speak, for example.

8. **To set up the pop-up menu with a list of possible voices, double-click it. Then, for each item in the menu, double-click *it* and enter an appropriate name (Figure 15-7 has a list of names).**

By default, the pop-up menu contains only three items. To add additional items—so you can include all possible voices in the menu—select Edit → Duplicate (⌘-D) for each new menu item you want to create.

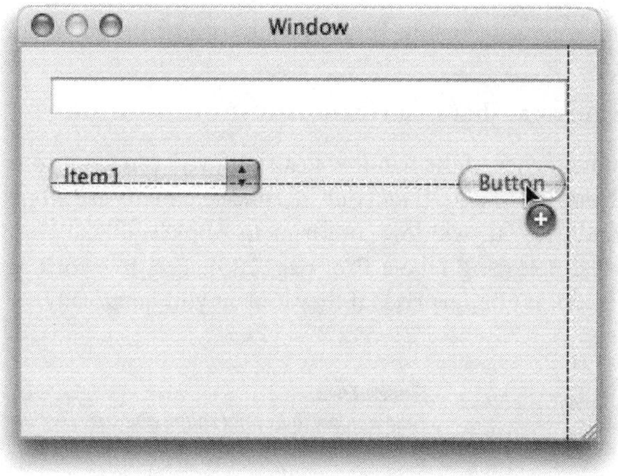

Figure 15-6:
If you drag the button in line with the pop-up menu, Interface Builder shows you they're on the same latitude with a dashed horizontal line.

Figure 15-7:
Enter these voice names into your pop-up menu. (You can find the same list in System Preferences → Speech → Default Voice.) Whatever voice is selected here when you close the pop-up menu is the same voice that'll be selected when you launch your program.

Tip: At this point, your interface is all laid out. To prove it, choose File → Test Interface (⌘-R). Interface Builder switches to testing mode, where you can click, type, and minimize the window to your heart's content.

Of course, none of the interface elements actually *do* anything yet, because you haven't written any code. Still, it's neat to be able to preview what your interface will look like when you actually run your program.

Once you've had enough testing, choose Interface Builder → Quit Application (⌘-Q).

9. **Resize your program window as shown in Figure 15-8.**

   If you drag the lower-right corner of the window just right, you can get it to snap 20 pixels away from the pop-up menu. If *all* your interface elements are 20 pixels from the edge of the window, your window conforms to Apple's official Human Interface Guidelines (see Interfacing Like a Pro, page 285). Feel free to brag to your friends about it—but don't be surprised if they look at you quizzically.

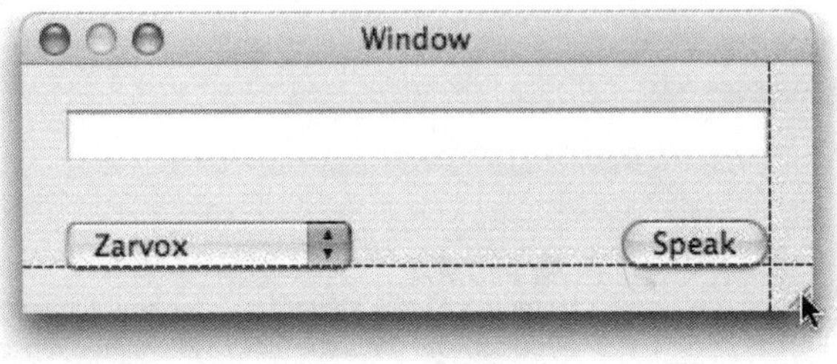

Figure 15-8:
Your window in its final shape and size. Feel free to resize the pop-up menu and button, though; as of right now, they're pretty far apart.

10. **Open Interface Builder's Inspector window by choosing Tools → Show Info (or by pressing Shift-⌘-I).**

    The Inspector lets you fine-tune the settings for your interface elements. The Inspector also lets you give your interface elements AppleScript names, so you can refer to them from your scripts.

11. **With the Inspector open, click the background of your program window.**

    Figure 15-9 details the changes you should make to the Inspector settings.

12. **In the pop-up menu at the top of the Inspector, choose AppleScript (⌘-7).**

    The Inspector → AppleScript pane lets you give your interface elements AppleScript names—a requirement if you want to be able to control these interface elements from your code. This pane also lets you associate interface elements with different scripts in your project, so that clicking a particular button runs a particular script, for example.

13. **Type *main* in the Name field.**

    That tells Interface Builder that you'll refer to this window as *window "main"* in your scripts.

14. Select the text field, and type *textToSpeak* in the Inspector's Name field.

    You'll refer to this text field as *text field "textToSpeak"* in your scripts.

15. Select the pop-up menu and name it *voiceMenu*.

    As you could probably guess, you'll refer to this as *popup button "voiceMenu"* in your scripts.

16. Select the button and give it the AppleScript name *speakButton*.

    Although you *won't* refer to this button in your scripts, it's always a good idea to give each interface element an AppleScript name. That way, if you decide to refer to the element later on—by sending it an AppleScript command—you won't have to come back to Interface Builder just to give the element an AppleScript name.

17. Under Event Handlers, turn on the "clicked" checkbox.

    That's the equivalent of telling Interface Builder, "When I click the Speak button, I want you to run a script."

18. Turn on the single checkbox under "Script" at the bottom of the Inspector (Figure 15-10).

    Now you're telling Interface Builder, "When I click the Speak button, I want you to run this *particular* script."

Figure 15-9:
Left: The window's Inspector, at first.

Right: The window's Inspector, after tweaking a few settings. First, give the window a title, so the window's title bar doesn't say "Window." Next, turn off the Resize checkbox, so you can't resize the window while your program's running. Finally, turn on the "Has texture" checkbox to give your window the cool, brushed-metal look from iTunes and iMovie.

19. **Finally, click Edit Script.**

Xcode comes forward, displaying a bare-bones script (Figure 15-11). The *clicked* handler in this script will run whenever you click the Speak button in your program.

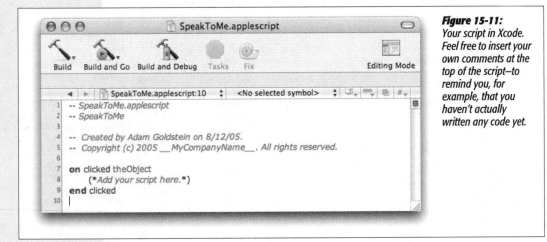

Figure 15-10:
With these checkboxes turned on, your program automatically runs SpeakToMe.applescript when you click the Speak button.

Figure 15-11:
Your script in Xcode. Feel free to insert your own comments at the top of the script—to remind you, for example, that you haven't actually written any code yet.

That's all there is to laying out an interface: dragging elements where you want them, tweaking settings in the Inspector, and linking interface elements to scripts. Now, when you run your program, everything will look exactly as you designed in Interface Builder.

Writing the Code

Before your program will actually *do* anything, you have to write the appropriate AppleScript commands. Luckily, it's not much harder to write a program-controlling script in Xcode than it is to write one in Script Editor. The only difference, of course, is that this time the program you're controlling is *yours,* and not some third-party program like TextEdit or FileMaker Pro.

To make your program work, fill in the code window from Figure 15-11 with the following commands (shown in bold):

```
--Part 1:
on clicked theObject
    --Part 2:
    tell window "main"
        --Part 3:
        set theText to (the content of text field "textToSpeak") as string
        --Part 4:
        set theVoice to (the title of popup button "voiceMenu") as string
    end tell
    --Part 5:
    say theText using theVoice
end clicked
```

Here's how the script works:

- **Part 1**—and the *on clicked* part in particular—indicates that this script should run when you click a button in your program. Of course, Xcode has no way of knowing *which* button should run this script—that's what Interface Builder is for (page 291).

- **Part 2** lets AppleScript know that you're about to send commands to your interface's *main* window (the window with the text field, pop-up menu, and button).

- **Part 3** puts the text that you entered in your program's text field into the *the-Text* variable. Later in your script, you'll have your Mac speak this text.

Tip: If you wanted to *change* what's in your program's text field—say, so you could update the text field with the word "talking" while your program is speaking—you'd use the *set* command instead of accessing *the content* of your text field.

• **Part 4** finds the voice you selected from the pop-up menu and puts that voice's name into the *theVoice* variable. You'll use this voice to tell AppleScript how to pronounce the text from part 3.

Note: The *as string* bit in parts 3 and 4 ensures that your *say* command (in part 5) will work properly. That's because *say*, as described on page 156, *requires* you to provide a string to speak out loud.

• **Part 5** is the meat of your script. This is where AppleScript takes the text from part 3—and the voice from part 4—and combines them to pronounce your text in a cheesy Mac voice.

Running the Program

Now that you've typed your commands, you can actually run your program. Simply choose Build → Build and Run (⌘-R). If Xcode asks to save your files, click Save All.

After a few moments, Xcode assembles your program and launches it. If you're not convinced that the Build command worked, just look in the Dock; you should see a new, generic icon to represent your program.

Soon after, you'll see your program's main window appear onscreen (Figure 15-12). Feel free to experiment by picking different voices, typing unusual sentences, and clicking Speak to hear them pronounced. When you've had enough of Apple's utterly synthesized voices, choose SpeakToMe → Quit Application (⌘-Q).

Figure 15-12:
Your very own AppleScript Studio application. For extra fun, choose a weird voice like Zarvox or Pipe Organ.

That's it! You now have a complete, self-contained AppleScript Studio application, ready to run whenever you are.

Tip: If you'd like to run your program *without* using Xcode, simply locate your project's folder (page 284) in the Finder, navigate to the Build subfolder, and double-click SpeakToMe. If you saved your project in the Developer folder, for example, your actual program would be in the Developer → SpeakToMe → Build folder.

To learn more about AppleScript Studio, check out Apple's special Web site for it: *www.apple.com/applescript/studio/*. In particular, look at the online documentation (for help with more advanced AppleScript Studio techniques) and the download-able example projects.

Tip: Dozens of AppleScript Studio examples are beyond the scope of Apple's Web site—or this book, for that matter. Luckily, they're not beyond the scope of Apple's *programmers;* you can find more than 30 example AppleScript Studio projects in your very own Developer → Examples → AppleScript Studio folder.

POWER USERS' CLINIC

Polishing Up an AppleScript Studio App

Although your AppleScript Studio program is a huge improvement on the ugliness that marks most plain Apple-Scripts, your program is still not up to the quality of, say, TextEdit. Little interface inconsistencies spring up all over the place: the About box has inaccurate information, the Help menu doesn't do anything, and so on. Although these interface quirks have no effect on how your program runs, they do have an effect on how your program *looks*—and in the era of Mac OS X, that's just as important.

Here's how to inject your program's interface with some vir-tual Botox:

- **Clean up your menu bar.** Although Interface Builder gives you a standard set of menus whenever you create a new project, the menus aren't custom-ized to your program's features. To fix the problem, open your program's interface in Interface Builder, double-click the menu items you want to modify (they're in the "MainMenu.nib - MainMenu" win-dow), and type new names for the menu items. At minimum, you should replace the word "Application" in the Application and Help menus with the actual name of your program (in this case, SpeakToMe).

- **Put correct information in the About box.** When you create a new project in Xcode, Mac OS X assumes that you don't care what your About box displays. That's why, right now, your About box says "Copyright 2005 __MyCompanyName__" or some similar nonsense.

  To fix the problem, open your project in Xcode and double-click InfoPlist.strings. You'll see a color-coded text file appear, filled with geeky names (CFBundle-ShortVersionString, for example). To change what ap-

pears in your About box, simply edit the string to the right of NSHumanReadableCopyright.

- **Make sure your program displays accurate information in the Finder's Info window.** By default, when you select your program in the Finder (page 294) and choose File → Get Info, you'll see a bunch of useless information—including Copyright 2005 __MyCompanyName__.

  If that text looks familiar, you shouldn't be sur-prised: it's the same information your program dis-played in its About box before you fixed it as described above. To fix the information in the Finder's *Info* window, you follow a similar proce-dure: open InfoPlist.strings in Xcode, and edit the string next to CFBundleGetInfoString.

- **Give your program a real icon.** No professional-quality program comes with a generic icon nowa-days. If you want your program to compete with the big boys—FileMaker Pro, Microsoft Word, and iTunes, for example—you'll need a memorable icon. Luckily, you can attach one quite simply: copy the image you want to use from a program like Photo-shop, select your program's *existing* icon in the Finder, choose File → Get Info, and paste the new image on top of the old icon in the upper-left cor-ner of the window. Touch-up complete!

Now that you have a pro-quality program, you can post it for the world to see. If you'd like to reach the widest audi-ence, post your program on a Web site like *www.versiontracker.com* or *www.macupdate.com* (both free)—they're gathering places for interested Mac fans.

Part Four: Appendixes

4

Appendix A, *AppleScript Support in Common Programs*

Appendix B, *Moving from HyperCard to AppleScript*

Appendix C, *Where to Go from Here*

AppleScript Support in Common Programs

If you're like most AppleScript fans, you'll want to have as many scriptable programs on your hard drive as possible. That way, if you want to do some complex task—say, laying out a book—you can use AppleScript to automate the process.

Of course, not every program supports AppleScript. And even among those that do, each supports a different *amount* of AppleScript automation. If you had to navigate the maze of AppleScript-supporting programs by yourself, you'd quickly go insane.

Don't worry, though. With this appendix at your side, you can easily check whether a common Mac OS X program supports AppleScript—and, if it doesn't, which competing programs support AppleScript better.

Databases

Program	Price	Web site	AppleScript support
AppleWorks	$80 (but included for free on iBooks and iMacs)	*www.apple.com/ appleworks/*	**Decent.** Although AppleWorks is great as an all-around text and graphics suite, its AppleScript support is not its strongest suit—especially for the AppleWorks database module. For example, AppleWorks lacks a scripting command for inserting pictures into a database.
FileMaker Pro	$300	*http://filemaker.com/ products/fm_home.html*	**Very Good.** As described on page 209, FileMaker excels at letting everyday users automate their databases with AppleScript. You can incorporate pictures, text, and files into your databases quite easily with FileMaker Pro.

Best choice for AppleScript: FileMaker Pro. If nothing else, FileMaker is simply a newer, more polished program—and its thorough AppleScript dictionary proves it.

Email Programs

Program	Price	Web site	AppleScript support
Entourage	Only available as part of the Microsoft Office suite ($400)	*www.microsoft.com/ mac/products/ entourage2004/ entourage2004.aspx*	**Excellent.** Microsoft Entourage supports many more features than Mac OS X Mail does. For example, you can use Entourage's *find* command to locate people who have a particular email suffix (like @apple.com).
Eudora	Free with advertisements, or $50 without advertisements	*www.eudora.com*	**Decent.** Eudora supports a fair number of AppleScript commands that Mail and Entourage do (like *reply*), but Eudora doesn't support some of the more advanced commands (like *connect to*, for automatically downloading your email).
Mail	Free, included with Mac OS X	*www.apple.com/ macosx/features/ mail/*	**Good.** Mail allows you to automate sending, receiving, and replying to email—all with AppleScript (page 186). Plus, you can use Mail to run scripts automatically when new email arrives (page 190). Still, Mail's AppleScript commands are quite complicated compared with, say, Entourage or Mailsmith.
Mailsmith	$99; free 30-day demo available for download	*www.barebones.com/ products/mailsmith*	**Exceptional!** Brought to you by the makers of BBEdit (see next page), Mailsmith is a powerful and extremely scriptable email application—so scriptable, in fact, that you can run AppleScripts when you click *existing* Mailsmith menu items, allowing you to customize the menu bar itself.

Best choice for AppleScript: Mailsmith. When it comes to the program with the most—and most useful—AppleScript commands, Mailsmith wins hands down over Mac OS X Mail and Microsoft Entourage.

Graphics Editors

Program	Price	Web site	AppleScript support
iPhoto	Included with Mac OS X, or as part of iLife ($50)	*www.apple.com/ilife/ iphoto/*	**Good.** Although iPhoto doesn't have the number of advanced filters that Photoshop does, iPhoto does have the advantage of being quite easy to use. And, as described on page 126, iPhoto allows a number of useful AppleScript commands.
Photoshop	$650	*www.adobe.com/ products/photoshop/*	**Very Good.** As described on page 131, Photoshop puts a huge range of AppleScript commands at your disposal. Sure, Photoshop isn't as easy to use as iPhoto—but if you're a graphics pro, power trumps ease of use.

Best choice for AppleScript: Photoshop. That is, if you don't mind clearing out your retirement account to buy it.

Page Layout Programs

Program	Price	Web site	AppleScript support
InDesign CS	$700	www.adobe.com/products/indesign/	**Very Good.** InDesign CS has an impressive set of AppleScript commands for laying out graphics, navigating your documents, fine-tuning your text, and much more.
QuarkXPress	$950	www.quark.com/products/xpress/	**Good.** QuarkXPress is a mainstay of the printing world, but its AppleScript dictionary isn't quite as comprehensive as InDesign's. For example, QuarkXPress can't automate adding Web links to your layout files like InDesign can.

Best choice for AppleScript: InDesign CS. Check out www.adobe.com/products/indesign/pdfs/indesign_cs_scripting_guide.pdf for a thorough guide to scripting InDesign to the fullest.

Plain Text Editors

Program	Price	Web site	AppleScript support
BBEdit	$200	www.barebones.com/products/bbedit/	**Exceptional!** Among programmers, Web designers, and other people who deal with plain text files everyday, BBEdit is a deity. Its AppleScript support is positively unbeatable: not only does BBEdit have an amazingly complete dictionary, it's also one of the only commercial programs that can *record* your actions as AppleScript commands (page 23).
SubEthaEdit	$35	www.codingmonkeys.de/subethaedit/	**Decent.** SubEthaEdit is a text editor that allows several people to edit the same file at once over a network. But if you want to automate small editing tasks on your own Mac, you'll be glad to know that SubEthaEdit has an AppleScript dictionary just waiting for your commands.
TextEdit	Free, included with Mac OS X	None	**Good.** Although TextEdit is supposed to be a word processor, it can work as a plain text editor in a pinch. Luckily, almost all the AppleScript commands that TextEdit supports for formatted files also work when you're just editing plain text files.

Best choice for AppleScript: BBEdit. Hands down. If you're looking for the gold standard in scriptability, you just found it.

If you're not willing to spend $200 on a text editor, take a look at TextWrangler (free, www.barebones.com/products/textwrangler/index.shtml), which includes all the same AppleScript commands as BBEdit, just without as many text-editing features.

Word Processors

A word processor, unlike a text editor, is a program that lets you lay out your documents in multiple fonts, colors, and sizes.

Program	Price	Web site	AppleScript support
Apple-Works	$80 (although included for free on iBooks and iMacs)	www.apple.com/appleworks/	**Decent.** AppleWorks is Apple's homegrown response to Microsoft Office. The AppleWorks scripting dictionary is nothing special, however; it lacks many of the timesaving commands from Word, like *save as* and *web page preview.*
Nisus Writer Express	$60 download, or $70 on a physical CD	www.nisus.com/Express/	**Good.** Writer Express has a number of power-user features, like the ability to select noncontiguous sections of text and apply a single font to all of them. Writer Express's AppleScript support, though, is virtually identical to TextEdit's.
Tex-Edit Plus	$15 shareware	www.tex-edit.com/ index.html#Tex-Edit%20Plus	**Very good.** Tex-Edit Plus is a favorite of Mac shareware fans worldwide–not least for its thorough AppleScript support. You can search for text, add sounds, and even autocapitalize words in your documents, all with AppleScript commands from Tex-Edit's dictionary.
TextEdit	Free, included with Mac OS X	None	**Good.** TextEdit is a simple, elegant word processor with a decent selection of useful AppleScript commands (page 59).
OpenOffice	Free	http://porting.openoffice.org/ mac/	**Nonexistent.** Although OpenOffice is a handy program for opening and saving Microsoft Office files, it doesn't support a single AppleScript command.
Word	$230 alone, or $400 as part of the Microsoft Office suite	www.microsoft.com/mac/ products/word2004/ word2004.aspx	**Very good.** As described on page 66, Word supports tons of AppleScript commands, from querying the built-in thesaurus to unleashing the word-count feature.

Best choice for AppleScript: Word. Although TextEdit wins on simplicity and style, you can't beat Word on raw power. (The same applies for other Office programs, too; Microsoft PowerPoint, the computerized-slideshow program, is infinitely more scriptable than Apple's Keynote, while Microsoft Excel, the spreadsheet program, is far more scriptable than AppleWorks.)

Web Browsers

For a detailed breakdown of the various choices in Mac OS X Web browsing, see page 176. If you're too lazy to flip back, though, here's the essence: Safari (page 175) works fine if you want to use fairly simple AppleScript commands, but a commercial program like OmniWeb (www.omnigroup.com/applications/omniweb/) is better suited for power scripters.

Moving from HyperCard to AppleScript

Back in the days before DVDs, iPods, and take-out sushi, everyday Mac fans used HyperCard to write simple automation programs. Sure, HyperCard couldn't command *other* programs, but its simplicity and power made HyperCard a favorite tool for thousands of budding programmers.

In addition, HyperCard was one of the first programming tools to let people build their program's interface through drag-and-drop—more than a decade before Interface Builder came along (page 285). *HyperTalk,* the programming language for HyperCard, was highly regarded for its English-like syntax and shallow learning curve. And even hard-core programmers respected HyperCard *stacks* (interfaces bundled with code) for their small file size.

Unfortunately, Apple stopped supporting HyperCard soon before releasing Mac OS X. If you happen to be one of the Mac fans who depends on HyperCard for everyday work, therefore, you're left with only a few choices:

- **Continue using HyperCard in Mac OS X's Classic mode.** *Classic* is Apple's buzzword to describe Mac OS 9 programs running in Mac OS X. Unfortunately, since HyperCard wasn't designed for Mac OS X, using HyperCard in Classic is likely to result in a major slowdown of your code. Plus, you'll continue to see HyperCard's old, gray, Mac OS 9–style windows—a scourge on the attractive interface of Mac OS X.

- **Buy a Mac OS X program that can open HyperCard stacks.** Such programs include SuperCard ($180, *www.supercard.us*) and Revolution ($150–$900 depending on license, *http://revolution.runrev.com/*). Unfortunately, neither program is *perfect* at importing HyperCard stacks into Mac OS X, so you may have to spend a while updating sections of code to be Mac OS X–compatible.

- **Rewrite your HyperCard stacks with AppleScript.** Since AppleScript and HyperTalk are fairly similar languages, you can rewrite your HyperCard stacks in AppleScript pretty easily.

Note: If your HyperCard stacks are full of interface elements, you'd probably be better off rewriting your stacks in AppleScript *Studio* (Chapter 15) than simply reprogramming your stacks in Script Editor. That's because plain ol' AppleScript doesn't allow for complex interfaces.

On the other hand, if your HyperCard stacks are simple (say, just based around a button or two) it's easier to rewrite your code in Script Editor than to deal with the complexities of Xcode and Interface Builder (page 283).

If you decide to pursue the converting-to-AppleScript route, you'll be glad to have the rest of this appendix at your side. The following pages address the most common syntax differences between HyperTalk and AppleScript, so you can bring your stale code from the confines of Mac OS 9 to the bright, shining future of Mac OS X.

Note: The rest of this appendix assumes that you know how to program in HyperCard proficiently. There's no explanation of what specific HyperTalk commands do, because you can find in-depth explanations in a book like *The HyperTalk Language Guide* (Addison Wesley, 1988).

If you *don't* know HyperCard, though, don't sweat it. HyperCard is unsupported by Apple, and there's little reason to create new programs with it unless you're nostalgic for the era of black and white Macs.

Data Types

AppleScript and HyperCard can both handle a variety of data types (strings, numbers, and so on). However, both languages have a different way of checking what *kind* of data is stored in a value or variable.

In HyperCard, if you want to check what kind of data something is, you use the command *is a*, like this:

```
if 4 is a number then
    --Do whatever
end if
```

In AppleScript, you use the *class* keyword to accomplish the same data checking:

```
if (the class of 4) is number then
    --Do whatever
end if
```

Dialog Boxes

In HyperTalk, there are two commands for displaying dialog boxes: *answer* and *ask*. You use *answer* when you want to just present information onscreen, like this:

```
answer "Fortune cookie says: You will enjoy good health."
```

On the other hand, when you want to use HyperCard dialog boxes to *get* information, you use *ask,* like this:

```
ask "How old are you?"
put it into theAge --The variable "theAge" now holds your dialog box response
```

In AppleScript, however, you use the *display dialog* command to accomplish both tasks, like this:

```
display dialog "Fortune cookie says: You will enjoy good health."
set theAge to the text returned of (display dialog "How old are you?" ¬
     default answer "")
```

Existence

When you want to check whether a file or folder exists using HyperTalk, you use the command *there is:*

```
there is a folder "Macintosh HD:Applications:"
```

In AppleScript, you use the keyword *exists* (page 47)—and you must direct your command at the Finder:

```
tell application "Finder"
    exists folder "Macintosh HD:Applications:"
end tell
```

Numbers

Although AppleScript and HyperTalk deal with math operations the same way (with symbols like + for addition, / for division, and so on), HyperTalk has a few keywords—like *add* and *multiply*—that simply aren't supported in AppleScript. For example, if you have a variable named *myNumber* in HyperTalk, you can use the following commands:

```
add 2 to myNumber
multiply myNumber by 5
```

AppleScript can't understand either of those commands, though. To accomplish the same job in AppleScript, you'd have to write this:

```
set myNumber to myNumber + 2
set myNumber to myNumber * 5
```

Note: Another feature that AppleScript lacks is the ability to use trigonometric functions like *sin, cos,* and *tan* (which work just fine in HyperTalk). If you need those commands for your script, download a trigonometry scripting addition (page 50).

Pausing

In HyperTalk, when you want to halt the progress of a script temporarily, you use the *wait* command, like this:

```
wait 2 seconds
```

In AppleScript, you use *delay* (page 151):

```
delay 2
```

Ranges

In HyperTalk, when you want to get a portion of a string or list, you use the keyword *to*, like this:

```
character 1 to 10 of "Fried octopus" --Would return "Fried octo"
```

In AppleScript, however, you achieve the same job with the word *through* (page 107), like this:

```
characters 1 through 10 of "Fried octopus"
```

Note: In HyperTalk, you refer the type of information you're getting in the singular–*character,* for example. In AppleScript, you refer to the same type of information in the plural (*characters,* in this example).

Repeat Statements

Most *repeat* statements (page 71) work the same way with either HyperTalk or AppleScript. There are a couple kinds of statements, however, that use slightly different syntax depending on the programming language you use.

For example, in HyperCard, some people insert the word *for* into their *repeat* statements, like this:

```
repeat for 10 times
    --Do things
end repeat
```

The fact is, the word *for* is unnecessary in HyperTalk. And in AppleScript, you're simply not allowed to use the word *for* in your *repeat* statements at all.

The other difference with *repeat* statements comes when you want to increment a variable each time your loop runs. In HyperTalk, you'd use the following syntax to increment a variable (*theAge*) from 10 to 20:

```
repeat with age=10 to 20
    --Each time this part runs, "age" will be one greater than before
end repeat
```

In AppleScript, the syntax is slightly different:

```
repeat with age from 10 to 20
    --Each time this part runs, "age" will be one greater than before
end repeat
```

Subroutines

In HyperTalk, you define a subroutine like this:

```
on triple someNumber
    return someNumber * 3
end triple
```

And run it like this:

```
triple 10 --Would return 30
```

In AppleScript, however, you define a subroutine like this (page 85):

```
on triple(someNumber)
    return someNumber * 3
end triple
```

And run it like this:

```
triple(10)
```

As you can see, the difference with HyperTalk is that you don't type parentheses around the value you want to perform a subroutine on.

Variables

HyperTalk and AppleScript have a lot in common when it comes to variables. In both languages, variables can hold similar kinds of information—strings, numbers, and so on. And in both languages, you have to use the keyword *global* when you want the ability to access a particular variable from multiple subroutines in your script (page 193).

The difference comes when you want to assign a *value* to a variable. In HyperTalk, you use the keyword *put,* like this:

```
put 33 into myAge
```

In AppleScript, you can use *put,* too—but, because of habit, most people don't. Instead, the more popular AppleScript way of assigning variables is to use *set* (page 54), like this:

```
set myAge to 33
```

Now, go forth and script!

Where to Go from Here

Each script in this book is a self-contained lesson, teaching you how to perform a certain task with AppleScript. Taken together, the lessons in this book could form the curriculum of AppleScript High.

If you're interested in pursuing AppleScript further, however, you'll want to graduate to more advanced scripts. And if you want to learn more obscure techniques—like, say, querying complex online databases (page 200)—you'll want a little more guidance than this book can provide.

Luckily, the Mac world is teeming with information on AppleScript. From Web sites to email lists, dozens of sources are just *aching* to provide you with Apple-Script information at your slightest whim.

Web Sites

Information stored on the Internet is fast, convenient, and—in large part—free. With a Web browser before you, AppleScript information is no more than a few clicks away.

AppleScript Sites

- *www.apple.com/applescript.* Apple's very own AppleScript home page. Be sure to check out the Resources link for a thorough list of AppleScript links elsewhere on the Web.

Tip: See *www.apple.com/applescript/guidebook/sbrt/* for a list of helpful AppleScript subroutines (page 85).

- *www.applescriptsourcebook.com.* A general-purpose AppleScript Web site run by expert Bill Cheeseman.

- *http://developer.apple.com/documentation/AppleScript/.* Another Apple Web page devoted to AppleScript. This one's meant more for programmers than for everyday Mac fans.

Tip: The AppleScript Language Guide, available from *http://developer.apple.com/documentation/ AppleScript/Conceptual/AppleScriptLangGuide/,* is a handy reference to all the nuances of AppleScript syntax.

- *www.google.com.* The world-famous search engine. If a particular AppleScript feature confuses you—say, using escape sequences (page 59)—do a search for something like *applescript escape sequences,* and browse through the results.

- *www.macosxhints.com.* A site filled with tips for Mac OS X power users. (A number of the tricks involve creative uses for AppleScripts.)

Tip: If you prefer your timesaving tricks in book form, check out Mac OS X Power Hound, Panther Edition by Rob Griffiths (O'Reilly/Pogue Press, 2004).

- *www.macscripter.net.* A popular site for AppleScript geeks, with tons of example code, a searchable database of scripting additions (page 50), and a bulletin board (*http://bbs.applescript.net/*) for posting questions.

- *www.scriptweb.org.* Links to dozens of different Web pages on all facets of Mac scripting.

- *http://developer.apple.com/technotes/tn2002/tn2065.html.* Apple's Technical Note TN2065 has everything you've ever wanted to know about the *do shell script* command—and more. If you're thinking about linking AppleScript with Mac OS X's Unix core, you shouldn't miss this TechNote.

Other Mac Programming Sites

- *www.cocoadev.com.* Beginner lessons on Cocoa, one of Apple's more advanced Mac OS X programming languages.

- *http://developer.apple.com.* Apple's *own* site for Mac programmers, including hundreds of sample code segments and technical documents.

- *www.macdevcenter.com.* Macintosh programming and scripting tutorials.

Discussion Lists

If you have questions about AppleScript—or enjoy reading other people's questions and answers—you should subscribe to an AppleScript discussion list. You'll receive an email every day, recapping the day's discussion. And if you have a question of your own, you can send it to a designated email address to have the question forwarded to everyone on the list (and, hopefully, answered by someone).

- **applescript-users** is an Apple-sponsored list for general discussion about AppleScript. You can subscribe to the mailing list at *http://lists.apple.com/mailman/listinfo/applescript-users*.

- **applescript-studio** is an Apple-sponsored list for talking about AppleScript *Studio*. You can subscribe at *http://lists.apple.com/mailman/listinfo/applescript-studio*.

- **macscrpt** is the original mailing list on Mac scripting languages, and a popular hangout for scripting pros. Subscribe at *http://listserv.dartmouth.edu/scripts/wa.exe?SUBED1=macscrpt&A=1*.

Books

Although Web sites and email lists are convenient for discovering tidbits of information, there's often no substitute for a physical book. Books—especially those in the following list—cover a single topic more thoroughly than a Web site ever could.

- *Mac OS X: The Missing Manual, Panther Edition* by David Pogue (O'Reilly/Pogue Press, 2004). A helpful guide to absolutely *every* important feature in Mac OS X.

- *Danny Goodman's AppleScript Handbook, 2nd Edition* by Danny Goodman (Random House, 1995). Even though it's an old AppleScript book, the detailed language explanations from this book are still pertinent today.

- *AppleScript: The Definitive Guide* by Matt Neuberg (O'Reilly, 2004). A very thorough AppleScript reference with in-depth explanations of all the language's features.

- *Learning Cocoa with Objective-C* by James Duncan Davidson & Apple Computer, Inc. (O'Reilly, 2003). An introduction to Cocoa, Apple's preferred program-writing language for Mac OS X.

- *Learning Unix for Mac OS X Panther, 2nd Edition* by Dave Taylor & Brian Jepson (O'Reilly, 2004). A guide to the various Unix programs included with Mac OS X. If you use the *do shell script* command often (page 256), you'll want this book.

- *AppleScript: A Comprehensive Guide to Scripting and Automation on Mac OS X* by Hanaan Rosenthal (Friends of Ed, 2004). This book teaches AppleScript using real-world examples, illustrating how the language is used.

With these sources by your side, AppleScript should never confuse you again. Now for the best part: writing your own scripts!

Index

Symbols

"..." (quotation marks), 47
& (concatenation symbol), 56
(*...*) multi-line comments, 42
- - (single-line comments), 42
/ (used to denote POSIX/Unix file paths), 76
: (used to denote file paths), 76
\ escape symbol, 59
\" escape symbol, 59
\n escape symbol, 59
\r escape symbol, 59
\t escape symbol, 59
~/ (used to denote user's Home folder), 76
¬ (line-continuation symbol), 55
... (ellipsis, creating), 214

A

A class name can't go after this identifier
          compiler error, 266
AAC audio file format, 153
About Convert/Print Window script, 12
About Finder Scripts submenu, 6
About Internet Services script, 9
About These Scripts command (Script
          Editor), 28
Accounts command, 11, 77
Action Clauses command (Script Editor), 28
actions (Photoshop)
     recording, 131
     wrapping in AppleScript, 133

Actions command (Photoshop), 132
activate command, 19, 111, 237, 241
Activity Monitor, 109
ADC (Apple Developer Connection), 276
add - new item alert script, 224
Add Bookmark command, 95, 183
add command, 127
Add to File Names script, 7
Add to File/Folder Names script, 6, 8
Address Book
     adding contacts to group, 185
     copying information to FileMaker Pro
          database, 212–216
     creating group, 186
     dictionary, 185
     writing plug-ins, 184
Address Book Plug-Ins folder, 184
Address Book scripts, 5
Adjustments menu (Photoshop), 133
administrator accounts, 258
Adobe Photoshop CS folder, 132
AE Monitor Web site, 44
AIFF audio file format, 153
AirPort, 174
     cards, 171
     signal strength, 172
alert, folder action, 222
alias keyword, 77
.app files, 31
Apple Events, 44

Apple Human Interface Guidelines (HIG)
    Web site, 285
Apple Lossless audio file format, 153
Apple online retail shop, 13
Apple Stock Quote (Yahoo) script, 13
Apple Store script, 13
AppleScript
    additional resources, 309–311
    controlling files using, 75
    examples CD, 24
    folder, 3, 6
    home page, 309
    making work with Web services, 200
    numbers, 305
    text handling, 65
    variables, 307
    versus HyperTalk, 303–307
    Web site, 6
.applescript files, 31
AppleScript Help script, 5
AppleScript pane (Inspector), 290
AppleScript Related Sites script, 14
AppleScript Studio, 281–295
    creating new project, 283
    Interface Builder, using with, 285–293
    interface design, 285–293
    overview, 281
    polishing up application, 295
    using Xcode with, 293–295
    Web site, 294
    writing code in, 293
AppleScript Website script, 6
applescript-studio discussion list, 311
applescript-users discussion list, 311
AppleWorks, 299
Application Bundles, 34
application script menus, 12
apply to all subfolders script, 225
as keyword, 271
at the front keywords, 61
Audible Web site, 159
audio file formats, 153
Auto Color command (Photoshop), 133
Auto Contrast command (Photoshop), 133
Auto Levels command (Photoshop), 133
automating button clicks, 241

B

backing up files, 91
Backup 2.0 Web site, 92
Basics folder, 31
batch renaming, 8, 113
beep command, 152
Berkowitz, Paul, 74

black text in Script Editor, 27
Block Pop-Up Windows command, 240, 241
blue text in Script Editor, 27
Bookmarks Bar menu, 183
Boolean values, 91
browsers
    Camino, 176
    Firefox, 176
    iCab, 176
    Internet Explorer, 176
    Mozilla, 176
    Netscape, 176
    OmniWeb, 176
    Opera, 176
    scripting, 176
    (see also Safari)
browsing, 302
Build and Debug command (Xcode), 279
Build and Run command (Xcode), 279, 284, 294
Build command, 294
Build profile info web page script, 6

C

cal command, 257
calendar, 262
call soap command, 200
call xmlrpc command, 200
Camino, 176
Carbon Copy Cloner Web site, 92
Card and Columns command (Address
    Book), 186
Change Case of Item Names script, 7
Changing Info Color script (DVD
    Player), 169
chat program (see iChat)
check for new mail command, 187
Check Spelling as You Type command, 28
Check Spelling command, 27
Cheeseman, Bill, 310
choose file command, 77, 97, 134, 197
choose file name command, 196
choose folder command, 98
choose from list command, 191
    every keyword, 109
    merging file lists, 116
choose URL command, 197, 198
chown Unix program, 258
class keyword (AppleScript), 304
Classes list command (Photoshop), 135
clicking tab buttons, 243
the clipboard keywords, 160
Clock command, 157
close - close sub-folders script, 224
CNN script, 14

Cocoa, beginner lessons, 310
coercion operation, 108
coercions, common, 272
colored text in Script Editor, 26
ColorSync folder, 30
ColorSync submenu (Script Menu), 6
command prompt, Unix, 252
Comment Tags command (Script Editor), 28
comments in AppleScript, 27
compiler errors, 266
compiling files, 24
concatenating lists, 115
concatenating strings, 56
Conditionals command (Script Editor), 28
Connect to Server command, 196, 198
convert - PostScript to PDF script, 225
convert command, 155
Convert to PDF/PostScript script, 12
converting music, 153
Copy command, 40, 42, 184
copy command, 215
Copy Phone Number to Clipboard script, 184
CoreServices folder, 138, 258
count command, 67, 238
Count Messages in All Mailboxes script, 10
Crazy Message Text script, 10
Create LDAP Server script, 11
Create New Mail Account script, 11
Create New Message script, 11
cron program, 261, 263
Current Date & Time script, 9
current date command, 62, 63, 156
Current Temperature by Zipcode script, 9
Current Temperature script, 14
Current Work folder, 45
Customize Toolbar command, 25

D

database, AppleScript, 203–217
    getting file information, 206
    making simple, 204–206
    searching, 205
default answers, 54
default responses, 55
Default Voice command, 15
Default Voice tab, 156
defaults command, 253
defaults Unix program, 251
delay command, 151
delete command, 94, 155
Desktop & Screen Saver command, 192
Desktop folder, 77
desktop icons, increasing size, 233
Desktop Pictures folder, 81, 139

Developer Tools
    obtaining and installing, 275
    (see also Xcode)
dialog boxes and scripts, 60
Dialogs command (Script Editor), 28
dictionaries
    checking whether a program has one, 238
    overview, 48
    scripting programs that don't have, 237–250
    (see also program dictionary)
diffuse glow filter (Photoshop), 135
digital cameras, 125
discussion lists, 310
disks, list folder command, 118
Display All Accounts and Preferences script, 11
display dialog command, 266
    buttons option, 60
    default answer option, 54
    default button option, 60
    dialogResponse variable, 60
    displaying numbers, 41
    giving up after option, 60
    lists and, 108
    multiple commands, 41
    scripting additions and, 50
    with icon option, 60
divider bar, 25
do JavaScript command, 180
do script command, 253
do shell script, Unix without Terminal, 256
do Visual Basic command, 74
Documents folder, 93, 225
Download Weather Map script, 14
Drop Box folder, 224
droplets, 141, 154
duplicate command, 92
DVD Player program, 169
DVD Player Scripts folder, 169
DVD scripts, 169

E

Editing pane, 36
editors, 38
    Script Debugger, 38
    Script Editor (see Script Editor)
    TextEdit (see TextEdit)
    Xcode (see Xcode)
else statement, 48
Enable Folder Actions command, 222
end command, 79
end if command, 47, 79
end repeat command, 79

end tell command, 47, 79
Erase Deleted Messages command
        (Mail), 189
error command, 275
Error Handlers command (Script Editor), 28
error statement tricks Web site, 274
error statements, 274
errors
    discovering, 274
    isolating and handling, 273
    preventing, 271–272
escape sequences, 58
Event Log, 29
Event Log History, 269–271
Event Log History command, 269
event logs, 267–269
Example Scripts icon, 4
examples CD, 24
Execute AppleScript command, 158
exists command, 47, 67, 271
exit repeat command, 271
Expected "" but found end of script
        compiler error, 266
Expected "tell", etc. but found "if" compiler
        error, 266
Expected end of line but found " compiler
        error, 266
Expected end of line but found identifier
        compiler error, 266
Expected end of line, etc. but found "tell"
        compiler error, 266
extending AppleScript's menu control, 240

F

file extensions, missing, 7
file information scripts, 206–209
FileMaker Pro
    copying Address Book information to
        database, 212–216
    creating new database, 210
    entering information into database, 211–
        216
        manually, 211
    Insert File command, 215
    New Database command, 210
    scripting, 209–217
    ScriptMaker, 217
    Sort Records command, 216
    sorting records, 216–218
files
    backing up, 91
    controlling, 75–103
    deleting, 94

displaying folders, 78
extensions, 76, 101
folders, 76
moving, 88–90
paths, 77
    notation, 76
POSIX, 77
saving, 100
saving all documents at once, 103
filter command, 135
filtering database information, 209
filtering images, 135
Find command, 25, 122, 185
Finder scripts, 6–8
Finder Scripts folder, 30
Finder window
    changing view of, 80
    settings, 82
Finder Windows – Hide All script, 7
Finder Windows – Show All script, 7
Firefox, 176
fit to pages command, 69, 70, 71
Flatten Image command (Photoshop), 135
Folder Action Scripts folder, 222, 223, 225
folder actions, 4, 8
Folder Actions Handlers command (Script
        Editor), 28
folder actions scripts, 221–235
    add - new item alert, 224
    apply to all subfolders, 225
    close - close sub-folders, 224
    convert - PostScript to PDF, 225
    Image - Add Icon, 225
    Image - Duplicate as JPEG/PNG/TIFF, 226
    Image - Flip Horizontal/Vertical, 226
    Image - Info to Comment, 226
    Image - Rotate Left/Right, 226
    open - show comments in dialog, 226
    setup, 234
    subfolders, 225
    Web site, 235
Folder Actions Setup command, 234
Folder Actions Setup icon, 4
Folder Actions submenu, 8
folder icons, 78
Font Sampler script, 9
FontSync profiles, 8
FontSync Scripts submenu, 8
formats, converting, 143
forward command, 190
Full Key Codes, 250
Function Key pop-up menu
        (Photoshop), 132

G

generate command, 61
Get Info command, 89
Get New Mail command, 187
Get Result of AppleScript command, 73
Get Size of IMAP Mailbox script, 11
get synonym info object command, 122
global Script Menu, 12
global variables, 307
Go to Chapter script (DVD Player), 169
Go to Time script (DVD Player), 169
graphical database program, 209
graphics (see images)
gray text in Script Editor, 27
GUI Scripting, 13, 238–250
    automating button clicks, 241
    clicking tab buttons, 243
    controlling menus, 240
    enabling, 239
    PreFab UI Browser, 247
    System Events, 239

H

handlers (see subroutines)
Hearing tab (System Preferences), 152
HetimaOsaxOpener plug-in, 37
Hide Navigation Bar command, 32
Hide Toolbar command, 26
History pane, 37
History, clearing, 270
HyperCard
    data types, 304
    moving to AppleScript, 303–307
HyperTalk
    checking if files/folders exist, 305
    dialog boxes, 304
    numbers, 305
    pausing scripts, 306
    ranges, 306
    subroutines, 307
    variables, 307
    versus AppleScript, 303–307

I

IBM's ViaVoice, 162
iCal, 176
    New Calendar command, 262
    New Event command, 262
    scheduling scripts with, 262
iChat, 191–195
    modifying when screen saver is on, 191
    status message setting, 193–195

Icons folder, 95
if statement, 89, 111
iLife Web site, 126
Image - Add Icon script, 225
Image - Duplicate as JPEG/PNG/TIFF
    script, 226
Image - Flip Horizontal/Vertical script, 226
Image - Info to Comment script, 226
Image - Rotate Left/Right script, 226
Image Events, 137–145
    bugs in, 140
Image Events scripts, 137–145
Image Manipulation command (Script
    Editor), 28
images
    converting, 125
    converting formats, 143
    creating a droplet, 141
    filtering, 135
    getting dimensions, 138
    getting random, 128
    JPEG2 format, 145
    making look surreal, 135
    opening, 125
    organizing and editing, 125–145
    padding, 140
    slideshows, 130
    (see also Photoshop)
Import Addresses script, 11
Importing command (iTunes), 153
Info Field, 29
info for command, 206, 207
    properties, 208
info for record, properties, 208
Info Scripts submenu, 9
information record properties, complete
    list, 209
inheritance, 83
Insert File command (FileMaker Pro), 215
Inspector, 290
Install Script Menu, 4
instant messaging
    signing up for new account, 191
    (see also iChat)
Interface Builder
    Inspector window, 290
    Quit Application command, 290
    Show Info command, 290
    Test Interface command, 290
    using with AppleScript Studio, 285–293
interface hierarchies, 245–248
Internal Modem command, 172
Internet and network scripts, 171–200
Internet Connect, 171–175
Internet Explorer, 176

Internet Scripts submenu, 9
Internet Services folder, 16
iPhoto scripts, 126–131
it keyword, 136
it statement, 136
Iterate Items command (Script Editor), 28
iTunes
    converting music files, 153
    converting song files, 152
    Library, 153
    Music folder, 154
    playing tracks, 148
    preferences, 153
    rating songs, 148
    scripts, 147–155
    skipping tracks, 150

J

JavaScript code, running in Safari, 180
JPEG2 format, 145

K

key down command, 249, 250
key up command, 249, 250
Keyboard Maestro Web site, 157
keyboard shortcuts
    Actions command (Photoshop), 132
    AppleScript pane (Inspector), 290
    Build and Debug command (Xcode), 279
    Build and Run command (Xcode), 279
    Copy command, 42
    Customize Toolbar command, 25
    Duplicate command, 289
    Event Log History command, 269
    Find command, 185
    Get Info command, 89
    Library command, 46
    Move to Trash command, 96
    New Calendar command (iCal), 262
    New command, 166
    New Event command (iCal), 262
    New Smart Playlist command, 150
    Open Dictionary command, 44
    Paste command, 233
    Quit Application command, 290
    Result History command, 37
    Save As command, 20
    Script Editor Preferences command, 35
    Script Menu, 19
    Select All command, 161
    Show Info command (Interface
        Builder), 290
    Show View Options command, 233

Test Interface command, 290
    View Source command, 177
    zooming in and out, 249
Keychains, 199–201
keystroke command, 248

L

Late Night JavaScript Web site, 44
Late Night Software's JavaScript, 180
launch command, 237
Library window, 46
Line Wrap preferences, 36
line-continuation symbol, 55
lists, 105–124
    adding items one at a time, 119
    adding multiple items at once, 119
    additional uses, 124
    as keyword, 108
    batch renaming, 113
    choose application command, 112
    choose from list command, 107
    common commands, 106
    concatenating, 115
    count command, 107
    display dialog command, 113
    displaying, 107
    every keyword, 109
    getting from other programs, 121
    getting selected items, 108
    inputting, 119
    item keyword, 106
    items keyword, 106
    iterating, 112
    list folder command, 118
    list processing, 112
    merging file lists, 116
    Microsoft Word and, 122–124
    nested, 106
    noncontiguous items, 107
    other uses for, 124
    preserving in a variable, 106
    processes, 110
    repeat statement, 113
    repeat with statements, 113
    set command, 106
    single-item, 105
    text item delimiters, 120
    TextEdit and, 121
load script command, 137
log command, 267
logging events, 267–269
Loop Movie script (DVD Player), 169

M

Mac Help command, 171
Mac OS X settings, tweaking hidden, 251
Macintouch script, 14
macscrpt discussion list, 311
MacUpdate Web site, 295
MacWeek script, 14
Mail, 186–191
    checking for new messages, 187
    Erase Deleted Messages command, 189
    finding mailboxes with unread
        messages, 188–191
    Get Mail button, 187
    mailboxes, 187
    Rules command, 190
    scripts, 10
    special rules feature, 190
make command, 80, 89, 238
    handling errors with, 90
    with properties option, 203
Make New AppleScript command
        (Safari), 181
make new command, 61
make new document command, 61
Make New Script command, 73
Make Plain Text command, 179
man Unix program, 253
Manage SMTP Servers script, 11
menus, extending AppleScript's menu
        control, 240
merging file lists, 116
Microsoft Word
    adapting TextEdit scripts, 67
    AppleScript support, 66
    fit to pages command, 69
    lists and, 122–124
    miscounting, 68
    scripting, 66–71
        count and every keywords, 68
Mimic PC monitor script, 6
motion blur filter (Photoshop), 135
move command, 88, 90, 155
Move to Trash command, 96
movies
    including with script, 165
    presenting full-screen, 164
    rotating, 167
    (see also QuickTime)
Movies folder, 166
Mozilla, 176
MP3 audio file format, 153
multi-line comments, 42
multiple script menus, 12

music
    converting, 153
    (see also iTunes)
Music folder, 159, 224
My iDisk command, 197

N

Navigation Bar, 32
Navigation Scripts subfolder, 12
nested lists, 106
Netscape, 176
new album command, 126
New Calendar command (iCal), 262
New Database command (FileMaker
        Pro), 210
New Event command (iCal), 262
New Finder Window command, 4
New Project command (Xcode), 276
New Smart Album command, 127
New Smart Playlist command, 150
New Tab command, 177
noncontiguous items in a list, 107

O

Old Desktop folder, 90, 233
OmniWeb, 176
    Web site, 302
open - show comments in dialog script, 226
open command, 77, 80
Open Dictionary command, 44, 46, 59, 109, 112
open location command, 175, 176, 199
Open Script Editor script, 6, 21
Open Script Folder script (DVD Player), 169
Open Scripting Architecture Extension (see
        osax), 50
Open Scripts Folder command, 16
Open URL command, 72
opening folder handler, 230
Opera, 176
osascript command, 260
osax (scripting addition), 50

P

passwords, 197–201
    Keychains, 199–201
Paste command, 233
path notation, 76
PDF format, converting documents to, 125
personal information managers (PIMs), 183
photos (see images)
Photoshop
    Actions command, 132

Photoshop (*continued*)
Adjustments menu, 133
Auto Color command, 133
Auto Contrast command, 133
Auto Levels command, 133
Classes list command, 135
commands, 134
Filter Suite, 134
filters, 135
Flatten Image command, 135
Function Key pop-up menu, 132
recording actions, 131
Save for Web command, 133
scripts, 131–137
(see also images)
pico, Unix text editor, 255
pictures (see images)
Pictures folder, 224
play command, 148
playpause command, 148
plug-ins, 37
Plug-ins command, 38
portable operating system interface (POSIX), 77
POSIX files, 77
PreFab UI Browser Web site, 247
Preferred Playback script (DVD Player), 169
present command, 164
scale option, 165
preserving a list in a variable, 106
Preview, 125
Preview Movie script (DVD Player), 169
Print Window command, 13
Print Window/Window with Subfolders script, 13
printing scripts, 12
Printing Scripts submenu, 12
processes, 110
produce command, 61
program dictionary, 18, 44
overview, 48
Standard Suite, 45
programmers, Web site for Apple, 310

Q

QuickTime
keystrokes, 165
Player, 164
scripts, 164–169
(see also movies)
Quit Application command (Interface Builder), 290
quit command, 237

R

Random Info Color script (DVD Player), 169
random number command, 130
random numbers Web site, 130
ranges, 306
AppleScript, 306
HyperTalk, 306
record data type, 203
record notation scripts, 203
recording scripts, 23
Remove profile from image script, 6
Remove Script Menu icon, 4
Repeat Routines command (Script Editor), 28
repeat statement, 70, 71, 151, 271, 306
repeat until statement, 151
Replace Text in Item Names script, 7
reply command, 190
Reset Windows script (DVD Player), 169
Resources folder, 34, 166
Result History command, 37
Retrospect Desktop Web site, 91
reveal command, 96
rotate command, 168
Rule Actions script, 11
Rules command (Mail), 190
Run as AppleScript command (Safari), 74, 180
run script command, 137
run VB macro command, 74

S

Safari, 175–183, 302
icons, 95
Make New AppleScript command, 181
preferences, 176
Run as AppleScript command, 180
running JavaScript code in, 180
Save All command, 103
Save As command, 20, 64
Save As PDF command, 34, 125
Save command, 64, 100
saving all documents at once, 103
TextEdit and, 102
Save for Web command (Photoshop), 133
say command, 156, 294
saving to option, 159
.scpt files, 31
screen saver, enabling, 192
screen zooming feature, 249
Script Assistant, 36
Script Bundles, 34
script bundles, 50

Script Debugger, 38
Script Editor, 21–38, 72
  .scpt files, 31
  adding your own shortcut menus, 28
  alternatives, 38
  Application Bundles, 34
  black text, 27
  blue text, 27
  colored text in, 26
  Compile button, 24, 40
  copying code, 73
  divider bar, 25
  Event Log, 29
  folder, 38
  Get Result of AppleScript command, 73
  gray text, 27
  icon, 4
  Info Field, 29
  Library window, 46
  Navigation Bar, 32
  plain text files, 34
  plug-ins, 37
  preferences, 35–38
    Editing, 36
    Formatting, 36
    General, 35
    History, 37
  Preferences command, 35
  Record button, 23
  Run button, 24
  Script Bundles, 34
  Script Field (see Script Field)
  script formats
    applications, 31, 33
    script files, 31
    text documents, 31, 34
  shortcut menus, 28
  starting, 21
  Stop button, 23
  Tabs section, 36
  toolbar, 22–26
Script Field, 26
  shortcut menus, 28
script files, 31
script formats, 30
  applications, 31, 33
  script files, 31
  text documents, 31, 34
Script Menu
  AboutFinder scripts submenu, 6
  adding new scripts, 15
  Address Book scripts, 5
  Basics submenu, 5
    AppleScript Help script, 5
    AppleScript Website script, 6
    Open Script Editor script, 6

  ColorSync submenu, 6
    Build profile info web page script, 6
    Mimic PC monitor script, 6
    Remove profile from image script, 6
  customizing, 14–17
  Finder scripts submenu, 6
    Add to File/Folder Names script, 6
    Change Case of Item Names script, 7
    Finder Windows – Hide All script, 7
    Finder Windows – Show All script, 7
    Replace Text in Item Names script, 7
    Switch to Finder script, 7
    Trim File/Folder Names script, 8
  Folder Actions submenu, 8
  FontSync Scripts submenu, 8
  hidden tricks, 19
  Info Scripts submenu, 9
    Current Date & Time script, 9
    Font Sampler script, 9
  Internet Scripts submenu, 9
    About Internet Services scripts, 9
    Current Temperature by Zipcode
      script, 9
    Stock Quote script, 9
  Mail Scripts submenu, 10
    Count Messages in All Mailboxes
      script, 10
    Crazy Message Text script, 10
    Create LDAP Server script, 11
    Create New Mail Account script, 11
    Create New Message script, 11
    Display All Accounts and Preferences
      script, 11
    Get Size of IMAP Mailbox script, 11
    Import Addresses script, 11
    Manage SMTP Servers script, 11
    Rule Actions script, 11
  Navigation Scripts subfolder, 12
  Printing Scripts submenu, 12
    About Convert/Print Window scripts, 12
    Convert to PDF/PostScript script, 12
    Print Window/Window with Subfolders
      script, 13
  rearranging submenus, 16, 17
  Script Editor submenu, 13
  Sherlock Scripts submenu, 13
  tricks, 19
  UI Element Scripts submenu, 13
  URLs submenu, 13
    Apple Stock Quote (Yahoo) script, 13
    Apple Store script, 13
    AppleScript Related Sites script, 14
    CNN script, 14
    Download Weather Map script, 14
    Macintouch script, 14
    MacWeek script, 14

script samples
    About Convert/Print Window, 12
    About Internet Services, 9
    Add to File Names, 7
    Add to File/Folder Names, 6, 8
    Apple Stock Quote (Yahoo), 13
    Apple Store, 13
    AppleScript Help, 5
    AppleScript Related Sites, 14
    AppleScript Website, 6
    Build profile info web page, 6
    Change Case of Item Names, 7
    CNN, 14
    Convert to PDF/PostScript, 12
    Count Messages in All Mailboxes, 10
    Crazy Message Text, 10
    Create LDAP Server, 11
    Create New Mail Account, 11
    Create New Message, 11
    Current Date & Time, 9
    Current Temperature, 14
    Current Temperature by Zipcode, 9
    Display All Accounts and Preferences, 11
    Download Weather Map, 14
    Finder Windows – Hide All, 7
    folder action scripts (see folder actions
        scripts)
    Font Sampler, 9
    Get Size of IMAP Mailbox, 11
    Import Addresses, 11
    Macintouch, 14
    MacWeek, 14
    mail scripts, 10
    Manage SMTP Servers, 11
    Open Script Editor, 6
    Print Window/Window with Subfolders, 13
    printing scripts, 12
    Remove profile from image, 6
    Replace Text in Item Names, 7
    Rule Actions, 11
    Script Editor, 13
    Sherlock scripts, 13
    Stock Quote, 9
    Switch to Finder, 7
    Trim File/Folder Names, 8
    UI scripts, 13
    URL scripts, 13
script support in common programs, 299–302
    AppleWorks, 302
    BBEdit, 301
    Entourage, 300
    Eudora, 300
    FileMaker Pro, 299
    InDesign CS, 301
    iPhoto, 300
    Mail, 300
    Mailsmith, 300
    Nisus Writer Express, 302
    OmniWeb, 302
    OpenOffice, 302
    Photoshop, 300
    QuarkXPress, 301
    Safari, 302
    SubEthaEdit, 301
    Tex-Edit Plus, 302
    TextEdit, 301, 302
    Word, 302
**scripting programs that don't have
        dictionaries**, 237–250
ScriptingAdditions folder, 50
ScriptMaker, 217
scripts
    activating program from dialog box, 110
    adapting existing script to be droplet, 142
    adapting TextEdit scripts to Microsoft
        Word, 67
    adding items to list one at a time, 119
    adding multiple items to list, 119
    automating typing function keys from, 250
    batch renaming, 113
    beeping, 152
    changing network name, 242
    checking for existence of file extension, 114
    checking for new messages in Mail, 187
    checking whether TextEdit has
        dictionary, 238
    choose application command example, 112
    cleaning desktop, 261
    coercion example, 108
    common list commands
        count command, 107
        item keyword, 106
    concatenation, 115
    converting Clipboard text into audio, 159
    converting images, 143
    converting iTunes files using drag and
        drop, 154
    counting words, 67
    creating Address Book group, 186
    creating database record, 203
    creating lists, 105
    creating new email message in preferred
        email program, 199
    default application property, 208
    discovering errors, 274
    displaying iChat status message, 193
    displaying lists, 107
    displaying name of every running program
        in a dialog box, 110
    displaying other dialog box, 47

downloading files, 195
eliminating oversized buttons, 228
emulating keystrokes, 248
encoding database records, 205
extending AppleScript's menu control to any
    program, 240
filtering images, 135
finding Address Book contacts, 185
finding best Internet signal, 173
finding mailboxes with unread
    messages, 188
finding unrated songs, 149
fit to pages command example, 69
folder action (see folder actions scripts)
getting image dimensions, 138
getting list of only modified documents from
    TextEdit, 122
getting lists from TextEdit, 121
getting selected item from list, 108
getting synonyms of a word from Microsoft
    Word, 122
handling errors, 273
identifying name of program that's
    designated to open particular
    file, 209
if statement example, 111
including movies with, 166
integrating Address Book with FileMaker
    Pro, 212
it statement example, 136
kind property, 208
list processing, 113
listing passwords saved in Keychain, 199
loading multiple Web sites
    automatically, 175
logging notifications, 267
merging file lists, 116
moving old desktop files, 233
name property, 208
nested lists, 106
notifying iChat when screen saver is on, 191
noting important events, 266
open location command example, 199
opening a file in pico, 254
opening folder, 229
packaging blob-creating Unix
    command, 254
padding an image, 140
pausing, 306
playing iTunes tracks, 148
playing slideshow, 131
QuickTime movie playing modes, 165
random numbers, 130
recording, 23
referring to specific pixel on screen, 124

repeat statement example, 71
retrieving password to Keychain key, 200
rotating movies, 167
running cal from AppleScript, 257
running in Safari's Address bar, 181
running JavaScript code in Safari, 180
running one script from another, 137
running Unix program without
    Terminal, 256
running uptime from AppleScript, 252
running uptime in current Terminal
    window, 253
saving all documents, 103
saving all TextEdit documents every 10
    minutes, 278
saving in TextEdit, 102
scheduling with iCal, 262
searching AppleScript database, 205
selecting tab in tab group, 243
sending files to Trash, 232
setting status to away only if screen saver is
    running, 192
setting values inside database record, 204
showing QuickTime movie full-screen, 164
skipping iTunes tracks, 151
sorting Filemaker records, 217
speaking current date and time, 156
speaking from, 156
speaking into sound file, 159
storing position and size of window
    onscreen, 124
testing exists command, 47
Text Suite example, 65
uploading files, 196
using handlers, 141
using open command, 49
using Script Editor's Library, 46
using speech recognition, 162, 163
using tell statements, 43
viewing plain-text version of Web site, 178
viewing Web site code, 177
wrapping actions in, 133
writing Address Book plug-ins, 184
zooming in and out, 249
Scripts command, 15
Scripts folder, 4, 15, 17
Select All command, 155, 161
Services menu, 72
set command, 54, 293
set the end command, 119
setting up, 3–20
Sharing command, 242
Sherlock scripts, 13
Shopping Lists folder, 225
shortcut menus, 28

shortcuts, AppleScript, 79
Show Info command (Interface Builder), 290
Show Navigation Bar command, 32
Show Song File command, 96
Show Standard Info script (DVD Player), 169
Show Toolbar command, 26
Show View Options command, 88, 233
Show Wide Info script (DVD Player), 169
single-item lists, 105
single-line comments, 42
slideshows, 130
Smart Albums, 127
Smile editor Web site, 38
SOAP scripts, 200
Sort Records command (FileMaker Pro), 216
sorting FileMaker records, 216, 218
sound, 95
sound and video scripts, 147–169
Sound Effects tab, 95, 152
Sounds folder, 117
SpeakToMe, 294
speech
    converting text in Clipboard into audio, 159
    generation, 163
    linking to a keyboard shortcut, 157
    listen for command, 161
    making a file speak, 159
    reading multiple emails, 160
    recognition, 163
    scripts, 155–163
    speaking from a script, 156
Speech Recognition tab, 162
speech-recognition Web site, 163
SpeechRecognitionServer program, 162
standard accounts, 258
Standard Additions dictionary, 209
Start Speaking command, 155
Startup Items pane, 34
Stickies, running services from, 74
Sticky Keys feature, 244
Stock Quote script, 9
String Comparison command (Script
        Editor), 28
string notation, 54
subroutines, 85–88, 307
    running instead of tell statement, 87
superuser accounts, 258
Surrealify an Image script, 137
Switch to Finder script, 7
System Events, 239
    classes, 240
    commands, 240

T

tell application command, 47
Tell Blocks command (Script Editor), 28
tell statements, 43
Terminal program, 252–256
    changing system settings, 253
    running AppleScript commands from, 261
    Unix without, 256–257
Test Interface command (Interface
        Builder), 290
testing and debugging scripts, 265–280
    compiling, 265
    error command, 275
    error prevention, 271
    errors, isolating and handling, 273
    Event Log, 267
    Event Log History, 269
    event notification, 266
    try statement, 273
    Xcode debugger, 275–280
text
    manipulating, 53–74
        concatenation, 56
        escape sequences, 58
        TextEdit, 59–66
    returned from dialog boxes, 54
    running scripts from, 72
Text Editing command (Xcode), 278
text item delimiters, 120
Text Suite, 65
    script example, 65
TextEdit
    adapting scripts, 67
    saving in, 102
    Services menu, 72
    Text Suite, 65
TextEdit scripting, 59–66
toolbar, 22–26
top program (Unix), 256
Trim File/Folder Names script, 8
try statement
    multiple commands in, 274
twirl filter (Photoshop), 135
typing function keys, 250

U

UI Element Scripts, 13, 250
UI scripts, 13
UIElementInspector tool, 247
UIElementInspector tool Web site, 245
Universal Access command, 239, 244
universal commands, 237

Unix
  AppleScript and, 251–264
  cron program, 261
  running AppleScripts from, 259
  scheduling AppleScript commands, 261
  superuser commands, 258
  system settings, 253
  text editing, 254
  without Terminal, 256–257
upload command, 197
uptime command, 253
uptime Unix program, 251
URL Access Scripting, 195–199
URL scripts, 13
URLs submenu, 13
Utilities folder, 109
Utilities folder command, 12

V

variables, 307
  string notation and, 54
  uses in scripts, 56
VersionTracker Web site, 295
ViaVoice, 162
View Source command, 177
Visual Basic
  macros, 74
  running from AppleScript, 74
Visual Basic, scripts and, 74
volume-up key, 95

W

WAV audio file format, 153
Web services scripts, 200
**Web services, making AppleScript work
      with**, 200
Web sites
  AE Monitor, 44
  Apple Human Interface Guidelines
      (HIG), 285
  Apple online retail shop, 13
  AppleScript, 6
  AppleScript Studio, 294
  Audible, 159
  Backup 2.0, 92
  Carbon Copy Cloner, 92
  error statement tricks, 274
  folder actions scripts, 235
  iLife, 126
  Keyboard Maestro, 157
  Late Night JavaScript, 44
  Mac Update, 295
  OmniWeb, 302
  PreFab UI Browser, 247
  random numbers, 130
  Retrospect Desktop, 91
  Smile editor, 38
  speech recognition, 163
  UIElementInspector tool, 245
  Versiontracker, 295
Where is iCa? compiler error, 266
windows
  moving, 84
  working with multiple, 83
wireless base station, 172
Word (see Microsoft Word)
Word Count command, 67, 68
word counting, 64
word processors, 302

X

Xcode, 38, 275–280
  Build and Debug command, 279
  Build and Run command, 279, 284, 294
  creating new project, 276
  New Project command, 276
  stepping through code, 279
  Text Editing command, 278
XML-RPC scripts, 200

Z

zooming in and out, 249

Colophon

Genevieve d'Entremont was the production editor and proofreader for *Apple-Script: The Missing Manual*. Linley Dolby was the copyeditor. Phil Dangler and Claire Cloutier provided quality control. Reg Aubry wrote the index.

Ellie Volckhausen designed the cover of this book, based on a series design by David Freedman. Rose Cassano created the cover illustration with Adobe Illustrator CS. Ellie Volckhausen produced the cover layout with Adobe InDesign CS using Adobe's Minion and Gill Sans fonts.

Phil Simpson designed the interior layout. This book was converted by Andrew Savikas and Joe Wizda to FrameMaker 5.5.6 with a format conversion tool created by Erik Ray, Jason McIntosh, Neil Walls, and Mike Sierra that uses Perl and XML technologies. The text font is Adobe Minion; the heading font is Adobe Formata Condensed; and the code font is LucasFont's TheSans Mono Condensed. The illustrations that appear in the book were produced by Robert Romano and Jessamyn Read using Macromedia FreeHand MX and Adobe Photoshop CS.

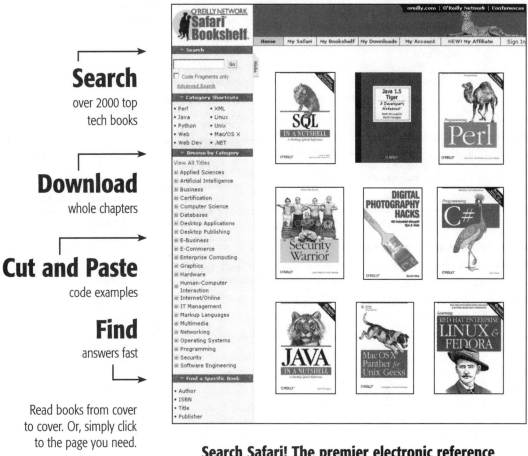

Keep in touch with O'Reilly

1. Download examples from our books

To find example files for a book, go to:

www.oreilly.com/catalog

select the book, and follow the "Examples" link.

2. Register your O'Reilly books

Register your book at *register.oreilly.com*

Why register your books?
Once you've registered your O'Reilly books you can:

- Win O'Reilly books, T-shirts or discount coupons in our monthly drawing.
- Get special offers available only to registered O'Reilly customers.
- Get catalogs announcing new books (US and UK only).
- Get email notification of new editions of the O'Reilly books you own.

3. Join our email lists

Sign up to get topic-specific email announcements of new books and conferences, special offers, and O'Reilly Network technology newsletters at:

elists.oreilly.com

It's easy to customize your free elists subscription so you'll get exactly the O'Reilly news you want.

4. Get the latest news, tips, and tools

www.oreilly.com

- "Top 100 Sites on the Web"—PC Magazine
- CIO Magazine's Web Business 50 Awards

Our web site contains a library of comprehensive product information (including book excerpts and tables of contents), downloadable software, background articles, interviews with technology leaders, links to relevant sites, book cover art, and more.

5. Work for O'Reilly

Check out our web site for current employment opportunities:

jobs.oreilly.com

6. Contact us

O'Reilly Media
1005 Gravenstein Hwy North
Sebastopol, CA 95472 USA

TEL: 707-827-7000 or 800-998-9938
(6am to 5pm PST)

FAX: 707-829-0104

order@oreilly.com
For answers to problems regarding your order or our products. To place a book order online, visit:

www.oreilly.com/order_new

catalog@oreilly.com
To request a copy of our latest catalog.

booktech@oreilly.com
For book content technical questions or corrections.

corporate@oreilly.com
For educational, library, government, and corporate sales.

proposals@oreilly.com
To submit new book proposals to our editors and product managers.

international@oreilly.com
For information about our international distributors or translation queries. For a list of our distributors outside of North America check out:

international.oreilly.com/distributors.html

adoption@oreilly.com
For information about academic use of O'Reilly books, visit:

academic.oreilly.com

O'REILLY®

Our books are available at most retail and online bookstores.
To order direct: 1-800-998-9938 • *order@oreilly.com* • *www.oreilly.com*
Online editions of most O'Reilly titles are available by subscription at *safari.oreilly.com*